Praise for Linda Aronson's *Screenwriting*

'A lucid and eminently useful atlas of screenwriting technique. All the vague confusing things that teachers and studio executives say about flashback, turning points and multiple protagonists are whipped into coherent shape here, in a comprehensive, precise and extremely practical theory. An essential tool in any writer's kit.'
Christopher Vogler, author of *The Writer's Journey*

'A very clear and intelligent analysis of what's going on in film structure and the advances of the last ten years. Terrific handling of *Pulp Fiction* and flashback. A genuine advance in the theoretical knowledge of film structure and a very clear coverage of the basics. A big advance on the standard texts. They say you can't teach an old dog new tricks, but I learnt a thing or two.'
David Williamson, playwright and film writer

'A unique and in-depth screenwriting book that is a MUST for the modern screenwriter. It sits on my desk.'
Screenwriters Utopia, US

'I really love this book. Her analysis of eight major features, followed by commentary of common script problems is worth the price of admission or cover price of this book alone. But the entire 300 pages maintains this level of quality and depth of analysis. Very strongly recommended.'
Script Magazine, US

'Linda Aronson provides screenwriters with invaluable detailed strategies to lay bare the workings of the craft. She has constructed a remarkable guide to take you from that mind-numbing first blank page, over all the hurdles, through to polishing the final draft.'
Jane Scott, Producer (*Mao's Last Dancer, Shine, Crocodile Dundee I and II, Goodbye Paradise*)

'An illuminating introduction into new forms of film writing that challenges us to keep up with the innovators.'
Jamie Sherry, *The Screenwriters' Guru Guide*, Writers' Guild of Great Britain

'There's only one book worth reading on screenwriting structure, by the way: *Screenwriting Updated* by Linda Aronson. She's published one of the only two credible explications of *Pulp Fiction*.'
Joe Clark

'Tired of the Syd Field and Robert McKee dyad? Screenwriter Linda Aronson has a new nuts-and-bolts book that could leave the other gurus searching for day jobs.'
Erick Opeka Austin Film Resource, Texas

'[*Screenwriting Updated*] . . . was intended as a guide to writing for TV and film, but it's very applicable to the games industry. The focus is on the structure of a story and gives practical strategies for creating or improving your narratives.'
Game On, US

THE 21ST CENTURY SCREENPLAY

A Comprehensive Guide to Writing Tomorrow's Films

LINDA ARONSON

SILMAN-JAMES PRESS • LOS ANGELES

First U.S. printing (originally published in Australia by Allen & Unwin, 2010)
10 9 8 7 6 5 4 3 2

Library of Congress Cataloging-in-Publication Data

Aronson, Linda, 1950-
The 21st-century screenplay : a comprehensive guide to writing tomorrow's
films / by Linda Aronson.
    p. cm.
Includes index.
ISBN 978-1-935247-03-6 (alk. paper)
1. Motion picture authorship. 2. Motion picture plays--Technique. I.
Title. II. Title: Twenty-first century screenplay.
PN1996.A76 2010b
808.2'3--dc22

                            2010052727

Internal design by fisheye design
Set in 11/14.5 pt Minion by Post Pre-press Group, Australia

Printed in the United States of America

Silman-James Press
1181 Angelo Drive
Beverly Hills, CA 90210

Contents

List of figures

List of development strategies

Foreword

Uncharted Territory

For any artist the act of creation is always a journey into uncharted territory. In the twenty-first century no artists are more aware of this than screenwriters. We know that the landscape of our profession is changing. As we set out on the journey to write the next great screenplay, we are always mindful of those who have gone before us and eager to learn from their travellers' tales. In recent years we have seen vast audiences gravitating towards innovative television shows such as *Lost* and *The Wire*. We have noticed cinema audiences flocking to unconventional movies such as *Pan's Labyrinth* and *Slumdog Millionaire*. We have also noticed that these unconventional works have been winning not only audiences but also awards. We are being challenged by a bewildering set of variations on traditional narrative forms. At the same time we are struggling to understand a complex global marketplace, continual developments in new technologies, and the emergence of multiplatform distribution systems. It is a very confusing world. We are invited to imagine stories large enough for IMAX screens and small enough for mobile phones. We need to be masters of linear narrative forms and pioneers in experimental story structures. We can see that the world of the screenwriter is changing and we know that the old maps don't help us anymore. As we each set out on our journeys seeking as always to generate new ideas, develop unforgettable characters, and create effective dramatic stories, we are more than a little confused by the breakdown of old paradigms. In these circumstances we are fortunate that Linda Aronson has stepped forward with a travel guide in the form of her new book *The 21st-Century Screenplay: A comprehensive guide to writing tomorrow's films*.

The seeds of this book were planted in Linda Aronson's previous work called *Screenwriting Updated*, which was first published almost ten years ago. *The 21st-Century Screenplay* is half the size again of its predecessor and incorporates a more detailed analysis of the traditional and emerging models for structuring a screenplay.

The 21st-Century Screenplay is presented in the most user-friendly and practical manner. Topics include Getting Ideas, Conventional Narrative Structure, Practical Plotting, Parallel Narrative (ensemble and time jump films), Films with Structural Flaws and Getting It on the Page. The book provides practical advice on screenplay structure using classical and contemporary examples such as *The African Queen, The Piano, Eternal Sunshine of the Spotless Mind, 21 Grams, Babel, The Hours, Run Lola Run, The Butterfly Effect* and *City of God*.

Screenwriters are familiar with the fear of the blank page and the terrifying array of options that confront us as we embark on a creative journey. The good news is that Linda Aronson's book is about solutions. She identifies the challenges and provides helpful examples and illuminating diagrams that prompt us to overcome the obstacles. She provides advice on core writing skills such as dialogue, subtext, plotting beats and writing treatments. She also offers in-depth analysis of popular genres such as romantic comedy, journey films, short films, and the special demands of adaptation. The book also contains a provocative chapter on flawed films ('Lost in the Telling') providing a critical analysis of films such as *The Insider, Syriana* and *Gods and Monsters*.

Without being prescriptive the book provides models and templates which are designed to serve as guides to the art of structuring a narrative that will engage an audience, maintain interest and communicate meaning.

Linda Aronson is a multi-talented, award-winning writer of plays, screenplays, television drama and young adult fiction (the latter published in many languages). She has written widely for the screen in the United Kingdom, Australia, New Zealand and the United States. Her credits include *Kostas*, directed by Paul Cox, the much-loved Australian stage play with music *Dinkum Assorted*, which premiered at the Sydney Opera House, the acclaimed comic novels for young adults *Kelp: A comedy of love, seaweed and Rupert Murdoch* (which won the Sanderson Book Prize), *Rude Health, Plain Rude* and *Naturally Rude*, and an extensive range of TV drama including Australian Writers' Guild AWGIE Award-winning episodes of *Singles* and *Learned Friends* for television. Linda is also a highly regarded teacher of screenwriting. Having taught widely for many years in Australia, she now acts as a script consultant internationally and presents guest lectures for major organisations in places all over the world, including Los Angeles, New York, London, Paris, Berlin, Dublin, Johannesburg, Prague, Stockholm, Copenhagen, Singapore and Auckland. Her remarkable body of work covers the mainstream as well as the margins of her profession and this experience gives authority to her voice. Linda's respect for the traditions of her art and her love of the conventions of her trade are balanced by her enthusiasm for the most innovative and experimental works of contemporary cinema and television. As a writer and teacher she is an authority on the pleasures of the well-trodden path and the thrill of the road less travelled. She also delights in the challenge of exploring totally uncharted territory.

As a screenwriting teacher at New York University I recommend a broad spectrum of textbooks to my students. I tend to the view that most of these books offer something of value and each of them is essentially as good as the person who reads them. In the case of Linda Aronson's work I make an exception. *The 21st-Century Screenplay* addresses areas not covered by others. The book provides the services of a personal script editor, dramaturg or even co-writer. It functions as a manual as well as a road map. *The 21st-Century Screenplay* is an essential guide for the twenty-first-century screenwriter. When setting out on a journey it always helps to take a map. *The 21st-Century Screenplay* is a special kind of road map because it encourages us to explore uncharted territory. Enjoy this book. Don't leave home without it.

Paul Thompson
Associate Professor
Film and Television
New York University

Preface

When I first thought about writing this book several years ago my intention was simply to write a new edition of *Scriptwriting Updated: New and conventional ways of writing for the screen*, which had first seen the light of day in 2000. However, it rapidly became clear that too much had changed since then for this to be desirable or even possible. For a start, parallel narrative films had proliferated at an astonishing rate all over the world. Screenwriters like Guillermo Arriaga, Paul Haggis, David Hare, Charlie Kaufman, Bràulio Mantovani and Christopher Nolan had pushed the boundaries of narrative even further, creating ever more complex script structures in films like *21 Grams*, *Crash*, *The Hours*, *Eternal Sunshine of the Spotless Mind*, *City of God* and *Memento*, films that, excitingly, displayed consistent patterns that meant writers could use them as templates. Obviously, any book I wrote had to explain these. But over and above all of this I needed to include all the new ideas, subtleties and changes of mind I'd become aware of in myself during those ten years—all of which, I should say, had been immeasurably assisted by the penetrating, enthusiastic and thought-provoking feedback I'd had from the literally hundreds of fine writers of all backgrounds and all levels of experience I'd met when I'd acted as a mentor in various script and writer development programs and when (with delight and no small surprise), I found myself invited to give lectures on *Scriptwriting Updated* to filmmakers' organisations and film schools and universities all over the world.

As well as inspiring me with new ideas, the feedback from those filmmakers on what they liked about *Screenwriting Updated* was invaluable. They kept kept saying how much they valued practicality and ease of reference during writing. Hence, in *The 21st-Century Screenplay*, I have focused even more on these things. I have increased the number of case studies and invented hypothetical examples to illustrate typical craft problems. I've also opted for very short chapters, which, I've found through teaching, make topics not only easier to find but also to absorb.

The result has been a much larger book than *Scriptwriting Updated*, one that takes the theories and practical techniques of *Scriptwriting Updated* much further and includes so much that either does not appear in *Scriptwriting*

Updated or is so condensed, or massively expanded or otherwise altered that the final book, *The 21st-Century Screenplay*, consists, in essence, of new or significantly changed material bookended by the opening and closing chapters of *Scriptwriting Updated*. Even so, the opening 'Getting Ideas' section from *Scriptwriting Updated* appears in *The 21st-Century Screenplay* with a new chapter called 'What film are we in?' (about preventing problems before first draft), while the last section, 'Getting It on the Page' is enlarged by new material on how to create subtext.

In the part of the book that deals with conventional narrative, in response to the strongly positive feedback on my development strategies method of constructing a three-act narrative, I have rethought, polished and expanded the existing strategies, adding new ones to cover new content about devising the second and third act, inner and outer story and voice-over. Since so many readers found my analysis of *The Piano* useful, it remains unchanged except for comment on its inner story/outer story content. A new, and I think extremely important, addition in the book is a section called 'Practical Plotting', which explains through examples a range of vital, day-to-day writing techniques (like picking and condensing story beats), things that are usually learnt only through practice. In this section readers familiar with my work will notice fragments from *Scriptwriting Updated* and from my craft skills newsletters, as well as extracts from an article that first appeared in 'Script Mechanics: Understanding and fixing the script' in Tom Jeffrey's *Film Business* (Allen & Unwin, 2006) and extracts from another article 'Characters in search of a plot' that first appeared in *Newswrite*, the journal of the NSW Writers' Centre.

Probably the most significant and far-reaching change relates to Part 4 of the book, which deals with parallel narrative (that is, films that use multiple stories and/or non-linearity). In response to requests from those many writers all over the world who are passionately interested in the topic, this part has been massively extended and rearranged to cover six, not four, main categories of parallel narrative, with many sub-categories. And for greater clarity, the material that remains from *Scriptwriting Updated* has been almost completely re-drafted.

Part 4 now includes two entirely new categories of parallel narrative. The first I term 'Double journeys' (films like *Brokeback Mountain*, *The Lemon Tree*, *The Lives of Others* and *The Departed*, that follow two characters travelling towards or apart from each other, or in parallel, and thus require two separate action lines). The second I've named 'Fractured tandem' (films like *21 Grams*, *The Hours*, *Crash* and *Babel*, which consist of equally weighted stories running in tandem but in a fractured form). Fractured tandem is particularly exciting because, as I explain, it can successfully handle stories that are exposition-heavy and contain truncated or practically non-existent second acts (stories rightly considered unsuitable for the conventional three-act, one-hero paradigm). This has made some writers joke that I have announced 'the death of the second act'. I haven't, I have just pointed out how a certain non-linear structure can insert pace, connection, meaning and closure into story material that does not possess it by virtue of the chronological progression of increasingly suspenseful events. Based on this extraordinary characteristic, I have also described how fractured tandem can be used both as a remedy for certain kinds of problematic three-act, one-hero structures and to insert suspense into didactic tandem narrative films (which often set out to depict social wrongs, so end up being predictable).

Two other new and lengthy sections had their origins in a single chapter in *Scriptwriting Updated*, the chapter devoted to tandem and sequential narrative. Tandem narrative (equally weighted stories running simultaneously in the same time frame, the form of films like *Nashville*, *Traffic* and *Lantana*) is now dealt with next to an expanded section on multiple protagonist form because I feel both are forms of ensemble films. I explain how the widespread misapprehension that ensemble films either do not need structure (because they are 'character driven') or must have a single hero (resulting in weak and redundant hero figures) has been responsible for many films that are characters in search of a plot. Sequential narrative (which I now term 'consecutive stories' narrative to differentiate it from a theory that emerged after *Scriptwriting Updated* about devising linear three-act films in sequences) is the form of films like *Rashomon*, *Run Lola Run* and *The Circle* and, in fractured forms (which I term 'portmanteau' forms), is the structure of films like *Pulp Fiction*, *The Butterfly Effect* and *City of God*. I split consecutive stories form into four sub-categories and explain how the portmanteau versions act in a similar way to fractured tandem, having the capacity to turn a series of stories that lack normal connection and chronologically building drama into a coherent, suspenseful film. Also included in the consecutive stories section is a chapter on the consecutive stories structure of Homer's *Odyssey*, which, fascinatingly, may, I think, provide a very useful structure not only for journey stories and biographies in feature films, but for television mini-series.

However, it is the flashback section that is now the biggest of all. It includes several new sub-categories of flashback. Most significant is 'preview flashback', the form used in films like *Michael Clayton*, *Goodfellas* and *Walk the Line*, a most useful form, in which a scene from late in the film is inserted at the start as a hook before the film plays from start to finish chronologically. The flashback section also discusses hybridisation (which is happening all the time) and contains many case studies, including detailed analyses of *Memento*, *Eternal Sunshine of the Spotless Mind* and *The Constant Gardener*.

Since the first question that writers always ask about parallel narrative is 'Which structure suits my film?' I have a chapter at the start of Part 4 entitled exactly that, designed as a starting point for planning. As another aid to planning, each category and sub-category of parallel narrative is followed by suggestions on how to use existing films as templates. Hence, if you want to write a film structured like *21 Grams* or *City of God* or *Pulp Fiction*, you will find practical suggestions about how to plan and assemble it.

Finally 'Lost in the Telling', a very popular chapter in *Scriptwriting Updated* dealing with the structural weaknesses in various problem films, returns with a section on parallel narrative films that don't achieve their potential including my theories on how to use forms like flashback and fractured tandem to fix certain script types that don't work in linear form.

Lack of space has unfortunately necessitated cuts, including my charts of flashback films, showing how and when the stories jump between time frames. I will make these available on my website at <www.lindaaronson.net>.

In the matter of style, I am conscious that in my effort to be clear and concise, particularly for the benefit of my readers whose first language is not English, I might sometimes sound dogmatic. This is unintentional. I don't believe in grand theories and unbreakable rules. I believe that scriptwriting, like all art forms, is always changing and reinventing itself and that is something to celebrate. My view is well expressed by David Hare, who says: 'Although there are rules, there are also no rules that can't be broken if they're broken brilliantly enough' and I fully expect to have my theories proved inadequate by some brilliant writer's narrative breakthroughs, indeed, I look forward to it. Hence, as much as possible I have tried to preface advice by qualifications like 'You might try' or 'Your best bet', but after a while such constructions become ponderous and hinder clarity. Where I don't qualify my statements, readers should remember that I am just one writer expressing a personal opinion. That said, on the occasions where I use a flat 'don't' the usage is conscious and is there because I'm discussing areas in which I have seen many writers come to grief. In such cases, 'don't' properly should read 'proceed with extreme caution'.

So many individuals and institutions contributed in so many ways to the planning and development of this book that I cannot mention them all.

Particular thanks for sharing so generously of their time and expertise must go to Guillermo Arriaga, Andrew Bovell, Charles Harris, Simon Johnstone, J. Mira Kopell, Lisa Ohlin, Danny Rubin, Linda Seger, Robin Swicord, Paul Thompson, Roger Tucker and Martin Winkler. For their ongoing encouragement over the years I thank Jim Fox, Judy Holland, Julian Henriques, Pavel Jech, Tony Morphett, Phil Parker, Susan Rogers, Robert Smith, Duncan Thompson, Christopher Vogler, Kees Vroege, David Williamson and Kate Woods.

Institutions and organisations whose dynamic, enthusiastic people welcomed and inspired me (very necessary to someone writing in isolation) include AFTRS, the American Film Institute, the Australian Writers' Guild, CEEA (Paris), Columbia University, Danish National Film School, DFFB (Berlin), Digital Media Academy (Singapore), FAMU (Czech Republic), Goldsmiths' College (University of London), Leeds Metropolitan University, London College of Communication (University of the Arts, London), Monash University (South Africa), National Film and Television School UK, New Producers' Alliance (London), New South Wales Writers' Centre, New Zealand Film Commission, New Zealand Writers Guild Foundation, New York University, POEM (Finland), QPIX, RMIT, Royal Holloway College (University of London), SP*RK (Screen Australia), the Screen Producers Association of Australia, Screen Training Ireland, Sources 2 (Berlin), the Swedish Film Institute, The London Screenwriters' Workshop, The Script Factory (London), University of California, Berkeley, University of Ljubljana and UTS.

Very special thanks must go to a small group of people. Thanks go to Paul Thompson for his constant support and for writing such a kind foreword. They go to my publisher Elizabeth Weiss, for her patience and good humour as the book took longer and longer to arrive and to editors Aziza Kuypers, Ann Lennox and all at Allen & Unwin for their talent and professionalism. They go to my agent Geoffrey Radford for always being at the end of the phone, wherever, whenever. Finally and crucially they go to Lisa and Mark Aronson, without whose limitless commitment, encouragement and advice—not to mention legendary proof-reading skills—I would still be writing this book, probably from a padded cell.

I owe an enormous debt to you all.

Linda Aronson
1 March 2010
Sydney

Part 1
Getting Ideas

Chapter 1
Creativity and general problem solving

THERE ARE MANY THINGS that a writer cannot control in the film industry. What we can control are the ideas we choose for our scripts. The most important ingredient in screenwriting is a first-rate film idea. This may sound obvious, but in fact many very talented writers do not fulfil their potential to write world-class scripts because they choose ideas which, while interesting and deeply felt, unfortunately, are simply not strikingly original enough for the highly competitive, expensive medium of feature film, particularly now that feature film has to compete for market share with drama from an ever-increasing number of platforms. Of course, we should all be passionately committed to the films we are writing, but there is no point in writing a script that has no chance of being made, and this means asking the hard questions, and asking them early. The question to ask is not so much 'Do I passionately want to write a film on this topic?' but rather, 'Is my film so vividly original that audiences all over the world will go to the cinema on a wet Monday night to see it?' (This is particularly important for art-house films, as they already have a limited demographic.) If it is not, ask yourself whether you want to invest a couple of years of your life in a script only to have producers tell you that you're a terrific writer but unfortunately your script won't find a market.

All of us, experienced writers and newcomers, need to take on competition in the way that Olympic athletes do: calmly, consciously and consistently aiming high, pushing our imagination and talent to the limits. In practical terms, we can try to do this by employing targeted brainstorming to get good ideas then meticulously planning our script structure.

Getting good ideas

The two perennial writing problems in scriptwriting are getting good ideas and structuring them properly. The enemy is pressure, particularly pressure of time, because it triggers a panic reflex that tempts us either to use clichés or to write story material that strains credibility.

The fact that so many clichéd and unbelievable films are made every year is testament to the power of this panic reflex. It would be reassuring if all of these weak films were made by inferior talents, but the sobering reality is that the people creating and funding such films—the people seduced and dazzled by what will appear to the rest of the world and, eventually, to themselves as a second-rate movie—are usually highly talented, sophisticated and commercially savvy people with a string of successful credits; otherwise they would not be in the position of making films in the first place. The lesson is that pressure has the power to warp the judgment of the best of us. We can all make stupid mistakes. Unfortunately, as we can't slow the industry down, the pressure is not going to go away. Time pressures have been part of the dramatist's job description since at least Shakespeare's day, and the reality for scriptwriters is that the job is not just about talent but about a capacity to be talented on command and to a deadline.

So what can we do? Well, we can ignore the problem and hope that it will never happen to us. A more sensible choice is to realise that at some point it will, then attempt to define and pinpoint what is going on intellectually when we make stress-related writing mistakes, and also when we are writing well. That way, not only should we be able to short-circuit the stress-related impulses towards cliché and the incredible, but hopefully—if we can just work out what's occurring mentally when we are writing well—we may be able to reproduce the process to order, and find techniques that will help us to be creative at speed, under pressure and for long periods of time. As Jack London succinctly put it, you can't wait for inspiration: you have to go after it with a club.

De Bono's creativity theories and screenwriting

Many accounts of the actual writing process exist, all remarkably similar. They describe an interaction between imagination and technique, a dual process whereby a logical, craft-skilled part of the writer's mind works to filter and make sense of streams of ideas, images and words coming from another part of the mind, usually loosely termed the 'imagination', 'subconscious', 'right brain' or, in earlier times, 'fancy'.

Interestingly, this division between imagination and technique, instantly recognisable to all kinds of writers, is also recognisable in terms of Edward de Bono's ground-breaking theories about the workings of creativity in *Lateral Thinking* (1970). In fact, de Bono's theories provide such a useful breakdown of the writing process as described by all manner of writers over the centuries that they can be used in a very practical way to pinpoint how good writing happens, and how poor writing can be improved.

VERTICAL AND LATERAL THINKING

De Bono describes two sorts of creativity, instantly recognisable to writers from their own work patterns. The first, 'vertical thinking', is a step-by-step logic that results in 'right' and 'wrong' answers. It's the sort of thought process that we apply in arithmetic, and writers use it for such tasks as judging whether a plot point is credible, or whether a piece of dialogue sounds lifelike. The poet Coleridge called it 'the organizing spirit of imagination'. We call it craft or technique. Its negative side is that it can push us to produce technically correct clichés. Vertical thinking makes up the 'ninety per cent perspiration' side of the writing process. The steps are depicted in Figure 1.1.

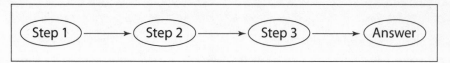

Figure 1.1 Vertical thinking

The second sort of imaginative thought process, 'lateral thinking', makes up the 'ten per cent inspiration'. It is a generative and very personal, associational, stream-of-consciousness thought process that is concerned with providing as many answers as possible, regardless of quality. The lateral mind is what is unique about each writer. In the old days it was called the writer's 'fancy' or 'muse'. It is what is at work when we write about emotions or intuit clever links between disparate things and, because it lacks any judgment, it is also what is at work when our work becomes 'over the top' or unfocused. Figure 1.2 depicts the lateral imagination in action, responding to a stimulus by accessing masses of connections, logical or otherwise.

Good writing seems to happen when craft (provided by vertical thinking) and the writer's unique view of the world (provided by lateral thinking) are inextricably mixed to produce a work of striking originality. For screenwriters who regularly work under pressure of time, in the rush to finish a script it is easy to either underuse the two sorts of thought process, or else to use each for the wrong jobs. The result is writing that is less original and less technically skilled than it needs to be.

What causes weak writing

Few of us have escaped the depressing experience of finding that something we thought to be a fine piece of writing turns out, in the cold light of day, to be clichéd or unbelievable or just simply over the top. How precisely does this happen? How can a fine, experienced writer produce technically correct

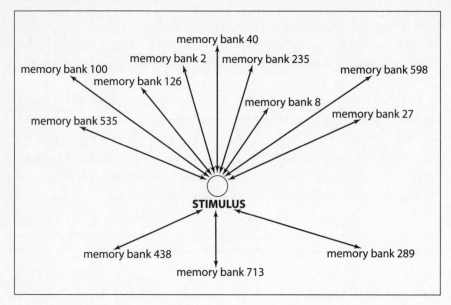

Figure 1.2 Lateral thinking in action

but clichéd material? How can an exciting new writer let a good idea fizzle out into cliché, or become incredible or silly? How is it that we do not recognise poor work at the time of writing?

Weak writing seems to happen when there is an imbalance between vertical and lateral thinking (often caused by pressure of time).

THE DANGERS OF BEING TOO VERTICAL

Being too vertical can make writers produce clichés without being aware of it. Because vertical thinking is based on experience, learnt skills and logic, it can only repeat and classify information that it has encountered before—in the case of screenwriting, what it has encountered before on screen. Functioning as it does on facts, accuracy and the idea of 'right' and 'wrong' information, vertical thinking tends to seize upon the first possible solution to any problem and stop there, quite uncritically, convinced that this is the 'right' answer. In screenwriting, the effect is to make the writer, even a fine one, produce a cliché and be happy with it; for example, creating a female character so weak it can only be described as 'love interest'. In all areas of screenwriting requiring originality (premise, characters, backstory, dialogue etc.), vertical thinking can only suggest what has been done before on screen. Hence, an over-reliance on vertical thinking will always pull towards cliché.

For example, given the problem of writing the screenplay for a film centred on a police station, busy professional writers unconsciously locked into vertical thinking will conclude that the 'right' way to do it (because this is what we've all seen before), is to have a range of stereotypical characters with stereotypical backstories, speech and plotlines (the rebel cop with the bad marriage paired with the conservative cop with the good marriage; the disapproving chief detective who constantly threatens the rebel with dismissal; the cynical, uniformed female cop, and so on).

In addition to the cliché problem, the emotional authenticity of stories and characters created by vertical thinking is always shaky because the writer is not getting into the characters' heads and trying to feel the emotion. Instead, the emotions and dialogue are being unconsciously copied from our memory of other films and television shows, which the vertical thinking mindset convinces us is what people say and feel in the given situation.

Overdependence on vertical thinking often happens through exhaustion (particularly for storyliners/consultants on television series), and is a perennial problem for established writers, making them write 'on automatic pilot' without being aware of it.

In *Selling Your Screenplay* (1988), Carl Sautter gave an interesting example of vertical thinking at work when he was story editor on the US TV drama series *Moonlighting*. Part of his job was to listen to writers pitching story ideas. He commented:

> I was astonished that almost every writer pitched variations of exactly the same plots. The most popular: Maddie and David are trapped together. Each writer pitched this isolation idea with fervour, confident that it was the most original and compelling notion of all time.

I heard a similar and equally frightening story from a judge in a short-film competition, where a staggering number of the many hundreds of films submitted had essentially the same plot. This had a person arriving at their car to find a stranger doing something bad to it (unlocking it, giving it a parking ticket etc.) and then the person assaulting the stranger, only to find that the car is not theirs. A similarly high percentage of the films in the competition indicated 'morning' by a close-up of a beeping alarm clock and a hand coming into frame to switch it off.

THE DANGERS OF BEING TOO LATERAL

An over-reliance on lateral thinking makes the script pull towards the incredible, silly, repetitive, unfocused and overly emotional. Lateral thinking is prone to all kinds of problems connected with poor technique and the 'real', because lateral thinking has no interest in such things; indeed, it lacks any kind of critical faculty at all. Lateral thinking pushes the writer to write for the sake of writing, unconcerned about structure, focus, repetition, intelligibility and redundancy. It falls in love with its own cleverness in devising dialogue or ideas or jokes, and doesn't know when to stop. In plot and characterisation, this means it is unable to discriminate between what is real and what is over the top. It is at work in all of those thriller films where the audience finds itself thinking: 'Why don't these people just call the police?' or 'Why are they walking into what is so obviously a trap?' In characterisation, being too lateral will pull us towards writing material that is maudlin. It will frequently make the writer too visible, and often lead to the preachy and the overt.

Because its whole approach is that more is better (quantity rather than quality), it can unwittingly produce the same scene (in essence) over and over again. Actor–writers are highly prone to this fault because lateral thinking is the major imaginative skill they have to use in improvisation, and when they come to write they automatically resort to it. This means that they tend to create a unique character and keep showing it doing the same thing over and over again. *Mr Saturday Night*, produced, written and directed by Billy Crystal, is a good example (see pp. 434–7).

Lateral thinking can also pull the writer to write in 'real time', meaning they create scenes as they would actually happen in real life, and not to cleverly push the plot and characterisation forward under the guise of naturalism. Lateral thinking cannot monitor how much exposition or backstory to include or when. It doesn't know when enough is enough. It typically produces scripts with several apparent endings before the real one.

WHY IS IT SO EASY TO GET VERTICAL AND LATERAL THINKING OUT OF BALANCE?

In their separate ways, vertical and lateral thinking are immensely seductive (see Figure 1.3 for a comparison of both approaches). Each creates an enormous, but false, sense of self-confidence. What makes things worse is that, in the pressured world of the film industry, the process of stopping to check that vertical and lateral thinking are in balance is counter-intuitive. Our every instinct is to jump at the first half-decent idea, whether it is a cliché resulting from vertical thinking or a half-baked idea resulting from lateral thinking. At every turn there is pressure to get something on paper. And of course, once scenes and dialogue are on the page, it is almost impossible for a writer to throw them away. The result is that writers can easily become deeply committed to ideas—just because they were the first ideas that occurred to them—that do not do them justice.

While both new and experienced writers are capable of imbalances in either direction, stress will typically make the more experienced writer rely on vertical thinking's craft skills, forget originality and jump with relief at the first half-decent idea so as to get at least something on paper. Meanwhile, the less experienced writer will typically get carried away on the imaginative roller coaster that is lateral thinking, exuberantly throwing credibility and all critical faculties to the wind.

Vertical thinking is seductive because its quick answers make the writer feel totally in control. Lateral thinking is seductive because its lack of self-criticism not only results in fluent, fast writing, but convinces the writer that everything they have written is wonderful. In both cases, the combination of fluency and self-confidence is hard for any writer to resist.

And writers are not the only ones to succumb to an imbalance of this kind: the fact that there are so many scripts that are unbelievable or clichéd means that directors, producers and network executives are also susceptible. Indeed, one often hears producers suggesting clichés because they feel that clichés are part of the genre ('... then a rookie girl journalist comes in to investigate and she falls in love with him!'). The hard economic truth is that imbalances between vertical and lateral thinking cost the film industry many millions of dollars a year.

VERTICAL		LATERAL	
Advantages	Dangers	Advantages	Dangers
Provides credible plotting	Can become clichéd	Can give original ideas at every stage of plotting	Can become unfocused
Has good structural sense	Can become overstructured	Pushes to transcend limits and clichés of structure	Can become unstructured
Has good sense of the everyday	Can become mundane	Will pick up the archetypal, mythical	Can become incredible, silly
Has good sense of naturalism	Can become predictable, boring	Will provide unusual ideas	Can become incredible
Sense of unity, perfectionism	Can cause rigidity, lack of originality	Provides a personal voice	Can become overly subjective

VERTICAL		LATERAL	
Advantages	Dangers	Advantages	Dangers
Good critical sense	Can become overcritical	Open to all ideas	Lacks capacity for criticism
Strong intellectual content	Can be overly theoretical	Provides powerful emotions	Can result in melodrama
Commercial instinct	Can be overcautious	Provides original voice	No commercial instinct

Figure 1.3 Advantages and dangers of vertical and lateral thinking

How to use vertical and lateral thinking

Successful pieces of screenwriting—perhaps of all sorts of writing—are always credible but highly original, which means, in the words of Carl Sautter, they are always 'real but unusual'. While they might take a traditional genre or situation, just as *Strictly Ballroom* takes the Cinderella story, they will always give it a strikingly new twist. Even if the work produced is avant-garde and non-naturalistic, the 'real but unusual' factor applies because what is 'real' in such cases is an emotional or intellectual reality, or sometimes both.

This balance between real and unusual seems to be a key to success in everything from the initial idea through to things like structure, characterisation and dialogue. In fact, it's useful to follow Carl Sautter's advice and think of the phrase 'real but unusual' as a motto for writing generally.

We can use lateral and vertical thinking processes to give us these 'real but unusual' components. 'Real' seems to be linked with vertical, and 'unusual' with lateral. To achieve a balance between the real and the unusual during writing, we can consciously switch between lateral, which can generate new and original ideas, and vertical, which, with its logic and analytical skills, can monitor the credibility and appropriateness of suggestions created by lateral. The trick is to know which jobs are best done with which process.

An analogy is driving a car. You can't drive a car without alternating between the brake and the accelerator. To 'drive' a script, alternate the accelerator pedal (lateral thinking, which drives the script forward by originality and emotion) with the brake pedal (logical vertical thinking, which keeps the script in control—that is, structured and 'real'). It is easy to be either too cliché (using only the vertical imagination), in which case the 'car' will grind to a halt, or too emotional, unstructured and over the top (using only lateral), in which case the 'car' will go off the road.

The development strategies method

Is there any way to control the balance between vertical and lateral thinking so that we can write to our best? While of course no method is absolutely foolproof, it is possible to duplicate the process that happens when vertical and lateral are working well together. This process breaks down into three steps which are repeated over and over again:

1 **Vertical thinking defines the task**; for example, inventing a speech for a particular character that will get across specific plot and theme details while remaining credibly in character.
2 **Lateral thinking brainstorms the task**, running through a number of possibilities and making as many original connections as possible.
3 **Vertical thinking chooses the best 'real but unusual' answer**.

Development Strategies 1 and 2: Diagnosis and general problem solving

From my work with writers and producers I have created a set of questions and reminders I call development strategies which copy this natural three-step problem-solving, imagination-boosting process. There is a wide range of development strategies in this book. Their aim is to stop our naturally highly active imaginations running away with themselves by consciously keeping lateral and vertical thinking functioning methodically in tandem. Development Strategies 1 and 2, described in the following pages, are designed to assist with general writing problems. They help with getting original ideas at every stage of the writing process by consciously firing the imagination with a variety of good triggers while ensuring that the resultant ideas are based in human truths and presented with sound technique. They can help with everything from getting a good idea for a film to creating a powerful speech. Later development strategies help to pinpoint the specific originality of the idea, act as reminders about common traps, and form a step-by-step method to create and revise a classic three-act narrative.

However, there is one very big problem with the development strategies: our own natural overwhelming urge to write—write now, and write quickly. Every dramatist is a natural storyteller and what we want to do is invent characters and make them talk. To slow down and ponder options is completely counter-intuitive; indeed, for many writers, particularly new writers, it is actively panic-inducing, because the all-pervasive myth about writing is that talent means speed and fluency, and speed and fluency automatically mean brilliance. Not always. They often mean recycled clichés or a writer out of control. All art requires focus and control. Ten per cent inspiration, ninety per cent perspiration.

DEVELOPMENT STRATEGY 1: DEFINING THE TASK AT HAND

It is frighteningly easy to jump in and start writing before you really know what writing task you have on your hands. Be conscious that your instinct for survival will push you to rush. Resist that instinct. Think: 'What am I supposed to be doing here? What is the problem here?' For example, if you are asked to submit ideas for a low-budget thriller film, have you defined to yourself precisely what the demands and potential pitfalls of a low-budget thriller are? Or, if you're writing a romantic comedy requiring two enemies to fall in love, have you planned a series of plausible steps to make that credible? Again, if you feel there is something wrong with your film's opening, before you start pulling it apart, have you tried to define as precisely as possible where the problem might be? Or, if you are writing a scene, have you defined to yourself precisely what you need to do in this scene before you start putting in the dialogue?

Development Strategy 1

DEFINE THE TASK AT HAND

Questions to ask:
- Do I know the task (for example, what film we're in, the point of this scene)?
- What am I supposed to be doing here?
- Do I understand the definitions? (For example, do I really understand any technical jargon being used?)

Use Development Strategy 1 to help define to yourself whatever task you have at hand. Once you are clear about what the task involves, you can use Development Strategy 2 to brainstorm a range of ideas from which to choose.

DEVELOPMENT STRATEGY 2: BRAINSTORMING THE BEST 'REAL BUT UNUSUAL' REMEDY

Once Development Strategy 1 has provided a range of questions that need to be asked, you can use Development Strategy 2 to brainstorm a range of 'real but unusual' answers for filtering later. It is important to realise that brainstorming, being lateral, is counter-intuitive, particularly in the situation when it is most needed; that is, a crisis. In a crisis, every vertical-thinking instinct will (a) be pushing us to jump at the first possible answer, which is likely to be a cliché and (b) be trying to filter out the more extreme or silly ideas coming from the lateral imagination. This can mean that potentially excellent ideas get thrown out along with the rubbish, so do not let vertical thinking hijack the process.

Development Strategy 2

BRAINSTORM THE BEST 'REAL BUT UNUSUAL' REMEDY

Allow lateral thinking to generate original or unusual ideas to be filtered by vertical thinking.

Questions to ask:

- Is what I am creating credible enough?
- Is what I am creating unusual enough?
- Have I let lateral thinking generate enough ideas?
- Once I have got all the lateral ideas, am I using vertical thinking to filter out poor ones?

The crucial thing to remember about this ideas-generating stage of the process is that any idea, however weak or crazy it may seem, is acceptable because it can lead by association to something useful. As writers, we are so used to rejecting substandard ideas immediately that at first this is a difficult process. It can feel like a rejection of our hard-earned skills of discernment. But in fact the process is liberating and empowering: instead of finding ideas by default ('this one isn't good enough, that one isn't good enough, this one is okay, let's go with it . . .') we end up with a range of good ideas from which to choose.

It takes discipline and practice to brainstorm in a crisis, because brainstorming requires you to 'daydream' about a problem rather than take action. It is rather like being faced with a charging tiger and asking yourself not to run but to consider the patterns on the tiger's coat.

To use Development Strategy 2 to maximum effect, writers need to stay calm and give themselves permission to think of silly or outrageous answers on the way towards exciting and original ideas. One simple way to control the panic instinct that says brainstorming is a waste of time is to use a stopwatch to set a time for brainstorming—even ten minutes can produce a fund of ideas.

DROWNING IN IDEAS?

As you start to practise brainstorming for ideas over the following chapters, you may well start to feel overwhelmed by the sheer volume of choice you create for yourself. You may feel that your head is spinning and wonder how on earth you will ever pick an idea and get started on the writing. This is particularly likely if you are a writer who hitherto has written without a plan. Don't panic. Later I will be explaining strategies you can use to choose the best ideas. For now, revel in your wonderful imagination. Enjoy the fact that never again will you need to be hostage to the first idea that comes to you blind, in your panic or enthusiasm, to the fact that it might be clichéd or over the top. You can be confident of creating a whole range of ideas even under extreme pressure.

Chapter 2
Triggering good ideas fast from screen models

THE TRICK TO GETTING good ideas at speed is to realise that imagination is reactive. We are used to thinking of the imagination as something overwhelmingly proactive, a powerful force that takes us over and dominates our lives. And so it is, once it has got an idea to run with. But if as writers we look back at how we got the ideas for our original work, almost invariably the answer is that something in the world around us—an event, a story read in the newspaper or told by a friend, an anecdote, a thought—provoked in us a response that demanded a story.

The business of getting an idea for a story was a reaction in response to a stimulus from the outside world; it did not come from inside us. This process is accurately described when we say of writers that something 'fired' or 'caught' their imagination. It's also what the ancients were thinking about when they spoke of the idea of a muse, which was a separate, and petulant, supernatural entity in charge of ideas.

Someone once asked Chekhov how he got ideas for his short stories. He pushed an ashtray across the table and said: 'Do you want a story about an ashtray? You'll get one tomorrow morning'. Chekhov may or may not have been irritated with his questioner, but either way this is a description of story triggering.

To experience how triggers can fire the imagination, try this simple task. First of all, give yourself ten seconds to think of as many one-sentence film ideas as possible. The chances are you will be lucky if you have one or two. Now give yourself ten seconds to think of film ideas on the topic 'earthquake'. This external stimulus will make it much easier to make connections and produce ideas. Finally, give yourself ten seconds to think of film ideas that combine 'earthquake' with another stimulus, say, a theme like 'self-esteem', or a simple plot model like a Cinderella story. You will find that the extra connections make it surprisingly easy to think of ideas (although the quality of many will be poor).

This associational activity is what happens naturally in the creative process. As we screen professionals rarely have time to wait for the Great Idea to come to us, we can artificially create the natural stimulus/reaction process ourselves, just as Chekhov did, by using vertical thinking to pick a stimulus that we then run past our lateral imagination so as to trigger associations and unusual connections. We can catch our own imagination and be our own muse.

This chapter and the next deal with using Development Strategies 1 and 2 in combination with a variety of story triggers to kick-start lateral thinking and get a wealth of story ideas at speed for three-act scripts. They also introduce Development Strategy 3, which is about pinpointing the components of a specific genre, and Development Strategy 4, which shows how to get more ideas by consciously making links between very different things. This chapter looks at using screen models (genre) to trigger plot ideas. The next chapter looks at other triggers, including fairytale, myth and fable, real-life events, characters, themes, events and random combinations of ideas.

Isn't a model a fast track to cliché?

Before we look at models we need to ask the obvious question: why use them? Isn't a model (particularly something like genre) a fast track to cliché? Why, in a search for the new and unusual, are we returning to formats that some would say have been done to death?

Unfortunately, it is a sad fact of writing life that any model, after a while, can produce or mask clichés. But this is not the fault of the model. It is because the writer has unconsciously let vertical thinking take over and pre-empt lateral imagination. Models are successful patterns that audiences enjoy and, in some cases, have been enjoying for thousands of years. The chances are that audiences will like them again, as long as lateral thinking is brought into play to push the boundaries and give the format a new and original slant. *Hamlet* was a commercially commissioned piece of formula writing, written within the very rigid format of revenge tragedy, a genre akin to the modern-day mafia or gangster movie, full of murder and betrayal. As usual, Shakespeare transcended formula and stereotypical characterisation. The trick for writers is to avoid being kidnapped by vertical thinking and pushed into a weak rehash of the pattern.

Writing to a screen model

Screenwriters are so often asked to write to models that it makes sense to deal with that approach first. Television series and serials, and nowadays online drama serials, are the most obvious examples of writing to models, but writing feature films often requires writing to a model or genre. Typical writing-to-model tasks would be the following:

1 ideas for a low-budget romance (feature)
2 the premise for a 50-minute television drama series
3 ideas for a package of three science fiction telemovies for the teen market
4 ideas for an online comedy serial

The way to get lots of ideas for models, as we might expect, is to know how and when to use lateral and vertical thinking. For experienced writers the hardest part will be to switch vertical thinking off after it has defined the requirements of the model, so that it is not allowed to generate ideas but only to choose them after lateral brainstorming. For newer writers, the temptation will be to sidestep the vertical task of defining the model's requirements and jump straight into lateral brainstorming.

The two-pronged approach can be summed up quite simply: define the model, then give yourself permission to brainstorm it freely and uncritically through a variety of triggers. Keep all the ideas so that later, when you are completely sure you have brainstormed enough, you can select the best, but vary the story trigger. The same trigger, used over and over again, is likely to be hijacked by vertical thinking, so that you think you are brainstorming but in fact you are only producing clichés and ideas that you had the last time you used the trigger (this is typically what is happening when TV storyliners go into burn-out).

Give yourself as much time as possible to work on this vital ideas part of the project. Remember, a good idea virtually writes itself. If you choose a poor idea, you will be spending a huge amount of time trying to make it sparkle.

Rejecting the first idea

This stage of the process is not about getting complete plots for films. It is about getting a wealth of one-sentence story ideas/fragments from which you can choose later. Moving into plotting too early can pre-empt the creative process. It is frighteningly easy to commit to a poor idea just because it was the first one that came to mind. As we've seen, the first idea is usually a derivative one springing from the vertical imagination. Instant, second-rate ideas are one of the great traps of vertical thinking and one of the great dangers facing experienced writers whose craft skills are extensively developed and who, as a consequence, can so easily drop into automatic pilot. Matters of detailed plotting come later.

Getting ideas for a film

As an example of how this works, let's look at the low-budget romance feature film. As we've seen, getting good ideas is all about finding useful triggers for lateral thinking. A model of the simplest kind, like the words 'low-budget feature romance', can sometimes act as a good trigger in itself. So this is where to start. Remember, all you are looking for at this stage are one-sentence ideas. Keep to one sentence because if you start to plot a whole story you will commit to it, thereby shutting out a whole range of other potential stories.

STEP 1

Reminding yourself that finding the right idea is going to take some time, relax and apply Development Strategy 1: Define the task at hand (see p. 12) so that you can brainstorm ideas. Make sure you know what the task is. While the task might seem obvious, consciously define it for yourself because that precision helps vertical thinking to keep you unpanicked.

Here the task is 'to think of ideas for a low-budget feature romance'. You will immediately notice that business issues are present, but don't allow them to inhibit the next stage of the process, which is brainstorming. Put them aside for later or, even better, jot down a memo on a separate piece of paper.

STEP 2

Having pinpointed the task, utilise Development Strategy 2: Brainstorm the best 'real but unusual' remedy (see p. 13) to come up with as many one-sentence ideas for a feature romance as possible. Ask yourself whether what you are plotting is unusual enough. Have you let lateral thinking generate enough ideas? Are you letting vertical considerations—such as business issues or quality—limit you?

Before brainstorming, consciously shed preconceptions about what a romance should be. Give yourself permission to be flippant, grim, ironic—anything, so long as you keep yourself open to all ideas. Also, consciously shed anxieties about quality or your inner critic may paralyse you. Think quantity not quality. Quality issues come later. Try for twenty one-sentence ideas, letting your imagination bounce off each. Here are a few random, even ridiculous, ideas on the topic of a 'real but unusual' romance.

1   A postal worker falls in love with a letter, which could be developed to a postal worker falling for the addressee, or for the sender (because this person has beautiful handwriting or the letter smells engaging) or for a person mistaken for the sender.

2   An elephant falls for an ant, which takes up the idea of opposites

or unlikely people attracting each other, such as the power-broker falling for a powerless person, an old person falling for a younger person, people of different races becoming attracted, the Romeo and Juliet idea.

3 A divorced couple falls in love again (used in *It's Complicated*).

4 Two murderers fall in love.

5 A person falls in love with their disease, which could be developed to a person who functions by thinking of themselves as weak or victimised finding strength through falling in love with someone who challenges that approach.

STEP 3
Write all these ideas down, even if you hate them. Sometimes they will later lead you to better ideas elsewhere.

STEP 4
Get other triggers from the model. Why? Because, while a limited model like 'romance feature' can sometimes trigger excellent ideas, usually stress will cut in and make us switch into vertical thinking before our lateral imagination has had a chance to work properly. The result is limited, cliched ideas.

To help yourself find a range of other triggers, you can use Development Strategy 1. For example, having defined the task as 'getting ideas for a feature romance', you can define it more precisely by asking 'What *is* a feature romance?' In other words, what are the story components of a feature romance? Logical vertical thinking will give us answers like these:

- setting (place and era)
- personal details of lovers (age, class, occupation etc.)
- the way lovers meet
- non-human barriers to lovers (social, health, misunderstandings, distance etc.)
- rivals to lovers
- ending—happy or sad?
- point of view (one or other of the lovers, a friend, a parent, a rival etc.)

Each of these character and plot components can be run past the lateral imagination as a trigger for brainstorming. Let's look at an example. We will take the idea of a 'real but unusual' setting for a feature romance. Switching to lateral thinking, we might get the following examples:

- Mars, outer space, spaceship, flying saucer
- zoo—lovers as animals, actually or symbolically?
- place of work—office, factory, bakery, garage, car yard, ferry depot, houses in the same street, chemistry lab, cancer ward, Alcoholics Anonymous meeting, deathbed, radioactive dump, school, university, gardens, parks, racing stables
- building site, studio, garbage dump, recycling facility, symphony orchestra, theatre, cinema, roller-skating rink, sports field, restaurant, hotel, bank
- desert island, emotional island of some sort, railway station (when both parties are stranded and/or emotionally isolated)
- on the internet—two people in different towns or countries
- medieval era or some other period in history, or a museum where both are enthusiasts for a particular era
- a cult setting of some kind, perhaps a religious cult setting (but period might be too expensive)
- fantasy land, fairy land, psychiatric hospital, beauty parlour
- big house—one lover rich, the other a servant
- small country town, big country town, big city, small rural pocket in big city
- cemetery, funeral parlour, shoe store, clothes store, shopping centre (he's the butcher and she's the newsagent)
- old people's home, children's playgroup, children's sports club
- health farm, resort, people out of context (will love last?)
- archaeological dig or the jungle (or the city as jungle)—beware budget
- a swamp, the desert, after a plane crash at the South Pole
- parrots in love

Already, the range of ideas has opened up enormously. The ideas show everything from the mundane (lovers meeting at a resort) to the apparently bizarre (parrots in love). But it is important to realise that without the mass of other ideas surrounding it, 'lovers meeting at a resort' might not have seemed so weak. As for 'parrots in love', while it looks out of place here, it could look quite respectable as an idea for an animated children's film. Also, while of itself it seems unpromising, it could be the feeder idea for another concept. This could be a comedy romance about two scientists fighting to become the first to document the mating habits of a rare parrot. Staying open to tragedy permits ideas like love in a cancer ward, which lifts the topic into a whole new range of emotions.

You can now go on to brainstorm each of the components. This will give you a huge range of ideas.

STEP 5

When you feel you have enough ideas from all of your triggers, take your favourite six or so and hand them back to your vertical imagination for a 'business issues' check. This is another way of defining the task. It requires you to define the business components your idea needs to have to be genuinely a 'low-budget feature romance'.

- low budget, so must not require expensive locations, special effects etc.
- must not be period because of the expense
- must not be written with expensive actors in mind
- is it my producer's kind of product (if a producer is attached at this stage)?
- is it to be aimed at a certain demographic? Should I choose?
- are there any co-production issues that might affect ingredients of the story (location, actors etc.)?

If a producer is already involved in the project, that person will probably appreciate receiving and perhaps contributing to this list. Lists like these are very helpful in helping the collaboration process run smoothly because they ensure that everybody knows what the writer is supposed to be doing.

Genre and audience expectations

Now that you have six or so story ideas, you need to double-check that you know 'what film we're in' so that you can give the audience the best possible version of the model it expects. In this instance, the model is a genre. Before you start making any detailed plans about a film in a particular genre, take a moment to identify elements and audience expectations of that genre. This will give you further details about plot and characterisation requirements. It will also remind you of the exact ways in which the script needs to grab the emotions and intellect of the audience; that a thriller must be *extremely* thrilling, and that a spy story must be full of suspense and a 'whodunit' must keep us guessing. Genre is a promise to the audience, and you must fulfil that promise in a real but unusual way.

This might all seem very obvious. In fact pressure makes it very easy to rush into creating specifics of storyline while forgetting the core requirements of the genre or, more precisely, what experience the audience is looking for when they come to this sort of film. The sort of questions that have to be asked, quite cold-bloodedly, are things like: 'Before I go any further, is my film actually exciting enough for a thriller?' or 'Before I commit to this who-dunit, does it really have enough twists and turns?' Such things can never be assumed.

All of this can be aided by a simple device, Development Strategy 3.

Development Strategy 3: The genre equation

Development Strategy 3 is actually a development of the 'real but unusual' rule that we've seen is a useful screenwriter's motto. It is the first development strategy to have a highly specific function, and its function is to make sure that the writer knows enough about the demands, clichés and nuances of any chosen genre to recreate it in a powerfully original way that will ful-fil—and hopefully exceed—the audience's expectations. Because it focuses on the scenario that could develop from the idea, it shifts the idea closer towards creation of a complete story with a proper structure. While it is still too early at this stage to start close plotting any of the ideas, it is useful to begin considering the general demands of a genre. Doing so helps filter out inappropriate ideas and shift more promising ideas to the top of the pile. It is much better to pinpoint the demands of genre before close plotting one particular story because choosing a story means you have emotionally com-mitted to it. This could blind you to its inadequacy as a vehicle for the genre you have to write in.

But what if the writer wants to play games with the audience's genre expectations? This certainly can be done but, just as we need to understand the form before we copy it, we must also understand the form before we play tricks with it. Development Strategy 3 is actually a kind of equation: *genre = pattern + relevant emotion + real + unusual*

Development Strategy 3

THE GENRE EQUATION

Identify the pattern or genre you are writing in, remembering 'the genre equation' which is:

genre = pattern + relevant emotion + real + unusual

Questions to ask:
- Am I including events and characters that will provoke high levels of the right emotion (for example, fear, amusement, suspense)?
- Have I identified all the components of the pattern?

- What plot and character points must I have for the audience to identify this as the chosen pattern?
- Have I identified the danger areas of the genre (for example, cliché, credibility gaps)?
- Have I run Development Strategy 2 to make sure I have got a highly unusual but credible version of the pattern?

The components of a genre

Development Strategy 3 asks us to pinpoint the components of a genre. How can we do that? There is an old comedy writer's rule that runs 'silly plus real is funny, but silly plus silly is stupid'. For example, in a successful comedy like *Muriel's Wedding* a plain girl agrees to a loveless arranged marriage (credibly 'real', vertical thinking) for the comically ridiculous reason that she is desperate to have a white wedding ('unusual', silly lateral thinking). The result is a premise that is engagingly funny. But if *Muriel's Wedding* had been about a girl who thinks, in a comically ridiculous way, that she's from the planet Zong and, also in a comically ridiculous way, is desperate for a white wedding, the result would have been stupid. This sound advice is another way of saying that if you remove vertical thinking from the equation, your comedy goes 'over the top'. There is also the obvious point that if you remove lateral thinking, the 'unusual' component of the comedy, all you will have is a completely vertical equation of 'real plus real', which is not funny at all.

Just as we can describe comedy films as being 'silly plus real', we can also define thrillers as 'exciting plus real', and tragedies as 'deeply sad plus real'. That gives us the emotion we want to arouse in our audience, but it also reminds us that an overdose of the relevant emotion will wreck any film; 'deeply sad plus deeply sad' will be over the top. The 'real' must always be there.

If we add to this equation the basic pattern of the specific genre (the pattern of a spy film, for example, is 'what spies do', and the pattern of a love story is that 'people fall in love'), we have a quick way to prove that our film is reaching the audience via the emotions and story patterns associated with that genre. Or alternatively, that it is playing games with story patterns and emotions (as in *Pulp Fiction*, which adds comedy and the mundane to the normal gangster movie pattern of fear, excitement and underworld atmosphere). Playing games with genre is of course entirely permissible; in fact it is the premise behind all film spoofs and many cult films.

We can even create a table to remind us of this (see Figure 2.1). Pattern components and credibility are handled by vertical thinking and emotion and originality are handled by lateral thinking.

Genre	Pattern components + emotion + credibility + originality
Comedy	Pattern components + silliness + real + unusual
Thriller	Pattern components + fear + real + unusual
Action story	Pattern components + excitement + real + unusual
Love story	Pattern components + romance + real + unusual
Tragedy	Pattern components + pain + real + unusual

Figure 2.1 Breaking down genres into tasks

Using the method shown in Figure 2.1, you could create a chart for yourself that identified the basic elements that you have to include in your film—then use it as a brainstorming tool. If, for example, you are planning a war film, jot down the elements you have to include (particular pattern, plus relevant emotion etc.) and note down ideas for them as shown in Figure 2.2.

War story	Pattern (normal components of war story)	Emotion (Fear, dread, triumph, anger, sorrow, desire for revenge etc.)	Real	Unusual
Historical war or invented war? Civil war? Internal, mental war? War with invaders from space?	Done from one side or both sides? Involving a mission? Explaining strategy? Include battle scenes, tender scenes, thoughtful scenes, scenes explaining cause of conflict etc. Message? Structure?	Many different instances of all the emotions, delivered suspensefully.	Research (into historical events if applicable, into robotics or space travel etc.)	Possibilities: usual war, unusual protagonists, unusual quest, unusual perspective on events (non-combatant?) Machine? Use an interesting narrative structure like flashback?

Figure 2.2 Genre table for a war movie

Expect clichés and plan to tackle them

Development Strategy 3 can also help you with clichés. Every genre contains its own clichés and pitfalls. Rather than ignore the possibility of these occurring in your script, expect them to appear and ready yourself to remove them: forewarned is forearmed. For example, if you are writing a science fiction movie, take a few moments to note down what was wrong with the bad science fiction movies you have seen. As you proceed with the script, check from time to time that you haven't inserted clichés or fallen into the pitfalls because this is an occupational hazard. When you find a cliché, either put a new spin on it or dump it. When you're in a pitfall, define it and brainstorm yourself out of it.

Chapter 3
Triggering good ideas fast from other models

Combining genres

An interesting way to avoid cliché and find new and interesting patterns is to combine genres. This approach can produce a wealth of interesting ideas. It is dealt with at length in Ken Dancyger and Jeff Rush's absorbing book, *Alternative Scriptwriting* (1995), but the theory in essence is to brainstorm the plot possibilities of combining different genres (for example, combining a gangster film with a war story, or combining a love story with a spy film) and see what interesting plot combinations suggest themselves. Interesting structural combinations might also suggest themselves as a result of the process, as for example in the case of *The English Patient*, which uses flashbacks to tell its combination of love and war stories.

Inventing genres

Brainstorming of the kind demonstrated in Chapter 2 with the low-budget feature can be used equally well with other genres. In fact an interesting brainstorming exercise is to think up new genres, then use them as triggers. For example, you might brainstorm literal and figurative treatments of the 'buried treasure' movie, the 'other woman' movie, the 'pride before a fall' movie or the Samson movie (hero destroyed by passion gets revenge), and so on. Be careful not to be drawn into close plotting of one or two ideas. The purpose is still to generate as many ideas as possible.

Getting good ideas fast from fairytale, myth and fable

Stories that have engaged audiences for hundreds or thousands of years make excellent models. Myths, fairytales and fables are actually ready-made templates and easier to use than genres because not only do they specify the protagonist, supporting characters and details of scenario, they also possess a very sound, traditional three-act narrative structure. While, to modern minds, using an existing story might seem like a form of plagiarism, in fact inventing stories from scratch is a relatively recent idea, and for writers before, after and including Shakespeare, using an existing story was the norm, the issue being how the story was made relevant to modern times.

The screen industry continues this tradition to its great profit. One very dominant fairytale, particularly in mainstream cinema, is 'Cinderella', which appears in everything from *Pretty Woman* to *The Killing Fields* to *Slumdog Millionaire* (with the television show *Who Wants to be a Millionaire?* playing the part of fairy godmother).

FOUR WAYS OF GETTING STORY IDEAS FROM 'CINDERELLA'

METHOD 1: CINDERELLA AS . . .

Think 'Cinderella as . . .' then insert a social role, type, thing, even a place. For example: Cinderella as . . . astronaut, pessimist, painting, mountain village etc.

METHOD 2: ONE-SENTENCE PLOT TEMPLATE

Create a plot template, underline its changeable components, then brainstorm each component to get new storylines: for example, 'Likeable, oppressed person encounters fairy godmother figure whose actions help them achieve their greatest wish.' Then, for example, you could brainstorm twenty different kinds of 'greatest wish'.

METHOD 3: SUMMARISING PART OF THE ACTION

Create a template that summarises a striking part of the action, then brainstorm the changeable components of that template. For example: 'Magic turned a poor servant into a glamorous, wealthy person for a short time, after which things returned to normal.' Try swapping 'magic' for, say, 'technology', 'natural disaster' or 'the government' etc.

METHOD 4: THE TWIST ENDING

Reverse or significantly change the fairytale's ending; for example, marriage to the prince becomes another form of slavery. To find a good twist ending, define the underlying assumptions of the fairytale and question them.

FAIRYTALES AS TEMPLATES FOR THRILLERS

While 'Cinderella' is probably the most common fairytale used in the film industry, others are evident, most often as thriller templates. For example, 'Little Red Riding Hood' is the prototype villain-in-disguise story (for example, *Psycho*). 'The Three Little Pigs' is the prototype serial killer film (*Home*

Alone is a comic inversion) and 'Jack and the Beanstalk' is the prototype spy and heist story (for example, *Being John Malkovich*). To get ideas for a thriller, brainstorm 'real but unusual' versions via the four methods used with 'Cinderella'.

MYTH, FABLE AND LITERATURE
THE HERO'S JOURNEY
It is impossible to talk about the use of myth in film without mentioning Christopher Vogler's brilliant and seminal book *The Writer's Journey* (1992). Vogler takes the ancient and very pervasive myth of the 'hero of a thousand faces' (in which the hero has to go into another dangerous world to save the tribe and achieve personal salvation) and demonstrates how its scenario, its protagonist and its range of compelling archetypes can be identified in modern screenplays of all kinds, from action movies to subtle psychological dramas, as well as being used as a template for new screenplays. The book is compulsory reading, but to summarise:

- The hero's journey is a circular one, starting and ending at home with a trip to a special world in the middle.
- On the way, the hero meets a range of people, good and bad, who are archetypes; that is, they stand for typical human types or roles.

The most frequently appearing archetypes are:
- mentor (a wise old man or woman)
- threshold guardian (a fierce person guarding the entrance to the special world)
- herald (a person who introduces the hero to the quest)
- shape shifter (a person who keeps changing their role)
- shadow (the hero's main enemy—a reverse image of the hero)
- trickster (sometimes a helper, sometimes a hindrance)

SUMMARY OF THE HERO'S JOURNEY PLOT
The hero receives a summons to adventure, but is reluctant to go into the special world. Events force the hero to go, taking a magic talisman given by a mentor or teacher. The hero defeats the threshold guardian at the first door into the special world, and goes through. The hero encounters new challenges, new friends and new enemies, eventually passing through the second door, which leads to the innermost cave and the great ordeal, in which the hero is face to face with death. The hero gets the treasure and starts back for the normal world, passing through a third door and experiencing a resurrection.

There is a final great battle and the hero experiences victory, returning with the treasure to the normal world.

The huge advantage of this model is that it provides not only a traditional structure and a specific scenario, but a range of strongly defined characters with pressing needs and clear roles to play in the progress of the protagonist. This not only ensures that the characters have the makings of an interesting psychology, but also that each character acts to impel the protagonist forward in the plot. This really is character-driven drama!

Brainstorm different versions of the actual journey (including metaphorical ones, such as illness as a journey), the archetypes and the steps in the journey.

USING MYTHS, FABLES AND LITERATURE

Myths, fables, and literary works are excellent triggers. For example, the Icarus story could be summarised and brainstormed as: 'someone too vain to heed warnings against a strong power is destroyed'. Ancient myths make good models for gangster and war stories. Arthurian legends are good for lawyer/detective/adventure/western movies. Fables and parable are ideal because they provide a scenario with a message. Ancient love stories like 'Orpheus and Eurydice' can be templates, as, perennially, can *Romeo and Juliet* and indeed all of Shakespeare's plays. (If this seems like plagiarism, remember that Shakespeare and his colleagues were also guilty of it and did it all the time. Shakespeare's *Merchant of Venice* is his answer to a very similar play by Christopher Marlowe called *The Jew of Malta*. *The Jew of Malta* was doing such good business at a rival theatre that Shakespeare was told to write something similar.) The classic comedies of Molière and Ben Jonson provide excellent triggers for comedy.

REDEMPTION AND *THE PILGRIM'S PROGRESS*

It is said that the US pilgrim fathers took two books with them from Plymouth: the Bible, and John Bunyan's allegorical novel, *The Pilgrim's Progress*, in which the protagonist, who stands for all humanity (at least, all non-conformist Protestant humanity), is changed for the better by experience, successfully achieving his goal (heaven) through ordeal. Perfectibility, an achievable goal and growth by self-discipline to redemption is deeply embedded in US culture, including its films. It is even present in a movie like *Pulp Fiction*. So pervasive is it that US scriptwriting theories often present growth and redemption in the protagonist as the inevitable subject-matter of a film. However, many cultures, in response to the socio-political realities in their part of the world, just don't believe in humanity as restricted only by its inner failings. They are fatalistic and pessimistic, and their films actively pursue more depressing protagonist's journeys, with little learnt or changeable, which is an entirely valid alternative response. Neither optimism nor redemption is obligatory. They are merely options.

Development Strategy 4: Finding non-narrative triggers

Almost anything can act to trigger lateral thinking—even a road sign reading WRONG WAY. So strong is our ability to find patterns that the results of combining random words together to find stories can seem eerily predestined.

Try brainstorming anecdotes, newspaper snippets, cryptic headlines, job ads, personal ads, street names, names in a telephone directory, proverbs, common phrases or billboards and the question 'what if...?'. Brainstorm interesting character types from occupation or social role. Brainstorm characters defined by emotional state; predicament; flaws; ambition; one of the 'seven deadly sins'; or astrological signs. Brainstorm weddings, funerals, journeys, holidays, war, accidents, divorce, departures, a mission etc. Photographs, music, art works and other sensory stimuli are good triggers, as are themes like poverty, parenthood, loss, ambition, the insanity of war etc. Try throwing disparate ideas together and waiting for a pattern to form. For instance, throw 'love story' together with a word picked at random from a dictionary; for example, love story/gravity, love story/intrusion, love story/expatriate. Development Strategy 4 will remind you what to ask.

Development Strategy 4

FIND NON-NARRATIVE TRIGGERS

Throw disparate ideas together and wait for a pattern to form.

Questions to ask:
- Could I find a better idea by trying for more combinations or via another method; for example, finding a trigger in a newspaper headline or through combining random words in a dictionary?
- Are the new ideas I get this way 'real plus unusual'?

Chapter 4
What film are we in?

A FILM IS A multi-million-dollar venture. While nobody would start pouring the foundations for a multi-million-dollar building without detailed plans, scripts are often set in concrete before those creating them have decided precisely what they want to create.

Of course, many very experienced screenwriters say they write without a plan. However, in my experience, these people don't for a second mean they sit down and start writing immediately the initial idea comes to them, not stopping until they finish the first draft (although very occasionally that does happen). On the contrary, when you ask them what preparation they did, normally you will find that they were profoundly and passionately immersed in the project long before they started writing (in other words, their plans were mental). You will also usually find that they rewrite extensively as they go. Most importantly, you will usually also find that they possess enormous experience, high skill levels and an awe-inspiring combination of objectivity and mental toughness that permits them to get to the end of one draft then almost instantly junk it and start all over again. For experienced screenwriters, starting without a plan often boils down to starting without being sure of the details of the ending or how they will get to the ending. Guillermo Arriaga is like this. Often cited as a purely intuitive writer, he is actually a master-craftsman who, far from dashing off his scripts, starts off with a lot of ideas in his head and meticulously reworks and condenses as he goes. Although he commences writing with plotlines incompletely formed, he states that by page ten he knows 'what the story is' (professional writer's shorthand for knowing a great deal about the film). Significantly, his daily writing process involves constant and ruthless rewriting. As for intuition, decision-making expert Herbert Simon's observation that 'intuition is analytical thinking frozen into habit and into the capacity for rapid response through recognition of familiar kinds of situations' is appropriate here. Which is to say that we shouldn't be at all surprised that experienced writers like Arriaga don't have to plan as much as newer writers and can modify on the run: they've been doing it for years. Arriaga was writing non-linear novels long before he wrote *Amores Perros*. The complicated narratives used by Paul Haggis in *Crash* and Stephen Gaghan in *Traffic* sprang from years of experience.

Inevitably, your script will change in the writing, but however tempting it is to dash straight from idea to writing scenes, avoid it. It's worryingly easy even for very experienced writers to commit to a plot that does not properly transmit the strengths of the idea or the message they are trying to get across. Once you have taken a path it is very hard to turn back, and by taking one path you have lost the opportunity to take many others. Because you are a good writer, your weak plot will probably be quite good, but not the best you are capable of. Then, tragically, because it's very hard to throw away a draft, the inadequate plot is there to stay. For everyone involved in developing the script, the shaky, inappropriate plot becomes what the film *is*, and keeping it intact becomes a point of honour, a matter of principle and an expression of artistic integrity. A new plot, even though it would transmit the ideas and story material infinitely better and result in an altogether better film, becomes unthinkable. Occasionally, the script will get made and be damned with faint praise. More often it will lurch through the early stages of development and end up in a bottom drawer, a huge waste of time, money and talent.

Don't drift into months or years of effort on writing that is less than your best. Instead, stop, take stock and spend some time pinpointing the inherent strengths of the idea and working out what you are trying to say through your film. In film industry jargon, this process is known as establishing 'what film we're in'.

What can go wrong and how to prevent it
PITCH FEVER

One of the most common places for a discrepancy to creep in between idea and plot is before even a word of the script has been written; that is, in the creation of the pitch. A pitch is a hymn of praise to a script invented to attract finance. These days, a pitch is often mandatory at a very early stage of a script's development; indeed, sometimes (and worryingly) development finance is even decided at public pitching competitions.

While a pitch is supposed to be a statement of intent about an unfinished or even unwritten script, what often happens is that, bizarrely, somewhere along the line intention becomes taken as achievement. The script is not *going to become* a brilliant thriller: it already is. Alas, persistently asserting that your script is a riveting, heart-stopping and strikingly original thriller about industrial espionage does not make it so—but this is exactly what people do.

Everyone involved starts to believe their own publicity. Hard questions are never asked about the script, with the result that in a surprising number of cases the finished script bears little relation to the high-powered pitch (even in basic matters like plot) but the team on the film are blind to this. I call this pitch fever. Here is an example (exaggerated for ease of understanding) of how a pitch can differ from the real film (both have been invented by me).

PITCH FOR *FINDING BECKY*, A FEATURE FILM

Annie Miller's got everything: good looks, brains, a top job as a journalist on a top paper. Then suddenly everything changes. Out of the blue arrives Becky. Tough and streetwise, Becky's nineteen, on the run, and desperate to keep the three-year-old girl she calls her sister. She trusts nobody—and nobody had better trust her. As Annie struggles to gain Becky's trust, she starts to find out things that shake her bright and privileged world. When she finally discovers Becky's terrible secret, she's thrown into a dark world of pain and vice she could never have imagined. In a heart-stopping race against time, Annie battles to save the girl whom, but for the grace of God, she might have been. A powerful and moving story about two women, chance, and unthinkable evil.

This, for all its prose clichés, promises an exciting, intricately plotted psychological thriller with some good action sequences. However, the script that follows might well go something like this.

SYNOPSIS OF WHAT ACTUALLY HAPPENS IN *FINDING BECKY*

Open on buzzing alarm and a hand turning it off. It's Annie, a nice, pretty young journalist. We see her at work. We see her having a drink with friends after work. We see her shopping and joking with a jolly middle-aged male delicatessen owner who clearly knows and likes her. She spends the evening watching TV and eating ice cream out of a tub. Domestic incidents occur including Annie at a launderette, Annie washing her face and staring in a mirror, Annie not having anything to wear etc.

Annie has a day off. She comes out of her house and finds a baby's necklace in the gutter. She looks everywhere for the child who owns it and finds the child and her mother, Becky, in a nearby park. Becky is a very young single parent with no-one to turn to. The child has lost their house keys.

The two women look everywhere for the keys and find them. In the course of the hunt they get to know each other. Becky tells

Annie about her shocking history of incest. It turns out that Becky always loved writing and wants to be a journalist.

The child's drug-addict father turns up. He wants money and is threatening. The two women run away with the child. They spend the whole day hiding in a variety of interesting/funny/weird places, meeting many interesting people, escaping cleverly and with witty dialogue. Finally, at night they hide in a visually interesting place such as a deserted factory with many ladders and lift shafts. There is a hunt scene. The child cries out for its father, who finds them. Annie wrestles him to the ground, finding a strength she never knew she had. The father is killed horribly by piece of factory equipment. Cut to Becky, rehabilitated and living with Annie, getting her first newspaper story published.

This is not depicting the pitch at all. It is not even a story, it is two women running around. Worryingly, dressed up with punchy dialogue and fast-paced action sequences from a good writer, this implausible, cliché-ridden collection of episodes will at first sight look much better than it is. People involved with the script, already believing it to be what the pitch says it is, will keep pointing out the wonderful dialogue (and it will be wonderful) and that great bit where Becky king-hits the Sumo wrestler (which will indeed be good). However, the problem in trying to make it better is that everyone on the film is hearing the pitch and no-one, in any real sense, is reading the script.

The rewrites that have been done (and often there will be many) will be addressing details such as whether the father drowned or was crushed, not tackling the overarching problem; namely, that the script opens with a string of clichés, then becomes not a rising, suspenseful or even plausible story dealing with the strong human issues promised by the pitch but, well—two women running around. Is Annie struggling to gain Becky's trust? No, Becky almost instantly volunteers the information about incest to Annie, a complete stranger, the act either of someone mentally unbalanced or operating a con. 'Dark world of pain and vice?' No. 'Heart-stopping race against time?' No. 'Chance and unthinkable evil?' No: two women running around.

Any writer whose talent can shine through a terrible storyline like *Finding Becky* is probably, with a better plot, capable of excellence. The waste of a slab of their writing life on things like *Finding Becky* is saddening. Unfortunately, when a film like this gets to the screen the audience will instantly see its weaknesses and the film will fail—to the surprise of those who made it and felt only the strength of the idea.

THE PLOT IS NOT HOLY

The problem with *Finding Becky* is that it has the wrong plot, a plot probably launched into with a lot of passion, a fair degree of panic (possibly even during an actual pitch competition) and certainly insufficient thought.

Passion is a vital requirement for a career in the film industry; however, art is about control and focus—about getting the passion in your head and heart actually onto the page. With a film project that you love, it's all too easy to get swept along by hope and enthusiasm without properly understanding what the film is really about, thus what your plot needs to contain. The plot serves the ideas. *The plot is not holy.* What is holy and inviolate is the idea. If the plot does not properly service the idea, the plot must be changed.

GETTING SWEPT AWAY

Weak film adaptations of books often happen because those creating the script love the novel so much that they invest a bald and meandering screenplay adaptation with all the richness they recall from the novel. Soon, the faulty plot becomes sacrosanct (for more about issues surrounding adaptation, see pp. 155–8).

The same thing can occur with a writer who launches prematurely into writing in the grip of a passionately felt idea. The writer can't pick the weak plot because the act of reading the script rekindles the powerful emotions that provided the idea in the first place. Once again, the weak plot has become the project.

By all means defend your project, but don't defend a pile of A4 paper with your project's name on it. Don't defend something just because it's there.

Strategies that help

MIND MAP

To understand why an idea resonates with you so passionately you need to isolate the idea's main themes and the story ideas it's giving you, then brainstorm connections. Linda Seger calls this clustering and regards it as a way of increasing the commercial viability of the script by finding the universal themes. In *Lateral Thinking*, Edward de Bono calls it identifying the dominant idea, and regards the notion of making connections from it as a way of ceasing to be dominated by it or by the mental clichés it calls up. Use a mind map as a starting point for clustering; that is, to articulate as many different reasons as possible why the idea might have appealed to you. These might surprise you. For example, you might find the idea compelling because it threatens you.

Here is a mind map on the theme of poverty.

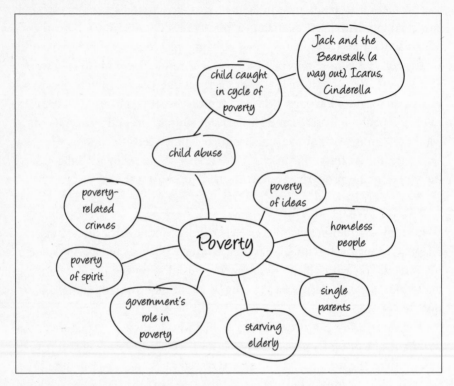

Figure 4.1 Mind map on the theme of poverty

HOW TO CREATE A MIND MAP

Brainstorm associations from each of the ideas thrown up in the process. For example, a theme of war might suggest rivalry, hence images of chess or battle which might form symbols, or the bases for scenes. Chess pieces might suggest plots for two warring generals, or the suffering of the foot soldiers. List the emotions that the ideas or images might create. Let these trigger more symbols and images. Expect some clichés to appear—just ignore them. You might not fully understand your attraction to the idea until later in the writing.

THE SPARK

To avoid being kidnapped by the pitch; indeed, even before you think about inventing the pitch, it's sensible to find what I call the spark. The spark is what makes your film irresistible—what will make people go out on a wet Monday night to see it. I named it the spark because it will be whatever makes people's eyes light up when you describe your film. These elements are what your audience wants and what you must deliver (or lose your audience).

In *Sideways*, the spark is 'an offbeat love story featuring less-than-perfect couples who like wine, with a lot of action in vineyards'. The spark elements are 'offbeat love story', 'less-than-perfect couples', 'wine' and 'vineyards'.

To exploit that idea, the filmmakers gave the audience a lot of 'offbeat love story', 'wine', 'less-than-perfect couples' and 'vineyards'. So, the trick is to try to define your spark and give your audience lots of it. If your spark is 'a romantic comedy on Mars', you need to have lots of 'romantic comedy' and lots of 'on Mars'. For example, if your couple has a picnic that goes comically wrong, it must go comically wrong in a way that is specifically Martian.

Defining for yourself what exactly your film's spark is will help you at every step of script development. It will:

- tell you what film you are in and make sure writer, producer and director are all in the same film
- give you a clear writing plan
- give you the pitch, the marketing tool and usually a clear pointer to the demographic and genre
- provide you with a safety check you can keep running to make sure that the film is achieving to its potential

HOW TO FIND YOUR SPARK

List what you, personally, think is vividly original and utterly irresistible about the idea then write the blurb for the DVD cover. Then try it on people. Surprisingly often, what makes your listeners' eyes light up will be an aside or just something you toss in on the spur of the moment. If so, make sure you emphasise that element in the script. This is why the spark is so much more useful for development and pitching purposes than a logline (an arresting, one-sentence description of what happens in the film)—because it springs from audience feedback, whereas a logline is invented in the absence of the audience, hoping to please it.

If no eyes light up, either you haven't yet got the spark or you aren't describing it properly. Keep trying, because if you cannot excite an audience you don't yet have a film. And if you don't know what you're selling, you can't write it (or, indeed, properly sell it).

CONTENTS OF THE SPARK

The spark can be one thing or a combination of several. It can be characters in a sight gag, as in *Twins* ('two comically dissimilar men are identical twins'). In a genre film, it's often the spin on the formula (for example, 'it's a film about a bank robbery—by paraplegics'). It can be a stylistic issue, as in

American Splendor, where animation, adaptation, original drama and documentary are combined. In some films, such as *Men in Black*, it happens in the opening moments as the hook (a moment of high interest to 'hook' the audience): 'aliens (hostile and friendly) are on earth in disguise and a special police force controls their activities'. Alternatively, it can happen some way into the movie, as in *Tootsie*, where the spark is 'an out-of-work actor pretends to be a woman to get a part'. Sometimes a major part of the spark is the cast, particularly a big-name star, or a celluloid hero (such as James Bond).

Even if you know the spark, it's surprisingly easy to forget it, so keep checking. If, in your romantic comedy on Mars, you've got distracted into, say, planning excellent scenes about the mother, back on earth, of one of the partners, either dump the mother scenes and come back to Mars and the romance or, if you think the earth scenes are better than the Mars scenes, seriously think about dumping Mars and making the film about the earthbound mother. Whenever you are stuck, go back to the spark, and make sure your script is serving it.

THE HEAT

The heat is one very specific aspect of the spark, to do with plot. The heat of a film is the crucial character and/or plot ingredient that gives the idea its attraction. For example, the heat of the film *Gran Torino* is the developing warmth between a bigoted, elderly Caucasian man and a family of South East Asians. Your plot must stay with the heat. The moment you leave the heat, your film will flag. Define the heat and stick with it.

A NEW WORLD

A useful set of ingredients and motto for a successful film are: 'powerful and universally recognisable emotions set in a new world—a world that we haven't seen on film before'. The new world is often a physical one, because new physical worlds, whether Californian vineyards or Mumbai before the Indian IT boom, have so much to interest us. However, the new world can also be of the mind (as in *A Beautiful Mind*). It can be a genre film set in a new world (just as the *Star Wars* movies relocated the western to deep space) or, like *Babe*, *Charlotte's Web*, *Wall-E* or the *Happy Feet* and *Toy Story* films, it can take us into the world of other creatures.

So, double-check that the world of your film is somehow new. If it isn't, think about relocating it in a new world because often you can, with wonderful results. A new world can mean new physical location, different era, different sex and/or age of main characters. If you are doing a world that is commonly seen (for example, the world of gangsters), show us a new side.

MESSAGE AND SCENARIO

Films are always 'about' two things:

1 **The scenario**; that is, 'what happens'. In other words, it is the way the spark is best carried through the action (for example, in *Twins*, the scenario is 'two comically dissimilar identical twins are comically involved in a road movie about escaping gangsters and finding their mother').

2 **The message**; that is, the themes and deeper meanings that the scenario naturally leads us to (in *Twins*, this is 'in the process each twin finds his better self and understands the power of family and brotherhood').

However, if you ask writers what their script is about, they will often just tell you the film's message, and assume that their scenario demonstrates it when actually it doesn't, in much the same way that people can believe a script illustrates a pitch when it doesn't. They will assert that, say, their film is all about father/son relationships when there is only one scene on fathers and sons. Just declaring that your film is about something doesn't make it so. Scenario is vital in film because film operates like parable or fable—scenario delivers message. You can't get the right message across unless you have an appropriate scenario. You can't transmit the message of 'The Three Little Pigs' by making the climax that Pig Three was adopted.

Differentiating between message and scenario—understanding your message and seeing the scenario as the means to carry that message—helps enormously to keep intention and execution together. Also, you need to understand your film's scenario and message so that later you know the function of each scene and can therefore cut redundancies or find a cheaper way to transmit the same plot, character and thematic information. One of the most frequent problems in any kind of writing is not getting what's in your head onto the page. Pinpointing your message and scenario is one of the most reliable ways of making sure your script transmits what you actually intend.

BUT WHICH COMES FIRST?

It doesn't matter. Often writers start out knowing the message of their film but not the scenario (for example, 'I want to write a film about the lack of trust and betrayal in marriage'). Others start out knowing the scenario or, more often, the start or climax of the scenario, but not its message (such as, 'A couple goes away on holiday, starts to fight, meets up with a stranger and ends up murdering him'). Sometimes film ideas come from a character idea (as did *Twins*). Character ideas are particularly difficult to turn into films or stories because the writer needs to invent both message and scenario. Whether you are starting from message or scenario, or character or heat, work hard to isolate the message, because this will tell you where to go in your scenario and what to emphasise. Be aware that the process can be difficult and is ongoing—often you have an intuition that you don't understand.

INTERDEPENDENCE OF SCENARIO AND MESSAGE
In *Twins*, the two men finding out about the importance of family could have been done through all kinds of other plots than the one that was actually used, the one involving gangsters, a long car journey and a hunt for a valuable, top-secret engine. Why the plot was useful was because it put the comically different twins together in a car in an adventure (thus providing endless opportunities for sight gags), gave them a girlfriend each, and put them into comic peril. If you isolate the message you give yourself a chance to play with different plots and choose the best.

Message and scenario exist in a symbiotic relationship. They nurture and focus each other—so much so that in the best pieces of writing it is impossible to imagine any other scenario that would do the job as well (think of *Memento*).

IS 'THEME' THE SAME THING AS 'MESSAGE'?
For me, theme is part of message. My definition of message is deliberately wide: 'anything and everything in the film connected with a philosophical comment about life'. I keep it this wide because the term 'message' is such a descriptive one, so provides a constant reminder for writers that a moral or some kind of comment should exist alongside the story or else audiences will get testy because they feel the film has no point. For more precise definitions and observations of a film's philosophical component, see Linda Seger's fascinating book, *Advanced Screenwriting* (2003), which breaks down what I call message into what she calls 'the theme' and 'issues arising from the theme' in Chapter 6, perceptively called: 'What it's really about'.

WHAT IF MY FILM HAS NO MESSAGE?
Even hero movies and horror films have a message—even if it's as simple as 'this action hero can always triumph over evil' or 'scientists should not meddle with nature'. Defining the message in films like these helps you give the audience a good example of the genre they've come to see, reminding

you that, for example, in your sci-fi horror movie, the scenario must depict the scientist meddling and the terrible consequences. This sounds simple. In fact, it's worryingly easy to forget.

THE SCENARIO
As we'll see, the scenario is divided into two plotlines that deal with the protagonist's public and private life. The film's main plot will be the 'adventure' and its other plot will deal with the protagonist's relationships. Sometimes a third will deal with the outer manifestations of an inner flaw.

WRITE ONE SENTENCE DESCRIBING EACH
Very early in the script's life, write one sentence describing the message and one describing the scenario—not as loglines or selling tools, but as a means of keeping you focused on what exactly you are creating. It is much easier to write thirty pages about what your film is about than two sentences. If you change what your script is about either in terms of message or scenario (or both), change your sentences. Narrative sentences (see pp. 64–7) will help here. Sometimes you won't know everything about the message until you're into a second draft. That's what drafts are for. Persist. The spark will always help. Keep reminding yourself of the spark and the heat and keep asking 'What is this film about, plot-wise and message-wise?' and 'Is this plot the best way of transmitting that message?' If scenes are coming to you, brainstorm what they might be transmitting. If the message is coming to you, brainstorm various plots that could illustrate your message and don't forget the genre equation.

Part 2
Conventional Narrative Structure

Chapter 5
Overview of conventional narrative structure

IN THE LAST CHAPTER I talked about message and scenario. To summarise, the message is what you want to say (even if it's as simple as 'this superhero is amazing'), the scenario is how you say it. Structure is the business of creating the best scenario to carry and display the message and it consists of a series of proven techniques to manipulate the very difficult and demanding audience that is sitting out there ready at every moment to reject your film.

Structure is emotion

Conventional narrative structure in screenwriting is today generally accepted to involve a three-act, linear chronological one-story piece about a single protagonist on a suspenseful journey towards a goal (and, often, as we've seen, redemption). This sounds very dry, but probably the most important thing to understand about script structure of all kinds, conventional or otherwise, is that it is all about emotion; specifically, about controlling and directing audience emotions in the most calculating and coldblooded of ways so that the audience will react exactly as the writer wishes at the precise moment the writer dictates. Film is a very emotional medium. Audiences come to the cinema specifically to laugh, weep or gasp in suspense (sometimes expecting intellectual content, sometimes not) but—and this is where our problem lies—they do none of these things easily. They do them only as a result of carefully calculated narrative tricks. We present them with a protagonist (a hero, male or female) who suffers emotional shock after emotional shock. Technical-sounding terms like 'turning points' are just another way of reminding the writer that to get the audience engaged the protagonist needs a big shock or a joyful revelation at key moments in the 100–120 precious minutes. Turning points in script structure, conventional and non-conventional, are always moments of great emotion for the character and thus the audience. A character is faced with a life-changing surprise. A character is faced with disaster at all sides.

Interestingly, Guillermo Arriaga, while he has limited patience with much screenwriting theory, says he consciously creates his scene breaks at moments of high emotion. Creating scene breaks and larger act breaks at moments of extreme emotion is exactly what structural models are intended to help you to do. The more you know about structure, the more you can control and focus audience emotions.

The limits of the conventional model

The first thing that needs to be said about what is accepted as the conventional structure for films (that is, the linear three-act model) is that it is not the only one. This flies in the face of the received wisdom but I believe it to be true, and, while it means we have a lot more structure to learn about, it also means that filmmakers who are writing outside the conventional form need not be trapped in the frustrating position of trying to fit square pegs in round holes, something that ends either in poor films, or, more commonly, in scripts abandoned. Other structures are out there to suit their purposes.

Before starting our discussion about conventional narrative, I want to look briefly at what, in my view, the conventional structure is good at, not good at, and other valid story structures that exist outside of it (structures I will look at later in the book).

Many years ago, when I first encountered conventional screenwriting theory I had spent some years writing for stage, film and television. While I could see instantly the storytelling value of the one-hero, three-act model with its built-in rising suspense to a powerful climax, I was puzzled because the theories assumed that this paradigm was the only one possible.

From my work in other dramatic forms I knew that good stories about groups and involving several storylines, each with a separate protagonist with a different point of view, were pleasing stage and TV audiences every day. I knew that in television we routinely split stories up into five acts or seven acts and audiences also liked this and wanted more. I knew that flashbacks and other time jumps (forbidden, even deemed 'lazy') could work powerfully. I knew that films did not have to be about the spiritual improvement of one individual and could have a social agenda and end less than optimistically, indeed be heartbreakingly pessimistic, to great acclaim.

I knew that there always had been many successful films that did not fit the one-hero linear pattern—classics such as *Citizen Kane*, *The Magnificent Seven* and almost every war film and film about a troubled family that has ever been made (because these are characteristically about the actions and interactions of a group). I knew that dramatic masterpieces from Shakespeare to Ibsen and Chekhov involved group stories: *A Midsummer Nights' Dream* is not about one hero, and Chekhov wrote about three sisters, not one.

Finally, while I knew that Aristotle's *Poetics* was often cited to prove that conventional linear narrative was, and remains, the only method of storytelling in Western civilisation, I knew that Homer's *Odyssey*, the iconic journey story of Western culture, is non-linear and episodic. Moreover, I knew that in *Poetics* Aristotle actually speaks admiringly of the *Odyssey*'s structure, he just feels it is inappropriate for the stage.

With all this in mind, the question for me was how then could the one-hero, three-act 'conventional' narrative model be the only true model for film, as was so often assumed?

CHOOSE THE STRUCTURE TO SUIT THE STORY MATERIAL

I have come to a number of conclusions over the years. These are:

- The three-act one-hero linear model is an excellent and extraordinarily versatile model, capable of producing films as diverse yet vividly original as *Juno*, *Children of Heaven*, *Goodbye Lenin* and the wonderful *Synecdoche, New York*.
- The three-act, single-protagonist model is not the only one: others have always been in use and are completely valid.
- The conventional model is the most *prevalent* model, the most *streamlined* model, the *basic* model and, crucially, the *safest* model (safety not being something to sneeze at in a high-risk, high-cost industry like film) because it builds in a fast pace and rising suspenseful chronological build to closure. In contrast, ensemble and non-linear models always struggle with pace, connection, meaning and closure.
- There is no reason why the three-act model needs to be optimistic, nor why its protagonist needs to improve or be redeemed (although usually the protagonist does need to undergo change).
- While conventional narrative is a wonderfully useful model, it only works for a certain kind of film. This film is chronological, has a long central development section and involves only one protagonist and one point of view. It covers a brief time span, gets off to a very quick start and always builds directly and suspensefully to a final climax.

If you want to write films that don't fit the conventional model; for example, ensemble films (such as *American Beauty*, *Traffic* and *Crash*), or flashback films (*Atonement*, *Slumdog Millionaire* and *Citizen Kane*, for example), or complex, non-linear films (such as *Pulp Fiction*, *21 Grams*, *The Sweet Hereafter* or *The Butterfly Effect*), or in fact any film that needs to be exposition-heavy, or have multiple protagonists, or time jumps, or several narratives, the conventional linear template will not work. In this case you need one of the parallel narrative forms.

Excitingly, all of the parallel narrative forms work by splitting, reassembling and sometimes either truncating or doubling the conventional three-act narrative structure, hence they can be planned and written within a reasonable time frame.

This is all good news. While we continue to have the ever-reliable conventional three-act paradigm at our disposal (in both its optimistic and pessimistic forms), we no longer have to stick exclusively to that. We don't have to choose our story material to fit one template. We have many templates to choose from, each of which suits a different kind of story, philosophy of life and message. And, even more exciting, because all of the parallel narrative forms are based on the three-act structure, we already have the building blocks to construct films in these other structural forms. This is even more reason to understand as much as possible about conventional narrative.

The basics of conventional (three-act) structure

The standard method of approaching conventional structure is to take a structural model (described in detail in a book or by a teacher) and try to fit the story fragments into it, adding more until the structure is complete. The advantage of this method is that the structure, being proven, is likely to transmit the story well, and the process of construction itself is a problem-solving exercise because it reveals the gaps and weaknesses in the story. The disadvantage of the method is that, however good the structural model—however good the book—if we persistently use only one methodology, vertical thinking will take over the process and short-circuit any original thinking without our ever realising it. It will use the method to recycle not only industry clichés but also our own old ideas, generated on the previous occasions when we used the same method. And this is not the fault of the method. It is caused by our own innate panic reflex towards shortcuts and clichéd vertical thinking.

For today's working writer, the reality is that no one method of creating a three-act structure is usable for a lifetime to the exclusion of all others. We must never allow ourselves to think we have 'the method' to handle structure, and we must force ourselves to outwit our talent (which will permit us to do a reasonably good job on all kinds of weak and clichéd ideas) by challenging it with new approaches so that rather than chug along at eighty per cent capacity, it can achieve its full potential.

Later chapters in this part of the book provide a series of practical techniques for creating a conventional three-act structure, including more development strategies. Because these strategies work on asking and answering questions, they demand brainstorming. They frequently cross-refer to other structural approaches, so they're useful. But, like all methods, they can become mechanical, and special effort must be taken to maintain concentration.

Screenplay structure equals good timing. All theories of screenwriting structure, whether linear or otherwise, boil down to the same basic storytelling problem: how to keep a live audience engaged for an evening. Film is a performing art constructed and executed in the absence of its audience, hence scriptwriting is the art of second-guessing that absent audience. Poor structure can alienate an audience in the same way that a good joke can be wrecked by poor telling. Thus, script structure is largely to do with 'good timing': knowing how and when to build up suspense, knowing how long to delay before delivering the crucial line, understanding the impact of energy and pause, and so on. Time also impinges in another, more basic way, which is that because audiences experience screenwriting within a time-imposed framework, sitting down at 8.30 pm and getting up at 10 pm, the film will always present itself to them with a beginning, middle and end. No matter how unconventional the structure or content, no matter how many time jumps or complex multiple narratives, time itself imposes this rigid structure and writers have to cope with it as best they can, creating a powerful start at 8.30 pm, a gripping middle between 9 and 9.45 pm, and a suspenseful climax at 10 pm. Terrifyingly, the longer the audience sits, the harder the screenwriter has to work to keep its attention, which means the cleverer/more moving/more unexpected the rising plot needs to be. Even worse, all this has to be worked out at two or three years' remove.

In fact everything about film—about moving pictures—is connected with time and movement in time; that is to say action in every sense. Film consists of movement in all ways: physical, emotional and spiritual. In screenwriting, story is movement and our characters move through their own mental landscape.

Some books on scriptwriting actually specify the page number in the script where structural high points should happen. Many writers find this worryingly rigid. But if you think of it not as a matter of pages but of screen time, it makes sense, because what is actually being said is that a script needs a twist or turn every ten to fifteen minutes, otherwise the audience will get bored—which is really just common sense.

BEATS OR STORY STEPS

Any narrative, linear or non-linear, is a series of consequences arising from an initial event or action. It's a chain reaction. All theories of script structure depend on the notion of a 'beat', which is a step forward in the plot. What is a beat? For example, in 'Little Red Riding Hood', Red Riding Hood's normal life is beat one. Her mother's instruction to take food to her grandmother is beat two. Meeting the wolf is beat three, and so on. A scene is not a beat. The easiest way to understand a scene is that if you have to move the camera and crew to another place, it's the end of a scene. It might take Little Red Riding Hood some scenes to gather food for her grandmother, as she goes to the grocer, to the baker, to the butcher, and so on. All of those scenes are part of the same beat and often you will need several scenes to show one beat. However, you must make sure you need all these scenes or the film will lose pace. When you feel a film is slow it's usually because the film is stuck on the same beat, saying the same thing in slightly different ways. This is an easy mistake. For example, if character X announces that he is going to make a phone call, explaining what he'll say, then makes the call exactly as he's just described, it's the same beat in two different ways.

Estimate about seventy to eighty beats for one hundred minutes of film. This total includes all of the beats in each storyline (main plot and subplots), and you will often have to combine beats from different plotlines in one scene to get them all in. Close plotting, which we'll deal with later, is how to order, combine and condense beats to tell the richest version of your story. It's a core screenwriting skill and requires ingenuity and practice.

CHRONOLOGICAL BUILD TO CLOSURE

As I've said, the great advantage of conventional three-act narrative is that it uses only those stories that start quickly and build steadily and chronologically to climax, which is definitely the safest to get the audience interested at 8.30 pm, more interested at 9 pm and on the edge of their seats at 9.55 pm. It chooses story material that quickly introduces the characters and their problems (providing a strong first act), shows the characters' problems growing increasingly complicated (providing a long second act) and reveals the characters' problems resolved in a climax at the end of the third act (although some theories split the middle into two acts, making the final act number four). Within this large 'beginning, long middle, end' structure are all sorts of twists and turns—devices which experience shows to have worked with audiences in the past. Hence, if you plan your three-act narrative and follow its rules about choice of story and the way you tell that story, you have a very good chance of getting a script with all the necessary pace, suspenseful build to climax and characterisation opportunities.

But aren't all good films like this? Don't they all have great beginnings, middles and ends? Yes, but as I have implied, many very good films do not have these things inbuilt chronologically and would be seriously lacking in suspense if told in a linear way from start to finish. They need to achieve their pace and rising suspense via non-linearity. *21 Grams*, for example, would be extremely boring if told chronologically because the lengthy but necessary pre-accident scenes would seem pointless. Only with hindsight can they play as unbearably poignant, and the film's non-linearity provides that hindsight experience.

THE DRAMATIC HIGH POINTS OF CONVENTIONAL NARRATIVE

Essentially, a conventional narrative film divides up its beats so that it has an opening hook followed by dramatic high points at the end of the first act, second act (or, if a four-act model is being used, at the end of the third act) and at the climax, which occurs just before the end of the film and resolves the central dilemma of the story.

As mentioned in Chapter 4, a good example of a hook is the opening of *Men in Black*, where a group of manual labourers turn out to be aliens. Another is the wild chase scenes that always open a James Bond movie. Early on in the film, either *as* the hook, or *after* the hook, there will be an event which changes the normal scheme of things and forces the protagonist in a new direction, effectively starting the story. This is called a 'catalyst', 'inciting incident' or 'disturbance'. I prefer the term 'disturbance'; first because it's a constant reminder that *an action* (rather than something internal like a thought or a feeling) has to occur in the physical world to fracture the protagonist's normality (because that's something we can actually *see*) and second and most importantly, it suggests that this change is the start of many in the protagonist's life. To me, 'catalyst' and 'inciting incident' imply that only one change need occur. Often this is what is wrong with weak stories, particularly those that start to experience difficulties in the second act. They simply don't have a complex enough story to last a hundred minutes.

Sometimes the disturbance is an apparently harmless event that leads to serious trouble (as in *Thelma and Louise*, where the disturbance is two women going off alone together on holiday, stopping *en route* at a bar). Sometimes the disturbance is a violent event in itself (as in *The African Queen*, where Sunday morning prayers are interrupted by a murderous attack). Once the disturbance has occurred, the suspense builds through one crisis to another as the film progresses towards its end, in what is sometimes described as a rising three-act structure, with the climax being the most suspenseful moment of the film. This makes sense, of course, because putting the moment of highest tension any earlier would make the action fizzle.

The main crises are often called 'plot points' or 'turning points'. I prefer the latter because it is more descriptive. Turning points are turns in the story's direction that cause turning points in the main characters' lives. Hence, we have the first-act turning point (the dramatic high point occurring at the end of the first act), the second-act turning point, which occurs at the end of the second act, and the climax, which occurs at the end of the film. Some theorists also include 'the midpoint', which is a major event in the middle of the film that turns the protagonist's life around.

In *Thelma and Louise*, the first-act turning point occurs when Louise kills the man who is attempting to rape Thelma, turning the film in a completely new direction and creating a shocking problem for the two women.

While the first-act turning point is usually a major shock, some conventionally structured films choose a more subdued, less startling first-act turning point as part of their overall message. For example, the consciously gentle *Ladies in Lavender* has as its first-act turning point the revelation that the cultured young man is an accomplished violinist (but note that this is still a kind of surprise). Even the deliberately restrained *Samson and Delilah*, a poignant love story about two Australian Aboriginal teenagers, has a sudden death as its first-act turning point.

Traditionally, the second-act turning point is the point at which the protagonist is physically or metaphorically closest to death (in *Thelma and Louise*, it is when Louise is told by the detective that she and Thelma are being charged with murder, which carries the death penalty). The third act, traditionally, is the protagonist's battle to win (Thelma and Louise rebel against the society that represses them, particularly the truck driver, who represents all sexist men), with the battle decided in a climax. The climax answers the question raised in the first-act turning point; hence, Thelma and Louise commit suicide (climax) which answers the question, 'How will Thelma and Louise react now that they have killed a man?'.

The disturbance, the two turning points, the midpoint and the climax form the spine of the story, so writers often try to pick them early. This is not as hard as it might sound, because moments of high drama are often among the earliest fragments to present themselves. Really, once you know the two turning points and the climax, you have your film.

Charles Harris, who wrote and directed *Paradise Grove*, believes that all turning points are followed by the protagonist's decision to act, so he adds a second step to the second-act turning point; namely, the protagonist's decision to fight back (in *Thelma and Louise*, it is the women's decision not to give themselves up). As we'll see in later chapters, this second step is not only very useful in constructing conventional narrative, it's vital in understanding how to split up non-linear parallel narrative.

VISUALISING THE THREE-ACT STRUCTURE

To visualise the three/four-act division with all its subdivisions, writers have developed a range of different diagrams. Each presents a different circuit breaker for subjectivity, and can be enormously useful. But it should be remembered that while depicting a script diagrammatically in its entirety is an excellent tool for the writer, the piece of screen drama that we produce is not experienced by the audience statically and in its entirety, like a painting. It is experienced as a sequence of events—moving pictures—that have to keep the audience's attention. So, however wonderful the third act might be, the audience cannot see it until it has sat through the first and second acts. And if the first and second acts are poor, the audience will not stay for the third one.

While this might seem glaringly obvious, it is actually very easy to be so taken up with what comes later in the script that you write a very poor beginning, thinking of it merely as a way of setting up the excellence that is to come. This happens all the time with television series, where the writers get so taken up with later episodes that they perceive the first episode merely as the set-up. The result is a weak first episode that loses its audience forever.

Actually, the importance of movement and the fact that a film is absorbed as a sequence is reflected in many of the diagrams commonly used by writers to depict and plan the traditional structure that they want to produce. The diagrams are all related to movement and a journey—travelling a road, moving full circle, climbing a mountain range. They all depict the protagonist progressing through a mental landscape.

THE MOUNTAIN

Frequently, to remind us that a film must build to a third-act climax, the rising action of the traditional three-act structure is depicted as a mountain range with the second act (as is common) being about the same length as the other two combined. Linda Seger, best known for her fine book on scriptwriting called *Making a Good Script Great* (3rd edition, 2010), is one of the theorists who use models like this one.

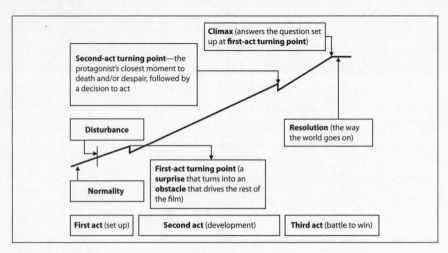

Figure 5.1 The three-act structure as a mountain

THE CIRCLE

Yet another way of depicting the three-act structure is to show the protagonist's adventure as a circle, returning to the point where it started. This is the case with Christopher Vogler's hero's journey model, the steps of which have been outlined on pp. 28–9. Figure 5.2 provides a much simplified model. Christopher Vogler splits the narrative into four, not three acts, and the hero proceeds through specific stages or trials on the journey, each of which is represented in the proper diagrams in *The Writer's Journey* by notches on the circle.

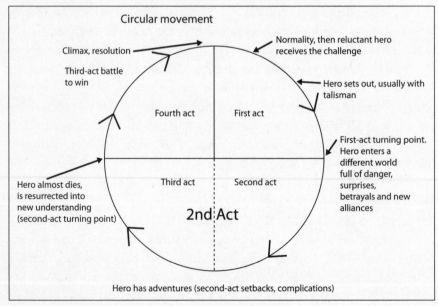

Figure 5.2 Christopher Vogler's hero's journey (simplified)

ROAD OR TIMELINE

A third way of depicting a conventional three-act structure is by a diagram
that resembles a road and is really a kind of timeline.

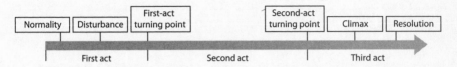

Figure 5.3 The three-act structure as a road or timeline

THE IMPORTANCE OF THE PROTAGONIST

Notice that the movement implied in all of the above diagrams is that of
the single protagonist—because the main task of conventional screenwriting structure is perceived to be creating the journey, the 'adventure', of one
protagonist (we'll look at structures that permit the journeys of several protagonists later). This is very easy to forget. The audience needs to walk each
step with this protagonist, in their shoes, and each step has to lead audience
and protagonist in a specific direction. It is very easy for a writer to slip from
being inside the protagonist to being inside another character, and start to
follow that character (which you can do in parallel narrative structures but
not in the conventional model). Some theorists actually feel that the protagonist should be in every scene of a conventional structure.

THE BASIC SMILEY/THOMPSON NINE-POINT STORY
STRUCTURE

The nine-point Smiley/Thompson structure is an enormously helpful model
for finding the basic shape of your three-act conventional screenplay (see
Figure 5.4). I first came across it many years ago in a class on stage writing
run by Paul Thompson of New York University, who says that he developed
it from Sam Smiley's book on playwriting. While Paul Thompson has now
significantly extended his model to include fourteen points (see Figure 5.7),
I find that the basic nine-point model remains an extremely useful structural
method, particularly at the start of the development process, but also later,
when it can be used as a diagnostic checklist. Its great strength is that it breaks
the three/four-act form into nine basic steps according to *what the protagonist is doing* in the script in response to events. This is excellent, because it
constructs the film around the actions of its main character, thus forces the
writer to think of the film in terms of the protagonist's *actions,* to create a
story with rising suspense, as opposed to a character just doing things.

In the following chapters, I've built on a range of structural approaches, my own and those of others, including the basic Smiley/Thompson model (Figure 5.4), to create a range of script development strategies, which, put together, will help create a solid outline for a conventional linear film.

Act one
1.   Normality
2.   Disturbance
3.   Protagonist
4.   Plan
5.   Surprise . . . which turns into the . . .
6.   Obstacle

End of act one

Acts two and three
7.   Complication, substories, more surprises and obstacles creating acts two and three
8.   Climax (end of act three)
9.   Resolution (how the world goes on)

Figure 5.4 Basic Smiley/Thompson nine-point plan

Figure 5.5 shows how the nine-point plan compares with the three-act model.

		Act one
1. Normality 2. Protagonist 3. Disturbance	=	The set-up
4. Plan	=	Actions in response to the disturbance
5. Surprise . . . which turns into the	=	First-act turning point, end of act one
6. Obstacle		
		End of act one
		Acts two and three
7. Complications, substories	=	Acts two and three
8. Climax	=	At the end of act three
9. Resolution	=	How the world goes on

Figure 5.5 Nine-point plan compared with three-act model

'CINDERELLA' STRUCTURED ACCORDING TO THE BASIC NINE-POINT
PLAN

Figure 5.6 shows 'Cinderella' broken down into the nine-point plan. I have
added an antagonist to the nine points to suggest the necessary protagonist/
antagonist conflict.

Normality	Cinderella is working as slave to her ugly sisters and wicked stepmother.
Protagonist	Cinderella
Disturbance	The household receives an invitation to the ball from the handsome prince, but Cinderella cannot go because she has no party clothes.
Plan	To go to the ball and meet the prince (but it seems impossible)
Antagonist	The status quo—'class distinction'—personified by ugly sisters and stepmother
	End of set-up
First-act turning point Surprise *which turns into* **Obstacle**	In an amazing physical surprise, Cinderella's hitherto unknown fairy godmother appears and provides clothes and transport for the ball, changing the entire direction of the story.
	BUT clothes and transport are provided only until midnight.
	End of first act
Second act Complications, substories, more surprises and obstacles	Cinderella goes to the ball, entrances the prince, forgets the time. (In some versions there is a ball every night for a week and she goes back to the ball several times, getting away before midnight every time except the last.)
Second-act turning point *(closest moment to utter despair)*	It's midnight. Her clothes turn into rags. She runs off in despair, leaving her shoe.
	End of act two

Third act	Cinderella returns to her old life, despairing of ever seeing the prince again. The prince announces that he will marry the woman whose foot fits the shoe. In some versions events keep preventing him from entering Cinderella's house. Finally, the prince arrives at the household but Cinderella is at first not allowed to try on the shoe. Cinderella fights back (her battle to win) by asking to try on the shoe.
Climax *(answering the question set up by the first-act turning point)*	The shoe fits. The prince says he will marry her.

Figure 5.6 'Cinderella' broken down into the basic Smiley/Thompson plan

Interestingly, in 'Cinderella', as in many fairy stories with a female protagonist, including 'Sleeping Beauty' and 'Little Red Riding Hood', the protagonist's decision to fight back and the battle to win are not pronounced; indeed, they are done largely by a male saviour. Modern films usually make the female more proactive.

ACTION LINE AND RELATIONSHIP LINE
So far I have been talking about conventional narrative as primarily concerned with the protagonist's adventure (known as the main plot or foreground story). However, in many scripts the script was inspired by its 'subplot' or 'background story'; that is, the protagonist's relationships. The classic example is *Witness*, which was specifically written to explore the emotional relationship between an Amish woman and an urbanised man. The main plot—in which the woman's son witnesses a murder and the urbanised man has to hide out on the Amish farm—is merely a means to bring the two together in a suspenseful situation, a way of permitting the subplot to happen.

MAIN PLOT AND SUBPLOT EQUAL
Because the relationship material is so important to the film I prefer to use my term 'action line' for the adventure (rather than the more commonly used terms 'main plot' or 'foreground story'), and my term 'relationship line' for the relationship material (rather than 'sub-plot' or 'background story'). As well as removing any suggestion that the adventure is more important than the relationship material, the term 'action line' is a helpful reminder that

this particular plotline must move from causative action to causative action. Meanwhile, the term 'relationship line' rather than 'subplot' acknowledges the great importance of relationship material in the film and is a helpful reminder that this plot must deal with a developing relationship (not, for example, just redundant, eternal bickering). I will use these terms from now on.

STRUCTURE OF THE RELATIONSHIP LINE

Structurally, the subplot has its own three-act structure, with catalyst/disturbance, first-act turning point, second-act turning point and climax. It is usually set up in the first act and developed extensively in the second act, after the first-act turning point has changed the protagonist's world. In many cases the relationship line can't happen until the second act because the protagonist does not meet the relevant relationship line characters until then. For example, in *The Station Agent*, Fin cannot meet Olivia and Joe until he moves to the train depot.

OTHER APPROACHES TO THE CONVENTIONAL LINEAR STRUCTURE

Many of the approaches to conventional linear structure consist of dividing the three-act action line in different ways—into nine, eleven, and so on. Check all of these out. There are many, many of them, all with a different perspective. Many writers find Frank Daniel's approach particularly useful, whereby you think of your script as seven crucial episodes. Another very productive method is the eight-part division recommended by Jack Epps Jnr, the writer of films like *Top Gun*, *Anaconda*, *Turner and Hooch* and *Legal Eagles*. Also extremely valuable are any approaches that describe the structure in terms of what the protagonist is being faced with and doing (this is one of the joys of Vogler's hero's journey model) because they are a useful reminder of the necessity of the plot to move forwards. Overleaf, in Figure 5.7, is Paul Thompson's extended version of the nine-point structure.

Without good structure, a good idea is nothing. The film industry is full of good film ideas that never reach the screen, also, sadly, many good ideas that reach the screen are so structurally flawed that they never achieve their full potential.

The following chapters provide a detailed, step-by-step guide for constructing the outline or 'beat sheet' for a simple-form three-act film, the map of your film you will use to take it to first draft. They also explain how to avoid common pitfalls and how, as far as possible, to be your own script doctor.

1. Balance
2. Disturbance
3. Person with a problem
4. Protagonist
5. Plan
6. The narrative question. What does the audience HOPE and FEAR?
7. Obstacles
8. Surprise(s)
9. Middle: character, relationships, themes + substories
10. Substories
11. More surprises
12. Major crisis A story, B story etc.
13. Major climax A story, B story etc.
14. Resolution

Figure 5.7 Extended version of the Smiley/Thompson plan

Chapter 6
Planning a conventional, three-act structure

SCREENWRITERS LOVE WRITING DIALOGUES and scenes. That's what we do. But, without a plan, you are unlikely to write a story that rises suspensefully to a climax within the permissible screen time. Ironically, your talent may pull you off track. Instead of taking Little Red Riding Hood from the grocer's into the woods to meet the wolf, you are likely write a wonderful but utterly irrelevant scene between the grocer and his gangster brother, leaving the audience thinking, irritably: 'What's the point of this?'

Assembling the fragments

It would be wonderful if the story behind a film presented itself in a logical way; starting at the beginning and proceeding neatly through to the end. Unfortunately, stories present in fragments—a character, a scene, a climax—and the writer's job is to interpret these fragments and impose some kind of order without pre-empting the creative process.

With a film script, as with a drawing or architectural plans, you start from a few bold strokes, move to a broad, general sketch, then gradually start filling in the detail.

The first step is to find a way of collecting and storing all the disconnected fragments—action line, relationship line, message, scenario, spark, new world, characterisation and all the other bits and pieces of the script—until they start to assume some kind of shape. Some writers have a special notebook. Some have a blackboard or notice board. Others write the fragments on pieces of paper which they then crumple into balls and toss into a basket until it is full. A lot of this is about psyching yourself into the right frame of mind, but in all cases there is a commitment to letting the lateral imagination do its spadework over as much time as possible without interference from logic. Screenwriters do not have the luxury of time permitted to novelists, but time given over to accumulating ideas is time well spent. The more fragments the better. You might like to write your spark on a piece of paper and post it above your desk.

THE BEAT SHEET, OUTLINE AND TREATMENT

What you are aiming for at this point is a 'beat sheet' or 'outline'—a step-by-step description in point form of the plot content (including action line and relationship line) of your whole film. This will provide the final map for your film before you embark on the micro-engineering task of writing your individual scenes, each of which has to be carefully selected to earn its keep and meticulously put together so that the film keeps its picky audience engaged. You won't be able to finish this for some time because it takes a great deal of work. The treatment is a prose description of the film often required by investors. In the chapters that follow there are various strategies that will help you construct your beat sheet, outline and treatment. For more on treatment writing see pp. 469–75.

Well-prepared beat sheets, outlines and treatments are lifesavers. They permit you to control the script rather than letting the script control you, or rather, letting your mood of the moment control you—because, if you construct your script as you go, you are at the mercy of how creative you happen to be on the day. Without them, one bad afternoon can see your characters heading off in a direction that is utterly wrong, but which you are then stuck with. Completed beat sheets and outlines permit you to immerse yourself in writing the minutiae of each individual scene to your best, allowing you to seed later plot issues and build cleverly to the end of each scene so that it jumps well to the next. The huge advantage of this is that if you get stuck on a difficult scene or have only a small amount of time to write that day, you can jump ahead to an easy scene or sequence and write that. Additionally, if you ever feel later that you have taken the wrong direction, you can go back to where you took that wrong direction and take the right one.

Screenwriter and University of California, Berkeley, lecturer J. Mira Kopell actually bases her teaching of feature film writing around the careful creation of a detailed outline.

Basic plan of your film

Use Figure 6.1, which is a basic plan of what your film has to contain and depict, to create a very simple plan of your film, to remind yourself about message and scenario and the way action line drives relationship line. Put a simple sentence or two into the message and scenario boxes outlining your rough ideas (for example, under scenario, write: 'ill-matched couple travel down river in Africa to blow up enemy war ship' and under message, 'triumph of human spirit, opposites can attract, love can change people'). Check that your rough idea of the scenario looks capable of depicting your message, and that your action line looks as if it will permit your relationship line to happen. You can keep coming back to it as you progress, adding more.

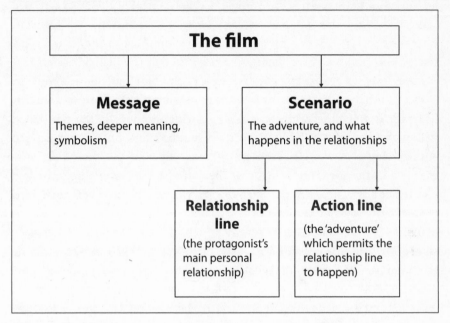

The film

Message
Themes, deeper meaning, symbolism

Scenario
The adventure, and what happens in the relationships

Relationship line
(the protagonist's main personal relationship)

Action line
(the 'adventure' which permits the relationship line to happen)

Figure 6.1 Basic plan of what your film has to contain and depict

USE THE DIAGRAMS

Use the mountain and circle diagrams, inserting notes about the steps of your story. You will keep modifying this. Every time you look at these, their shape will remind you of the fact that you are not creating random incidents, but are tracking one story's rising suspense to a climax.

MAKE STRUCTURE CHARTS

Simultaneously, start making a basic structure chart into which you can start inserting your fragments, trying to get them into some kind of loose chronological order and three-act structure. All that this requires is a page divided into three columns, labelled 'Act One', 'Act Two', 'Act Three'—or, even more simply, 'Beginning', 'Middle' and 'End' (these refer to the action line). Some of your ideas will be action line, others will be relationship line and some will concern message, character etc. Just put them all in. You will have to keep updating your charts and creating new ones. Keep them all for reference because you may go off course.

The point of structure charts is to keep options open while feeling your way towards the story. By all means think about possible scenes and note down every idea, but be aware that one strong scene can send the story in a direction that will later reveal itself to be quite wrong. You might well have scenes that you know, in your bones, are crucial to the story and will stay. Maybe they will, but, surprisingly, you may later find that you transmit your point more vividly with a condensed version. For example, writing a film about a mother investigating her serviceman son's suicide, your initial idea might be to spend the first part of the film showing the mother, after the funeral, driving across country to the military base to confront its commanding officer, meeting other grieving mothers on the way. Later, you might decide that the journey is a distraction and you can get a much stronger impact by making the mother publicly confront the officer very early on in the film, say actually at the son's funeral, where she can also briefly but powerfully interact with the grieving mothers, so you don't need the elaborate journey set-up.

Figure 6.2 depicts what a simple structure chart devised in the early stages of writing *Being John Malkovich* might have looked like had Charlie Kaufman used this method. Of course, the chart is entirely fictitious and Mr Kaufman might well have used a completely different approach. Note that a lot of options are wide open and much will be thrown out. Notice also how the content is put in the form of questions, so as to resist committing too early.

Development Strategies 5 and 6: Simple and advanced narrative sentences

I've created some development strategies to find the chain of events in the action line based on the Smiley/Thompson model called a 'narrative sentence'. A narrative sentence is a fill-in-the-gaps method of checking that the idea is developing into a proper story; that it is something more than a logline, half-idea or an ongoing normality, and that it is based on the actions of the protagonist. It's surprising how far down the track scripts can go without their writers having a real sense of what story is being told. The narrative sentence forces you to provide your story spine—unlike thirty-page treatments in which it is easy to ramble and avoid the hard narrative questions. It is very easy to spend twenty pages of your treatment giving a vivid account of the first ten minutes of your film, then use the remaining ten to give the baldest of explanations about what is to happen next.

First of all, try the simple narrative sentence.

Feature film: weird, thought-provoking comedy about being able to get into someone's head. Possible title—'The Portal'?		
Act one	**Act two**	**Act three**
Opening? Protag? A man.	Once inside person's head what can he do? Rob a bank? Seduce women? Or do women seduce him? What is his wife or girlfriend doing at the time?	John Malkovich realises something is happening? Or should this be earlier?
Peter? John? Craig?		John Malkovich dies with Craig, Maxine and Lotte in his head? They are trapped in a dead body?
Setting? What is protagonist doing before disturbance?		
Craig finds portal into someone's mind.	Personal story. Parents? Wife? Love story? Infidelity story? Any way of linking the two stories?	
Where is it? How does he find it? On a walk in the country? In a coat? In a suitcase? Under the bed?		Wife dies? Maxine shoots Craig?
	Maxine and Lotte attracted?	Happy ending? Or Craig loses everything? Craig killed by person whose mind he gets into? Craig going crazy, ending up a derelict?
What is Craig's job?	NB There must be some explanation of the portal somewhere.	
Is he married? Yes, has wife, Lotte, a meek woman.		
NB What is Craig's job? How can it fit in with the story?		Craig and his wife living happily ever after?
In act one he meets another woman? Maxine?		
Is there any philosophical content in this, or is it just science fiction? If philosophical content, what?		
What is the ending of act one? Finding the portal?		

Figure 6.2 Hypothetical structure chart for writing *Being John Malkovich*

Development Strategy 5

CREATE A SIMPLE NARRATIVE SENTENCE

Create a simple sentence to describe your story in terms of the protagonist's sequence of actions using the following model:

[Protagonist] faced with [problem] responds by [series of actions] and finally deals with [same problem as above] by [climax].

Questions to ask:
- Can I fit my story into this simple structure?
- Does this scenario fit my message?

As you go further into development, start trying to complete the advanced narrative sentence (which is really just the basic Smiley/Thompson nine-point plan rendered as a fill-in-the-gaps sentence).

Development Strategy 6

CREATE AN ADVANCED NARRATIVE SENTENCE

Fill in the gaps to describe your story in terms of the protagonist's sequence of actions.

[Describe protagonist], who is currently [describe normality], experiences [describe disturbance] responds by [describe plan in response to disturbance] but everything changes when [describe surprise that turns into the obstacle which drives the rest of the film] which causes [describe increasing complications] which are resolved ultimately by [describe climax] and the story ends [describe resolution].

Questions to ask:
- Can I fit my story into this more advanced structure?
- Does this scenario fit my message?

You will find filling in the gaps in both of these sentences difficult—naturally, because the sentences are summaries of your entire film. Expect to keep returning to them and modifying them as you proceed.

Narrative sentences can gradually be expanded to create your entire outline, in fact your whole thirty-page treatment, with the great advantage that the narrative is being built, as it were, from the inside out—from the skeleton outwards—so it will be very strong. Narrative sentences also permit an overview of your whole film. They allow you to think about structure but do not lock you into a scenario before you are ready. They also physically show you where the story's gaps are and prompt you to consider different ways of filling them (unlike treatments, where good prose can conceal poor structure).

NARRATIVE SENTENCES FOR RELATIONSHIP LINE

The narrative sentences mentioned above refer to the protagonist's adventure, the action line. The relationship line of your script also has a three-act structure, which we shall return to later, using the narrative sentences to help.

Chapter 7
Normality and disturbance (the set-up)

AS YOU ARE MAPPING out your script with structure charts and narrative sentences, you will need to fill in more detail. This is where the later development strategies come in. They are designed to help you create a plan for the simplest form of conventional rising three-act narrative. They are also useful as a starting point to check that an existing three-act script has the necessary structural elements in place and remedy problems if it has not.

Because a film is planned from the general to the particular—from a broad idea inwards to detail—sometimes the development strategies jump from one topic to another and back again. Rather than try to work on your script as you read through the strategies, read through them first, then go back and use them for reference as you plan the script.

When you actually start to apply the development strategies to your script, brainstorm each new one to get 'real but unusual' answers. Expect many of your first answers to be clichéd or uninspiring—but persist. You will use the development strategies again and again in the planning as more detail comes to you, referring to them in conjunction with your structure charts to create your final map for your film before you embark on writing scenes, your beat sheet or outline. For quick reference, use the list on pp. x–xi.

Getting a good set-up: Normality and disturbance

Your film is a chain reaction of events. The first event in the action line—the first step up the mountain or signpost along the road—is the disturbance. This simply means something unusual happening in the normality—the normal world—of the protagonist. The disturbance acts to give the protagonist a problem that the course of the film will answer, either happily or otherwise. These elements—protagonist, normality and disturbance, plus the problem that arises out of the disturbance—provide the set-up. A common failing of weak films is that they do not properly set up their story and main players. How is it possible to know whether a set-up is working properly?

TOO MUCH NORMALITY, TOO LITTLE DISTURBANCE

Set-up problems are normally caused by writers spending too much time on the normality. It is surprisingly easy to write material about an ongoing normality; that is, to write different scenarios or tableaux which describe an unchanging state (for example, different aspects of life in a country town) or character (the way a certain character typically behaves—say, losing their temper over trivialities) rather than creating a journey through which a character must travel.

Repeated normality—writing endless different versions of essentially the same scene—is also often seen in films about life stories, journeys or long-term relationships, because in such cases it is easy to mistake physical movement or movement of time for movement in plot and character.

Endlessly repeating the normality is something to which actor–writers are particularly prone because their training is to create a character, rather than a character moving through a scenario. A film that displays these faults very evidently is *Mr Saturday Night* written, directed and starring Billy Crystal. The film sets out to show an egotistical, self-destructive, but ultimately endearing comedian. But rather than create a plot that takes this character on a journey, the film ends up merely showing us different instances of the same thing; namely, a comedian being self-destructive. The film becomes boring because the comedian is not given a problem. Compare the film of John Osborne's play *The Entertainer*, in which Laurence Olivier plays an egotistical, self-destructive comedian who needs money, and therefore does a series of unscrupulous things. The crucial story elements here are 'a problem, a goal and a journey'.

To check that your film has a problem, a goal and a journey rather than multiple versions of essentially the same scene, use the simple narrative sentence, Development Strategy 5. While films that are slow often have too much normality before the disturbance, if the protagonist has been properly identified and is interesting enough, this can give the film an epic or art-house quality, as in *Kiss of the Spider Woman* or *Out of Africa*, and often the intention is exactly to be slow. But if poorly handled it can be disastrous. A simple way to understand what makes a disturbance is that the story cannot start until the disturbance happens. Think of shaggy dog stories. These always start with (say) the Englishman, the Scotsman and the Irishman in a specific situation, such as walking along a road. But the joke proper cannot start until something else occurs (for example, a lion appearing).

Think of the normality as your protagonist on the cusp of change, and the first part of the change is the disturbance. Consider starting your film on or just after the disturbance, as happens in *Juno* (where the opening shows Juno trying to prove her pregnancy test wrong) and *Gran Torino* (which opens on the funeral of Walt's wife, leaving him isolated, permitting the relationship with his neighbours to develop). Notice that in both films, the way we learn about the disturbance is in a dynamic, interesting scene set *after* the disturbance event—so the film opens with the action line already on its way. *Juno* is already pregnant and Walt's wife has already died. More lyrical films will often show longer normality, as in *The Station Agent*, where the disturbance, Henry's death, happens some time after the start.

Remember that a disturbance is not a feeling or mood ('John is feeling miserable')—it is an event. A useful rule of thumb is that a good disturbance cannot be described without a verb, often a verb of movement, disruption or change—the gunslinger *rides* into town, the detective *breaks* a leg, the novelist *receives* a mysterious letter, the missionaries are *attacked* by enemy soldiers. This rule makes up Development Strategy 7.

Development Strategy 7

MAKE SURE THE DISTURBANCE HAPPENS SOON AND INVOLVES REAL CHANGE

Describe the disturbance with a verb of movement, disruption or change.

Questions to ask:

- Is my disturbance 'real but unusual' (Development Strategy 2)?
- Is the verb to describe it a verb of movement or disruption, or is it a 'passive' verb like 'living', 'feeling', 'experiencing'? If it's the latter, you haven't got a proper disturbance in place yet.

Identifying the disturbance makes us understand the essence of the normality. For example, in *Being John Malkovich*, if we decide that the disturbance is Craig being forced to give up puppeteering to get a job in commerce, to get maximum dramatic effect we must do everything we can in the pre-disturbance minutes to establish Craig's normality as an unsuccessful but passionately committed puppeteer. The audience can only value the disturbance if they know what and how much it is disturbing. In practical terms this means that we must use every moment from the start of the film—titles included, if possible—to describe the normality. If you want a fast start, use the *Juno* and *Gran Torino* trick of implying the normality and disturbance through an energised scene after the disturbance event.

A film with a poor disturbance is usually a film with a poor action line because the disturbance is the first movement of the action line. As we'll see later, a poor action line means that the film has to function on a static relationship line.

Finding the action line

With the normality and disturbance in place, the next step is to start finding the chain of reactions created by the disturbance. The next question to ask is: 'Does the film have a story (action line) yet?'

A disturbance on its own does not mean there is a proper action line. An idea for a film 'about a reclusive actress living in Spain' is not yet a potential story because the statement describes only a normality. When the reclusive actress living in Spain catches a burglar, that constitutes a disturbance, but the story can't stop there. It is the consequence of the disturbance, the twists and turns that occur as a result of catching the burglar, that will provide the action line. *Many films that falter in the second act do so because they don't have enough story.* Technically, this is because the story has only a disturbance (a small change, something logical, that might have been expected) not a small change leading to unexpected, suspenseful consequences. A small change alone gives you only a small story.

Keep trying to work out the simple narrative sentence and use Development Strategy 8 to help.

Development Strategy 8

DISTINGUISH AN IDEA FROM A STORY

Make sure you have distinguished your idea from your action line.
Remember that an idea is a normality or a normality disturbed by an unusual event, and a story (action line) is a chain of reactions following an unusual event.

Questions to ask:
- Am I genuinely devising a story or am I simply devising different scenes to illustrate the same normality, or the same normality plus disturbance (for example, spending a long time on Walter being a widower before interacting with his neighbours)?
- What is the normality, and have I got too much of it?
- Is it on the cusp of change?
- What is the disturbance and is it really leading to the first-act turning point and a proper adventure?

Chapter 8
Action line or relationship line?

THIS CHAPTER IS ABOUT differentiating between action line and relationship line, developing the relationship line and then entwining the two.

As we saw with *Witness*, it's very common for writers to be impelled to write not because they have a strong action-line idea but because they want to deal with an interesting character or interpersonal relationship. That's fine. Neither action line nor relationship line is superior, but you need both, so you need to know which one is presenting itself to you. You also need to understand the precise way in which the two types of storylines are interdependent.

One way of confirming that the idea that's come to you is the beginnings of a relationship line is to ask yourself whether your idea is primarily that two people are forced together and quarrelling. If so, what you are feeling is your film's relationship line. Use Development Strategy 9 to check this.

Development Strategy 9

DIFFERENTIATE THE ACTION LINE AND THE RELATIONSHIP LINE

Remember that the relationship line deals with relationships and internal changes and is often what impels writers to write. If the story idea presents itself to you as a relationship or a change of character, you are sensing the film's relationship line and you need an action line to carry it.

Questions to ask:
- Is my idea based on relationships, particularly a conflict-ridden relationship, or a character undergoing internal change?
- Do I have an action line yet?
- Will the action-plot scenario I have chosen to carry the relationship line display it better than any other?

The action line causes the relationship line

A relationship cannot change until events force it to change, so you need to create a strong action line: a series of events that force change on your characters. If your action line does not provide events that can change the relationship, all your characters can do is bicker unproductively. A film with events that force the relationship to change is *The African Queen*. The developing love between Rose and Allnutt could not happen without the action line, the journey down the river. Without the river journey, those two characters would never have come together, and, cleverly, every incident on the journey marks a movement forward in their progression towards love. Compare this to *Guarding Tess*, a film where the action line does not permit the relationship line the filmmakers were after. *Guarding Tess* is supposed to be about how a feisty, wilful elderly widow of a US president and the young security guard who has to look after her move from mutual hostility to love and warmth. Unfortunately, the film's action line gives them no chance to change and bond. The characters spend a lot of time bickering, then Tess is kidnapped and the security guard has to find her. He does so in the final moments of the film, and the two behave as if there is great love between them, something quite implausible because the last time we saw them they disliked each other intensely. For a more detailed analysis of *Guarding Tess*, see pp. 415–16.

If *The African Queen* had been approached this way, we would have had Rose and Allnutt stuck in their roles as picky spinster and happy drunk, bickering at the mission, with the mission's destruction and the journey down the river starting only towards the very end of the film. Later in the book I reconstruct *The African Queen* without a journey down the river to show the importance of action line on relationship line (see pp. 137–9).

In a successful film, *the action line permits, indeed causes, the relationship line to happen*. A good action line not only forces the relationship-line characters together but keeps challenging them, individually and incrementally, in different ways. For the writer, this means choosing an action-line scenario that ensures that every incident is both relevant to the action-line 'adventure', and can progress the relationship line another step. However, you can't choose appropriate action-line incidents to carry the relationship line forward until you know where you want the relationship line to go; that is, where it starts and where it ends up.

Define where you want the relationship to go

To work out a simple progression for the relationship line, start by jotting down a simple 'relationship road', with signposts indicating the developmental steps of the relationship. Make sure the relationship does develop (that is, that the signposts show development and cannot be interchanged). The advantage of this is that it will lock proper incremental growth into the relationship line, preventing your relationship-line scenes from turning into unproductive bickering, as in *Guarding Tess*, something that can happen frighteningly easily. Creating this 'relationship road' actually overlaps with another approach we will come across later, the character arc. The character arc is about each individual's emotional journey (what's going on inside their heads and hearts), whereas the relationship line is about the external behaviour of two or more people, their public interaction.

Development Strategy 10

CREATE A RELATIONSHIP ROAD

List the steps in the relationship line from start to finish.

Questions to ask:

- What are the characters in the planned relationship like at the start of the film and what are they like at the end of the film?
- What hurdles can I put in the way of them coming together (or falling out)?
- What changes does each have to make—or does only one character change?

Peg your relationship line to the action-line timeline

Once you've got your 'relationship road' you have to find scenes that show each step. There is a fast and reliable way to do this (and to also make sure the action line and relationship line are interwoven, as they must be). Simply go to your action line, work out its timeline, and peg your relationship line to events in that timeline. *The action line always arrives with some kind of timeline, with some scenes already built in.* For example, in a comedy heist story about John and Anna falling in love in the process of planning and robbing a bank, the characters have to (a) decide to commit the robbery, (b) plan it, (c) execute it and (d) either get away with the money or get caught. There will have to be scenes involving all of this—the characters will scope out the bank, assemble the gang, discuss the *modus operandi* and do the robbery.

By contrast, while we know that John and Anna will gradually fall in love, we don't know the progression, or where, when and how that love happens. We do know, however, that 'the action line permits the relationship line to happen', so the heist will *cause* the falling in love. To plan the love story, work out the action line heist (your charts and other planning tools described in

Chapter 6 will help), then find places in it where the progression of the love story could credibly happen. If you need the pair to feel sudden rapport, find an event in the heist story that causes it. If you need them to quarrel, find a reason in the heist story; make the quarrel be triggered by something in the heist. You will find that the heist story will act as a story trigger for brainstorming (heist + love story + real + unusual).

As you are going through this pegging process, think about what events in the action line can cause your characters' relationships to change. By sketching in ideas, you will find a genuine story about your characters' changing relationship is beginning to form. To further enhance that story, start to plan it out as a three-act structure, because this will build in rising suspense, making it even more powerful. The disturbance will be the start of the relationship, the first-act turning point will be the surprise/obstacle in the path of the relationship, and the second act will show a variety of hurdles in the way of the relationship. The relationship's lowest point will occur at a second-act turning point before the characters in the relationship come together for a final great effort in their action-line struggle. In the climax of the action line they will normally encounter the climax of the relationship line, which will be the moment of truth for their relationship, the point to which the whole film has been leading them, emotionally. For example, in the closing moments of *The African Queen* just as Rose and Allnutt, moments before their scheduled execution, are being married (climax of the relationship line), the drifting wreckage of *The African Queen* hits the side of the German ship they were seeking to destroy, and blows it up (climax of the action line). Rose and Allnutt could have been married either before or after the blowing up of the ship. To combine the two increases the energy of the film.

Use all of your tools to map out the action-line three-act structure (the mountain, the circle, the nine-point Smiley/Thompson model and the simple and advanced narrative sentences) to peg both lines together.

Development Strategy 11

PEG THE RELATIONSHIP LINE TO THE ACTION LINE AND START CREATING A THREE-ACT STRUCTURE FOR THE RELATIONSHIP LINE

Write a timeline of the action line in point form then find events in the action line where steps in the relationship line can be credibly and logically caused and can happen.

Questions to ask:
- Have I written a timeline of the action line?
- Have I found events on the timeline where action-line progression can happen?
- Have I found good relationship scenes to insert into action-line events?
- Is my relationship-line movement tied closely to my main plot's movement?
- Are the scenes in the relationship line genuinely moving the relationship forward, or am I duplicating the same interaction?
- Have I started to identify and develop the three-act structure of my relationship line, tracking the relationship through its disturbance, first- and second-act turning points and climax?

Linda Seger's book *Making a Good Script Great* has some very useful discussion and diagrams on interweaving the action and relationship lines, particularly on how the two three-act structures interact, in Chapter 3, 'What subplots do' (although notice that she has a rather different take on story lines, and uses different terminology, so that my 'relationship line' is referred to as a 'subplot'). You will continue to work on interweaving as you go.

Climax in inner/outer story films

As I've said, in most linear films, the climaxes of relationship line and action line occur in the same event. There are, though, certain films in which action line and relationship line climax in different scenes. These are films in which a character's inner flaw has caused the story (as in *The Piano*, where the flaw is Ada's refusal to talk except through the piano). They involve a mechanism termed 'inner story/outer story'. Their heat is in the problems the protagonist's flaw causes, and in how the protagonist overcomes the flaw and becomes a more balanced person. Inner story/outer story is related to another character development component in films, called 'the character arc'. We'll look at inner story/outer story and character arcs when we look at characterisation.

WHAT IF I DON'T YET HAVE AN ACTION LINE?

What happens if you don't yet have an action line, just an interesting character? Good questions to ask here are: What attracted you to this character in the first place? What do you want to transmit about the character to the audience? What is new, exciting or interesting about the character? What is the new world you are showing us?

Frank Daniel's suggestion for finding a story to fit a character was to identify the character's weakest point and construct a plot around that, a good recipe as your film will then be truly character-driven. Having identified the weakest point, put the character in precisely the situation where this will be most exercised. The more that events demand of characters—the more your characters are put on the line, the more they are tormented—the more intrigued the audience will be (as long as you keep it real).

ACTION MOVIES

It's important to be aware that some genres require fewer beats overall, particularly action films, for the simple reason that they do not have the available screen time. The actual plots of most action films are very simple because so much screen time has to be devoted to chases, fights, amazing escapes and the like. These stop the plot because nothing can go forward until the 'Will they get away?/Won't they get away?' of the action sequence is resolved. Once the chase/entry/burglary has been concluded, the plot can continue—but not until then.

Because there is less room for complexity, the steps that are there must be as original as possible, particularly in the relationship line. In many action movies the relationship line is often as simple as a developing romance between the male hero and the woman he has to save or capture. Other forms of simple relationship line occur in 'buddy movies', in which the relationship line concerns the growing friendship between two partners both involved in the physical chasing of the action plot. Conflict between the pair energises the film—without it, they have only the external enemy. Poor action movies often display very clichéd relationship lines, whereas good action movies usually have interesting, witty or surprising ones (after all, *The African Queen*, one of the great screen love stories, is for all intents and purposes an action movie).

Relationship lines in action films need careful thought because they are restricted quite seriously by the genre's inbuilt demand that they happen 'on the move', as part of the chase or journey. There is simply not enough time to remove the protagonist from the scene of the action in order to interact with another character—for example, a spouse at home. An interesting example of an action movie where a spouse is physically removed from home and put next to the protagonist is in the Arnold Schwarzenegger film *True Lies*.

Chapter 9
Protagonists and characters who seem like protagonists but are not

CONVENTIONAL NARRATIVE IS ALL about the protagonist's journey. The story cannot start until the protagonist is identified and shown in their normal life (in their normality), and the story cannot move forward until a disturbance fractures the protagonist's normality and forces them into a course of action.

In practical terms, this means that films that do not establish their protagonists early try the audience's patience. A striking example is *Jaws 3*, which takes twelve minutes to do this. Often, delays of this sort are related to the fact that the filmmakers involved do not really know what film they are in, so are not properly focused on whose story to follow.

Interestingly, establishing the protagonist early is the mark of successful films across all cultures. While films from some cultures often take a long while to get to their disturbance or their first-act turning point and have very low-key plots, they will almost always set up their protagonist early, so the audience knows whose story it is following. A good example is *Tulpan*, in which the young protagonist, who wants to marry Tulpan, is set up in the film's opening moments in a marriage interview.

Until the audience knows who the protagonist is—whose story we're in— the film is in limbo. Writers need to know whose story we're in in order to create the right plot for that character and get it up and going. Audiences, and writers, need to know who is climbing the mountain, hence whose shoes we are inside. Giving this job to the wrong character can make plot and characterisation fall apart.

But who is the protagonist?

While the protagonist is central to the conventional paradigm, and filmmakers are always talking about this character, it can actually be very difficult to work out who the protagonist is, both in your own story material and in films generally. For example, who is the single protagonist in *Thelma and Louise*? In *Pulp Fiction*? In *The Big Chill*? Conventional screenwriting theory is often quite vague on the topic. Here is what is generally accepted about the protagonist.

- There is only one protagonist.
- The film is the protagonist's story, the protagonist is who the film is 'about'.
- The protagonist is on screen most of the time.
- The protagonist is the most interesting character.
- The protagonist drives the action and makes the decisions.
- The protagonist is not passive and reactive.
- The protagonist has a normal person's point of view.
- The protagonist is the person whose head we are inside, whose shoes we are in and with whom we identify.
- The protagonist does not die (except occasionally at the very end of the film, as in *Thelma and Louise* or *The English Patient*, because they have to be around at the end of their own story. The film *Il Postino* has the protagonist's death followed by a sort of coda, or conclusion).
- The protagonist is the one whose life is being made difficult and the person who is making it difficult for them is the antagonist.
- The protagonist is central to the film's dramatic high points and is the one climbing the three-act mountain.
- The action line cannot start until the protagonist is established.
- The protagonist is the person who changes most, who goes on a spiritual journey of change and growth, learning as a result of the film's action.
- Whoever speaks in voice-over is the protagonist for the duration of the flashback.
- The protagonist is the protagonist in both action and relationship lines.

As soon as you start to test this definition, you run into problems because, for a start, while the conventional wisdom is that a film can only have one protagonist, actually many films have multiple protagonists. As we'll see later, all of the parallel narrative forms (tandem, multiple protagonist, double journeys, double narrative flashback, consecutive stories and fractured tandem) have multiple protagonists, but so do buddy movies.

If you think that in buddy films like *Thelma and Louise* and the *Lethal Weapon* series both buddies seem to be playing the part of protagonist, working together to evade a common enemy, you are right. In these films, both buddies are protagonists in the action line (the adventure). However, in the *relationship* line the more normal of the two (let's call this person Buddy 1) always has their life made difficult by their partner, Buddy 2, who is a wild card, moreover their erratic behaviour probably caused the adventure in the first place. What this means is that the more normal of the two buddies (e.g. Louise) is the protagonist in both action and relationship lines, while Buddy 2 (e.g. Thelma) is a protagonist in the action line, in the adventure when the two are under attack, but an antagonist in the relationship line. The conflict between the two buddies stops them from becoming Tweedledum and Tweedledee, identical twins.

SUPERHEROES

The second way in which the definition fails to work is in the matter of the protagonist always being not only the most interesting person in the film, but also someone who reflects the 'normal' point of view and, in addition, the character who most changes and grows. This is definitely not the case in superhero films. In James Bond films, the most interesting character and also the character whom the film is about, is James Bond. But Bond is emphatically not normal, does not change and grow, and does not undertake a journey of the spirit into self-knowledge (although Bond in *Quantum of Solace* did change, to the chagrin of many fans).

OUTSIDERS

The problem doesn't stop with superheroes. Both King Kong and Raymond in *Rain Man* are the most interesting characters in their respective films, but both, like Bond, are emphatically not like normal people, and neither change nor grow, nor are able to undertake a journey into self-knowledge. The characters who change are not these two, but the people who come into contact with them.

The rules continue to break down when applied to films like *Sophie's Choice* and *The Shawshank Redemption*. Sophie and Andy are clearly the most interesting characters, but if we were in their shoes there wouldn't be a film—because we would know the surprise denouements. In these, as in *Rain Man* and *King Kong*, it is the characters who are observing them who are normal, who change, and, as the central point of the film, are changed by them.

MENTOR ANTAGONISTS

There is a pattern in these films. It is that a normal, often quite weak person, achieves spiritual growth through the influence of a mentor figure, a fascinating, enigmatic outsider with a wisdom born of pain, who, while clearly the most interesting character in the film and the person the film is about, is neither normal, nor a person whose shoes we can be inside, nor a person who changes and grows. We see it in *Rain Man*, *Sophie's Choice*, *King Kong*, *The Shawshank Redemption*, *The Elephant Man*, *Scent of a Woman*, *Clubland* (aka *Introducing the Dwights*), *Jean de Florette*, *Dead Poets' Society*, *Balzac and the Little Chinese Seamstress*, *The Motorcycle Diaries*, *The Green Mile* and many more, including, in an evil incarnation, the Hannibal Lecter films.

We can call this sort of film a 'mentor antagonist' film because the enigmatic mentor figure must be depicted from the outside, as an antagonist in both action line and relationship line, or the film will not work. Meanwhile, a much less interesting character plays the protagonist.

Why is this necessary? Probably the easiest way to explain it is to describe a personal experience. Some years ago I was commissioned to write a feature film about a bizarre and eccentric elderly fan dancer on a mission of revenge, from a producer's idea. I couldn't understand why, in my script, this woman kept turning into a 1950s-style housewife. Eventually, I realised the reason was that I had assumed that she, as the major character, was the protagonist. However, in trying to get inside her head to give her the normal point of view and understandable motives conventional wisdom says a protagonist must have, I had robbed her of her personality—her eccentricity, her 'differentness'. The defining and interesting thing about this woman was that she was the sort of character, like Raymond in *Rain Man*, who defied logic and could not change. To be depicted properly, with all the comedy and mystery that she deserved—to keep her unpredictable 'wild card' identity—she had to be seen from the outside.

The problem was solved by inventing a new protagonist who was an ordinary person (a truck driver), and making the fan dancer the antagonist in the action and relationship lines, a person who came into his life and dragged him into her comic journey of revenge, changing him but remaining unchanged as the two gradually and inevitably fell in love. The fan dancer remained the major character, but she was not the protagonist.

The most interesting character is not necessarily the protagonist

The moral of the story is that the most interesting character is not automatically the protagonist and, most importantly, there is no status in a character being the protagonist. Your star actor does not have to play the protagonist in a mentor antagonist film; in fact, the best part in many films is a mentor antagonist. From a writing point of view, protagonists and antagonists are simply technical devices for better demonstrating character. The protagonist is the character you are inside, the antagonist is the character you see from the outside. Some characters are better shown from the outside.

It is very easy to mistake a mentor antagonist for the protagonist because this sort of character is a driven, eccentric, dynamic troublemaker who is so much more interesting than the pallid, ordinary and often very young person who is their foil. But, as in my case, this can be disastrous, not only because it normalises the enigmatic outsider but because it wrecks both action and relationship lines.

To highlight this, let's rewrite *Scent of a Woman* with the danger-seeking blind war veteran as the protagonist. If we made the veteran the protagonist, we would have to get into his head and capture his point of view and his motives. This would make him normal and remove his danger and mystery. Having removed the mystery from the veteran by making him the protagonist, we have to cast the student who comes to look after him into the role of antagonist. But this person is not an antagonist. He is mild and ineffectual. He has to be, otherwise he would stop the veteran leaving—he would prevail. We can understand him and relate to his consternation at being stuck with a blind man on a rampage—although it is now hard to see the new 'normalised' veteran as somebody who would go on a rampage.

What has happened here in making the veteran the protagonist and the student the antagonist is that we ended up with two 'normal', almost identical people. There is no conflict or mystery, so the whole premise of the story starts to fall apart because it is not believable that the veteran does what he is supposed to do. This is exactly why my fan dancer turned into Doris Day. *Wedlock* is a film that suffers from exactly this problem of a protagonist and an antagonist who are both 'everyperson'. Had *Wedlock* turned its bland thief protagonist into a remote, possibly psychopathic, mentor antagonist and made his uninteresting love interest female partner a protagonist, the film would have had a lot more energy. Other films that might have benefited from being constructed as mentor antagonist films are *Gods and Monsters* and *The Insider* (see pp. 438–9, 412–13).

How to pick if you have a mentor antagonist

If your film involves a normal but passive and reactive person being pulled reluctantly into an adventure (often a physical journey as well as an emotional journey) by a dominant, eccentric, unpredictable and often dangerous teacher figure, a figure characterised by their strange behaviour or world view, a person who is strikingly different from everyone else, who effects great changes around them but often changes little themselves, who possesses a unique wisdom (often born of suffering)—realise that your wild-card character is probably a mentor antagonist and not a protagonist.

The protagonist will be the normal person who is changed by the mentor.

That normal person will be the protagonist climbing the mountain, and we will stay in the normal person's shoes while the teacher figure, the mentor antagonist, remains always a mystery.

Stories about children with a difficult parent are usually mentor antagonist stories with the parent as mentor antagonist to the child protagonist, as, usually, are films that have someone's name in the title. Typically, as in *Scent of a Woman* and *Rain Man*, the mentor antagonist takes the protagonist on a dangerous adventure (action line) while teaching them and forging an emotional bond (relationship line). In this sort of scenario there will be minor antagonists whom the protagonist and mentor evade or defeat.

Sometimes, though, the mentor antagonist figure is the first character that comes to you (as with me in the fan dancer story). Here, to properly explore that character, you will have to invent a 'normal' protagonist, to be irritated by and learn from the charismatic mentor antagonist. As we shall see, several forms of double narrative flashback (that is, flashback that has a full plot in the past and a full plot in the present, as in *Slumdog Millionaire*, *Shine* and *Citizen Kane*) use mentor antagonists in the story set in the present). The character in most jeopardy is usually the protagonist. Notice that mentor antagonists actively cause the adventure.

The weak protagonist is still a protagonist

The weak protagonist in mentor antagonist films will still show all of the characteristics of the protagonist *except* that:

- they do not drive the action or make the decisions
- they are reactive rather than proactive
- they are not the most interesting character

They are still normal, and they are still the character to whom the nine-point Smiley/Thompson model event happens, who climbs the three-act mountain and who goes to the other world and back.

Development Strategy 12

IDENTIFY THE PROTAGONIST

Be careful to pick the right protagonist.

Questions to ask:

- Is the answer to the question 'Whose story is this?', 'The story of the character I think is the protagonist'? (If the story is another character's story, that other character might be the protagonist.)

- Is my protagonist the POV character?
- Is my protagonist leading the action and proactive not reactive (except in mentor antagonist stories)?
- Is my protagonist the voice of normality?
- Is my protagonist around at the end of their own story?
- Does my protagonist make the decisions, or if not, are they being troubled by a charismatic mentor antagonist?
- Have I established this character for the audience early on?
- Am I using flashbacks (in which case I need to look at chapters 34–41)?
- Is the character speaking in voice-over the protagonist? (Because anyone speaking in voice-over automatically becomes protagonist for the duration of the voice-over.)
- Is my protagonist centrally involved in the disturbance, first- and second-act turning point, and climax?
- Is my protagonist the same in the action and relationship lines?

Writing mentor antagonists requires a change of mindset

The reason you want to write about your mentor antagonist is because you're fascinated by them. But, as we've seen, to keep them enigmatic you have to create a protagonist who will inevitably be a character in whom you are not really interested and who, almost by definition, is not particularly interesting. And not only do you have to create this rather ordinary protagonist, but you also have to get inside their head, you have to tell the story from their point of view and *make your film their story*.

The change of mental focus here can be very difficult because you need to invest yourself into, essentially, a different film. However, if you don't achieve it, your enigmatic outsider will not work. Keep telling yourself it is the pro-tagonist's story. Map out their mountain. Construct the story around their emotional journey.

The Mercutio character

In trying to identify your protagonist, beware of what I call the 'Mercutio character', who is not the protagonist but initially feels as though they are. I took the name from the friend of Romeo who is unexpectedly killed early on in *Romeo and Juliet*. Shakespeare is often said to have killed off Mercutio because he was potentially more interesting than Romeo, the hero. The Mer-cutio character is a charismatic and likeable individual who appears early in the film and is usually a friend—sometimes a partner or spouse—of the pro-tagonist. The death early on of this person—usually as a result of defending or assisting the protagonist—forms the first-act turning point, impelling the protagonist (who is filled with remorse and/or thoughts of vengeance) to respond in a way that drives the story forward. In the basic Smiley/Thompson model, this death is the surprise which becomes the obstacle. Classic Mercutio characters are the young man who dies in *The Battleship Potemkin*, the first woman murdered in *Psycho*, and the British soldier killed in *The Crying Game*. The Mercutio character is actually an antagonist.

In most films your protagonist will conform to the conventional model

Mostly, your protagonist in a conventional narrative will not be a mentor antagonist. They will be a normal proactive protagonist who conforms to the list above. However, check that your material is not inherently a buddy movie, an ensemble or double journey film, a superhero film or a film involving a Mercutio character or a mentor antagonist. Ensemble and double journey films require parallel narrative forms.

Things to remember about protagonists

- The most interesting character in the film is not necessarily the protagonist, they can be a mentor antagonist, with a less interesting character being the protagonist.
- There is no extra status involved in one character rather than another being the protagonist; both are technical devices. Staying on the outside of a character creates mystery, and sometimes the most interesting character is interesting precisely because they are a mystery (like Raymond, Sophie and Andy). Frequently, the star of the film (in every sense) is the mentor antagonist.
- Mercutio characters can confuse you. Their job is to create the first-act turning point crisis for the real protagonist, usually by their death. You can pick them because they die or disappear from the action early.
- You can have multiple protagonists but you will probably need a parallel narrative form (see Part 4).

Chapter 10
One protagonist, many antagonists

THE TECHNICAL, STORYTELLING REASON that you need to know your antagonists is so that you can depict them from the outside as threats to your protagonist, thus creating the drama of the film.

Antagonists become easier to understand and identify once you realise that a conventional three-act film has only one protagonist but two or more antagonists. This is because there has to be one antagonist in the relationship line and at least one antagonist in the action line. Spy films show this pattern very clearly. For example, in a James Bond film Bond is the protagonist and the action line will typically show an arch-villain as Bond's major antagonist, with minor antagonists in the form of henchmen who appear in sequence for Bond to defeat. Meanwhile, Bond's relationship line will involve a beautiful female antagonist who usually starts out as his enemy but ends up his lover.

While we tend to think of antagonists as creatures of the action line, in fact the most complex antagonists are actually relationship-line antagonists. For this reason we will look at them first. But before doing so, we can establish a number of important facts about antagonists generally.

General facts about antagonists
- As we have seen above while looking at the mentor antagonist, antagonists are not necessarily less interesting than protagonists; in fact they are often the reason the film is written. A major antagonist must be at least an equal match for the protagonist and is often stronger.
- Antagonists (particularly minor antagonists) often die before the end of the film. Major antagonists die only at the end (but see also Mercutio character above).
- While antagonists need not be the protagonist's enemy (indeed, they can be friends or lovers), antagonists always cause trouble or change for the protagonist. Their job is to create a conflict situation, often a major life change for the protagonist, thereby driving the plot.

- A rule of thumb for picking an antagonist is to look for situations in which one character is causing another character problems and behaving in a way no normal or reasonable person would. The instigator will normally be the antagonist, and the person being caused problems will be the protagonist.
- The antagonist is powerfully driven and the antagonist's wishes, at least initially, are directly opposed to the protagonist's.
- Mentor antagonists are characters best seen from the outside. They feel as if they may be protagonists but in fact, they actually cause trouble to a weaker or less interesting protagonist.
- Multiple antagonists (and multiple protagonists) often occur in parallel narrative films, where typically the films focus on many different points of view. I deal with these later in the section on parallel narrative.

Relationship-line antagonists

So, there are action-line antagonists and relationship-line antagonists. We'll deal with the latter first.

On a very practical note, relationship-line antagonists are very useful because their presence with the protagonist permits the protagonist's thoughts to be transmitted to the audience by way of dialogue. Plots involving lone protagonists often create a relationship line between the protagonist and the main action-line antagonist in order to give the film some emotional content. This has the practical side effect of allowing both to discuss their plans and feelings. This happens in *The Fugitive*, in which the Marshall starts out an enemy and gradually comes to respect the protagonist and believe in his innocence. Other antagonists in *The Fugitive* are the one-armed man and, in an interesting twist, the doctor's friend (who looked initially like a relationship-line antagonist), who turns out to be an enemy. This phenomenon also occurs in *The Juror*, in which the Demi Moore character and the criminal hunting her become involved in an intense emotional relationship.

LOVE, FRIENDSHIP AND CLICHÉ

Often protagonist and relationship-line antagonist start out enemies in the relationship line and end up friends or lovers. In the action line they often end up, as in buddy movies, both fighting the action-line antagonists. Protagonists and relationship-line antagonists so often fall in love that this is a serious danger area for cliché and sketchy 'love interest'. Writers have to work very hard to reinvent the antagonist–protagonist love affair and inject it with genuine suspense, particularly in action movies or romantic comedies, because the moment audiences see a warring couple engaged in a comic or dramatic adventure, they suspect the ending is going to provide reconciliation and true love. One way of creating change is via 'the prude turns action hero' model.

THE PRUDE TURNS ACTION HERO

Antagonists of all sorts always cause the protagonist trouble. That's their job: they are antagonistic. The 'prude who becomes an action hero' or, more precisely, 'the prude who becomes a sexually unrepressed action hero' causes trouble through changing from being meek to being highly aggressive. Such characters are normally women, and part of their transformation involves rejecting sexual repression and becoming openly sexual. Typical examples are Rose in *The African Queen*, Thelma in *Thelma and Louise*, Lotte, Craig's wife, in *Being John Malkovich* and, in *True Lies*, Helen, the wife of the Arnold Schwarzenegger character. Characters like this normally come into their own in the second act, and it is here that their extreme change causes major problems for the protagonist.

To help avoid cliché in your relationship line, you could take the idea of an extreme change seen in the 'prude to action hero' and invent other kinds of character transformations that could cause the protagonist trouble. For example, you could reverse prude to action hero to make your relationship line antagonist be an action hero turned into prude, or an atheist who finds religion, or a conservative who becomes revolutionary and so on. Simply brainstorm notions of profound character change. Always make sure that conflict between the antagonist and protagonist in a relationship line is productive, driving the plot, and does not turn into redundant bickering.

THE LOADED GUN

It can help with developing relationship-line antagonists to think of them as 'loaded guns', people who could change in many and unexpected ways, and do. In *Thelma and Louise*, Thelma's transformation causes tragedy, but tracking the deeds of 'prude to action hero' antagonists is often used successfully for comedy. This happens in *The African Queen* and *True Lies*.

Relationship-line antagonists don't always change, of course. In *Planes, Trains and Automobiles*, it is the tense, fastidious protagonist who changes.

Notice that the dramatic value, the impact, of the antagonist's change lies in its unpredictability. The protagonist in a film always changes. We expect and understand their change, partly because we see it from the inside, from the protagonist's point of view, and partly because the change is more logical because the protagonist is a normal person, with a normal point of view. Louise's change in *Thelma and Louise* is a logical result of what happens to the two women on their journey. Given Louise's personal history, her behaviour is utterly logical. This is quite unlike Thelma's behaviour, where the change from innocent prude to action hero could not have been predicted. So, make sure your antagonist's transformation is utterly unexpected. Don't seed an expectation of it.

Action-line antagonists

Action-line antagonists are normally a lot simpler to write than relationship-line antagonists. They typically change little and, in extreme forms, like the robot antagonist in *Terminator II*, are so focused on one aim that they are physically unstoppable.

Action lines usually have a number of antagonists. This is particularly necessary in films where the action line places the major antagonist at a physical distance from the protagonist. In these cases you need agents of the major antagonist close to the protagonist causing them trouble. This is obvious in action movies (in James Bond films, Mr Big obviously needs heavies on the ground to harrass Bond) but it also applies in more subtle films. In *Thelma and Louise* the main antagonists are the hunter, the sheriff, other lawmen and Thelma's husband, but these are all at a distance so there needs to be more antagonists close at hand. The rapist, the hitchhiker, the highway patrolman, and the boorish truck driver all fulfil this function.

If your film has an antagonist at a physical distance from the protagonist, you will need either to create secondary antagonists who can cause trouble at close hand or find a way to bring the major antagonist into close physical proximity.

NON-HUMAN FORCE AS ANTAGONIST

An antagonist in an action line can be a force of nature (for example, a volcano or a hurricane) or a social force (for example, class prejudice), but it normally has human agents, actual people whose actions help the non-human force to cause the protagonist trouble. In *The African Queen* the river is an antagonist, but there are human antagonists in the form of the German army and navy. Often, films that have a non-human enemy are mission films involving a group of characters on a quest to save humanity. In this instance, the antagonism occurs within the group so there is not as great a need for external human antagonists. Films like these are usually structured in multiple protagonist/antagonist form, a parallel narrative form, which we look at later.

Development Strategy 13

IDENTIFY THE ANTAGONIST

Pick the right antagonist(s) for the relationship and action lines.

Questions to ask:

General

- Are my antagonists characters that make life difficult for the protagonist?
- Am I depicting my antagonists from the outside?
- Am I mistaking a Mercutio character for a major antagonist?
- Do my major antagonists at least equal the protagonist in strength, intelligence etc.?
- Are my antagonists powerfully driven with wishes that are, at least initially, directly opposed to the protagonist's?

Flashbacks and ensemble stories/multiple antagonist structure

- Does my film use flashback narrative or have a group involved in a mission, reunion or siege? If so, it might need a parallel narrative structure (see Part 4).

Relationship-line antagonist

- Are my antagonist and protagonist sufficiently different from each other?
- Is there conflict, emotional involvement of some kind, and increasing closeness?
- If I have a love affair, is it clichéd and am I creating an antagonist that is merely a 'love interest'?
- Is the protagonist/antagonist conflict productive rather than just being redundant bickering?
- Does my antagonist assist the protagonist in action-line battles against a common enemy?
- Are the changes my antagonist goes through interesting but credible, 'real but unusual'? Further to this, am I using a 'prude who turns into action hero' model and, if so, is it a 'real but unusual' rendering? Should I incorporate some other massive character turnabout (for example, 'atheist finds religion')?

Action-line antagonists

- If my action-line antagonist is remote from the action, do they have agents?
- Alternatively, do they start to get emotionally closer to the protagonist?
- If my action-line antagonist is non-human, does it have human agents?

Mentor antagonists

- Is my antagonist a mentor? If so, do they teach the protagonist new values?
- Am I depicting the mentor antagonist from the outside so that they can remain a mystery?
- Should they be the antagonist in both the action and relationship lines?

Chapter 11
Characterisation

IN FILM, A CHARACTER *is* what it *does* (whereas in fiction a character tends to be what it observes and thinks). While character in film must always be demonstrated through a story, this is exactly what most writers find the hardest thing to do—to invent and construct a story that will illustrate their characters in a way that interests the world. This is because for every writer who is inspired by plot but who struggles with character, there will be twenty who struggle with plot but are terrific at character. Hence, the main problem for most writers is not to find characters but to control them.

Writers often spend massive amounts of time exploring their characters' pasts and inner states, but do it in a vacuum, in isolation from the plot. They get into character like actors into a pre-existing role; something that is exhausting (although extremely interesting), but very often doesn't actually transfer to the script—it doesn't lead to the creation of a chain of events that actually demonstrates that character's personality on the screen. This might be best understood by an example from television writing: you can spend a huge amount of time creating character profiles but at some point you need to invent plots for episodes, the stories that will actually depict your characters being what you intend them to be.

Character exploration is always lengthy, so it must be time well spent. To make sure your character exploration actually transfers to your plotlines, giving you scenes that genuinely illustrate your characters, I'd suggest that you begin not as many experts suggest, by working from the inside out, from a character's psychology to their actions, spending a lot of time looking at characters in isolation from the story in which they appear, but that instead you work more intuitively, feeling your way back from your characters' actions to their motivation, using your storylines (even thought they might not yet be fully developed) as if you were a police psychologist using a suspect's behaviour as a way to get inside their heads. Think about what your characters *do* and *might do*, rather than what they *are*. For example, rather than decide that your character is 'insecure' in the abstract, think what actions in your existing plot might already indicate insecurity, or how you might angle the plot to demonstrate insecurity. Development Strategy 14 will help here.

Development Strategy 14

FIND OUT WHAT THE PLOT TELLS YOU ABOUT CHARACTERS

Work out a broad outline of your characters' personalities through what you can deduce through your plot.

Questions to ask:
- What do I know about my character from their actions?
- How would my character react in situations involving danger, love, aggression, temptation etc?
- What would my character never do?

When you have found out what your plot is telling you about your character, you can start to use a 'character chart' to work out the psychological cause of the behaviour. A character chart is a dossier on a character's past and present, containing their public, private and inner lives. Character charts involve you listing, methodically, details about the character's past life. They help you to make your characters more complex and more original. They also help you to avoid clichés, particularly in minor characters, which can creep in just because there is so much else to think about in a script. Character charts are a very tedious job, but, in the middle of all the drudgery, you will suddenly have new insights and think of new and useful aspects of the character that you can use.

Figure 11.1 shows the sort of chart that might help. There will be overlap between public and private qualities. For example, 'has trouble mixing' has both a public and private dimension. This is not a problem because the point of the chart is not to separate the public and private, merely to force consideration of them.

Charts work to help you get inside your character by throwing stimuli at the lateral imagination to create 'real but unusual' connections. Connections may not happen immediately, but persist and they will.

Character development is an ongoing process that should occur simultaneously with structural planning. It takes time. It is often only after a couple of drafts that a character's motivation will be entirely clear or you will fully understand the human foibles that are being depicted in the script.

Character demands in the script as a whole

The audience needs to know (so your chart needs to tell you):

- where the character has come from psychologically (social and family background)
- the character's weaknesses, strengths, areas of vulnerability
- the public roles of the character—job, family etc.
- current events driving the character

Character demands in each scene

The audience needs to know:

- what the character wants out of each scene
- who has the power in the scene
- what the character is trying to hide in each scene

Past			Present		
Personal	**Public**	**Internal**	**Personal**	**Public**	**Internal**
Date, place of birth? Where grew up? Family? Relationships with family? Unpleasant and pleasant aspects of childhood? Major family events in childhood?	Class of family? Education? How family was regarded? How character came across to others? What jobs? Hobbies? Political/social beliefs? Shy or outgoing? Crucial events witnessed?	Personality flaws? What secrets? What did this person hate talking about? Emotional crises in childhood?	Family still alive? Contact, good or bad, with family? Has partner? Children? Where lives and lifestyle? Any personal crises at the moment?	Job? Financial state? How good at job? How happy in job? Enjoys workplace? Fits in socially and in workplace? Hobbies? Political beliefs? Passions? Pet hates? Ambitions? Shy or outgoing? People most loves, hates, pities, fears?	Problems at work or socially? Grudges? Secrets? Fears? Damage carried from past, if any? What does this person hate talking about? Optimist or pessimist?

Figure 11.1 Character chart

Use Development Strategy 15 to help you with character charts.

Development Strategy 15

GET INTO CHARACTER

Devise character charts by asking who, why and how, remembering
to think 'real but unusual'. You need to think about the protagonist/
antagonist's background, how it might drive their motives, and how they
try to fulfil their aims.

Questions to ask:
- Do I understand these characters well enough?
- Are they and their dilemmas 'real but unusual'?
- Am I unconsciously giving them clichéd motives or actions? If so, how
  can I pull against the cliché?

MAKING YOUR CHARACTERS TALK

Many writers feel that making the character speak helps them to better
understand their character. Do this by creating a scene that puts your character in a stressful situation but which cannot occur in your film (or you will
want to keep it). Write a scene about, say, how they would react to someone
pushing ahead of them in a queue.

FINDING INTERESTING CHARACTERS AND AVOIDING CLICHÉS

To avoid clichéd characters or to kick-start your creativity if you are feeling
exhausted with the script, try the following methods.
- Think of a new version of a character from myth, fairytale, fable or
  genre. Look in newspapers, especially articles and advertisements, for
  characters or roles that sound interesting.
- Think of a social stereotype and pull against it.
- Consider new versions of archetypes; for example, Christopher
  Vogler's archetypes in the hero's journey (see Chapter 3).
- Think of putting opposite personalities in conflict.
- Define a character through its flaws.

Character arc and inner/outer story

As we've seen above, the action line permits the relationship line to happen.
So far I have been talking as if all of the plot material about the protagonist's
interpersonal relationships amounts to one thing called 'the relationship line'.

The relationship line is actually made up of two interwoven plotlines.

1 **The protagonist's external dealings with people close to him/her** (for example, the external incidents in *The African Queen* that show Rose and Allnutt falling in love).

2 **'The character arc'**; that is, the protagonist's internal journey (emotional, psychological and spiritual) caused by events in the action line and relationship line (the internal changes that take place in Rose and Allnutt as a result of the love and the adventure on the river).

Some films have a third component to the relationship line, the inner/outer story component I mentioned earlier, whereby a protagonist's inner flaw creates the action line. We'll look at that in a moment.

The character arc (the protagonist's changing heart)

Think of the character arc as 'the protagonist's changing heart'. If the story is a feature film, the character arc is the emotional and psychological journey travelled by the character in the whole film. If it is a thirteen-part television series, it is the journey travelled in the whole thirteen episodes. If it is a feature film trilogy, such as *Lord of the Rings*, it is the journey travelled in the entire trilogy. The character arc occurs in response to the action line (the adventure) and the relationship line (close relationships formed or tested or both during the adventure). For example, in *Tootsie*, Michael's character arc tracks his growing awareness of how women are exploited and his increasing understanding and appreciation of his feminine side. Sometimes his increasing awareness happens as a result of actions in the relationship line (where he is interacting with a number of people he either loves or who want some kind of romantic or sexual relationship with him). Sometimes it happens as a result of events he experiences in the action line (which is, the plot involving him passing himself off as a female actor in a soap opera).

As we've seen, some film cultures prefer the emotional/psychological journey to be a positive one towards self-knowledge and emotional growth. Other cultures prefer a negative journey. Most films (apart from superhero films) need character change to give the film point, depth and interest.

How character arcs can improve your film

Specifically, character arcs can help where the film is starting to slow or meander; where there are clearly characters in search of a plot; or where the characters seem two-dimensional. They can:

- create a proper plot by pointing to the kind of actions that are necessary to depict the movement of the character through its arc (for example, if you have a town full of characters in search of a story, finding the character arc of your protagonist and other main characters will suggest actions and events that you can craft into a compelling story)

- make a character more complex, interesting and emotionally engaging (a character who is unchanging can only grab the audience through their actions, whereas a character that is performing actions and also changing as a result of their actions can interest the audience on several levels)

- focus the film thematically, hence enrich it and deepen it

How to pick or create the character arc

Sometimes this is easy because the story will come with a ready-made character arc, as in *Tootsie*, where the plot is clearly all about a man whose actions make him become more sensitive to women. But in other stories you might have to search out or even invent a character arc. This is often the case in action films, but it can also be true of films that are all about relationships. For example, you might be writing an intense film about a marriage break-up, but have got so immersed in creating events and quarrels that you have lost sight of the exact journey that each of the partners is travelling emotionally. This is likely to mean that your film won't really have a point or a focus. It may end up a sequence of intense, realistic but ultimately repetitive quarrels. Some action movies don't need character arcs, but a surprising number do have them and they can often add another and very interesting dimension to the film.

To create or find a character arc, work out where, emotionally and psychologically, you want your character to finish, then work out from that where you want them to start. The bigger the character arc the more dramatic the film. Characters in art-house films have smaller character arcs. Create a simple, logical step-by-step list of the characters' emotional movement from the start of the film to the end. The start of the film will be their furthest point from change. The climax will be the precise moment of final change.

Look for places in the action line and relationship line where you can show the changes. Use Development Strategy 16 to help.

Development Strategy 16

CREATE A CHARACTER ARC

Create a character arc to plan your characters' emotional and psychological progression.

Questions to ask:

- Do I know where I want my characters to start and finish emotionally and psychologically?
- Have I created a step-by-step map of the progression?
- Can I find places in the action and relationship lines to cause and show each step?

Inner story and outer story

For practical purposes, outer story is the action line, while inner story is a particular kind of character arc that occurs in one particular kind of story in which the film's action line is caused specifically by a protagonist's inner flaw. The flaw causes a series of external events, often very dramatic, that ultimately helps the protagonist to overcome the inner flaw. In *The Piano*, Ada's inner flaw is her refusal to talk. The outer story—the action line—is about what happens and what she does when she is kept away from the piano. The events in the action line (outer story) initially put her into great difficulty, but gradually help her, in her inner story, her character arc, to overcome her flaw, her wish for silence. In other words, finding love with Baines makes her feel able to reject silence. This rejection is shown in a cleverly symbolic scene in which Ada is accidentally dragged overboard by the sinking piano. Faced with the option of being pulled into death and eternal silence by the piano, she consciously rejects silence by releasing her foot from the rope that links her to the piano.

INNER STORY/OUTER STORY FILMS HAVE TWO ENDINGS

The big structural difference about inner story/outer story films is that they have two climaxes; the climax of the outer story (the action line) and the climax of the inner story (the character arc). The outer story has its climax first, with the external events caused by the flaw resolved. The inner-story climax comes afterwards, with the protagonist understanding the error of their ways and rejecting the flaw. There can be a dangerous loss of pace between the two climaxes—something you can feel in *The Piano* as a hiatus, an anticlimax, between Stewart letting Ada go with Baines and the sinking-piano scene. Try to make the two climaxes happen as close together as you can, or the film will flag.

Some theorists would take inner story and outer story further, arguing that it is present in all films. This seems to work on the assumption that all films are optimistic, but many cultures are fatalistic and this is reflected in their films.

'Character-driven' films

Before we leave character issues, we need to look at the notion of the 'character-driven' film. 'Character-driven' is a much-misunderstood term. Properly, it means 'action line driven by the demands of the character'. It means that character dictates the action line and that the function of the action line is to demonstrate character. Thus, a James Bond plot will be carefully invented and put together to give James Bond the opportunity to react as only James Bond would. A Mr Bean plot will be carefully constructed to give Mr Bean the chance to behave as only Mr Bean would. The action line must permit the character to display what is characteristic about them.

Unfortunately, character-driven is often taken to mean 'you don't need an action line plot; just put an interesting group together and you will have a film'. This results in characters in search of a plot, technically speaking; characters locked into an endlessly repeating normality, just being themselves. Fascinating as they may be (or rather, fascinating as they may be for us as writers to write, because they are actually not fascinating to watch), characters in a film can't just stand around behaving normally or wander about bumping into each other and talking (it's surprising how many unsuccessful films are exactly that). They need a strong action line to illustrate their character in action and, to interweave those stories, very careful planning. Even restrained art-house films like *Meantime*, *The Station Agent*, *Children of Heaven* and *Samson and Delilah* have action lines to demonstrate their characters. Film is not about character, but character demonstrated through action.

Chapter 12
The plan and first-act turning point

THE PLAN IS THE protagonist's response to the disturbance, and the first-act turning point (the surprise that *turns into* the obstacle) is a shock that turns that plan upside down. The complications constitute the second act, which is, at base, a series of incidents that happen in response to the disturbance, thereby taking the protagonist to their lowest point.

The plan has a very important function. It has to mislead the audience so that the first-act turning point comes as the biggest surprise it can be. It's very useful if the first-act turning point is as big a shock as possible (as long as it's credible) because the bigger the shock the more energy you are injecting into the film, hence the more fuel you have to drive the story for its one hundred minutes.

A film with an excellent plan section is *The Player*, in which the protagonist puts into play an elaborate plan to prevent himself from being harmed and, in a shock that comes completely out of the blue (the shock being the first-act turning point), he ends up harming someone else, and this act on his part drives the rest of the story.

It's very easy to forget to lead the audience away from the first-act turning point. Since you, as writer, know what's going to happen in the story and are concentrating on trying to make it happen, you can find yourself writing *towards*, rather than *away from* the first-act turning point surprise, thereby reducing its impact. For example, in *The Player*, this would have resulted in the protagonist stating aloud his fears that he might harm someone.

A more common problem is not giving your characters sufficient to do between the disturbance and the first-act turning point surprise, so they are more or less hanging around waiting for the surprise to happen. Remember that your characters do not know that the surprise/obstacle is about to happen, so think how they might logically react to the disturbance, brainstorming possible responses, and find credible plans that make the story look as if it will go in the opposite direction from the path it actually takes. For example, if you were writing a modern-day *Jack and the Beanstalk* story, you would make much of Jack's plans to retrieve the cow so that the beanstalk came as a shock. Your plan section will be short, but effective. Both action line and relationship line have a plan in response to the disturbance, and in each a plan that misleads the audience will inject great power into the first-act turning point.

Development Strategy 17

INSERT A MISLEADING PLAN

Brainstorm a logical, credible response for the protagonist to have to the disturbance that will lead the audience off track so that the first-act turning point comes as more of a surprise.

Questions to ask:
- Have I got a good 'false' plan?
- Am I really leading the audience off track?
- Do I have plan sections in both action and relationship lines?

The first-act turning point (what the film is 'about')

Fascinatingly, if you ask people what happens in a film—what it's 'about' in terms of scenario—they will usually describe its first-act turning point scene. They will say that *Thelma and Louise* is about 'two women going away on holiday who shoot a rapist and go on the run'. They will say that *Tootsie* is about 'an actor who dresses up as a woman to get a part'. What they are actually picking is the part of the set-up that creates the start of the world-seizing story. In terms of the basic Smiley/Thompson model, they are picking the surprise that will turn into the obstacle. What this means in practical, diagnostic terms is that, in a conventional linear film, your first-act turning point scene will contain the essence of the film's appeal. It will be what makes it original and interesting. It will be what your film is 'about', scenario-wise.

Arguably, the first-act turning point is the most important component of your conventional narrative film because it delivers on screen the core ingredient that will sell your film and also sets the stage for the complications that give us the film's story (told in the second act). It is also your compass, since, if you know what your first-act turning point is you have your film—because the first-act turning point raises a question that the rest of the film seeks to answer, a question that is finally answered in the film's climax. How will

Thelma and Louise cope with having murdered a man? The climax answers that question: suicide.

Climax and first-act turning point are linked. If you know your first-act turning point you know the central issue of your climax, and if you know your climax you can infer your first-act turning point.

If your first-act turning point scene is boring or doesn't really connect to your climax, either you haven't picked the natural first-act turning point of your idea or you don't yet have one (this often happens in films that originated in one interesting character). Either way, you know you haven't yet pinned down what it is about your film that will grab an audience.

In films that flag in the second act, the loss of pace is often caused by a weak or non-existent first-act turning point. The film is relying for its story content just on a disturbance or inciting incident that is simply not interesting enough to drive one and half to two hours of story.

ONE STRIKING AND UNPREDICTABLE SCENE

My feeling is that the first-act turning point is one (and one only) striking, unusual scene, often utterly unpredictable, containing one moment—a few seconds—that shows us the world has changed for the protagonist. It is not a feeling, not a sequence of events (although it may be preceded by a sequence of causative events); it is a physical event that shocks the audience, giving them a completely unexpected surprise. It is the moment the rapist dies in *Thelma and Louise*, the moment we see Michael in *Tootsie* striding down the street dressed up as Dorothy. It makes people sit up in their seats. It makes them feel the film has really started. Quieter films still have their world-changing moment, although it might not be so shocking. In *Samson and Delilah*, it is the actual moment when Delilah realises her grandmother is dead. In *Children of Heaven*, it is the actual moment when we see the little boy realise he could win a pair of shoes in the foot race. In the French film *The Secret of the Grain*, it is the moment we realise that the protagonist has decided to open a couscous restaurant. Why just one moment? Because this is drama, not fiction, and we show rather than tell.

Knowing that the first-act turning point is one world-changing moment is enormously useful because you can pick whether you've got it or still need it. Traditionally, it happens about twenty minutes into the script (frequently earlier these days) and it turns the plot in a new direction, lifting the stakes for the protagonist by pushing them into a new, highly emotionally charged situation that forces them to take action in a way they did not plan.

VOGLER'S ENTRY INTO ANOTHER WORLD

A good way to test whether you have a first-act turning point in place is to use Christopher Vogler's idea that the protagonist enters a new world, physical or metaphorical, or both, at the first-act turning point, stepping into it in that one crucial moment of truth.

Do Thelma and Louise enter a new world at their first-act turning point? Yes: the moment the man dies, they step into the world of the fugitive. Does Michael enter a new world at his first-act turning point? Yes: the moment he starts posing as a woman, he steps into the world of women and the world of deceit and lies. Do the protagonists in *Samson and Delilah*, *Children of Heaven* and *The Secret of the Grain* enter a new world? Yes. If your protagonist is not forced into a new world by the first-act turning point, you haven't yet got a proper first-act turning point.

LINDA SEGER ON TURNING POINTS

Linda Seger has interesting material on turning points in *Making a Good Script Great*, in which she explains that a turning point should kick the action into an unexpected direction, push the protagonist deeper into the problem and raise the central question again but with added, surprising complications.

THE SURPRISE THAT TURNS INTO THE OBSTACLE

A crucial part of the surprise is that *it turns into the obstacle that drives the rest of the film*. This part of the Smiley/Thompson structure is an absolute gem. Whatever your surprise is, it must *become* the film's central problem, and if it can't, it's not a first-act turning point and you will need either to add some element to it, or to find a new one.

It's very easy to invent a surprise which is definitely interesting and definitely surprising but which has nothing to do with the rest of the film, so check it in the following way. If your planned first-act turning point is a person getting sacked, ask: 'Is my film about what happens to someone who gets sacked?' If it is, fine. If it isn't, you haven't yet got your first-act turning point, you've just got an unconnected surprise and that will not give you the big problem that will fill up two hours of screen time.

Compare *Thelma and Louise*. If we ask the question 'Is *Thelma and Louise* about what happens to two women who shoot a rapist?', the answer is yes. The same is true of *Tootsie*. 'Is *Tootsie* about an actor who dresses up as a woman to get a part?' Yes, it is. You may spend a long while finding a good first-act turning point.

DON'T DELAY THE FIRST-ACT TURNING POINT

A delayed first-act turning point can cause boredom and massively damage a film—as in *Prelude to a Kiss*, where it appears about an hour into the film (see pp. 416–17). A story with a very lengthy set-up might be better told in parallel narrative (see how *Prelude to a Kiss* might have worked in a non-linear structure p. 417–18).

MAKE SURE THE DISTURBANCE LEADS TO IT

Crucially, the first-act turning point can only happen directly or indirectly because of the film's disturbance, so choose a disturbance that will give you the first-act turning point you need.

Development Strategy 18

FIND THE FIRST-ACT TURNING POINT SCENE (SURPRISE/OBSTACLE)

Make sure the surprise is an actual, physical surprise—an event—and that the protagonist's change of heart or decision is triggered by this physical surprise. Also make sure the scene represents an entry in another world by the protagonist, either physically or metaphorically.

Questions to ask:

- Have I made the protagonist experience a physical, world-changing surprise in one scene at about twenty minutes into the film (possibly earlier)?
- Does my surprise cause/turn into the obstacle that drives the rest of the film?
- Does my surprise raise the question that the rest of the film explores?
- Does my first-act turning point have all the effects described by Linda Seger?
- Is my first-act turning point scene what the film is 'about' in terms of scenario?
- Is my first-act turning point the moment when the protagonist enters another world physically or metaphorically?

Chapter 13
The second act

THE SECOND ACT—THE FILM'S middle—is universally regarded as the hardest part of the script to write. While writing *Don Giovanni*, considered by many to be the greatest opera of all time, Mozart wrote in despair to his father that he was utterly stuck in the second act and felt as if he'd never finish it. If the second act had Mozart fazed, perhaps the rest of us can take heart.

It's all about complications and things getting worse

All of the many theories about how to write the second act come down to finding a range of complications in the protagonist's story that keep it powerfully interesting for an hour of screen time, then lead it to a gripping third act, which is the protagonist's battle to win against the odds.

Linda Seger has excellent material in *Making a Good Script Great* on different sorts of obstructions and other ways of creating a compelling second and third act. These include, using her terms: barriers, reversals and complications; methods for choosing the right settings and scenarios; using scene sequences to bump up the pace; using foreshadowing and payoff; and many other practical and detailed methods to tackle the business of stymying the protagonist. This is obligatory reading. Another useful concept is the midpoint, first, I believe, pinpointed by Syd Field and picked up by people like Jack Epps Jnr as a point midway through the second act when the story takes a radical twist.

In an online interview on 13 November 2008, Michael Halperin, who wrote *Writing the Second Act*, adds a different and very useful perspective by observing that the second act 'involves suspicions, miscues, anxieties, game plan and all the other elements comprising the dramatic romantic and comedy genre'.

Robert McKee takes another and very useful slant by explaining second-act mechanics in terms of different sorts of conflict impelling complications and forward story movement. As we've seen, Christopher Vogler describes the second act as a journey into another world and suggests archetypes that people it and actions that occur as the protagonist seeks a real or metaphorical treasure. This is very useful because it provides the protagonist and other characters with an agenda that writers can simply flesh out. These are just some of the many approaches to the second act, all of which deserve investigation.

The second act *is* the story

While all writers acknowledge the importance of the first act in creating a good set-up for the second act, the second act itself tends to be regarded in isolation, as a trackless desert in the film's middle through which we have to struggle before the third act and resolution.

However, rather than thinking of the second act as the film's middle, it's more useful and accurate to think of it as the real start of the story, as making up most of the story, following on from a first-act set-up and ending at the moment a long way down the line at the second-act turning point, when the protagonist decides to fight back against the odds in a final battle that ends in the film's climax.

If we look at the second act this way we can see that, as I've said earlier, many scripts that start to fall apart in the second act do so not so much because the second act is hard to write but because the script didn't have a strong enough story in the first place. It did not have a story sufficiently interesting to be elaborated upon and developed for an hour-long second act. Our world-seizing story actually begins properly only in act two.

WORKING FROM THE OUTSIDE IN

The first-act turning point sets up what the story is 'about', and the second and third acts tell that story. Because the story really starts at the second act, I suggest looking at the second act in terms of what frames it—working from the outside in, calculating the needs of the second act by reference to the first-act turning point at one end, and the second-act turning point at the other. Each of these in its different way is enormously useful with content and construction of the second act.

GETTING GOOD COMPLICATIONS FROM THE FIRST-ACT TURNING POINT

Use the first-act turning point plus logic to get good complications. If you use your lateral imagination to get ideas for complications you will find it time consuming and ineffective. Also, you will tend to grab the first half-decent ideas that come to you. Instead, use your vertical imagination and, using the first-act turning point, ask yourself 'What logically could happen to a protagonist faced with the problem mine is faced with at the first-act turning point?', then list as many 'real but unusual' ways as possible that this goal or problem could be obstructed, creating conflict of an emotional or physical kind for the protagonist.

Take *Tootsie*. Here, the protagonist's goal or problem at the first-act turning point is that he is impersonating a woman for professional success. If you ask what obstructions could happen to a man who is trying to pass himself off as a woman, you can get a long list of possible complications in less than a minute. For example: the protagonist falls in love with a woman and can't declare his love; the protagonist declares his love for the woman and the woman thinks he's a lesbian; a man who thinks the protagonist is a woman falls in love with him; a man who thinks the protagonist is a woman tries to press physical advances on him; the protagonist is mistaken for a cross-dresser; the protagonist finds keeping make-up and costume in order difficult and time-consuming; the protagonist's friends think he has deserted them; the protagonist is thought to be gay; a gay man makes a pass at the protagonist; a lesbian makes a pass at the protagonist; the protagonist is raped.

Apart from the last three options (which are too confronting for the light romantic comedy that *Tootsie* sets out to be) the list above provides all of the plot complications that actually occur in *Tootsie*.

The same method could have been used to find the second-act complications in *The Piano*. The protagonist's problem or goal as it presents itself at the first-act turning point is that her means of expression, the piano, is stuck on a beach and therefore unavailable to her. Her need is to get the piano back. If you look at the second-act complications of *The Piano* (see pp. 121–3) you will see that each event is an obstruction to Ada's goal of getting the piano back to express herself, including falling in love with Baines (because by then she wants the piano *and* Baines).

Make sure the complications are different

When devising second-act complications, make sure that the obstructions hindering the protagonist are genuinely different rather than different versions of the same obstruction. For example, in a script where the protagonist is shut in an underground dungeon and has to get out, three different instances of the protagonist being stopped by guards and killing them are not different obstructions. They are three different versions of the same obstruction: guards. Genuinely different obstructions would be the protagonist first obstructed by guards, then by fear of heights, then by a booby-trapped gate, and so on.

Development Strategy 19

DEVISE SECOND-ACT COMPLICATIONS VIA THE FIRST-ACT TURNING POINT

To get a range of interesting second-act complications, first define the protagonist's dilemma after the first-act turning point, then brainstorm as many 'real but unusual' ways as possible that this dilemma could be increased. Note that the dilemma can change or be added to.

Questions to ask:
- Do I understand the problem caused for the protagonist by the first-act turning point?
- Am I writing obstructions that are 'real but unusual'?
- Do I have a lot of different obstructions rather than many versions of the same obstruction?
- Could I increase the obstructions by a clever twist to the protagonist's dilemma?

Using the second-act turning point as a destination

To understand how to use the second-act turning point as a way to find the content of the second act we need to look back at the actual mechanics of the second-act turning point. The first part of the second-act turning point is the closest moment to physical and emotional death, and the second part is the decision to act. Therefore, if John is your protagonist, you know that between the first-act turning point and the first part of the second-act turning point you have to take John to his lowest point as the direct result of complications arising out of the first-act turning point. This means you've got a clear destination for John. You might not know how you'll get him there, but you know where he has to be. Everything in his life, personal and public, has got to be disastrous at the first part of the second-act turning point, after which he will decide to fight back.

BUT WHY DOES THE PROTAGONIST HAVE TO REACH THIS NADIR?

Your protagonist has to reach this low point because your story's got to be more interesting and suspenseful than it was at the first-act turning point or it will fizzle (which happens in *The Crying Game*). If you've given John a fascinating problem at the first-act turning point (as you should have) you have to do something much bigger again at second-act turning point. The closest point to disaster, to death, is as suspenseful as a story can get.

SECOND-ACT TURNING POINT PART 1 (THE WORST MOMENT)

Just as the first-act turning point is a physical event, one amazing scene, so the protagonist's worst possible moment is also a physical event, an actual moment, that occurs in one scene. While the whole film leads up to it and while it may occur at the end of a complex sequence, the worst possible moment itself will be just a few seconds where the protagonist hits rock bottom. The worst possible moment may be something as dramatic as the protagonist being tortured, or having a gun put in their face. It may be someone telling them that a loved one has died or they have lost the crucial court case. It may be a sudden horrified understanding of something that happened earlier on. But something visibly happens on screen. The relationship line also has a worst possible moment, of course. Usually both terrible moments happen in the same scene, but sometimes they happen separately.

SECOND-ACT TURNING POINT PART 2 (DECISION TO FIGHT BACK)

The second step in the second-act turning point is that the protagonist decides to fight back and starts to do so. Why a decision to fight back? Because it is vital to maintain suspense. Curiously, while an audience will get increasingly anxious as things worsen for the protagonist, eventually they will reach a point where they disengage emotionally and move from empathy (feeling as if they are inside the protagonist's shoes) to pity, where they are on the outside of the protagonist, who is now a hopeless case, a victim. If things continue to get worse for the protagonist, the audience can even start to get bored and irritated, feeling preached at or otherwise manipulated.

Endless disasters befalling the protagonist slow the film right down and alienate the audience—because, in the end, they rob the film of suspense. Suspense requires the possibility of change. If there is only hopelessness the film becomes predictable.

To get the audience back on the edge of their seats you have to get them emotionally engaged again with the protagonist, which means you have to introduce hope (hence suspense). In practice, you have to turn your protagonist into a fighter. The protagonist, bruised and battered, has to decide to fight back against impossible odds—and if the odds aren't high enough, you must go back and make them so.

The protagonist does not need to win. Your climax can be catastrophic (like the climax in *The Secret of the Grain*) or muted (as in *Tulpan*), but as far as I can tell an attempt to fight back from a hopeless position at the second-act turning point, however brief, seems to be obligatory to maintain suspense. Films as different as *Slumdog Millionaire*, *Children of Heaven*, *Gran Torino*, *Samson and Delilah* and *Synecdoche, New York* all provide excellent examples of a protagonist relentlessly fighting back against impossible odds; in fact, astonishing escapes are a recurring feature of *Slumdog Millionaire*.

Sometimes writers actually want the ending of their film to be predictably catastrophic, but step cautiously. Make a film too predictable and people don't need to stay and watch.

Like the first-act turning point surprise and the second-act turning point worst possible moment, the decision to fight back must be seen to happen on screen. We must *see* the protagonist take the first step in the battle to win because in film we show rather than tell. The act itself can be as simple as picking up the phone.

Parts 1 and 2 of the second-act turning point can happen in the same scene. Part 1 is your beacon for act two, telling you where you must take the protagonist. Part 2 helps you set up the third act.

HOW TO GET THE PROTAGONIST TO THE LOWEST POINT
How, then, do you get the protagonist to their lowest point? Two things can lead you in the wrong direction here. First of all, as we've seen, you can use lateral imagination alone to think of things that can go wrong. This is unlikely to give you the rich variety that you need. Second, you can fall into the trap of seeing complications as a sequence of things happening on the same emotional plane rather than a downward progression, during which, with increasing tension and suspense, things get worse and worse, and finally hit rock bottom.

Proceed here by making a list of what the protagonist has to have lost by the second-act turning point (how things can go from bad to worse to catastrophic). What exactly has to be lost? Their loved ones? Their credibility? Their belongings? Their safety? Their good name? Work this out, then brainstorm how you can make it all happen. Make your complications occur in order of increasing seriousness, to create a good downwards progression.

Development Strategy 20

SECOND-ACT TURNING POINT PART 1: PROTAGONIST'S WORST POSSIBLE MOMENT

To find the protagonist's worst possible moment, look for the step in the plot where the protagonist reaches their lowest possible point, emotionally and/or physically. Invent one if you don't have one. Then make the protagonist decide to fight back.

Questions to ask:

- Have I found the protagonist's lowest point?
- Do I have to invent or expand one (think 'real but unusual')?
- Is my second-act turning point bigger and more dramatic than the first-act turning point?
- Does it fulfil the requirements of a turning point in restating the protagonist's problem and turning them in a new direction?
- Have I shown the worst possible moment in one scene?

When you have got your protagonist to their lowest ebb, use Development Strategy 21 to work out how to show their decision to fight back.

Development Strategy 21

SECOND-ACT TURNING POINT PART 2: DECISION TO FIGHT BACK

Make sure you have got the protagonist to the worst possible moment, then make them decide to fight back, and start a battle to win (that battle will happen in the third act).

Questions to ask:

- Have I made my protagonist decide to fight back against high odds?
- Have I started the fight-back in a clever and suspenseful way?
- Will this action lead to the battle to win (third act) and the climax?
- Have I shown the decision to act in one scene, via the protagonist taking the first step in the battle to win?

The second-act relationship line

It's often said that the protagonist's relationships come to the fore in the second act. This isn't surprising really, as often the protagonist barely knows the relationship line characters until the start of this act, and sometimes has not even met them. In *The Station Agent*, as we've seen, Fin doesn't meet Joe or

Olivia until the start of the second act (which begins after he inherits the station building). In cases like these, the three-act structure of the relationship line cannot actually start until the second act, so its dramatic high points occur some time after their equivalents in the action line.

CHECKING THAT THE RELATIONSHIP LINE IS MOVING

It's easy for the relationship line to stop developing and get jammed in the same place. A good way to check whether this is happening is to see if any of the relationship sequences can be swapped around. If major scenes or sequences can be swapped between acts without a problem, the relationship line is static. The best scenes often contain the action and relationship lines together, so that each informs the other. If the relationship line is not moving, it could be because the action line is not permitting movement, in which case you will need to change the action line to get the possibilities of progression you require.

Hang on to the idea that the action line permits the relationship line to happen and choose your action line events so that they force changes on the relationship.

Development Strategy 22

CHECK THAT THE RELATIONSHIP LINE IS MOVING

Write a narrative sentence for the relationship line to make sure it is moving, rather than restating the same relationship point in different ways.

Questions to ask:

- Does every incident in the relationship line take the relationship forward, or am I duplicating the same interaction over and over again?
- Could I swap around any of the relationship scenes? (If so, the relationship line is not moving.)
- Is my relationship line's movement tied closely to the movement of my action line?
- If my action line isn't helping my relationship line, do I need to change the action line?

The second act can be condensed

Interestingly, in folk tales, the second act (and also part of the third act) is always the bit of the story that is condensed or expanded. For example, in the various versions of 'Cinderella', Cinderella may attend the ball on one night or attend several balls on a series of different nights. Our ability to condense the second act—or even remove it—will become very important later when we look at non-linear and group stories, which often condense or lose the second act almost entirely.

How can something as important as the second act be condensed? We can condense it precisely because it consists of complications—different things that can go wrong as the result of the problem caused by the first-act turning point. The essential dramatic moments in the second act of 'Cinderella' are its start (the first-act turning point, going to the ball) and its second-act turning point (running away from the ball) and if you want to tell 'Cinderella', you must keep these. However, you can remove the rest and still have a story.

Understanding just how to cut the second act, particularly how to use the huge energy of the second-act turning point scenes (the protagonist's worst moment and the decision to act), is the key to understanding and structuring films with time jumps and flashbacks.

Chapter 14
The third act: Climax, resolution, symbolism and myth

THE THIRD ACT IS triggered by the two-step second-act turning point. The third act is the battle to win. We must be on the edge of our seats throughout act three until the very end of the climax scene, which is when we finally know whether the protagonist has succeeded or failed.

Build the suspense by loading the dice against the protagonist from the start of the second act onwards, consciously factoring in clever twists and turns in action line and relationship line. The second-act turning point will have left the protagonist bereft and damaged, so, in act three, you will need to make the audience feel that the damage might be fixed and the protagonist made happy (even if your intention is to do the exact opposite). Without hope there will be no suspense.

The climax

The climax might well be the scene that made you write the film in the first place. If so, remember that however much you are dying to write it, you have to earn a climax. Horror, tears or helpless laughter are not won easily.

Note that (except in inner/outer story films, where the inner story has to be resolved after the action-line climax), the climax is the story's major dilemma resolved in one make-or-break moment. Like the turning points, the climax is always *seen on screen* as one physical moment, one crucial, win-or-lose scene, even if it is preceded by a spectacular battle or chase. This one scene provides 'the point' of the film in both action line and relationship line. For example, the climax of *Gran Torino* (Walt deliberately getting himself shot by the gang), is both the climax of the action line (how Walt defeats the gang) and the climax of the relationship line (how Walt, the inveterate racist, gives his life to save Theo and Sue, the Hmong neighbours he started out hating).

ANTICLIMAX WORKS TOO

Sometimes, to make a point, anticlimax is used. Life merely goes on, despite tragedy, or despite the lack of great triumphs, or despite the innocent being punished while the guilty go free. This is so in *Crimes and Misdemeanors*, *The Station Agent* and *Tulpan*. In all cases it works because the non-climax is actually a different but valid answer to the original dilemma or problem. A misdirected climax, as in *Guarding Tess*, is not an answer to anything, therefore is irritating.

KEEP UP THE PRESSURE

Maintain pressure up to and until the end of the climax scene. It is very easy for the writer to forget that the climax must genuinely be a 'do-or-die suspenseful battle', the culmination of a whole third-act struggle in which the protagonist (who almost always wins) could really die or lose the fight/the case/the lover. A good example of the writer not really believing in the plot and therefore creating a weak third act and climax occurs in the action comedy *Six Days Seven Nights*. This is a film about two people crashing a plane on a desert island and having adventures with drug smugglers while being assumed dead. The climax depicts the couple arriving back at their own memorial ceremony, which is being held at the island resort they originally left. So little attention was given to the notion of what would really happen if a couple died like this that no grieving relatives are even shown telephoning the resort, let alone attending the memorial service. This weakens the climax because it is incredible. Probably, the writer was distracted by looming plotting problems of writing the comic chaos of the plane's actual landing.

CLIMAX AND FIRST-ACT TURNING POINT

The climax should answer the question raised by the first-act turning point, as we've seen. It is quite common for the climax to shift a little from what you initially planned. If the two don't match, change one or the other.

Development Strategy 23

FIND THE CLIMAX AND FIRST-ACT TURNING POINT

Make the climax answer the problem posed by issues arising from the first-act turning point, or find the first-act turning point via the climax.

Questions to ask:

- Does my climax answer the problem set up by the first-act turning point?
- If I have no first-act turning point, what question is being resolved in my climax?

- Is my new first-act turning point what the film is 'about', and a good surprise/obstacle?
- Is the 'battle' in my climax being won (or lost) too easily; that is, is it genuinely exciting?
- Am I really exploring all the possibilities for suspense in the climax?
- Am I really writing as if the protagonist could actually die/lose their partner etc.?
- If my climax is an anticlimax, is this deliberate and will it work (or will it make the audience feel robbed)?
- Am I, as is necessary, presenting the new normality and ending the film soon after the climax?
- Are the action and the relationship lines coming to a climax in the same scene?
- Alternatively, if my film is an inner/outer story film, am I properly resolving both stories separately, with minimum hiatus?

Resolution and ending

Once the climax has been reached, we need to demonstrate the new normality in plot and subplot as economically as possible. Often this can be done in the same scene as the climax (although an inner/outer story, as we've seen, usually requires two endings). Sometimes, however, writers become so involved with the characters and story that they cannot leave them. This is particularly so with films carrying great emotional or autobiographical content from the writer or director.

Films that suffer from this syndrome often show multiple endings—that is, scene after scene following the climax, each of which feels like a farewell. These can significantly reduce the impact of the film, so, if there seem to be too many endings, blend them or choose the most pertinent.

Development Strategy 24

COME TO A RESOLUTION AND ENDING

Make the film end soon after the climax, to avoid loss of impact and inappropriate audience response (like boredom or amusement).

Questions to ask:

- Is my film displaying multiple endings?
- If there is autobiographical or strong personal material in the film, am I sufficiently distanced to decide which is the best sort of ending?

Going from the general shape to myth and symbolism

By now you will be starting to get a good general idea of your film's overall shape, through your many diagrams, plans and charts. Now, come back to the film's message by trying to find myth and symbolism in your plotlines. In most films, the message or deeper meaning is the reason you are writing the film, but it's very easy, given the complexity of structural planning and the detailed work of planning and writing scenes, to get distracted from the film's message, hence from its whole *raison d'être*.

SYMBOLISM AND MYTH

A film is a parable or fable, with the action transmitting a deeper meaning. In conventional narrative, the meaning is illustrated through what happens to the protagonist, so, as I've said, the script is a journey through the protagonist's mental landscape.

Sometimes a film idea will come to you with symbolism vividly in place but without you understanding what it means and you have to struggle to decipher what your subconscious is trying to tell you. For example, you might find yourself powerfully driven to write a film about a certain place or historical event, but you don't know quite why. At other times however you will want to write about a certain emotional or social phenomenon and need to find symbols and a scenario to fit the point you are making. This happened in the writing of Jane Campion's *The Piano*. Jane Campion says that her original idea for the film did not include a piano. She started out with an idea for a repressed woman who found her sexuality. She invented the piano as the device which could permit this to happen. The piano came at quite a late stage in the project. It's a brilliant symbol because it is an object that is strongly identified with both Victorian passion (think Chopin) and Victorian repression, and, in the New Zealand context, with the contrast between Western and indigenous cultures.

You can start to understand or create symbolism via the relationship line. Because symbolism is often strongly connected with the emotional, spiritual and psychological content of a film, the relationship line will usually give you clues about any symbols that might be appearing, and will guide you as to what symbols you need to include if you don't have any.

Setting a film against a dramatic natural landscape will almost always add a seriousness and sense of universality to the plot. The desert, the mountains, the sea—all these become metaphors for life, and the characters moving across them start to become symbolic of the human race locked in battles against fate and/or the elements. Even a comedy such as *Priscilla, Queen of the Desert* resonates with a higher seriousness because of its desert setting. Urban settings can also have a potent symbolic quality, as in *Blade Runner*.

Try to find objects like Campion's piano, that can be symbolic while also forming the centre of the plot. That way, the symbol is always present, so always resonating. As for myth, most stories have mythical counterparts because myths, like fairytales, tend to be about perennial human dilemmas. To find mythical elements, simply look for similarities in the script with stories in myth, and then boost the elements of myth in the script.

Development Strategy 25

USE SYMBOLISM AND MYTH

Look for any symbolism that is appearing and develop it. Think of symbols to enforce themes and ideas, particularly in the development of the relationship line.

Questions to ask:

- Are symbols and elements of myth already appearing in the script, particularly in the relationship line? If so, how can I develop them?
- Can I think of symbolism that will give the relationship line greater resonance?
- Have I set the film in a place that has useful symbolism?
- Have I inadvertently set up symbolism that might be counterproductive (for example, set a comedy against a background with dark symbolism)?
- Have I overdone the symbolism?

Preparing to write the outline

By now you should have a sound, basic structural plan for your film. However, because you have been so immersed in the *minutiae* of planning you are likely to have lost perspective on the film as whole. You're also probably exhausted. Use the following three tools to regain distance, focus, energy and self-confidence before you start work on the outline.

WHAT YOUR FILM HAS TO CONTAIN AND DEPICT

Figure 14.1 is an expanded version of Figure 6.1. Use it first to remind yourself of the material your film needs to contain and depict, then redraw the chart with the boxes empty and write into each box the relevant material in your film.

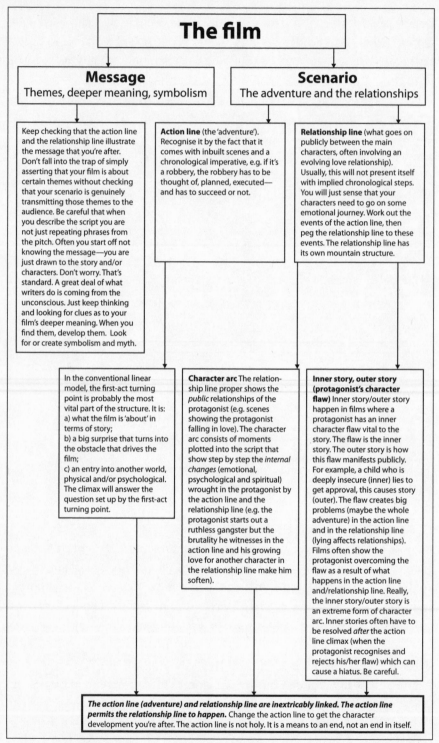

The film

Message
Themes, deeper meaning, symbolism

Scenario
The adventure and the relationships

Keep checking that the action line and the relationship line illustrate the message that you're after. Don't fall into the trap of simply asserting that your film is about certain themes without checking that your scenario is genuinely transmitting those themes to the audience. Be careful that when you describe the script you are not just repeating phrases from the pitch. Often you start off not knowing the message—you are just drawn to the story and/or characters. Don't worry. That's standard. A great deal of what writers do is coming from the unconscious. Just keep thinking and looking for clues as to your film's deeper meaning. When you find them, develop them. Look for or create symbolism and myth.

Action line (the 'adventure'). Recognise it by the fact that it comes with inbuilt scenes and a chronological imperative, e.g. if it's a robbery, the robbery has to be thought of, planned, executed— and has to succeed or not.

Relationship line (what goes on publicly between the main characters, often involving an evolving love relationship). Usually, this will not present itself with implied chronological steps. You will just sense that your characters need to go on some emotional journey. Work out the events of the action line, then peg the relationship line to these events. The relationship line has its own mountain structure.

In the conventional linear model, the first-act turning point is probably the most vital part of the structure. It is:
a) what the film is 'about' in terms of story;
b) a big surprise that turns into the obstacle that drives the film;
c) an entry into another world, physical and/or psychological. The climax will answer the question set up by the first-act turning point.

Character arc The relationship line proper shows the *public* relationships of the protagonist (e.g. scenes showing the protagonist falling in love). The character arc consists of moments plotted into the script that show step by step the *internal changes* (emotional, psychological and spiritual) wrought in the protagonist by the action line and the relationship line (e.g. the protagonist starts out a ruthless gangster but the brutality he witnesses in the action line and his growing love for another character in the relationship line make him soften).

Inner story, outer story (protagonist's character flaw) Inner story/outer story happen in films where a protagonist has an inner character flaw vital to the story. The flaw is the inner story. The outer story is how this flaw manifests publicly. For example, a child who is deeply insecure (inner) lies to get approval, this causes story (outer). The flaw creates big problems (maybe the whole adventure) in the action line and in the relationship line (lying affects relationships). Films often show the protagonist overcoming the flaw as a result of what happens in the action line and/or relationship line. Really, the inner story/outer story is an extreme form of character arc. Inner stories often have to be resolved *after* the action line climax (when the protagonist recognises and rejects his/her flaw) which can cause a hiatus. Be careful.

The action line (adventure) and relationship line are inextricably linked. The action line permits the relationship line to happen. Change the action line to get the character development you're after. The action line is not holy. It is a means to an end, not an end in itself.

Figure 14.1 What your film has to contain and depict (expanded version)

INDEX CARDS AND BEATS

The next step in planning the outline is to transfer your plans for the various plotlines onto index cards, using a different index card for each beat of each plot, numbering each one. You then set the cards out in order on a table, which will permit you to see the film in its entirety. You will be able to pick weaknesses and experiment with plot changes by the simple means of moving the cards around, which you will keep doing and doing again as you proceed.

Some writers use different coloured cards or a different numbering system for different plotlines, so they can easily pick whether there is enough of each plot, and if the various plots are being intertwined in a balanced way or being presented in clumps. You can also check the film's running time.

THE MAGIC LETTER

The story goes that legendary screenwriting teacher Frank Daniel used to advise all writers at the start of a script to write themselves a letter explaining why their film was going to be wonderful. They were then to place the letter into an envelope, seal it, and put it away until they had a serious problem with the script. At this point, in their greatest despair, they were to open the letter and there, miraculously, would be the answer.

This makes a lot of sense. The letter will not only contain the spark, but the spark written in detail and with passion and absolute conviction—all of the things, very probably, that you need to get you back on track.

Writing the outline

Now you can start to write a proper outline or 'beat sheet' in point form, thereby giving yourself another chance to check that your script has good bones before you start to flesh it out with scenes and dialogue. Your outline will go through several drafts. Point form will make it harder to waffle, and remind you that each new point must be a movement in the plot. As you proceed, see also Part 3, Practical Plotting and Part 6, Getting It on the Page. Chapter 15 provides a structural analysis of a conventional three-act structure film, *The Piano*, which you may also find useful for reference.

Chapter 15
Structural analysis of *The Piano*

THE PIANO IS A powerful and compelling film built on a fine three-act structure, involving inner and outer story and containing interesting use of myth and symbolism. It very usefully illustrates the structural components described in the previous section. Use the following structural analysis for reference and exercises. For example, as an exercise in understanding the narrative sentence and Vogler's hero's journey, apply them to *The Piano*.

ORIGINS

Jane Campion wanted to write about a repressed Victorian woman finding sexuality and self-expression. The plotline involving the arranged marriage and the lost piano came later. In other words, *The Piano* came from an idea for a character and relationship line, and the action line was invented to permit the relationship line to happen. This is very common.

Structural breakdown of the action line following the basic Smiley/Thompson nine-point plan/ three-act structure

ACT ONE

1 **Normality**: Ada's life in Scotland
2 **Disturbance**: going to New Zealand to be married
3 **Protagonist**: split between Ada and her daughter. Together they form one complete person, the protagonist. The child is both Ada's voice and her conscience. Note how Campion cuts constantly from Ada to the child, who either acts out what her mother is feeling—from dancing along the beach with joy when her mother is playing the piano with joy, to caressing the trees after her mother has caressed Baines, to cartwheeling at the end of the movie—or else acts out the opposite—most crucially, going to Stewart and not Baines with the piano key.

4 **Plan**: to continue her silent protest, expressing her emotions only through the piano

5 **Surprise**: that Ada is not allowed to bring the piano—her voice—from the beach to the house

6 **Obstacle**: because she is not allowed to bring the piano to the house, she is unfulfilled, she cannot 'speak'. She has to get the piano back to fulfil her plan (to express herself only through the piano). This is the problem/need that drives the rest of the film. Getting the piano back is what the film is 'about'.

The surprise plus the obstacle form the first-act turning point.

ACT TWO

7 **Complications**: act two contains all of the obstacles which prevent Ada from fulfilling her plan to express herself through the piano. It also provides a range of answers to the question posed by the first-act turning point: 'What will happen when a woman who expresses herself through playing the piano is prevented access to a piano?' Notice the barriers and reversals, and how the question changes when Ada falls in love with Baines, now needing both Baines and the piano.

- Stewart will not bring back the piano.
- Ada goes to Baines with a note about the piano, but he cannot read.
- When the child explains, Baines refuses to take her to the beach.
- Baines finally takes Ada to the beach to play the piano but does not bring it back.
- Baines offers Stewart some land in exchange for the piano on the condition that Ada teach him.
- The piano is dropped on its way back from the beach.
- Ada insists the piano is hers, but Stewart insists she give it up and teach Baines so he can have the land.
- Ada refuses to teach Baines because the piano must be out of tune which would distress her.
- The piano has been tuned, so she teaches him.
- Baines offers the bargain—one key per visit.
- The daughter wants to come in—she might betray them, thus prevent the bargain being paid out and the piano returned.
- Baines wants her to strip for him—five keys.

- The music-lesson sham is almost exposed at the Bluebeard play.
- Baines wants more—ten keys to lie with her.
- The little girl sees and caresses the trees, stopped by Stewart—will he find out? The little girl says 'I know why Mr Baines can't play the piano', but Stewart doesn't understand.
- Baines gives the piano back saying it's turning Ada into a whore and he wants her to love him.
- Stewart, thinking he'll have to pay for the piano, offers it back to Baines.
- Baines says he can keep it.
- Now Ada has got the piano back, she suddenly finds it is not enough for her—it will no longer fully express her emotions. She now needs Baines *and* the piano (note that now the complications involve not getting just the piano but getting Baines and the piano. Some analysts would call this act four).
- Ada goes to Baines. He tells her to go, opens the door for her to go, so she hits him. They make love.
- Stewart accidentally sees them! Will he stop them? Violently?
- Stewart does not stop them. He lies under the house listening. Baines says 'If you care, come back tomorrow.'
- When Ada goes back the next day, Stewart catches and tries to rape her.
- Maoris are bashing at the piano (if they destroy it, this is an obstruction).
- Stewart barricades Ada in the house.
- Ada starts playing the piano in her sleep (is this impending madness? If so, it will be a very effective obstruction to getting Baines and the piano).
- Ada tries to express her sexuality with Stewart (if she can, she won't need Baines).
- Baines is leaving in a few days (if he's gone, she can't have him).
- Ada keeps trying with Stewart but won't let him touch her. (Is she falling for him? This would obstruct her need for Baines.)
- Stewart is touched by Ada's advances. He takes down the barricades. (Is Ada falling in love with him?)
- Having taken down the barricades, Stewart gets her to promise not to see Baines (another obstruction).
- Ada writes: 'George, you have my heart, Ada McGrath' on a

piano key and gives it to the child to take to Baines—but the child takes it to Stewart.

- Second-act turning point: Stewart goes crazy, chops off Ada's fingertip, which stymies her because she cannot play properly. This is Ada's lowest point, her brush with death. Will Stewart kill her?

ACT THREE (COMPLICATIONS CONTINUE)

The battle to win: Can Ada fight back and win Baines and the piano?

- Stewart tries to initiate sex with Ada. (Will she? Has he beaten her into submission?)
- Ada stops him with a strange look (a late appearance of the decision to fight back). He sets off with his gun to see Baines. (Will he kill Baines?)

8 **Climax** (there are two, because the film involves inner/outer story)

- Outer story climax: Stewart tells Baines that Ada's telepathy asked him to let her go with Baines and tells Baines to take her. Ada and Baines leave with the piano.
- Inner story climax: Ada pushes the piano overboard, thereby rejecting it as her only instrument for expression! (Now she only has Baines.) But she catches her foot in the rope. It pulls her over into the sea where she seems destined to drown. She has to choose whether to live, and engage with the world, or die, thereby choosing utter, irreversible silence. She decides to live and speak, overcoming her flaw (notice the hiatus between the two climaxes).

9 **Resolution**: Ada is living with Baines. She is a music teacher with a silver fingertip (made by Baines), teaching herself to speak.

ACTION LINE, RELATIONSHIP LINE, INNER AND OUTER STORY

The action line (and outer story) is what actually happens to the piano—all of which is triggered by Ada's inner flaw; namely, that she insists on staying silent and communicating only via her daughter and her piano. The relationship line is the growing love between Ada and Baines. Ada's character arc, her journey, is an inner-story model, whereby through sexual awakening into sexual and emotional fulfilment she manages to overcome her inner flaw and reject silence and isolation. Note how the action line permits the relationship line (and inner story) to happen, and how the action line pulls the relationship line along.

PROTAGONIST AND ANTAGONIST

Ada is the protagonist. Stewart is primarily an action-line antagonist, with Baines the antagonist in the relationship line. When Baines and Ada fall in love, Stewart becomes the antagonist in their story. Baines is an antagonist who changes. The greatest change is in Ada, the protagonist.

STEWART BUYING MAORI LAND

There is another minor plot about Stewart buying Maori land. This serves to show Stewart as greedy and unresponsive, a man without spirituality and intuition. The Bluebeard play is a kind of symbolic set-up that pays off in the actual finger chopping. As normal, the second act is largely concerned with the relationship line.

UNITIES

The first big scene—in which Ada lands on the beach—is duplicated in the climax scene, where Ada and Baines are leaving and Ada chooses to live. Note also the unity in the script whereby Ada's first words and the opening words are: 'The voice you hear is my mind's voice at six years old'. Ada adds later in the same scene that: 'Silence affects everyone in the end'. The last words of the film are all about silence.

SYMBOLISM

The plots and setting of a good film are mental landscapes, metaphors for the characters' mental state. *The Piano* functions against the setting of two real landscapes which have enormous metaphorical/symbolic power as symbols of sexuality. These are water (particularly the ocean, but also rain and water generally) and the wild forest. Fire is another potent symbol, which Jane Campion does not use in this instance, except in the child's tall story about the death of her father, in which he is struck by lightning.

These images of storm, water, wild nature and fire are, of course, the stock in trade of Gothic fiction, which, like *The Piano*, is driven by repressed sexuality. In classic Gothic style, Campion uses symbols of wild nature to externalise sexual crisis—like a storm as the outward expression of Stewart's jealous rage just before he chops off the finger, and the pelting rain to accompany Stewart's rape. Note that the Maoris often appear naked or half-naked against water, which symbolises their relaxed attitude towards sexuality (compared with the over-dressed, repressed Europeans, whose clothes drag in the water and the mud). The Maoris actually call Stewart 'old dry-balls'. The uneducated Baines, who wears Maori tattoos on his face and is powerfully driven sexually, occupies the middle ground between the two races.

The piano is another symbol, this time of Western culture and the sublimated, controlled sexual passion of the nineteenth century. Jane Campion added the piano to the plot because she wanted a way to explore the dawning sexuality of a repressed Victorian woman. For Ada, the piano is her voice, her passions. Only when she is playing the piano can she speak. It is her emotional self, her passionate self, which Victorian society would seek to suppress. The juxtaposition of the piano against a raging sea operates on a powerful emotional level. The subliminal effect of these symbols—which flash up constantly and naturally in the background—is to reinforce the sexuality and passion of the plot. On a less primeval level, there is a whole symbolism of angels (Western asexual creatures), which starts the moment Ada and the little girl land on the beach and the Maoris say they look like angels, to the last part of the film where the angel's wings (Western asexuality) are swept back and forth through the ocean.

MYTHS

Many great films and novels link into folk tales and myths as well as Jungian archetypes. *The Piano* links into many powerful myths, most obviously 'Beauty and the Beast', and 'Sleeping Beauty' (awoken by a kiss).

To summarise, we can find elements of the following mythical/fairytale components:

- 'Beauty and the Beast'
- 'Sleeping Beauty'/enchanted princess
- Faustian bargain
- Folktales in which the protagonist is forced to perform onerous tasks, often nightly, to gain freedom
- Ada having a telepathic 'dark power'

Part 3
Practical Plotting

Chapter 16
The nature of the task

THE LAST CHAPTERS DEALT with broad structural issues. Now, as you start your outline, we need to explore the extraordinarily difficult task of scene-by-scene plotting, something often understandably neglected in screenwriting books because it is hard to explain in the abstract and is usually learnt only by experience. The key to understanding plotting is to realise that the inbuilt limits of the screenplay form make it, in technical writing terms, an excercise in micro-engineering.

A novelist focuses on creating the best piece of fiction they can. A screenwriter, on top of the massive task of telling a world-class story, is constantly focused on cutting, condensing, shaping, pumping up suspense, all just to get over what they want to say in 100 to 110 minutes, 120 at most. And this is the core of the problem. Normally, you have a maximum of two hours to grab and hold the imagination of the world with a powerful story, but you must:

- tell your story almost entirely by characters in action (with no help from prose narrative)
- tell everything in one sitting to an audience that gets restless after one slow scene and actively bored after two
- create never-failing, ever-rising suspense to a powerful climax (with no possibility, as a novelist, of quiet pauses at the end of chapter breaks)
- do it all to a budget

The impact of time

Even in terms of how long the story can be there is a problem. The business of dramatising action, of 'showing not telling', is inherently a very time-consuming way of transmitting a story. Take this simple sentence from a novel: 'They met by accident at the station and spoke tersely about custody of the children.' This will take a minimum of about forty-five seconds on film, probably more, depending on whether we know the characters and how much information the parents need to discuss.

Let's break this down. Five seconds or so at least will be needed at the start to establish the station and the presence of all of the characters, and probably another five seconds for a final shot of the scene. 'Spoke tersely about custody of the children' will involve a series of terse sentences and pauses, with the camera cutting between each face, every shot eating into screen time. If the children are there, which, for dramatic purposes, you will probably want them to be, you will need to provide time for the camera to record them perceiving and being upset by their parents' discord. You may want a child to interrupt and a parent to send the children out of earshot. You may want to see passers-by reacting, and so on.

What this means in practical terms is that you have time for only about a hundred small packets of information like the sentence above (about one per minute), possibly less since many of your 'sentences' will take a lot longer to transmit on screen than the example above. On top of all this, the plot of a film has to be a chain-reaction, with event A causing event B causing event C and so on, without irrelevancy or repetition. This kind of close plotting is actually extremely hard to do.

The need for words

Because the look of angst is also the look of indigestion, a further and serious restriction is that film cannot transmit detailed internal thought processes. This will affect not only how you tell your story but the kind of story you can tell (it's why *The Shipping News* was a brilliant exploration in prose narrative of a man's internal state but was probably never going to work as a film).

While occasionally you can do a bit of voice-over narrative, your characters must demonstrate their personalities, their responses and their thoughts primarily through action and credible dialogue couched in short speeches. That said, you must not be too cryptic because your audience cannot flick back a few pages if they get lost, and they must be able to absorb your film in one sitting (or at least understand and enjoy enough to come back for another viewing).

Budget

A novelist's imagination can run riot. A screenwriter has to write scenes that are affordable, and moreover be ready at the drop of a hat to relocate a scene so that it has exactly the same dramatic content but happens in a different, more convenient or cheaper location. Screenwriters learn tricks such as how to cut redundant characters (all actors have to be paid); how to write a period script so that scenes can be shot tight to conceal a twenty-first century background; how to write so that scenes involving a very busy actor occur only in limited locations, so the actor can be present for the minimum time. These are the hidden skills of screenwriting, vital for everyone's survival, but only noticed if they are missing.

Instruction manual

Finally, regardless of any issues of quality, a film script has to be an instruction manual instantly understandable on a first reading to a wide range of people. Anyone who's struggled to understand a kit furniture instruction manual knows that writing good instruction manuals is an art in itself. It calls for an astonishing degree of precision, particularly as the instructions must be brief so they don't interfere with any reader's visualisation of the script. In a nutshell, if you write in your script 'she falls into a brown study', a carpenter out there may be told to start building bookcases.

Becoming invisible

None of this is to suggest that writing a novel is easier, just that film writing requires a range of different skills from fiction, skills that are often hidden, because while novelists are normally a very vivid presence in their work, the good screenwriter disappears so far into the script that, if the job is well done, for those precious one hundred minutes the audience thinks it is looking at real life. A lot of this book is actually about the art of becoming invisible, of creating characters, story and, particularly, a way of telling your story—a structure—that transmits everything you want to say, whether your film is a conventional model or a parallel narrative.

For all of the reasons I have given here, writing a good script is difficult even for very experienced screenwriters. Moreover, it is difficult *every time* for experienced screenwriters because every script is a new recipe. In most spheres of life, people get taught the best way to do something, replicate it and get the product that's required. Replicate *The Reader* and you get *The Reader*. Our job is extrapolation, taking proven methods and techniques and combining and extending them in new ways to create material that is unique, vividly original and appealing to people all over the world. Not easy.

It's hard because it's hard

If all of this sound daunting, the message to everyone involved in the creative development of a film script is that if you are finding it hard, take heart. The reason it's hard is because, quite simply, it is. The script is not, like the rest of the film, the work of armies of experts. It comes out of a few heads, a few minds, and this really is both the joy of it and the nightmare. Our tools in creating it now and in all its future forms (forms we shall all have to tackle at some point in our working lives) are persistence, the willingness to learn from other writers, adaptability, an acceptance of our own fallibility, a readiness to rewrite as much and as often as it takes, and, finally, above all, careful planning.

Chapter 17
Close plotting: Beats, interweaving and condensing

IT'S ONE THING TO know that you want to write a powerful story about a robbery, another to know exactly what plot steps or beats you need to tell the story to its best, and even harder to know how many you can get into the screen time at your disposal, particularly if your film is a parallel narrative structure with several stories.

Close plotting is the art of picking, condensing and ordering beats and scenes to maximum effect (for an explanation of beats, see p. 50). As I've said, for 100 minutes of screen time you need about 70 to 80 beats. Simple arithmetic shows you how little time this would give you for each beat if you showed it separately. You don't. You combine beats from separate storylines. Hence, in, say, *Finding Nemo*, the relationship between father fish Marlin and his friend Dory is taken a beat further every time they together encounter and overcome a problem (a beat) in the action line (the hunt for Nemo).

To plot effectively, you need always to be thinking: 'condense, tighten, enrich'. You need to see individual scenes and sequences as means to an end, not ends in themselves. Specifically, you have to know how to:

- create a story as a chain reaction of events
- differentiate between a beat and a scene, and realise when you are just repeating different versions of the same beat
- use one scene to simultaneously drive a number of plots and transmit character information (which means you will often have two or more beats in one scene)
- choose carefully where your scenes are set to maximise what you can get across (for example, it might be more useful for your arguing husband and wife to argue in an office rather than at home so that a third and a fourth character can credibly walk in and, in the same scene, take other plots another step further)
- truncate (so that three slow scenes that happen over two days in five different places can be condensed into one scene on one morning in one location)

- think in terms not of simply 'a good scene', but of a good scene that packs in as much information as possible, as part of a continuously building action line that is pulling the relationship line along
- see your film as a series of simultaneously running plots, as if in an aerial view

Creating a chain of events: '. . . and then?'

A plot is a chain of events—a series of beats—leading to a climax, but it's easy to get stuck providing different versions of the same beat without realising it. Imagine you had to write an episode of the now defunct series *Seinfeld* (TV series are useful examples for plotting issues because everyone knows the characters and the kind of story material, which means the only issues are getting a good story and structuring it properly).

The comic pattern in *Seinfeld* was that a tiny event or act escalated comically into a major drama. Let's imagine Jerry has a new girlfriend. She's perfect except that she has enormous feet, which increasingly unnerve him. The large feet must somehow cause a story, that is, an escalating comic problem ending in a climax. The temptation will be for you to get stuck at the first beat ('Jerry notices her big feet and finds them unnerving'), persistently inventing funny ways in which the feet unnerve Jerry, rather than an adventure—that is, a set of consequences arising from the feet phobia. For example, the following are all versions of 'Jerry is unnerved by the big feet'.

- The girl keeps stepping on people's feet in a cinema queue then blaming others.
- Jerry starts to feel less manly because his feet are smaller than hers.
- The girl arrives wearing embarrassingly huge shoes.

These are not a story, they are different versions of the same beat—technically, a repeated disturbance—and, even if you write each brilliantly, the script will feel as if it's running on the spot. To create a chain of events, choose one of the three options that you like and ask: 'and then?' to start a story.

Let's say you opt for the cinema queue idea. Ask, 'and then?' Imagine your answer is 'Jerry, in the cinema queue, takes his girlfriend's side and gets into a quarrel with a strange woman'. Then ask, 'and then?' Your reply might be, 'The strange woman starts to stalk Jerry.' Then ask, 'and then?'

In all of your scripts, always ask: 'and then . . . and then . . . and then . . .?' consciously taking your story, step by step, to a climax (traceable to the very first step).

Condensing beats

To illustrate how to create storylines in beats and how to condense beats, let's look at another defunct American TV series, *Friends*. I've devised a six-beat plotline (a subplot) for Joey, one of the characters, then shown how to condense it.

WHAT DOES JOEY NEED IN HIS PLOT?

Plot illustrates character, so your first question must be: 'What does my character need in his plot to depict his character?' Joey is an actor, so it would be good to have a plot that includes acting. He is also kind, good-looking and obsessed with acting, but a little stupid and sometimes unintentionally insensitive to others. Our plot needs to depict all of these qualities.

JOEY'S STORY IN SIX STEPS OR BEATS

In our plot, Joey gets a job as a vegetable in a soup commercial and messes up in a typical Joey way. How do we turn that into a story with six beats? Here's one way.

1   Joey is auditioning with others for the role of a tomato in a soup commercial which will involve a lot of actors dressed as vegetables.
2   Joey gets a smaller part as a carrot. He's irritated by the arrogant man who got the job of the tomato and attracted by the gorgeous girl who is the cauliflower.
3   At rehearsals, Joey questions the motivation of the carrot. He forces the cast and director to have discussions about the psychology of their characters, particularly how the vegetables would interact in a crisis situation (getting mashed into a soup).
4   Rehearsals turn into therapy sessions. Everyone is talking about their bad childhoods, their terrible mothers etc.
5   The director starts to shoot the commercial, but then has a nervous attack, remembering his bad relationship with his brother. All of the vegetables start fighting, which Joey tries unsuccessfully to stop. Comic chaos.
6   Joey gets sacked, but a casting director gives him a role as an aggressive blackcurrant in a new fruit juice ad.

Notice that there is a clear story progression here, each point leading to the next. If each was just a different version of, say, 'Joey's suit is very tight and something funny happens', it would be a repeated disturbance and ultimately boring.

HOW COULD WE REDUCE THIS IF WE HAD TO?

Identify the essence, the heat of the idea. In comedy, this is what is funniest about it. Here, the heat is that Joey is so obsessed with acting that he discusses the motivation of a carrot, which upsets the director and actors and gets him sacked. Thus, whatever we do, we must keep 'Joey gets an acting job as a carrot' and 'the director has a nervous breakdown triggered by Joey discussing the carrot's motivation'. Other funny elements are the sight gags (vegetable costumes); Joey's jealousy of the tomato and attraction to the cauliflower; actors dressed as vegetables solemnly discussing the motivation of vegetables and remembering their traumatic childhoods.

We could easily tighten our plotline one beat by combining beats 1 and 2 and starting the scene at the end of the audition, so we open with Joey interacting with the tomato and cauliflower actors. That's actually faster, richer and funnier. If we have to lose more, the interaction with the tomato and cauliflower could be cut back; although, if we're clever, we can include it in the story elsewhere.

Joey's story as four beats could be:

1 Joey is at rehearsals for a soup commercial, where he has got the role of a carrot (although he wanted the role of tomato, and is antagonistic towards the tomato and flirtatious to the cauliflower). Joey questions the motivation of the carrot, and asks how all the vegetables would feel in a crisis situation like being made into soup.

2 The rehearsal has turned into a therapy session. Everyone is talking about their bad childhoods, their terrible mothers etc. (play on Joey's antagonism to the tomato and attraction to the cauliflower).

3 The director starts to shoot the commercial, but then has a nervous attack, remembering his bad relationship with his brother. All of the vegetables start to fight, as Joey unsuccessfully tries to stop them. Comic chaos.

4 Joey gets sacked, but a casting director gives him a role as an aggressive blackcurrant in a new fruit juice ad.

Joey's story as three beats could be:

1 Joey is at rehearsals for a new carrot juice (no longer a soup) involving only one actor, Joey, as the carrot. There are no other vegetable actors, only the crew and the director. Joey questions the motivation of the carrot and how it would feel in a crisis situation—like being made into carrot juice.

2 The director starts to shoot the commercial, but then has a nervous attack, remembering his bad relationship with his brother. Comic chaos.

3   Joey gets sacked, but the director gives him a role as an aggressive
    blackcurrant in a new fruit juice ad.

JOEY'S STORY IN TWO BEATS AND WITH TWO ACTORS AND ONE SET ONLY

You could get almost the same joke with just two actors and one set: Joey
and the director in the director's office (using only a corner set; again, much
cheaper) where Joey has come to discuss the commercial. You would lose
the big sight gags, but you could compensate by making the conversation
between Joey and the director funny in itself. Perhaps the director has a
funny facial twitch or is paranoid about spilling his coffee—whatever. Note
that including the shooting of the commercial means lots of extras as camera
crew etc. That's expensive and does not really add to the comedy.

1   Joey questions the motivation of the carrot and how it would feel in a
    crisis situation like being made into carrot juice.
2   The director and Joey discuss the carrot's motivation. The director
    has a nervous attack, remembering his bad relationship with his
    brother. Comic chaos (for example, the director bursts into tears,
    or curls up on the floor in a fetal position). End the story with Joey
    watching the director in amazement, or with Joey sneaking out,
    leaving the director.

The two-beat story isn't as rich and visual as the longer version, but it still
contains the story's heat, its core. Lack of screen time and budget will often
force you to condense your material and, actually, often the condensed version is better.

Story stranding

At some point you will have to interweave your stories. In certain films, usually
group films, there is so much story to transmit that each scene has to be carefully constructed so that it will transmit several story strands simultaneously.
For example, in a film about six gangsters, you will have a lot of interpersonal
plot beats to transmit as well as your main gang story (see pp. 218–33). Study
films and TV drama to learn about good and bad close plotting.

How the action line permits the relationship line to happen

To show how the action line permits the relationship line to happen, and to
illustrate a weak action line can destroy a film, I will retell *The African Queen*
without its wonderful action line, the journey down the river. In this new

version, Rose and Allnutt stay at the mission throughout, bickering and end-lessly reacting in character to each other's character flaws.

Technically, this means that they are stuck at the disturbance of the story, the destruction of the mission, and I have provided no first-act turning point, no building middle act to catastrophic second-act turning point, and no exciting 'battle to win' third act and climax. Notice that this new version has a sequence of events (in that the characters both do a series of things in character and in response to each other) *but there is not an incrementally building plot.* There is no real story.

Notice too how unconvincing the love story is in this new story. This is because a credible love story between two such different characters requires extenuating circumstances and my weak action line hasn't provided any.

THE AFRICAN QUEEN (WITH NO ACTION LINE)
(Each new number indicates a different segment or sequence.)
1   The mission is attacked.
2   Rose and Allnutt are the only survivors.
3   Rose and Allnutt bury the dead.
4   Rose makes Allnutt sleep in a shed.
5   Rose makes Allnutt rebuild the chapel and helps him. They have comical differences about how to build. Rose, who cannot admit she is wrong, keeps making mistakes in the building but making excuses for herself.
6   There is a storm and *The African Queen* breaks its mooring and sinks. Allnutt is thus stuck with Rose.
7   Allnutt drinks himself into a stupor.
8   Rose throws away all of Allnutt's gin.
9   They have a terrible argument and call each other hurtful names.
10 Germans come to the camp. Rose and Allnutt fight them off.
10a *Or* Germans come to the camp and Rose and Allnutt take one as a prisoner.
10b *Or* Rose falls ill. Allnutt nurses her back to health. She is a very bad invalid, but they fall in love.
10c *Or* Allnutt falls ill and Rose nurses him back to health.
11 Allnutt tell Rose about tragic events that happened to him as a boy. Rose tells him about her repressed childhood.
12 Allnutt restores Rose's harmonium. She is touched.
13 Rose makes a Union Jack flag and insists on flying it.
14 Now in love, they get married.

Notice how static this is. Notice how it consists of largely unconnected sequences that do not build on each other and which can be shuffled about without creating any problem in plot continuity (a clear sign that the plot is not moving). We might add a bit more excitement by having Rose and All-nutt keep a prisoner, but it would still be very static. We could combine some of these points to fool ourselves that we were adding energy. For example, we might write it so that the Germans creep up as Allnutt and Rose are quar-relling, so they are caught unawares. Our best hope for a plot here would probably be a story based around the conflicts and/or unity that might result from that German prisoner idea, but then the film might become a three-way piece, with a strong risk that the German prisoner could pull focus. Notice how the beginning of the film has a certain energy, because of the originality of the characters and setting, but it soon starts to grind to a halt. As for the love story, it is utterly implausible.

Good writing skills can mask storytelling problems

As I've commented about 'Finding Becky' (see pp. 33–4), what is really frightening is that while the weaknesses of this version are vividly evident because we all know the real *African Queen*, if you imagine the outline I've given with stylishly constructed scenes, witty dialogue, good characteri-sation and a range of moving and comic scenes, it could seem reasonably good. It would be much harder to pick the lack of proper plot. The writerly skills might well mask the utter lack of story, of step-by-step movement, and the repetitiveness of the action. It would feel slow but each scene taken sepa-rately would be good. It would be damned with faint praise as 'promising' with 'interesting characters'. But good characters do not make a good film. You need a story.

SIEGES ARE DIFFICULT

As a postscript, take note of the siege nature of my new *African Queen* plot. When you have a story that is inherently static, as all siege situations are, you have to work hard to create credible and interesting *emotional* conflict between the characters that are under siege.

COLLAPSING YOUR TURNING POINTS: *THE BETRAYED WIFE*

Often a plotline can be energised very powerfully by taking what at first sight looks like the first-act turning point and making it the disturbance, then turning the second-act turning point into part of a new first-act turning point, so as to put the protagonist in a very powerful dilemma. Your original third act will then become part of a new and more interesting second act. You will of course have to add a lot of plot.

For example, look at this plot outline.

1 **Protagonist**: An upright woman lawyer in her thirties is very much in love with and emotionally dependent upon her high-profile husband who happens to be a compulsive gambler.

2 **Disturbance**: Thugs arrive at their home and threaten her husband unless he pays off a massive debt.

3 **Plan**: The woman tries to raise money to pay off the debt but can't.

4 **First-act turning point**: The thugs arrive, capture the husband and tell the woman that she has to give them secret information about a case that her law firm is handling or her husband will be harmed.

5 **Second act**: She becomes involved in a complex scheme to get information for the thugs.

6 **Second-act turning point**: She is discovered, loses her job and finds out that the plan was her husband's idea, that he is not in danger, and that he has another woman.

7 **Third act**: She goes to the police, who initially don't believe her, but finally do.

8 **Climax**: She tells him that she is free of him, and can cope on her own.

This seems okay, although rather boring. It is not set in a new world, but possibly a good writer could cleverly insert new-world elements. Note that it has a surprise first-act turning point, a second-act turning point that takes the woman to a very low point, and a climax that pays off the first-act turning point. So, apparently, everything structurally necessary is in place.

But look how much more confronting and faster the story becomes if you collapse the turning points, so that the first-act turning point is combined with the weak disturbance and the second-act turning point becomes the first-act turning point.

1 **Protagonist**: Upright woman lawyer in her thirties is very much in love with and emotionally dependent upon her high-profile husband who happens to be a compulsive gambler.

2 **Disturbance** (originally first-act turning point): Thugs arrive at their home and tell the woman that her husband owes them a huge sum of money and she has to give them secret information about a case that her law firm is handling or her husband will be harmed.

3 **Plan**: She gets the information for the thugs.
4 **First-act turning point**: She is discovered, loses her job and finds that the plan was her husband's idea. He is not in danger from the thugs, and he has another woman.

Suddenly the woman has a much bigger problem, with many possible options opening out for the next part of the story. You could either build on your existing plot idea, or go in a completely new direction. Does the woman engage in revenge, and if so, how? Does the story become an action thriller? A psychological thriller? A horror story? Does the woman turn the tables on the husband and the other woman in some clever/shocking/horrific way? Note that this version gives you everything that you had in the original, but permits you to take it further.

Shifting where an event happens

Akin to collapsing turning points to get a more interesting and original story is using the story fragments that come to you at a different part of the film than the one you first thought of. For example, the fragment 'woman kills brutal husband' could be the start of a story, the middle of a story or its climax.

Don't lose the plot: Staying with the heat

Twins stays with its heat because it employs a story that throws the unlikely twins together and takes them on an adventure. This all sounds very obvious, but in practice it is quite easy to stray away from the heat. For example, imagine *Twins* with a plot that followed only one twin as he searched for a twin he knew existed but had never met. Imagine that the climax is that Arnold Schwarzenegger finds his identical twin, and the twin is—Danny de Vito! It's the same joke (non-identical identical twins) but the joke—the heat—hasn't been properly exploited so it falls flat. Note too that the story is not about identical twins having an adventure. It's a single-protagonist hunt story with a sight gag about non-identical identical twins right at the end.

A less extreme version of losing the heat would be a plot where for long periods of time we followed only one twin on an adventure.

Writing in code

Planning is always a process of logic trying to impose a shape on material from your unconscious. This can result in an odd phenomenon that I call 'writing in code'. It is often what is happening when good writers produce oddly weak plots but are passionate in defending them; the writer has attached a clichéd plot to a strong idea because their logical mind, trying to find an appropriate scenario to fit the combination of images, emotions and vague bits of scenes that are coming from the unconscious, has gone straight to memory banks and jumped on the most obvious scenario to fit the general theme.

For example, you might find yourself passionately inventing a tired melodramatic plot about a woman being pursued by a homicidal maniac and ending up at the first-act turning point imprisoned in a warehouse. You then find yourself drawn to write scenes about the husband having a separate adventure elsewhere. You occasionally insert scenes about the woman, showing her as she tries various ways to escape, but you don't enjoy writing these and, despite your best efforts, they remain slow and lifeless. Nothing seems to energise them, even though you try to the point of the ridiculous (she finds dynamite, but it doesn't work; she gets attacked by rats as she tries to dig her way out; a big chunk of wood falls, just missing her head; a passing stranger fails to hear her call etc.). However, you are positive you don't want your protagonist to escape (you know you want her kept under threat), and at the same time, you really want to write about her husband.

Strangely, what might be happening here is that what really interests you is 'a woman trapped in a difficult marriage'. However, you jumped at a plot too soon, and came up with the first 'woman trapped' scenario from your memory banks, which is a kidnap plot. Kidnap and siege plots often come up in these 'writing in code' situations, so if a siege or kidnap plot pops into your head, check that it really is giving you what you need.

In our 'woman in the warehouse' plot, to service what you're really interested in, you need a plot that will keep the woman in her threatened position in the marriage, *in close physical proximity* to the husband.

Picking writing in code is difficult, but you are usually conscious of being strongly pulled to write what you know is a tired plot which stops dead at the first-act turning point, while you want to follow another character who is equally if not more fascinating. If this happens, try dumping the old plot and finding a new one that puts the two characters that you're drawn to physically together and in conflict.

The trick when you are stuck like this is to check the spark and the heat, asking yourself, 'What is attracting me to this idea? What am I trying to do here? Is this plot going to give me the chance to explore what I want to explore? Do I know what I want to explore? What is this film about?' It's very easy to keep working on a plot because it was the first one that occurred to you. As I have said, there is nothing sacred about the plot. If it's not letting you do what you want, change it.

Just in passing, whenever you have a plot about two people in conflict, put them geographically close together if you can, because that prevents the plot jumping back and forth between different locations and also means the physical threat is increased. Menace from a distance is difficult.

Changing protagonists in the second act

Finding yourself wanting to change protagonists in the second act is not, however, always a sign of writing in code. It's a common problem in scripts written by writers used only to short-form writing. Not used to the marathon that is a feature film and unable to think of a chain of complications at the speed at which they normally work, they panic and change direction. Don't get distressed if this happens to you. Planning a film is usually a slow process. Simply go back to the first-act turning point and start working on complications arising from the surprise that turned into an obstacle. Alternatively, if you find your new protagonist more interesting than the first, go back and make your film about the new protagonist. Certain parallel narrative structures do indeed change protagonist and story, often having several of each, but very rarely does a parallel narrative film make its audience focus exclusively on one protagonist for twenty minutes without giving warning, via flashbacks or a prologue, that this film is unconventional. Audiences asked to invest in one protagonist and then swap to another without warning may simply feel that the film has, literally, lost the plot.

Chapter 18
Plotting: Tips, traps and rewriting

Voice-over

Voice-over narration is a wonderful but problematic device because it can easily get out of control. It is so attractively poetic, so lyrical, so full of character, that it is easy (particularly for scriptwriters, trained to keep words to a minimum) to get carried wildly off the point, inventing scenes simply to permit the narrator's purple prose to soar over endless, repetitive montages of the protagonist, often just in its normality. This can wreck your story, but, because the voice-over has become so much part of the fabric of the film, cutting it becomes difficult, both in structural terms and emotionally because usually you love the voice-over and have sweated blood to get it on the page.

To give yourself the best chance of writing powerful, apposite voice-over—to make it enrich rather than damage—first pinpoint exactly why you are using it. Work out precisely what your narrator is interested in and what exactly is his or her point in recounting their story. Then, instead of inserting the voice-over as you go, consciously put it aside while you plan, construct and write the first draft. When that's done, insert the voice-over. That way, the voice-over is servant to the story, rather than vice versa. You may have to tinker a bit with the internal content of scenes, but you will have a strong story, not just footage supporting a voice. Redundant voice-over is often a problem in adaptations of fiction.

'Do we need it?' A weak idea that skews the whole film

Surprisingly often, usually when they're working without a plan, writers will insert a weak or implausible bit of plot, not considering the ramifications—then adjust the entire script to fit the weak bit. For example, not thinking ahead, the writer creates a murder story in which character A is present when character B murders character C. This later causes problems because A would have told the police. Instead of just removing character A from the murder scene, the writer will often go to amazing lengths to explain why A didn't tell the police—creating a whole series of complicated and often implausible twists and turns that take the plot away from its heat.

When you are having plotting problems justifying characters' behaviour or some other plot element, go back to why you are having the problem. Ask 'What is this bit of plot adding to the story?' Then see whether you can substitute something that will perform the same function but be more original.

You can apply this approach to major structural issues. Imagine that you want to write a film about brotherly sacrifice and to illustrate this you have chosen a drug-smuggling plot in which one brother becomes a drug mule to buy his sibling out of massive debt. However, having got this story sketched out, you are struggling to find a new take on drug-smuggling. Stop and ask yourself what the drug plot is giving you. Could you get the same effect via a different, more inventive version of plotline (in a new world)? Could your protagonist be smuggling documents out of a brutal dictatorship? Body tissue across a continent? Alternatively, do you need a smuggling plot at all? Could one brother save the other by hacking into computer records? And does actual crime need to be involved? Could you get a similar level of threat by having the brother required to seduce or win over the creditor?

THE LITERARY 'DEVICE'

'Literary device' is a term you sometimes hear filmmakers use to explain a character or plotting point that they realise is weak or clumsy or clichéd but feel justified in using because its sole function is to set up some fascinating bit of the script, after which it will disappear, with no harm done.

Unfortunately, these devices have a way of skewing the whole film. For example, a common device of this sort is a clichéd or boring protagonist (say, a clichéd female journalist) inserted to explain the shift in the story from one milieu to another where the really interesting stuff will happen. Sounds fine, but because you have spent a lot of effort getting your audience interested in your clichéd Sally the Journalist—in telling the story from her point of view, and making this dreary character the hero and focus of your film— you can't dump her. A three-act linear narrative (as opposed to a multiple protagonist film) dictates that the character you set up as protagonist at the start of the film remains protagonist (unless you are doing something like *Psycho* or *The Crying Game*, where you have a Mercutio character who feels like a protagonist but whose death is actually the start of the real protagonist's story). You will have to keep Sally at the heart of your film (thereby robbing your interesting characters of screen time), all the while trying to keep your audience interested in her, which is very hard because she is a cliché. Additionally, in terms of casting, you're unlikely to attract a decent actor because the character is so weak.

If your plan is to take Sally to the new milieu and then dump her for another protagonist, why not open your film on the new protagonist? Why knowingly create a weak character or plot? Your audience may not stay around long enough to see the good bits. In *The Oyster Farmer* possibly Jack started out as a literary device (see pp. 426–7).

Black hats and white hats

A mundane but very important point to remember is that characters of about the same age and similarly dressed, particularly in uniforms and particularly in rapid action, can be very hard to tell apart. Characters in hats or helmets are particularly difficult because they have no visible hair colour or hair style, one of the fastest means of identification. Divers and pilots whose helmets cover their entire face so that only the eyes are visible are the hardest of all. Obviously, if we can't make out who is doing what and why, the film has problems. If you think your characters might be hard to recognise—because of their dress, because it's an opening scene, because it's a battle, or all or some of the above—be inventive. If you cannot make their clothes visibly different or give them clearly different hair or glasses, give them mannerisms. The more distinguishing marks between group members the better. This also applies to child characters who grow up during the film. *The Joy Luck Club* solves this problem by quarantining each group of women in a separate, self-contained storyline (see pp. 348–51).

Rewriting

A film industry mantra is 'writing is rewriting'. Yes and no. Rewriting is inevitable; it normally improves the script, and often you will lose count of the rewrites you do. In fact, usually you will look back and shudder at how you ever thought the previous draft was adequate. However, unfocused, repeated rewriting is a waste of time and money and can mean a script dies on the page. When a script dies like that it's usually because the writer (and others, if anyone else was involved) started into plotting without properly working out the spark, message and scenario—generally, what film they were in. Thus, the rewriting has been going in circles. Try to minimise rewriting by planning the script before the writing starts.

The big problem with rewriting is that even a good writer's worst writing is always respectable and will normally contain elements of genuine excellence. The urge will be to save what's written, even if it's not serving the spark (which may not have been properly identified anyway). Unfortunately, brilliant scenes that don't serve the spark have a habit of fizzling on the screen—which is how you can end up with a tepid film out of a wonderful idea.

TECHNIQUES FOR REWRITING

Rewriting requires a lot of work before even one new word gets written. It involves:

- 'un-thinking' or 'shedding' previous drafts
- considering, then choosing new options that will still fit with the spark, the message and the scenario
- exploring and making the new options your own
- writing up chosen options under pressure to world standards

Un-thinking takes strong nerves because you have to analyse and often reject material in which you're invested. Assume objectivity is going to be difficult. Don't rush into changes and, while reminding yourself that the plot is not holy, think very seriously about the implications of your changes. They could change the spark. They could change the protagonist, thus change the point of view of the story.

Often new options will mean refocusing the script very slightly, which in its way can be harder than refocusing it in a major way (you may forget tiny but crucial changes). Alternatively, rewrites caused by sudden budget or cast changes can mean you are left with as little as the theme and the chess pieces. In cases like these, you may have to find a new spark and start all over again. You may have a different protagonist, even a different genre. In a massive rewrite, a lot will have to go. Be aware that scenes or lines that worked brilliantly in draft two may now be redundant or slow the pace. Your adaptation may only now be 'inspired by' the original.

Rewriting can be depressing and requires endurance. However, the result when you get there is usually well worth it, and it comes with the territory.

In a crisis

- Give yourself permission to panic for a minute or two, then get on with the job.
- Go back to basics. Think: 'What am I supposed to be doing in this film/scene?', 'What film am I in?'
- This is when all of your notes on spark, heat, message and scenario, charts, versions of the genre equation, narrative sentences, index

cards, scene breakdowns, outlines etc. become immensely useful. Re-read them, double-check them.

- If you wrote yourself Frank Daniel's magic letter, open it and reinvigorate yourself.
- Go back to the script development strategies in this book to check you really do have the structure and character points in place.
- Is the first-act turning point still what the film is 'about'? Does the climax still answer the question of what the film is 'about'? Are your action and relationship lines properly in place and functioning?
- Have you erred from the original plan? If so, go back to it. If you prefer your new version, restructure the script to include it.
- Check that crucial material hasn't accidentally been left out after cuts and rewrites without you noticing; also, that scenes rendered redundant by cuts or new material have not been left in. This is very common after many drafts, and often explains why good filmmakers passionately defend shaky scripts. Redundant scenes can be left in while themes, even vital scenes, can be missing or deleted—all because everyone was concentrating on something else. I call this 'sixth draft syndrome'.
- Get people whose judgment you trust, and who understand your writing strengths and weaknesses, to comment. Be prepared for this to be painful.
- Remember the old-time Hollywood writer's question: 'Do you want it fast, or do you want it good?'

Using criticism to best advantage

When a script comes back from readers with a range of criticisms, writers often plunge straight into rewrites. This is understandable but very dangerous because it can mean changes are locked in before criticisms and problems have been properly diagnosed. Particularly dangerous is the fact that frequently producers and readers pick problems but misdiagnose them (as we've seen earlier, in Chapter 4, What film are we in?), so their suggestions are actively counterproductive.

Imagine a script coming back from readers with the general criticism that the female characters are too passive. Tackle the problem by going back to basics, with Development Strategy 1: Define the task at hand. Ask questions like: 'Do I know the task here? What is the next step? What is causing the problem? Am I sure that this really is the problem, or could it be only a symptom of another problem; for example, what film we're in?'

Although we know only a minimal amount about this particular script, we can open up a whole range of interesting plot and characterisation possibilities just by targeting the task, in this case, by asking three questions: what, precisely, is being criticised; is the readers' diagnosis accurate; what solutions are possible?

WHAT, PRECISELY, IS BEING CRITICISED?

You can't fix something until you know what it is you are supposed to fix. First of all, what is meant by 'passive'? One reader might simply mean they want to see the character engaged in more action. But a militant feminist might want the film's women to be politically active. So get your readers to give you a precise definition, with examples from the text.

IS THE DIAGNOSIS ACCURATE?

The old rule is: one person with a criticism can be ignored; two with the same criticism are a worry; three with the same criticism are right. That said, as we've seen, readers often criticise the symptoms of a cause, but mistake them for the cause itself, suggesting solutions that compound the problem. For example, in a 'writing in code' situation (see pp. 141–3) a producer might rightly pick that the second act of the woman-trapped-in-the-warehouse script is slow, but suggest adding more terrifying incidents in the warehouse, which will only worsen the situation.

As for the passivity that worries your readers, this might not be passivity *per se*, but a symptom of poor and clichéd plot and characterisation generally. So, a remedy would have to tackle significant plot and characterisation changes throughout, rather than fine-tuning to one set of characters. I've suggested a range of ways to instil energy in a script above. As ever, remember that the plot is not holy.

In summary, look carefully at all possible causes of the passivity problem. Also, check what, if anything, is good or useful about the passivity, so you can incorporate it in some other way. For example, the passivity might be the only factor forcing a weak male protagonist to act.

WHAT SOLUTIONS ARE POSSIBLE?

Here are just some possible responses to the charge 'passive female characters'.

1   Go to other readers.
2   Ditch the project.
3   Define the original themes and ideas behind the script and consider whether a different scenario would carry the ideas better;

for example, using an antagonist who changes massively, as in the 'prude to action hero' model.

4   If the film is a comedy, think of it as a tragedy, so as to spark ideas. If it is a tragedy, think of it as a comedy to spark ideas.

5   Remove all women from the plot.

6   Remove all men from the plot and make the entire cast female.

7   Reverse current male and female roles.

8   Combine characters to make them richer.

9   Pull against the stereotype; for example, if a female character is a stereotypical housewife, give her a non-stereotypical hobby, obsession or approach to life.

10   Make the women's passivity a comic or dramatic feature to be built upon; say, in a subplot (for example, the women's passivity means they do not notice something vital happening or, as in *The Stepford Wives*, the women's passivity is a vital clue in the plot).

11   Make the women passive-aggressive for added conflict.

12   Scrap all current female characters completely and invent new ones.

13   Keep the useful characteristics from the female characters and re-use them in new characters. For example, the plot might require a new female character to have the same profession as her earlier passive version.

14   Add a new character or twist to the plot which can somehow galvanise the passive female characters into action.

15   Think of unusual ways to make the women interact more dynamically with the men. For example, turn the male protagonist's wife into his mother, sister or daughter.

16   Give a female character her own perspective on the main plot, which might be in opposition to the male protagonist's perspective. For example, make the major antagonist a proactive female.

17   Look for a model for the story in folk tale, genre or myth that might help with new and interesting ideas for how the females could be more proactive.

18   Insert more conflict between characters generally.

CHOOSING A REAL BUT UNUSUAL ANSWER

The last step is to choose, out of all the possibilities, a 'real but unusual' answer. Check not only for the best answer, but for any chain-reaction effect. For example, will the story be completely distorted by the changes? Will new characters pull focus away from important male characters, and if so, how will you fix the balance? How will the changes affect audience expectations? Will women have to figure more prominently in the climax?

Notice that each of the eighteen possible responses could be used as a springboard to more detailed responses, which in turn are capable of being dramatised in a huge variety of ways. It is the ideas behind any rewrites that are being tackled.

While responses such as 'go to other readers' and 'ditch the project' may initially seem flippant, in fact they're sensible. Perhaps the current reader (or producer) is simply wrong for this project. Perhaps the project is indeed not worth pursuing. The essential message here is don't rush into changes.

Apprenticeship

Often, a new writer will start film school with a promising, unfinished and structurally flawed script. Two or three years later they are an infinitely better writer, but the script is no longer an adequate reflection of their mature talents and would take years to fix, if indeed it is fixable at all. Sometimes a script like that needs to be viewed as an apprenticeship. If it's genuinely good, throw yourself into it. If not, honour it, treasure it, but move on to something that permits you to write to your best and kick off your career.

Writing under pressure

It's typical of a writer's life that an important writing opportunity arises at the worst possible time. Here is a simple plan for writing when you are under pressure of time:

1   Work out how much time you can afford to devote to the writing, and create a plan with dates for completion of each stage of the work. Do not plan to do everything at the weekend or in a few consecutive days because the pressure on you will be too great. Instead, try to do a little each day. Remember that even a minute here and there can be used to brainstorm solutions to small problems. For example, a five-minute coffee break devoted to brainstorming the demands of the genre in which you plan to write will give you a huge amount of information. Added together, these minutes will move the work on its way, and also increase your confidence.

2   Consciously remind yourself that stress creates cliché. Look calmly at your strengths and weaknesses as a writer, and be aware that under stress you will make your normal mistakes. For example, if you have a weakness with structure, that weakness is liable to show

itself under stress. This is not being negative, it is being focused. Write yourself reminders about problem areas in the script or with technique and stick them over your desk.

3   If you are finding it hard, that's because it's hard.

4   Throughout the writing, make use of the development strategies. Start with number 1: Define the task at hand; that is, refresh your memory about the sort of material that is needed for the sort of script you have to write. Watch relevant films and read relevant scripts. Be aware of details.

5   Decide what the genre demands in terms of emotions and pattern.

6   If you are writing a short film, check that the story can be told in the length of screen time you have.

7   Check what specific limitations, if any, the piece of work might have; for example, no period pieces, no expensive effects etc.

8   Brainstorm and explore a range of ideas as shown in Chapters 2 and 3. Do not jump at your first idea because it will probably be a cliché. Later ideas are likely to be more original. Choose an idea that fits with the above points and is original and unclichéd.

9   Use the genre equation (Development Strategy 3).

10   Isolate your spark, 'new world' and heat, (see Chapter 4, What film are we in?).

11   Create structure charts.

12   If your story is about a group reunion, siege or mission, or is running multiple stories in parallel or consecutively, jumping about in time, or has flashbacks, see Part 4, Parallel Narrative.

13   Work out a simple story sentence (Development Strategy 5) which you keep developing. If you are writing a parallel narrative film, you will have a number of these.

14   Draw a 'structure mountain', putting in the turning points (see Figure 5.1, page 54). If you are writing a parallel narrative film, you will have a number of these.

15   Decide whether your story is an action line or relationship line and peg the relationship line to the action line (Development Strategy 11). In parallel narrative, there might be a number of action lines and relationship lines.

16   For any relationship line, draw a 'relationship road' (Development Strategy 10) with signposts indicating the developmental steps of the relationship. Make sure the relationship does develop (that is, that the signposts show development and cannot be interchanged).

17   If you are writing a non-linear and/or ensemble film, consult Part
     4 of this book, which deals with parallel narrative. You will need to
     think about: condensing your plotlines; a macro; pace, connection,
     meaning and closure.

18   Check that you have the right protagonist and antagonist, and that
     the antagonist is a worthy foil to your protagonist. Be aware that
     you might have to invent a protagonist to match a charismatic
     mentor antagonist.

19   Check that you have a good first-act turning point in your story or
     stories. Remember that it must be a physical 'surprise'. Remember
     that your first-act turning point is what the story is 'about'. If you
     know what your film is 'about', you will often have your first-act
     turning point without knowing it.

20   Make sure that the action does not slow down and meander after
     the first-act turning point.

21   Work out good second- and third-act complications. Work out
     complications logically by asking what obstacles could be put in
     the way of the protagonist after the first-act turning point. Create
     a downward progression to part 1 of the second-act turning point
     (protagonist's worst possible moment).

22   Check that your climax answers the problems raised by your
     disturbance and first-act turning point.

23   Make sure that your climax is powerful and worth your audience's
     effort.

24   If your antagonist is pursuing your protagonist from a distance,
     consider inserting a companion for the antagonist, so they have
     someone to whom they can express their aims and thoughts. Insert
     some relationship conflict between these two people.

25   Keep checking that you are exploiting the intrinsic drama and
     essence of your story (for example, if your story is a thriller, is
     it really thrilling?). Ask what is 'hot' (exciting, new, marketable)
     about your story, and make sure you are properly exploiting this.
     Try to leave enough time to edit your work. In your second draft,
     check that your story hasn't shifted so your climax no longer fits the
     first-act turning point.

26   In your second draft, run through all the development strategies
     and your other checklists again.

Stick to the spark

Just generally, if you are lost or there are problems, go back to the spark, and make sure your script is serving that spark. Keep using Development Strategy 3, the 'genre equation', to check that you know the pattern you need and the emotions you have to evoke. Similarly, use the strategies from Chapter 4: narrative sentences, message and scenario, and mind mapping.

Chapter 19
Genres with particular plotting problems
Adaptation of fiction

Many fine films have been adaptations of novels. Not surprisingly then, studios and independent producers often actively seek out novels for adaptation, assuming that a successful novel will automatically translate into a successful film. Unfortunately, this frequently isn't the case, not only because some novels are too long or too internal for film, but because there is a fundamentally different contract between writer and audience in film and fiction. The difference is this: for audiences, fiction is about the journey, film is about the destination. The same people who happily tell you that their favourite novel 'takes fifty pages to get going' will, if sitting in a cinema, get angry with slow scenes in seconds. We love novels that go off the point for a chapter to examine the protagonist's bizarre but utterly irrelevant Auntie Nellie. Do this in a film and the audience will get actively hostile. Many novels have very little plot and end in mid air, in a deliberate anticlimax. You just can't do that in feature film. The film audience demands from very early that your film has a story consisting of a chain-reaction of events and a 'point'—even if that point, as in *Mulholland Drive* or *Caché* (*Hidden*), is to question narrative conventions, including the notion of 'point' in itself.

Film needs to engage immediately and rise steadily and incrementally to a climax, but many novels, as well as starting slowly and ending in anticlimax, are episodic. Often, the only way film can insert the vital rising suspense into episodic story material is by using a parallel narrative form, for example flashback. This permits the episodes to be quarantined in flashbacks while a strong story in the present pulls the film forwards, thus preventing slowing. This will give you a good result, but it raises serious issues about staying true to the book. To make the film of the book you have pulled the book apart.

As for creating a climax from a novel that doesn't have one, the writer has three unattractive choices: first, copy the novel and write a script without a climax; second, invent a brand new climax; or third, angle the script so that an event of not much significance in the novel becomes the climax (which may mean ending the film before the novel ends, or adapting only one part of the novel). This can mean the novel's message is seriously distorted. All of this assumes that the novel has a through line and does not, as many novels do, change stories midway, in which case the scriptwriter has to somehow bridge the gap. I once had to insert an entire second act, with a whole new plotline, into a three-part miniseries adaptation of a novel because, as the novelist cheerfully admitted, the novel had no middle and the two halves were really two novellas, with only one character in common.

When it gets to this stage we are really into the territory of 'inspired by the novel', and the primary reason for adapting the novel for the screen in the first place—that the novel was successful—has gone because the novel is so massively changed.

The bottom line here is that a great novel may simply not transfer to film and adaptation is not just about dramatising good scenes from the book. In fact, frequently adaptation is an attempt to change apples into oranges. If the apples are actually capable of being changed into oranges and, more to the point, everyone is happy to get oranges, that's fine. If not, there are problems. The things to look for in any novel you plan to adapt are a strong through line, rising suspense and a climax.

ISSUES IN FICTION ADAPTATION

Novels always have to be condensed (novellas and short stories are a better prospect), hence episodic novels may end up reduced to one episode, changing them beyond recognition. Dialogue in novels is usually unnaturalistic and rambling and will usually require a complete rewrite. Characters might have to be deleted or combined. New characters may need to be invented to speak aloud content handled via prose narrative. Only novels which can make their point via a strong action line—as do Lord of the Rings and the Harry Potter books—are a reliable bet for screen adaptation, although note that the middle film in Lord of the Rings was, predictably, weaker than the rest.

Many novels feature mentor antagonists, with the narrator a weak protagonist. Sometimes this can be transferred as is to the screen. In other instances it might be best to eliminate the novel's narrator altogether and make the mentor antagonist of the book the film's protagonist.

Adaptation of fact/biographical films

Adaptation of factual/historical material involves picking out the 'story steps' or beats of a real story to create a piece of drama that will operate on the audience in the same way as a fictitious story. As with fiction, a narrator describing a real-life charismatic individual may need to be removed from the film, or the film rendered as a mentor antagonist structure (see a discussion of *The Insider* on this point on pp. 412–13).

Biographical scripts may have very serious problems as a result of the writer assuming that a life is of itself a story, and wanting to include everything that happened in the subject's life or, more often, everything involving famous people that happened. If this is the case, the film is likely to be confusing and ultimately boring. A common problem is spending time on various famous people who happened to be involved with the protagonist but have nothing to do with the story.

Biopics require you to take an angle on the subject's life. While many biopics span a person's whole life, it might be that what's interesting about the subject happened over just a few years. It can help if you find a character from myth, fairytale or great literature that resembles your character. This can give you a better handle on the character, and also suggest a plot. For example, is your character a Don Quixote character?

PARALLEL NARRATIVE
Life stories are often best served by one of the parallel narrative forms because these conceal episodic progression and permit time jumps, as well as stories running in past and present. We'll look at this issue later on.

Forms typically used are:
1 centre-split flashback (for example, *Goodfellas*)
2 double narrative flashback (as in *Shine*, *The Remains of the Day*, *Citizen Kane*, *The Life of David Gale*)
3 consecutive stories (as in *City of God*)
4 preview flashback (as in *Walk the Line*) is also a possibility.

HISTORICAL ACCURACY AND LIBEL
You need to be aware of the extent to which (if at all) you are going to elaborate upon the truth for dramatic effect. There can be legal problems involved in this form.

Checklist for planning adaptations of fiction or fact
1 Think very seriously about whether your material is suitable for adaptation. Success as a novel is no guarantee of success as a film.
2 Have someone on the development team who never reads the novel so they can check that the script works as a film.

3   Producers should note that their objectivity may be compromised because the reason they are making the film is usually because they are in love with the book.

4   Check whether the dominant story is an action line or relationship line (see Development Strategy 9). You must find a good action line rising in suspense to a climax. If you don't have one you will have to invent one, which may radically change the material.

5   Write short and advanced narrative sentence summaries of the action line and the relationship line. (At this stage aim for more than one version of each.)

6   Identify the protagonist(s) and antagonist(s), or list who they might be.

7   Be aware that the most interesting character might be a mentor antagonist.

8   Be aware that if the source material is about different versions of the same sort of character, there could be multiple antagonists or protagonists. If so, structure accordingly. You may need a parallel narrative form (see Part 4).

9   Consider whether a traditional three-act structure will be most useful, or whether one of the forms of parallel storytelling would better serve the source material.

10   Ask and answer the 'who, why, how?' questions about character. Complete character charts and pinpoint what it is that is most important to transmit.

11   With factual material, you will almost inevitably have to jettison a lot of the source material and probably add more to fill gaps. Attempt to pick out (a) some superfluous material and (b) some gaps.

12   If you are using a traditional three-act narrative structure, start planning the structure with the help of the development strategies; that is, identify the action line and relationship line structures: normality, disturbance, first- and second-act turning points, complications, climax and resolution.

If you intend to use parallel narrative, you will also need to follow these steps, but you may need to do it for stories in past and present, and you may need to invent a story in the present to best transmit a story in the past. I discuss this later in relation to double narrative flashback and other parallel narrative forms.

Comedy and satire

To write successful comedy and satire, you need a scenario which will best show your character's foibles. To do that, you must understand very specifically what those foibles are. You need to work out what is sometimes known as the character's comic or dramatic perspective—that is, what character flaw at once defines him or her and makes them funny. This is not a new technique. The classic comic satirists like Molière and Ben Jonson actually gave their characters surnames that summed up this comic perspective. So, go to character charts and put together a kind of identikit picture of each of your characters.

Very useful here is Frank Daniel's technique for creating an action line around a character's weakest point. This happens in the John Cleese journey film *Clockwise*, where an obsessively punctual man misses his train to a vital conference. The same trick appears in *A Fish Called Wanda*, in which huge mileage is derived from simple comic inversion of an animal lover who keeps accidentally killing animals. The technique is not restricted to comedy: *Hamlet* is all about an indecisive man asked to be decisive.

As we might expect, three is usually a good number for these sorts of comic events—two is too few and four is overkill. There are three dogs killed in *A Fish Called Wanda*, the comedy building to a climax with the third. The audience has fun in the anticipation, with anticipation working here as another form of suspense. Jokes in *The Simpsons* are often told in threes.

Journey films

Journeys seem like a natural fit to film because they involve a lot of action and built-in opportunities for interesting encounters. This is certainly true of fiction, and it's why the journey form (picaresque) is one of the oldest narrative forms.

However, while journeys may work in fiction, in film they often fail, partly because film journeys so easily fragment into episodic 'adventures', and partly because it is so easy for the writer to mistake the characters' physical movement for movement in plot and character. It is very easy to keep creating different versions of the same scene, featuring the same unchanged protagonist.

If there are no ongoing central action-line and relationship-line problems that the protagonist has to cope with in the course of the journey on the road—no 'incremental' plots—the writer is left to create a hundred minutes of random adventures on the road. Creating separate adventures is actually much harder than creating a rising three-act narrative because each new character or situation on the way has to be set up from scratch. Nothing appearing earlier in the script will assist here. It is back to square one every time.

The effect of this is that each stop on the protagonist's journey becomes one gag—one sketch—and new characters almost inevitably present as stereotypes (protagonist meets shyster, protagonist meets raunchy girl, protagonist meets thug etc.).

Monty Python and the Holy Grail—a weak journey movie made by some of the world's most brilliant comedians—shows how the process can defeat even the very best writers. Typical of poor journey movies, *Monty Python and the Holy Grail* has brilliant moments between long stretches of boredom. It is really a series of comic sketches. It gets boring because there is no plot to follow and the film is standing or falling on the strength of each individual sketch. Lack of action and relationship lines means that there is no story to engage in and hold—nothing, as it were, to go anywhere. The effect of this is to deprive the story of any suspense or urgency—because suspense and urgency can only come out of a sequence of events. Take suspense and urgency out of a scripted piece and you remove the audience's ability to care about the characters.

AN EMOTIONAL AS WELL AS PHYSICAL JOURNEY

Good journey films (like *Thelma and Louise*, *The African Queen* and *Planes, Trains and Automobiles*) are pleasing not only because they have a strong action line but because each step in the action line causes a change in the central characters, a step in their emotional journey, whether comic or tragic. *The Remains of the Day* offers a variant of that insofar that while each step of the journey provides a new insight into the protagonist in the present, each step also triggers a flashback that illuminates the present.

Clockwise is a lot more successful because it utilises a three-act narrative with the requisite rising suspense and climax, each comically catastrophic incident on the journey building to the next. Without a structure, the film would simply have involved a character driving towards the north of England, having adventures on the way.

TRY SHUFFLING YOUR SCENES

As I explained on p. 111, if you can shuffle your scenes without problem, by definition no plot or character movement has occurred. Nothing has changed. You can do this in *Cold Mountain*. The experiences of the returning hero can be juggled (for example, the incident with the Goat Woman could occur anywhere), therefore they are not properly leading to a climax. And while the returning lover says the journey changed him, it didn't. He travelled physically but not emotionally.

Cold Mountain, like many journey films, including *O Brother, Where Art Thou?* and *Last Orders*, would probably have worked better told in parallel narrative structure. Some journey films, particularly biographical films, which track an emotional journey across an entire lifetime, use multiple protagonists and flashback or other forms of non-linearity to boost suspense and overcome their tendency to fragment into episodes. There are actually quite a few different parallel narrative ways to depict physical and/or emotional journeys. (See double journey form, pp. 162, 174–5, 179, 246–51; preview and double narrative flashback, pp. 175, 258–67, 271–327; portmanteau, pp. 176, 180, 332, 335, 347–75.)

IDENTIFY THE RELATIONSHIP LINE FIRST

The best way to approach a journey film is to think of it first not in terms of its action line—that is, what physically happens on the journey—but in terms of its relationship line—where the journey will take the characters emotionally and spiritually. All good journey films are actually emotional journeys.

Once you know the characters' emotional journey, you can choose a suitable kind of journey as the action line that will best display it, then choose specific events on the basis of their capacity to move each character one emotional step forward while also pushing the action line one step forward. Each incident should cause the next.

TWO DIFFERENT KINDS OF JOURNEY MOVIE

There are two different kinds of journey movie regardless of whether buddies, multiple protagonists or a single hero are used. There are journeys in which the point of the story is unfinished business at the journey's end (as in *Priscilla, Queen of the Desert*) and there are journeys in which the story of the film is contained in the journey itself, and what happens at the journey's end is merely the inevitable climax of what has happened before (as in *Thelma and Louise* and *Planes, Trains and Automobiles*). Films that are about unfinished business at the journey's end will usually make the physical journey end with the end of the second act and use the third act to deal with the unfinished business, finalising it in the climax. Films that are about the journey itself will use the third act to depict the final battle in the journey, with the climax answering the questions raised by the adventures of the journey.

DOUBLE JOURNEY FILMS AND MULTIPLE PROTAGONIST QUESTS

Double journey films are a form of multiple protagonist film in which two characters journey either towards each other, or in parallel or apart (emotionally, physically or both), as in films like *Vicky Cristina Barcelona* or *Brokeback Mountain*. Because both characters are so often apart they need their own action line (see pp. 246–51). Journey films with many travellers, like *Priscilla, Queen of the Desert* or *Little Miss Sunshine*, are usually multiple protagonist quests, and involve many interwoven action and relationship lines (see pp. 177–8, 208–36).

Rites-of-passage and coming-of-age films

If your film could be one of these, you have a ready-made character arc involving a movement towards maturity. Your task is to keep the general emotions that we expect with rites of passage and coming of age, but somehow ring the changes. You are in well-trodden territory, so avoid clichés and sentimentality. A good practical definition of sentimentality is 'unearned emotion'.

The originality of both kinds of film, but particularly of coming-of-age films, rests in the originality of the 'world' in which the coming of age happens, and the specifics of the enforced 'growing up'. Charles Harris feels that the child figure in many coming-of-age films is surrounded by adults, most or all of whom are deeply flawed, and each of whom represents a different choice. The child figure can either choose to become like one of these adults, or to become something different, and the journey will usually involve the child figure realising the inadequacy of a number of characters and lifestyles.

In structural terms, this means that many coming-of-age films are group films. Those with multiple adult role models are really multiple antagonist films—more precisely, mentor antagonist films, as in *Tea with Mussolini* and *Dead Poets' Society*. There are, though, films like *Stand by Me* in which adults barely figure and these, structurally, are group quests (see pp. 177–8, 208–36).

Not surprisingly, rites-of-passage and coming-of-age films involving one crucial mentor (for example, *Scent of a Woman*, *Finding Forrester* and the fine *Clubland*, aka *Introducing the Dwights*) are mentor antagonist stories.

Romantic comedy

We have already looked a little at romantic comedy (see pp. 18–21, 37–8). The big plotting problem with romantic comedy is that you have a couple made for each other that you have to keep credibly apart for an hour and a half.

What normally sells a romantic comedy is a strikingly original action line set in a new world; that is, the story of two lovers meeting and interacting in a real but unusual way in a real but unusual context before finally coming together. The emotional journey they travel on the way (relationship line) is secondary because essentially it is always the same: 'couple meet, experience obstacles to their love, and [usually] end up together.' To avoid characters in search of a plot (relationship-line material without action line) think of the action line as an adventure, real or metaphorical—a journey down the river as in *The African Queen*. Keep reminding yourself that the action line permits the relationship line to happen. Action romantic comedies are usually like buddy movies, with the partners operating as joint protagonists in the action line (fighting the common foe) but as protagonist and antagonist in the relationship line.

HUNT FOR WHAT IS UNUSUAL

Originality is vital but very hard in well-worked genres such as romantic comedy. Find the spark and heat, and make sure they are unusual. Set your film in a new world. Hunt for what else could be unusual and original about the couple. One simple tool is to brainstorm the question: 'What can I do that hasn't been done before?' An unusual couple (for example, a couple of very different ages, a couple of animals, a couple from extremely different backgrounds) can add to the originality. Even if you're writing about two eligible young people, try to find what is unusual about them. Make the plot play on this unusual quality—in other words, stay with the heat. For example, if you're writing a romantic comedy about two young elephants, have comedy specifically associated with being an elephant in love. You will keep thinking of clichés because the genre is so well-worked. Don't panic. Expect clichés, and do the normal thing: junk them or find an amazing new twist.

The short film

Short films are worth mentioning here because they provide an excellent way for new filmmakers to get into the industry. But they are not easy, simply because there is so little time to impress. Short films need much thought and careful planning.

The essential ingredient of a short film, whatever its content, is impact. The short film must grab its audience and leave it with an overwhelmingly powerful impression or thought. Really, whether serious or comic, a short film is essentially 'one gag'. Consequently, while short films can be structured as traditional three-act narratives they often end on the first-act turning point—the surprise/obstacle—so they can leave the audience with a thought-provoking surprise. The structure here is: normality, protagonist, disturbance, plan, surprise/obstacle, end of film.

Short films are often written for competitive purposes—so compete. Aim as high as you can, because this will instantly put you ahead of most competitors, who are just writing the first film that occurs to them. Calmly set yourself the task of writing a short film that will stay with people for the rest of their lives. Keep thinking 'real but unusual' and brainstorm every moment of the film to find excellence. Utilise all the tools at your disposal (plot and style, sound, dialogue, setting, set details, costumes, camera angles). Plan every detail ahead to make best use of shooting time because disasters *will* happen on the day.

Make sure your story is tellable in the time you have. Don't create the first five minutes of a feature. Be careful that you are giving the audience the heat, not just feeling it yourself. Give your interesting character a plot that stays with the heat, that fans it. Thinking of it as a quest (successful or unsuccessful) or adventure is useful.

Go easy on symbolism and, if you are a writer–director, beware of getting obsessed with the camera. Once you've got a good story, then you can get excited about how you'll shoot it.

COMMON PROBLEMS IN SHORT FILMS

Don't lose focus. Don't explore characters and ideas that are not central to the film, or include inessential action. Make sure that everything on the screen is enriching and demonstrating the core idea. Stick with the protagonist and the antagonist. Don't get distracted by minor characters. Don't give long speeches or much time to characters that are only facilitating the action (for example, the doorman whose job is simply to open the door—indeed, check whether you actually need that doorman).

Crucially, get the most value out of screen time and budget. Transitions rarely earn their keep. A car driving up and stopping eats into shooting time but often adds nothing more than if you had opened on the stationary, newly arrived car. Often short films fizzle, not because the original idea is poor, but because the film's ending does not answer the question set up in the opening. If the film's topic and question is set up as: 'Will the protagonist succeed in robbing the bank?', the climax must address that (see also Part 6: Getting It on the Page).

Part 4
Parallel Narrative

Chapter 20
An introduction to parallel narrative

THESE DAYS, THE FILM industry is witnessing a noticeable increase in films that use several separate narratives running in parallel, often involving non-linearity, time jumps, large casts, or all of these. I call such films 'parallel narrative' films, and they include works like *Slumdog Millionaire, Milk, Babel, Pulp Fiction, Amores Perros, The Curious Case of Benjamin Button, Eternal Sunshine of the Spotless Mind, Memento, The Hours, The Jane Austen Book Club, Lantana, 21 Grams, The Sweet Hereafter, American Beauty, Crash, Traffic, The Usual Suspects, Magnolia, Shine* and many more.

Films like these used to be considered of interest only to art-house audiences, but increasingly they are dominating even mainstream competitions like the Academy Awards. Meanwhile, television, once the province of all things conventional, is also increasingly presenting more complex narrative forms to highly receptive audiences.

As artists we can't help but be excited about structures that blow open the conventional, chronological mono-protagonist narrative. But there is also a serious commercial application here. There is no reason why properly used, parallel narrative structures can't be used to give us new, exciting and highly commercial versions of every genre from love story to action blockbuster. As I explain below, even rearranging a predictable or meandering linear narrative into a non-linear model can inject excitement and suspense.

But how do we master parallel storytelling? Quite clearly, films that use multiple stories and time jumps can be spectacularly impressive. Unfortunately, they can also be spectacularly disastrous, if indeed they ever make it to the screen.

And these films are not only complex, they are paradoxical. For example, why do flashbacks in *The Remains of the Day* work to humanise and explain its central characters, while flashbacks in *Citizen Kane* show Kane as unfathomable, even sinister? How do *The Full Monty, American Beauty* and *Revolutionary Road* succeed so well when other ensemble films end up as characters in search of a plot? How can *21 Grams* work when it has a huge set-up and no real middle? If you are trying to create a film to showcase the talents of forty actors, just where do you start?

The triumph of the three-act structure is its capacity for creating strong narrative that builds towards a suspenseful climax. Any writer who rejects the classic model is instantly faced with the problem of finding new ways to solve the basic storytelling problems of suspenseful narrative, good characterisation, meaning and closure. So, if we depart from the three-act structure, how and where can we start? Are there any rules or guidelines? What are the structural pitfalls? How can the old knowledge help us to do something new? Everyone knows the old joke that all stories have a beginning, middle and end—not necessarily in that order—but are there guidelines any more specific than that?

Parallel narrative storytelling is based on three-act structure

As I have mentioned and will explain in detail in the following chapters, all of the unconventional narrative forms we find in today's films rely heavily on the traditional rising three-act model. This is even true of films with very complex structures such as *21 Grams*, *City of God*, *Memento* and *The Hours*. Parallel narrative films inevitably struggle with pace, connection, meaning and closure because they have so many plotlines to handle—plotlines (just to make the job more difficult) that often inherently lack rising tension. They solve these problems by creating pace and connection artificially, through splitting up, rearranging and sometimes multiplying or truncating three-act stories. This gives them the powerful opening, rising suspense, climax and closure (the strong beginning, suspenseful middle and gripping end) that they would otherwise lack. There are clear patterns and techniques that can be copied, so instead of relying on intuition, you can actually plan your parallel narrative film.

By using parallel narrative techniques we can create screenplays that would never work in three-act structure, even screenplays like *21 Grams* and *The Hours* that work excellently without what we would call a proper middle, using stories with second acts so truncated they scarcely exist. Since conventional structure is, as we've seen, all about the story's middle (its fascinating development of a first-act turning point problem leading to a third-act battle to win) this is quite amazing.

IN MEDIAS RES

While it's often asserted, referencing Aristotle's *Poetics*, that we should stick exclusively to the three-act, one-story, linear chronological form because this is the traditional Western narrative structure, in fact from ancient time onwards many great works, including the iconic journey model, Homer's *Odyssey*, written down centuries before Aristotle was born and possibly invented even earlier, have started at a crucial scene in the middle and used flashbacks. Moreover, this was a standard way to write epics. The term for it is *in medias res* (Latin for 'into the middle of things') and it was coined by the Roman poet Horace in his *Ars Poetica* when advising epic writers to use it—precisely because it grabbed and held the audience.

Homer's *Odyssey* is far closer to *Pulp Fiction* and *21 Grams* than it is to the Hollywood three-act paradigm. It starts in the middle, uses multiple protagonists, and tells Odysseus' adventures after leaving Troy in a massive flashback. Other authors using flashbacks are the ancient Greek novelists Heliodorus, in *Ethiopian Story*, and Antonius Diogenes, in *The Wonders Beyond Thule*. Virgil deliberately copied Homer in *Aeneid*. Non-linearity crops up all over the world in classic works like Dante's *Divine Comedy* and Milton's *Paradise Lost*. I gather from traditional oral storytellers around the world that they use it in their work too.

This is far from being merely of historical interest. What all of these ancient professional storytellers knew, I think, is that if you have a long, episodic, lopsided narrative, your best bet to hold a live audience is to use parallel narrative and non-linearity. In short: steal energy from the suspenseful parts of the story and inject it into the bits of the story that might play slow. You can see from the delightful but endlessly meandering *O Brother, Where Art Thou?* what happens when you try to tell the *Odyssey* chronologically.

So it's not coincidence that structure of the *Odyssey* closely resembles the structure of *Pulp Fiction* and *21 Grams* (the writer of which, Guillermo Arriaga, actually uses the term *in medias res* to describe his writing). All three are using non-linearity to create pace and unity in narratives that are inherently exposition heavy, fragmented, episodic and lacking in chronologically building suspense.

Terminology

We are so used to using the three-act linear narrative that film people often think of 'act one', 'act two' and 'act three' as being the same as 'beginning', 'middle' and 'end', and use the terms interchangeably. This can cause confusion when we're talking about parallel narrative where, for example, as in *Fight Club*, a scene from late in the film might appear at the start. In parallel narrative, 'beginning, middle and end' are what the audience experiences, regardless of whether the film is linear or whether scenes appear out of chronological order. Meanwhile, 'acts one, two and three' are the consecutive parts of the story in its linear form (which we can shift around to get a better beginning, middle and end).

Other terminology that might cause problems are complicated labels that I have invented like 'double narrative flashback', 'two-thirds preview flashback' and 'stories walking into the picture'. These terms are necessary because the task is not just to describe parallel narrative, but to establish guidelines for writing it. We need descriptive names, first to remind us precisely what each category does and how it's constructed, and second, so that we can all discuss them knowing exactly what we mean.

You need to know whether your idea is genuinely about two or more complete stories in the past and present (as are *Slumdog Millionaire*, *Fried Green Tomatoes* or *The Life of David Gale*) or whether, like *Michael Clayton*, your story is just a linear three-act structure with a chunk of action from two thirds of the way through the story stuck at the start to grab the audience. When, in your mystery story, your detective asks 'What were you doing on November 12?' you need to know whether your flashback should be twenty seconds or twenty minutes. In this, my precise, if inelegant, terminology is designed to help.

Chapter 21
Six categories of parallel narrative

ALTHOUGH HYBRIDISATION IS HAPPENING all the time and any analysis must take that into account, at present I think we can usefully isolate six different sorts of parallel narrative films, each structured differently and each transmitting a different philosophy. These six fall into two main categories: films that jump about in time and films that don't. The films that stay in one time frame are often called ensemble films, and there are three main kinds. The films that jump about in time are often called non-linear films, and there are two main kinds. Finally, there is a hybrid, which is very like one of the ensemble forms, but incorporates time jumps. These various forms are shown in Figure 21.1, but, I stress, we must expect hybridisation.

Form follows content

The joy for writers is that each of the categories and subcategories works best for different story material and philosophy. So, once you know your film's story content and philosophy, you will be able either to pick the best parallel narrative structure to transmit it or alternatively, to realise that you need a new hybrid.

For example, if you want to write about an enigmatic outsider whose past life is being studied by a character or characters in the present, your best bet is a form of flashback called 'double narrative flashback' (the form used in *Shine*, *Citizen Kane* and *Slumdog Millionaire*). However, if you want to write a film on the theme of poverty in the city, following a wide range of characters, your idea will probably be best served by tandem narrative (as in *Traffic* or *Lantana*). Again, if you want to write about several possible outcomes triggered by one event, the structure to use is one of the 'consecutive stories' forms as in *Rashomon*, *Atonement* or *Run Lola Run*. So, the thing to remember is that in parallel narrative, *form serves content*. You choose the structure that will best transmit your story and philosophy. Later in this chapter I give a general guide to the sort of stories that suit each structure.

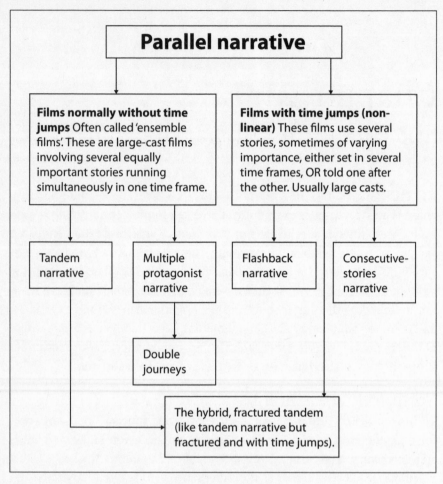

Figure 21.1 Types of parallel narrative film at present

Ensemble films

The distinguishing feature of standard ensemble films is that they have a large cast and a series of stories that run simultaneously and chronologically in the same time frame. While ensemble films like *Winged Creatures*, *The Hangover* and *Eternal Sunshine of the Spotless Mind* make use of flashback, typically ensemble films have no time jumps except perhaps a flashback as a framing device, or to transmit a slab of backstory.

A huge number of films from all over the world are ensemble stories; indeed, any DVD case photograph that gives equal prominence to three or more characters is liable to be one. Examples include *Nashville*, *Lantana*, *Little Miss Sunshine*, *American Beauty*, *Vicky Cristina Barcelona*, *Revolutionary Road*, *Love Actually*, *The Jane Austen Book Club*, *Traffic*, *After the*

Wedding, As It Is in Heaven, Caramel, The Full Monty, City of Hope, Monsoon Wedding, Death at a Funeral, In Bruges, The Big Chill and too many more to mention.

Despite the vast number of ensemble films being made, structural analysis of these films has been very limited. Such analysis as there is tends to operate on the premise that all ensemble films, sometimes all parallel narrative films, are the same; moreover, scrutiny often stops at a description of the film's action, and observations that these films have big casts and 'subplots'. Talk of subplots is not really useful in this context because a subplot presupposes a main plot, which many of these films just don't have in the regular sense of the term; that is, one hero on a single journey. Ensemble films all use several storylines, often of equal importance (as in *Traffic*, for example). And ensemble films are by no means all the same. There are major differences in structure and content, as we shall see later.

Ensemble stories are a different and equally valid form

The biggest problem for writers trying to write an ensemble film is that for the most part ensemble films are not recognised as being different from the conventional one hero/one journey model, let alone as forms that have their own structural mechanisms. Much script development all over the world is premised on this and it has caused great damage. This is not surprising. If you work on the assumption that film structure is always about one hero on a single journey towards spiritual improvement, you have only two options when you come to write a story that you know has multiple stories and a group of equally important characters. Either you say that because your ensemble story doesn't conform to the one hero/one story structure it can work without any structure at all (which results in films that are characters in search of a plot). Alternatively, you can try to force your ensemble story into the standard one-hero model—and end up with a redundant hero and your group in the background. As we'll see, tandem narrative films (same theme, different adventures) suffer most from the 'characters in search of a plot' syndrome, while multiple protagonist stories (same team, same adventure) suffer most from extraneous heroes.

Ensemble films are valid narrative forms with their own structural make-up. They are, and have always been, used all the time all over the world (including the US) whenever writers want to write about individuals in a social context or about society at large. They appear whenever scripts seek to explore the restrictions imposed by external social factors like class, race, religion, gender, law, family, peer group and the like. Almost all war films and films about troubled families are ensemble stories, as are almost all films about social minorities—inevitably because such films are about social interaction and about the demands of social roles and social responsibility.

While the spiritual journey of a sole individual is an important and perennial topic, as I have said earlier in connection with conventional narrative, there is absolutely no reason why all films should be about this, and indeed, in practice they aren't.

In the following chapters I analyse three different families of ensemble films, all different in structure and philosophy.

TANDEM NARRATIVE

Examples are: *Traffic, Lantana, Nashville, Caramel, City of Hope, Me and You and Everyone We Know, Love Actually, Pan's Labyrinth, Daybreak, Short Cuts* and *Crimes and Misdemeanors.*

The term 'in tandem' has come to mean 'at the same time', so tandem narrative is a good name for films that use equally important stories on the same theme, running simultaneously in the same time frame and geographical area, with the film's action jumping between stories. Tandem narrative films are usually didactic and span a wide range of society, the moral being that all of the characters are affected by the same socio-political problem or are impacted by the same social malaise. A good motto for these films is: 'same theme, different adventures'.

MULTIPLE PROTAGONIST NARRATIVE

Examples are: *Revolutionary Road, American Beauty, The Jane Austen Book Club, Mystic River, Little Miss Sunshine, Galaxy Quest, The Big Chill, Monsoon Wedding, After the Wedding, Ordinary People, Love! Valor! Compassion!, As It Is in Heaven, Last Orders, The Full Monty* and *Saving Private Ryan.*

These are films about a small team of people thrown together in a group 'adventure' which is specifically a quest, a reunion or a siege (emotional and/ or actual). Crucially, all of the main characters in these films are versions of the same protagonist. The motto here is: 'same team, same adventure'.

DOUBLE JOURNEYS NARRATIVE

Examples are: *Vicky Cristina Barcelona, Brokeback Mountain, The Proposition, The Queen, The Lives of Others, The Lemon Tree, The Departed* and *Finding Nemo.*

Double journey films are actually multiple protagonist films that deal with a very specific relationship; namely, two characters journeying either towards each other, in parallel, or apart (physically, emotionally or both). The motto here is: 'two lives in parallel'.

Films with time jumps (non-linear)

As I have mentioned, there are three sorts, flashback, a form I name 'consecutive stories' and a hybrid term 'fractured tandem'. We can expect more hybrids.

FLASHBACK

There are six varieties of flashback, some simple, some complex, each serving a different story purpose. Sometimes films will have several kinds.

1 **Flashback as illustration**: a simple backstory device, as when, for example, a detective asks: 'Where were you on the night of April 5?' and we flash back to what happened.

2 **Regret flashback**: non-chronological fragments from an unsuccessful love relationship (as in *Annie Hall* and *And When Did You Last See Your Father?*).

3 **Bookend flashback**: a scene or sequence in the present that appears at the start and the end of the film, 'bookending' the story (for example, *Saving Private Ryan* and *Fight Club*).

4 **Preview flashback**: the film starts on a scene or sequence midway or two-thirds through, then flashes back to the start, running through chronologically to the end (as in *Michael Clayton* and *Goodfellas*).

5 **Life-changing incident flashback**: one life-changing moment is revealed bit by bit in one flashback shown several times incrementally (for example, *Catch-22*).

6 **Double narrative flashback**: two or more complete stories centered on one enigmatic outsider are told in different time frames, with the action jumping back and forth between the two. Films in this form drop into two categories according to their view of human nature and each is structured differently. They are:
   • **Flashback as thwarted dream** (as in *Slumdog Millionaire*, *The English Patient*)
   • **Flashback as case history** (as in *Citizen Kane*, *The Usual Suspects*)

CONSECUTIVE STORIES (IN *SCRIPTWRITING UPDATED*, TERMED 'SEQUENTIAL NARRATIVE')

These are films that use separate stories (with separate protagonists) told one after the other, coming together at the end. Their point is to make a political or philosophical comment. There are four main sorts, and I've given them names that can be used as mottos.

1 **Stories walking into the picture**: new protagonists walk into shot and the film switches to their stories (e.g. *The Circle, Ten*)

2 **Different perspectives**: different versions of the same event (e.g. *Run Lola Run*); *or* different characters' views of the same events (e.g. *Rashomon*)

3 **Different consequences from the same event** (e.g. *Atonement*)

4 **Fractured frame/portmanteau**: several stories are split up and held within one story, which forms a frame (e.g. *Pulp Fiction, The Butterfly Effect, City of God, The Joy Luck Club*). Films in this form are actually fractured forms of either (a) stories walking into the film or (b) different-perspectives.

Hybrid

FRACTURED TANDEM

Fractured tandem runs equally important tandem narratives but fractures them, jumping between time frames. Examples are: *21 Grams, Babel, Crash, Three Burials of Melchiades Estrada* and *The Hours*. Essentially, it is tandem narrative chopped up and put together out of chronological sequence in order to pump up speed and transmit a philosophy about accidental tragedies and tragic, unforeseen consequences.

Autobiographical narrator using voice-over

The voice-over autobiographer narrator, honest or unreliable, can appear in all parallel narrative forms. It causes significant structural changes in double narrative flashback. Some films have a narrator who tells someone else's story, not their own, and who is either a minor player in the action, or simply an unidentified storyteller. Voice-over narrative can pull a parallel narrative off course as much as it can a conventional narrative, so should be used with care (see pp. 301–2).

Chapter 22
Which structure suits my film?

THE FIRST QUESTION WRITERS ask about parallel narrative is whether it suits their material. Later chapters provide detailed guidelines to writing in each of the parallel narrative forms with analyses of films in those forms and suggestions as to how you might use the structure of an individual film as a template. So, if you feel a structure like that of *The Joy Luck Club* or *21 Grams* might suit your story material, you will find practical suggestions for using it as a model. In this chapter I provide a checklist, but use it only as a starting point because (a) sometimes your material may be told in different ways, hence may suit a range of forms and (b) you might need to invent a hybrid.

Tandem narrative
Examples: *Traffic*, *Lantana*, *Gomorrah*, *Caramel*, *City of Hope*, *Nashville*, *Break of Day*

SUBJECT MATTER
If you are thinking: 'I want to show how a socio-political problem and/or human foibles affect a broad cross-section of society', this is probably the form for you. Tandem films contain equally important but separate stories (each with its own protagonist) running simultaneously on the same theme. If your material is a group of about six characters on a joint adventure with a shared goal, see the multiple protagonist form below. The mottos are useful here. Multiple protagonist form is: 'same team, same adventure'; tandem is: 'same theme, different adventures'.

Multiple protagonist
Examples: *The Full Monty*, *Burn After Reading*, *American Beauty*, *The Jane Austen Book Club*, *The Magnificent Seven*

SUBJECT MATTER

Multiple protagonist is probably the form you need if you feel you want to write about a group of people *or* an individual affected by a group *or* an individual affecting a group *or* a 'team' on a group quest, siege or reunion 'adventure'. The group's views and responses are always central to a multiple protagonist film. Not all films in which groups appear are multiple protagonist stories. Films like *The Counterfeiters* and *Four Weddings and a Funeral* that follow only one member of the group are one-hero stories, not multiple protagonist films.

Story material in multiple protagonist form is typically a quest, reunion or siege, or a combination of these, with subject matter as follows:

QUESTS

1 **'One last job'**: for example, *Ocean's Eleven*, *Space Cowboys*, *Crouching Tiger, Hidden Dragon*, *Sleepers*
2 **'Soldiers on a mission'**: for example, *Saving Private Ryan*, *The Magnificent Seven*, *Stand by Me*, *Galaxy Quest*, *The Band's Visit*
3 **'The Cinderella sports team'**: for example, *The Mighty Ducks*, *Brassed Off*, *A League of Their Own*
4 **'Let's put on a show'**: for example, *The Full Monty*, *The Commitments*, *Cosi*, *Little Miss Sunshine*, *Calendar Girls*
5 **'Group journeys'**: (group prison break, holiday etc.) for example, *The Great Escape*, *National Lampoon Vacation*, *City Slickers*

REUNIONS

1 **Weddings and funerals**: for example, *Monsoon Wedding*, *Death at a Funeral*, *The Big Chill*, *Radiance*
2 **Regular club/class**: for example, *The Jane Austen Book Club*, *Italian for Beginners*, *Love! Valor! Compassion!*, *The Dinner Guest*
3 **Seeking out the family/prodigal returns**: for example, *You Can Count on Me*, *All About My Mother*

SIEGE FILMS (EMOTIONAL AND ACTUAL)

1 **Troubled families**: for example, *To Live*, *Ordinary People*, *Little Miss Sunshine*
2 **Prisons, actual or metaphorical**: for example, *The Great Escape*, *Chicken Run*, *Paradise Grove*, *Deliverance*, *Cocoon*
   (Note: not all prison stories are multiple protagonist films. *The Shawshank Redemption* and *The Green Mile*, for example, are mentor antagonist films).

3 **Coming of age**: for example, *Tea with Mussolini*, *The Magnificent Seven*

4 **Save our town!**: for example, *Waking Ned Devine*, *Local Hero*, *The Swamp Dwellers*, *Italian for Beginners*, *Mystic River*, *As It Is in Heaven*

5 **Comic heist**: for example, *Burn After Reading*, *Ruthless People*

6 **Social siege**: for example, *American Beauty*, *Revolutionary Road*

Double journey
Examples: *The Lives of Others*, *Vicky Cristina Barcelona*, *Brokeback Mountain*, *The Lemon Tree*, *The Queen*, *The Departed*

SUBJECT MATTER
Use this for films involving two central characters, who are journeying either towards, apart or in parallel with each other physically, emotionally or both. Because they are seen so often apart, interacting with other characters, both travellers need their own plotline.

Double narrative flashback
Examples: *Slumdog Millionaire*, *Milk*, *Shine*, *Amadeus*, *Citizen Kane*

SUBJECT MATTER
These films always have at least one complete story in the present and one in the past and jump between the two for the whole film. Subject matter involves one or more of the following:

1 someone having to find out about the past of an enigmatic person, often dead, traumatised or unwilling to speak (for example, *Citizen Kane*, *The Bridges of Madison County*)

2 someone returning to scenes from their past but also having an adventure in the present (for example, *Remains of the Day*, *The End of the Affair*)

3 someone pursuing a lost dream from their past (for example, *Shine*, *Slumdog Millionaire*)

4 the life of a charismatic, larger-than-life individual (for example, *The Life of David Gale*, *Amadeus*)

Other flashback forms
There are several other flashback forms that are not double narrative. These are films that either: insert a linear narrative inside one scene or sequence from

the present (as in, for example, *The Green Mile, Fight Club, Titanic*) *or* take a scene from the middle or end of the film and put it at the start before running straight from beginning to end (as in, for example, *The Hangover, Goodfellas, Michael Clayton*) *or* show non-chronological fragments from a failed past relationship (as in, for example, *Annie Hall, And When Did You Last See Your Father?*). These forms are dealt with in a later chapter. Time jumps also appear in consecutive stories form and fractured tandem (see below).

Consecutive stories structure

Examples: *Run Lola Run, Groundhog Day, Atonement, Pulp Fiction*

SUBJECT MATTER

Use this for films that need complete or almost-complete stories (often on the notion of 'truth') appearing one after the other (even if the opening is traditional, or if there is a bookend frame), often with their own titles.

Sub-categories are:

1 **Stories walking into the picture**: that is, stories simply happening one after the other, linking at the end (as in *The Circle* and *Paris, je t'aime*)
2 **Different perspectives**: that is, different versions or points of view of the same events (as in *Run Lola Run, Vantage Point, Groundhog Day* and *Rashomon*)
3 **Different consequences**: that is, different outcomes from the same events (as in *Go* and *Atonement*)
4 **Fractured frame/portmanteau**: that is, fractured versions of one of the three above, using one split-up story to act like a bookend or a portmanteau (as in *Pulp Fiction, City of God* and *The Joy Luck Club*)

Fractured tandem structure

Examples: *21 Grams, Babel, The Hours, Three Burials of Melchiades Estrada, Crash, Rendition*

SUBJECT MATTER

These films involve fractured versions of equally important stories. This is probably the form for you if your subject matter involves:

1 unexpected, often tragic, connections between apparently or initially very disparate people, triggered by an accident or random event
2 several equally important stories, some or all fractured, running simultaneously sometimes in the same time frame, but often in several

3 consequences, chain reactions

Fractured tandem can also be used to inject suspense and a detective story element into predictable tandem narrative scripts.

Do you need parallel narrative at all?

Parallel narrative is so exciting that writers often seize upon it for the sheer joy of playing with multiple stories. However, wrongly used, parallel narrative can be actively destructive. A case in point is *Pay It Forward*, which has a very interesting story in the past but utilises a double narrative flashback structure that burdens the film with a redundant story in the present. The heat of *Pay It Forward* is the story in the past, about the relationships between a lonely young boy, his reclusive teacher and his single mother. The story in the present—of a journalist trying to trace a boy who invented the idea of repaying a favour by doing a favour to a complete stranger—simply interrupts its flow. The only narrative point of the story in the present is to explain what 'pay it forward' means. Once that's been explained, very early on, the story in the present adds nothing, in fact it actively reduces. *Vantage Point* has similar problems. Setting out to tell a story from eight different viewpoints, style triumphs over substance and the film ends up repeating the same tiny fragment of action again and again, before cutting, finally, to a car chase.

To make sure you need parallel narrative, pick out what, precisely, is the 'heat' of the film you're planning to write—that is, what its core ideas and interests are—and check that the structure you're considering actually services that heat.

Section 1
Tandem narrative

Chapter 23
Tandem narrative: An introduction

SUCCESSFUL TANDEM NARRATIVE FILMS consist of equally important stories (each with its own protagonist and each on the same socio-political theme) unfolding simultaneously and chronologically in the same time frame. The films are always didactic and typically deal with communities. In some the theme is more overtly political than others. If it is particularly political, the film will make its point by spanning a whole community from top to bottom, from the ruler to the beggar, often openly calling for change. Sometimes, like *Syriana*, it will even span different countries. Examples include: *Traffic*, *Nashville*, *Love Actually*, *Caramel*, *Independence Day*, *Daybreak*, *City of Hope*, *Lantana*, *Me and You and Everyone We Know*, *Syriana*, *Magnolia*, *Pan's Labyrinth*, *Short Cuts* and *Crimes and Misdemeanors*.

While the telling of equally weighted but often unconnected and very different stories alongside each other is revolutionary in mainstream film, in television it is standard, and television inherited it from the stage. It derives from the traditional and highly successful formula of 'main plot and two subplots' found in drama at least as far back as Shakespeare. Today, TV leads the way in using new narrative structures, using multiple and often only remotely connected stories told in parallel, incorporating techniques like time jumps, dream sequences and so on. It is no coincidence that tandem narrative writers like Stephen Gaghan (*Traffic*, *Syriana*) and Paul Haggis (*Crash*) have wide experience in TV writing.

Theme and moral are hugely important in these films, and the writing motto here is: 'same theme, different adventures', which reminds us that all the various stories have to illustrate the film's theme in different ways. In *Traffic*, the theme is the war on drugs. In *Lantana* it is trust and honesty in marital or quasi-marital relationships. In *Caramel*, it is the social pressures on a group of women friends in modern Beirut.

Always, the challenge with these films is to make them good stories, not just sermons, or variations on a theme (which in effect usually means characters in search of a plot).

Predictability

The elephant in the room as far as tandem narrative films are concerned is predictability, particularly in overtly political films, where the message unfortunately often comes over as: 'if anything bad can happen it will'. So, in *City of Hope*, will the ethical young councillor become involved in cronyism and nepotism? Yes. In *Traffic*, will the beautiful, talented schoolgirl become a junkie? Yes. In *Syriana*, will the decent young Muslim boys become terrorists? Yes. *Syriana*, for all its great performances and important topic, is a film that suffers from predictability (see Part 5, Lost in the Telling), as does *City of Hope*.

Earlier, talking about the second-act turning point, I explained that the protagonist's decision to fight back against the odds and the third-act battle to win were necessary to prevent the film becoming a predictable descent into catastrophe, resulting in zero suspense and a disengaged audience. However, the problem with overtly political tandem films is that they often need to show people not winning. They need to show typical (hence predictable) outcomes. If your film is about the suffering of the poor, it needs to depict the suffering of the poor. If it is about how heroin can wreck lives, it needs to show how heroin can wreck lives. However, if the only unpredictable elements in your film are how bad things will become and whether anyone at all will escape catastrophe, your film may well end up extremely boring. As we'll see, there are a number of ways of reducing predictability, but it is an inbuilt problem of the form, so needs constant attention.

Tandem films are all about connections

Connections are of paramount importance in tandem narrative. Audiences come to tandem films with the question: 'Why these stories?', expecting clever and thought-provoking links between all of the stories so they add together to create one coherent message. If you don't provide sufficient connections and a clear message, they are likely to reject the film, just as certain audiences rejected outright the fine fractured tandem narrative *Babel* because they felt the Japanese girl's story was insufficiently connected. It didn't matter that they loved everything else. The more connections, the more room for suspense and audience engagement, so, usually, the wider the appeal of the film.

Successful tandem films achieve connection, meaning and closure between their stories in a wide variety of ways. The evolution of *Nashville*, regarded by many as the iconic tandem narrative film from the US, provides some very useful insights into why connections are needed and how they can be formed. Luckily, in an interview available on the widescreen DVD of the film, Robert Altman describes very clearly how the film's structure evolved and, fascinatingly, reveals that from the beginning he and his team were focused on connections—because they knew that without them there wouldn't be a proper film.

Altman explains that *Nashville* came into being because United Artists had just bought a Nashville-based country music publishing company. They commissioned him to create a film about the city and its music. Altman decided to look at what he called 'the Hollywood syndrome' at work in Nashville and 'to take this country–western culture and a populist kind of culture [then] put [them] into a panorama [to] reflect American sensibilities and politics'. These were his themes and he organised his team so as to create a film about them. He sent writer Joan Tewkesbury to Nashville, and her diary of events (including the freeway pile-up) formed the spine of the film. However, as storytellers, Altman and his team knew this was not enough. The theme would not be properly transmitted just by providing a panorama of typical Nashville people in typical Nashville stories. To make a coherent film there had to be one overarching *story* that linked all of the stories and characters together, otherwise the film would become a series of vignettes— animated portraits without a moral or emotional point.

Consequently, and consciously, Altman chose a political campaign as the overarching story, and the team created a story about the campaign manager, who, together with a local lawyer, is organising public rallies and fundraisers for a politician seeking preselection for president as all of the other stories are going on. Obviously, the issue of who becomes president links everyone in a city, from top to bottom, so already the campaign story provides connection. However, to further knit the film together—to make the political story more

vivid and personal—each of the film's separate stories and each of its kalei-
doscope of characters actually intersects in some way with the campaign,
with the film's tragic climax happening at a political rally, at which all of the
characters are assembled either to watch or to perform.

He further linked the stories by what he called 'connecting tissue', meaning characters who could credibly move between the many stories and thus
link them, characters like the BBC reporter and the enigmatic bicycle man.

Notice how all of these are dynamic narrative devices, story devices; that
is, characters actually doing things towards a goal. This is our job as writers:
to create a fable, to get the message across through the scenario.

TYPES OF CONNECTION
Good tandem films are like a piece of fabric. The separate stories make the
horizontal threads, and the different kinds of connections between the stories provide the vertical threads that weave all the stories together. All good
tandem narrative films feature some or all of the following connections and
connection devices.

THEME AND MESSAGE
Theme is the most vital connection in tandem. All tandem narrative films are
didactic and have a socio-political theme (sometimes very political, sometimes not) illustrated differently through each separate story. Usually the
films are critical of society, and the message is a call for change; in less political films, a change of heart, in more political films, a change of social policy.

EPIC APPROACH—A WIDE RANGE OF TYPES WITHIN A CHOSEN SOCIAL GROUP
To reflect tandem narrative's concern with what's wrong with communities
and how we should fix it, tandem narrative films are often epic, panoramic,
spanning a wide range of social types, sometimes an entire society (as in
Traffic), sometimes a minority group (as in *Caramel*). Usually, the more
overtly political, the wider the social spread (as in *Syriana*, which spans several countries). The title *Me and You and Everyone We Know* says it all.

GEOGRAPHY AND TIME
Events happen in the same time frame and characters often literally walk into
and out of each other's stories (although characters may not always know
each other when they pass). Geography and time usually connect characters
in the film's final moments. In some cases, the final moments are the first

time characters from different stories connect (as in *Crimes and Misdemeanors*), which can provide an interesting and pleasing twist.

CHARACTERS APPEARING IN A NUMBER OF DIFFERENT STORIES

Characters play a part in several different stories. Hence, in *Lantana*, the police officer goes into all of the different couples' lives; in *Traffic*, the judge is involved with characters from a number of the stories; in *City of Hope*, characters are connected with each other by marriage, job and intersecting stories. This is Altman's 'connecting tissue'.

FACILITATING CHARACTERS

These are characters who talk a lot about other characters, providing crucial information. They may or may not appear in several stories. In *Nashville*, the BBC reporter making a documentary about Nashville was a conscious device inserted to provide information and connection. Altman says: 'We decided we needed a voice, a reporter to ask the questions that the audience has to know', a character who 'could touch everybody'.

DISASTER

Some kind of social catastrophe links all of the stories, symbolising the connections across community, either triggering the main story (*Independence Day*) or winding it up (*Nashville*). A final catastrophe coming out of the blue, though, can feel contrived (like the earthquake in *Short Cuts*). Conversely, a final catastrophe that is too clearly signalled and happens without a twist (as in, say, a film in which a range of different characters all finally board the same train, which crashes) can be boringly, even comically, predictable.

OBJECTS, BEHAVIOURS AND SIMILAR CHARACTERS

Stories may be connected by objects (for example, the same kind of flower appears in each); behaviours (for example, all characters are diabetic or all have tried to commit suicide) or similar backgrounds (for example, all characters have suffered unhappy childhoods). However, if the only connection you have between your stories is that, for example, a yellow rose figures in each, it is unlikely to have the same emotional punch as films that have more connections; indeed, it could appear whimsical.

TWO-STORY TANDEM NARRATIVE

Some tandem narrative films have only two stories, linked only at the start or end, sometimes both. The structure is specifically designed to transmit the film's themes and message, and pleasing suspense and closure of the film depend on how the two stories eventually connect. Examples are *Crimes and Misdemeanors* (two stories linked by a meeting at a wedding), *Pan's Labyrinth* (a small child's different realities meet in death) and *Sliding Doors* (two possible directions for a life). In all cases, suspense, connection, meaning and closure are achieved by the twist ending—so the twist needs to be clever.

THE MACRO PLOT: THE STRONGEST FORCE FOR CONNECTION

I have left the most important connecting device until last. This is the macro plot, the overarching plot that Altman and his team knew was necessary to create unity in *Nashville*. It is the strongest narrative device for connection in tandem narratives and needs to be looked at in depth.

Chapter 24
The macro in tandem narrative

WHEN WE FEEL A tandem narrative film is characters in search of a plot, the macro is the plot that's missing. Figure 24.1 shows how the plots are constructed in *Nashville*, with the film's macro, the political campaign story, being an overarching plot that, as well as linking all of the other stories, dynamically illustrates the film's theme, and brings the message home.

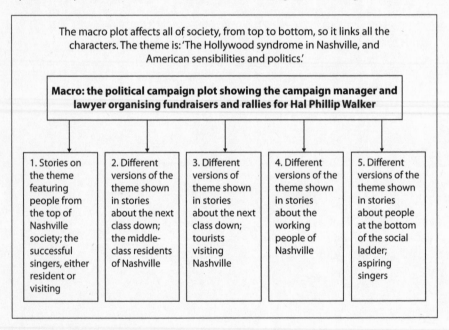

Figure 24.1 The plots in *Nashville*

In *Independence Day*, the macro is the alien invasion story (linking a variety of separate stories happening in different places). In *Lantana*, it's the murder investigation (linking a series of couples across a city). In *Traffic*, it's the judge's war on drugs (linking individuals and families across the US and Mexico), and in *City of Hope*, it is the attempts by crooked councillors to replace the ghetto with an upmarket shopping mall (linking everyone across the neighbourhood).

Dynamic connection

Imagine each of the films above without their macro plots. All that's left is a set of interesting stories loosely linked by the same theme: vignettes. There is no energising forward momentum. The macro adds energy, impact and vitally—*dynamic* connection. It occurs in most but not all tandem narrative films and is a very reliable way of providing thematic and story momentum, of adding, to both theme and action, 'a point'.

Technically, the macro operates like the action line—the adventure—in conventional narrative. It permits all of the other stories to happen—just as the journey down the river in *The African Queen* permitted the love story to happen.

In many tandem narratives, there is no strong connection between the various stories until the macro starts. Before that, all of the characters are just living their normal lives. The macro creates a common problem. All of the other stories are pegged to the macro and all are pulled by it towards a joint climax and successful closure, just as, in conventional narrative, the action line pulls the relationship line along. The macro affects the whole group, from top to bottom, richest to poorest, so links all of the characters.

About the macro
CRIME, DEATH AND THE TICKING CLOCK

Macros often involve crime, death and a ticking clock, logically, because these add jeopardy. Even *Caramel*, a very gentle tandem narrative film, has a macro involving a ticking clock and women involved in breaking society's rules.

THE MACRO NEEDS TO GET STARTED QUICKLY

Interestingly, many audiences felt *Lantana* was uncomfortably slow before the start of the murder plot. Writer Andrew Bovell and director Ray Lawrence knew this and took a calculated risk that the film would hold the audience's attention until this point. The gamble paid off, but it was a gamble. The lesson here is that the longer the macro takes to get started, the more risk there is of the audience getting restless.

MACRO AS A REPEATED RESPONSE

While crime and death do figure in many macros, the macro doesn't have to be heavy on crime, neither does it have to be a highly structured plot, it just has to involve a chain of actions that carry the film's message. *Caramel's* macro is not a proper story, not a plot building to a climax at all, yet it does the job of holding all the stories together and transmitting the message.

Caramel's macro is a series of fragments—actions—showing the women acting *as a group* to help each other when one of their number is suffering because of social mores. So, the women come as a group to comfort their friend whose married boyfriend does not turn up for the anniversary celebration she has set up. They accompany a member of the group to hospital to have an operation that fakes virginity. They help the elderly woman in the shop across the road look glamorous for her new boyfriend, and keep a watch on the demented old lady she has to care for. Note that the group acts, not just one or two of the group.

Must you have a macro?

A macro adds energy and focus to a tandem narrative film, but whether you use one depends on the kind of film you want to make. Sometimes you might want to make a more restrained and open-ended film. Without the murder investigation which is its macro, *Lantana* would simply be 'different versions of loyalty and honesty in romantic relationships', making the film quieter, slower and more meditative than it is—which would have been fine, just different. It would have been more like the Swedish film *Daybreak*, also on the theme of marital relationships, which does not have a macro. *Daybreak* is linked by time and place (all of the stories happen on the same night in the same city), and at the end the characters all pass each other on the street. The result is a very successful but restrained, cerebral, more art-house film.

The same is true of *Me and You and Everyone We Know*, which also has no macro. Its theme, demonstrated over a number of stories, is, in the words of writer–director Miranda July: 'children and adults trying to figure out how to touch each other, in every sense of the word'. The stories are poignant, innocent and gentle, which is remarkable because a significant part of the content deals with sexual interest and attraction between children and adults.

DREAD CAN ALMOST TAKE THE PLACE OF A MACRO

One of the interesting things about *Daybreak* and *Me and You and Everyone We Know* is that both, but particularly the latter, use the threat of something terrible possibly happening to the characters to energise the story by adding the magic ingredient, suspense.

Me and You and Everyone We Know is highly suspenseful because the threat of sexual assault against adults but also, shockingly, against children, hangs over the community, and we dread that the film will climax in an attack. This is handy to know: in a tandem narrative, a threat hanging over the community can create high levels of suspense because the audience assumes that the point of the film is to show the threat eventuating. Arriaga uses dread like this very effectively in *Babel*, as we'll see later.

The power of a macro

A macro in *Me and You and Everyone We Know* would logically have had to be an overarching plotline, linking all the stories that illustrated Ms July's theme of 'children and adults trying to figure out how to touch each other in every sense of the word'. It's hard to imagine any macro plot that would illustrate this theme apart from one involving actual sexual assault. This would have shifted the film into very dark territory, the territory of *Lantana*, to become an emotional thriller about violent sexual crime; more horrific than *Lantana*, actually, because it would need to be sexual crime involving children. Such a thing would have been a travesty of the delicate, gentle film Ms July wanted to make.

Interestingly, the film has its cake and eats it. Dread of an assault provides tension but lack of assault provides the warm delicate ending the director–writer was after. However, for someone who wanted to make a hard-hitting film about sexual assault, a macro would have provided the requisite impact. The trick here is to know what effect and what audience you are after.

POLITICAL CONTENT

Noticeably, all of the films that operate well without a macro are films that are not trying to push any strong reformist political line.

MACRO AS THE DIFFERENCE BETWEEN BIG SCREEN AND SMALL SCREEN?

Many tandem narratives that don't have macros were originally made as telemovies. This is interesting: is the macro therefore what makes a tandem narrative film a feature? Certainly, it is easier to market a film that has a strong macro plot, and films without a macro are definitely more art-house.

Only promise a macro and plot connection if you intend to pay it off

You don't need a macro but you do need connection and a coherent message. *Magnolia* is a remarkable and often very moving tandem narrative film containing nine complete and emotionally charged, high-jeopardy narratives all happening on the same day in California's San Fernando Valley. Each has a strong three-act structure building to a powerful climax. There is no macro.

Unfortunately, for many people its ending is unsatisfactory because while there are thematic connections between the stories (all characters are connected via a TV quiz show and all of the stories are about the difficulty of attaining love, particularly problematic parent–child relationships), and while all happen in the same geographical area, with all of the characters finally experiencing the same freak weather condition resulting in frogs raining down from the sky, there is no real coming-together of the stories, no answer to the questions: 'Why these stories in particular? Why not others?' The problem is exacerbated because the film starts with a kind of prologue listing three extraordinary coincidences, which sets up an expectation that the film will end with coincidence; indeed, suggests that the point of the film will be an amazing final coincidence involving all of the stories, possibly echoing the coincidences in the prologue, so that 'coincidence' becomes the macro. But there are no coincidences and the stories do not interconnect—even in the simple but pleasing way they do in *Daybreak*, by characters passing each other in the street unawares.

Certainly, a policeman who appears in two stories makes an appearance in a third because he happens to see a character from another story committing a crime (which, at a stretch, could be seen as a coincidence) but this is all. The plotlines just don't deal with the promised coincidence. This is unlike *Me and You and Everyone We Know*, which, having promised horrific climaxes, delivers by showing us climax scenes that might end horribly or sadly but actually end poignantly and in ways that are life-affirming.

So, while *Magnolia*'s direction is impressive and its performances and individual stories often magnificent, it's hard to pick the film's overall message, or point. What the frogs symbolise (if they are meant to be symbolic) is unclear. The linking device whereby all the cast sing the same song provides a kind of connection but does so by taking the film into surrealism, which has a distancing effect and inevitably undercuts the emotional impact created by naturalism. The unfortunate thing here is that very probably the lack of connection would not have been so noticeable if connection via coincidence hadn't been set up so strongly at the start as the film's theme. Had the prologue instead consisted of striking stories that were pertinent to the film's ending, closure might well have been very satisfactory indeed. As it is, you get the sense that the prologue and the raining frogs are a great opening and a great ending—to another film.

Perhaps the lessons here are that in tandem narrative:

- audiences assume there will be a connection between stories
- meaning and closure are created through connection

- you don't need a macro but you do need sufficient connection between the stories to explain why you chose those stories and no other
- either pay off on a specific promise of connection or don't promise it

Short Cuts: Some audiences love open-ended films

Short Cuts has no macro and, while it is a highly memorable film with wonderful performances, passion, and wit, it lacks pace, connection, clear meaning and closure. *Short Cuts* employs ten narratives about residents of Los Angeles. Characters are connected by chance, physical proximity or family relationships. Sometimes stories cross each other, but many stories lack suspense and there is often a choice to go for anticlimax and 'slice of life'. Technically, this results in some stories being internally repetitive, giving us an ongoing normality with redundant conflict. Predictably, this has the effect of slowing the film down.

The film opens with what seems like the set-up of a macro, as all the characters experience helicopters spraying Los Angeles with insecticide, but the insecticide story soon disappears altogether and one wonders why it was there at all. The film ends with an earthquake affecting all the characters, which, while it does provide connection of sorts, unfortunately feels a bit convenient. It should be said that many people loved *Short Cuts*' slowness, lack of suspense, documentary flavour and lack of overall final resolution. They loved the fact that there was no closure and life just goes on.

In the end, these are matters of taste. Interestingly, though, the films of Altman that are most widely celebrated, films like *Nashville* and *Gosford Park*, do have macros (in both cases, a murder story). So it could be argued that Altman at his most popular uses macros.

Chapter 25
Writing your tandem narrative film

IT'S VERY EASY TO write a directionless tandem narrative because we writers love to write characters. For example, imagine your initial idea is 'a film about homelessness'. Passionate about your topic, you will find it relatively easy to write, say, five stories involving a range of different interesting homeless people in different parts of the same city on the same day. However, while this may well give you an interesting and possibly very poignant script, it is unlikely to be a suspenseful one because your stories are not strongly connected and you do not have a major plotline pulling them all towards a joint climax (think of *Lantana* and *Nashville* without their macros). Your audience is likely to be a little distanced from your characters, particularly if your piece is very didactic (as we saw when looking at the second-act turning point, endless disasters remove suspense and create audience disengagement).

This may be transmitting exactly what you want. If so, that's fine. However, if you want greater audience engagement and more dynamism, probably your best chance is to add a macro; for example, 'city authorities have decided that all homeless people must be removed from the streets in preparation for the Olympic games'. Suddenly, your characters, rather than just being themselves, locked in their normality or being pulled by poverty into catastrophe, are faced with a threat and must react as only they would do. They have either to fight back or be crushed and both of these provide action and a building narrative. As writer, you are in a win-win situation. You still have all of your wonderful characters in their individual stories, but you have added suspense, and can explore your characters via action, as they engage in their different adventures on the film's theme. You will also have the chance to explore, dynamically, via a parable, a wide cross-section of society, from the decision-makers to the homeless, thereby setting your stories in their social context, as part of a flawed system.

Change of focus
The hardest thing about creating a good macro is that, unless your film idea has actually presented itself to you as a macro for a tandem narrative ('I want

to write a movie about how a country about to put on the Olympic Games clears the homeless off the streets'), to make the macro genuinely gripping and more than just a transparent connecting device, you have to completely refocus so that you see the film as being *about* its macro. The macro has to be what you would describe on the DVD cover. Instead of thinking of your film as a means to tell your series of separate stories about homelessness, you now have to see it as a film akin to my Olympic Games story idea. You have to think: 'city authorities are removing homeless people from the streets and trouble breaks out'. This way, instead of being characters in search of a plot, your film is defined by its overarching plot—which is genuinely an action line permitting a series of relationship lines to happen (as in *Traffic* or *Lantana*).

You can see this mental shift in Altman when, after describing his theme and the fact that he actually had to insert a political campaign to link the stories he set out to tell, he says in a complete reversal: 'We were doing a political campaign and everything else that happened in the film *Nashville* [was] just a bunch of stories that supported a bunch of characters.' In fact, as he's just described the individual stories in the film came before the political campaign, which was invented with the specific purpose of holding the stories together. What's happened here is that he's simply shifted his mental viewpoint. Now he's seeing the individual stories as ribs coming off the spine of the macro. The macro is now the film's *raison d'être*, not just something added on. That's exactly the mental shift, the change in point of view, that you need to happen because it means you are immersed in the macro. It then gets written better and the whole film is improved.

However, the viewpoint switch is hard and counter-intuitive. It resembles the difficult process you have to go through in creating a mentor antagonist film, when what interests you is the mentor antagonist but to properly tell their story you have to invent and get inside the head of a new, much less interesting protagonist. We'll see a similar phenomenon in flashback, where you want to tell a story set in a character's past but to create the necessary unfolding mystery for the audience you have to invent and immerse yourself in a new story, a second story, set in the present.

Avert predictability

As we've seen, the biggest problem hanging over tandem narrative films, particularly overtly political ones, is predictability. The first step towards averting predictability in your didactic tandem narrative is to accept that while you are passionate about transmitting your message, didacticism and predictability could kill your script. Next, accept that your audience may not share your beliefs. Reject the idea that your job is simply to catalogue a predictable descent into misery and disaster. Set yourself the task of constructing a clever fable—a parable—so full of surprises and so powerful that it will convert even those opposed to your views.

Surprises are the key. Think of using characters acting out of character—for example, a coward becomes brave or a teenager who looks set to become a hopeless junkie recovers while the teenager who seems set to recover becomes heavily addicted—although avoid clichés.

As long as you stay credible and unsentimental, you can make fate intervene to cause a sudden, unexpected twist, so that the drug lord dies a fluke death that sends the plot in a new direction, or an endangered child is suddenly removed by a grandparent. *Traffic* is full of twists and turns in character; most particularly, the survival of the apparently doomed Mexican policeman, his honour intact. This means we can accept the occasional predictable demise, like beautiful-talented-schoolgirl-to-hopeless-junkie.

The macro is usually your greatest weapon against predictability (the Mexican policeman's story is a crucial part of the macro in *Traffic*) because the macro is an action-line story, an adventure, which can be constructed to include suspenseful twists and turns while, in the background, in the individual stories, the social malaise can be seen causing the relentless descent from bad to worse that you want to display. For example, in our film about homelessness ('city authorities have decided that all homeless people must be removed from the streets in preparation for the Olympics') there can be all kinds of suspenseful elements in that macro plotline while, in the background, we run more conventional linear homelessness stories.

Another option is *Gomorrah*'s trick, whereby suspense is injected into a film about inevitable catastrophe by introducing the possibility of escape (hope) and a constant threat of double-crossing. Work for suspense, always remembering that suspense requires possibilities for escaping the threat. Consciously insert credible rays of hope that you can ultimately quash (or not, if you want to go for a twist ending).

Fractured tandem?

One radical, structural way to add pace to scenarios that might suffer from predictability and/or be exposition-heavy is to use fractured tandem, the form used in *21 Grams*; that is, to deliberately chop up the stories and tell them in a non-linear way. We will look at this later.

Great characters, real but unusual premise, new world

All films, tandem included, need fascinating characters, a real but unusual premise and an interesting new world. So, with our homeless movie, don't go for stereotypical homeless people; create something fascinating about them (think of how fascinating and unusual Arriaga makes El Chivo, the derelict–assassin in *Amores Perros*).

Technical plotting issues in tandem narrative

Tandem narrative, like all parallel narrative, runs several storylines in the screen time normally taken up by the one hero/one journey combination. Hence, you need to tell your stories very economically. The first step to creating and telling economical stories is to reduce each story to its key dramatic moments (its turning points and its climax), the point beyond which it ceases to be the story. That way, you know the minimum amount of the story you need to make it work, because there is a limit to how much you can remove from, say, 'Cinderella' before it ceases to be 'Cinderella'. We've discussed this earlier in the context of the second act. What, in effect, you can remove are the second-act complications. You cannot remove any more or the story is no longer 'Cinderella'.

TRUNCATION

Removing the middle of a story can work surprisingly well in tandem narrative, permitting you to include a greater number of connected stories, thus more versions of the theme. This happens in *Love Actually*, where none of the love stories has a real middle (which, coincidentally avoids romantic comedy's perennial plotting challenge, to keep the loving couple credibly apart). The other way you can truncate a story is to end it on its first-act turning point (in 'Cinderella', the arrival of the fairy godmother), which gives you a thought-provoking surprise, or on its second-act turning point (in 'Cinderella', losing the slipper at midnight) which gives you a tragedy. We'll look at the latter technique later in *City of Hope*. Truncation can also provide the film's point, as in *Crimes and Misdemeanors*, which cuts the third act of each of its stories (a romantic comedy and a film noir murder tale) to make the point that life is not like a Hollywood movie.

Ending at a turning point means ending at a moment of suspense. Fascinatingly, as we'll see, audiences don't seem to mind being left in mid air like this (although they might if the truncated story were central rather than peripheral).

Whether you intend to use whole stories or to truncate, work out the three-act structure of each, including its protagonist. A skeletal version is often fine; in fact, often you won't have time for much more. The macro will need three acts and major stories usually need to have three-act structures. Minor stories can often be truncated, depending on what you want them to say. For help in condensing plotlines see pp. 135–7.

INTERWEAVING PLOTS IN TANDEM NARRATIVES

Once you have worked out the key points of each of your stories, you need to plan how to interweave these stories. Tandem narrative films contain so many stories that you will often need to further several plotlines (plus character material) in one scene. Usually, tandem narratives solve this problem by creating scenes into which new characters can literally walk to start a new scene. This not only increases speed and continuity but reinforces the standard tandem message that society is interconnected and we are all affected by the problem at the centre of the film.

A good example of how to interweave stories occurs early on in *City of Hope*, where Sayles cleverly transmits backstory, character and relationship material and sets up later action—all in one brief sequence. Mike Rizzo, the jealous policeman, is driving along with his anti-corruption partner, Bill. Just as they are discussing Rizzo's refusal to stay away from his estranged wife Angela, the ambitious, oily detective O'Brien drives by and stops (this is his first appearance). The three men talk briefly, and O'Brien asks Mike and Bill first to harass Ramirez, whom we can infer to be a local criminal and second whether they are going to the mayor's fundraising dinner. As O'Brien leaves, Bill describes O'Brien's ambitions with contempt.

This extremely short scene transmits an extraordinary amount of information, and moreover, does it dynamically. It gives insights into Mike's jealousy (important for Nicky's story); it reveals Bill's honest and sensible character (important for when Mike shoots Nicky, and Bill talks about a cover-up); it shows O'Brien's oiliness, ruthlessness and ambition (important for the macro, for Joe's story and for Nicky's story); and it sets up the mayor's fundraising dinner, an event that is important at the end of the film (important for Wynn's story because Wynn and his followers storm the dinner to demand answers from the mayor). Thus, information vital to five plots is set up in seconds in a credible and unobtrusive way.

HOW TO INTERWEAVE

Do this at planning stage. Your index cards will help. Keep looking for ways to knit plots together. If your characters live in close physical proximity, exploit that. For example, if you need characters A and B to be quarrelling about character C, make it happen in the café that belongs to character D who has just come out of the kitchen after telling character E that their marriage is over. Meanwhile, Character F can be walking past the café window so that when A and B's scene in the café is finished, you can cut without explanation to character F in character G's apartment asking for a loan (see also Part 3, Practical Plotting).

ATTACH STORIES TO YOUR CHRONOLOGICAL MACRO

Structurally, your macro (if you have one) will be a big help because, being an action line, it has an inbuilt timeline (for example, the decision to remove the homeless, the plans, the attempts etc.) to which you can attach your various stories. Once you have worked out the macro's time-line, material for all of the plots, from the homeless to the government enforcers, will start to suggest itself. You might also want to write about other characters pulled into the macro; say, the kindly grocer who hands over food, or the angry road cleaner who hates the homeless. These are facilitating characters, Altman's connective tissue. Remember that every time the macro plot moves, it will pull the other stories along because it will create consequences, hence character reactions, hence suspense. Plan the macro's content carefully.

PROGRESSING YOUR STORIES

All of the stories in a tandem narrative progress simultaneously. Hence, if you have six stories, the first step in story 1 will be followed by the first step in story 2, the first step in story 3, and so on. When all the first steps have been provided, you will tell all of the second steps in your stories (although of course, you don't have to stick to the same order each time). Plot each step of each story, write each step on a card and arrange the cards to get good movement, always remembering to make characters walk into each other's stories where possible. The cards will also permit clever, dramatic cuts between stories.

Plan of action

Proceed as follows:

1   Set up normality in all plots except macro.
2   Set up first step in macro.
3   Set up first step in each story in response to first step of macro.
4   Set up second step in macro.

5 Set up second step in each story in response to second step of
   macro—and so on.

Of course, you can alter the order in which you visit each of the separate
non-macro stories. Try at all times to avoid predictability and work to factor
in surprise and suspense. Having a scene at or near the start that puts all or
many of the characters in the same place at the same time (as *Nashville* does)
has a unifying effect and tells us that we are in a group story.

Achieve rising suspense and emotion across storylines by using Robin
Swicord's technique of jumping stories so that the emotional level of the
scene you leave is the same as the emotional level of the scene you enter.
Sometimes a jump to a contrasting emotion works well too (see p. 234).

Creating a tandem narrative via actor improvisation

If you plan to improvise a film with a large number of actors, the form to
use is tandem narrative, because your actors can be divided into groups to
create different stories on the theme and connected to a macro you provide.
If you try to use more than about six actors in a multiple protagonist narrative—that is, a film about a team on the same adventure—you are likely to
find you do not have the screen time to give each character the large amount
of exposure the film requires. You can see this problem in action in the film
Parallel Lives (which was devised via actor improvisation) and is discussed in
Part 5, Lost in the Telling.

Working with good actors in an improvisational setting can produce
excellent results, but actors are not trained to invent plots and they should
not be expected to. Scripts produced in unfocused improvisation sessions
typically lack building plot and instead feature emotional exchanges such
as redundant quarrelling, tears and unexpected sexual liaisons. You can see
this happening in *Time Code*. It is the result of actors adrift without a plot or
backstory, trying, as they trained to do in improvisation sessions, to create
emotional situations out of the blue by means of confrontational behaviour.
Other results are plot clichés coming out of panicked vertical imagination
(sudden house fires or violence, long-lost relatives, characters discovering
that they are related), which in the excitement of the workshop situation, can
get locked into the plot.

To get the most from your actors in an improvisational situation, define
your theme and the location of your film and work with your actors to create vivid characters and interconnected stories that illustrate the theme. For

example, imagine the theme of the film is pollution. Divide the actors into groups, then ask each group to brainstorm towards a storyline based on the idea of people in some way connected to pollution. This could result in figurative treatments (for example, a relationship polluted by jealousy), or physical treatments (an asthma attack induced by the pollution, or a worker employed to dump pollutants).

If a macro plot is appropriate, either you or your actors can invent it. Your actors can suggest ways in which the macro could intersect with their stories. They can also suggest connections between the stories—connections by blood, by geography, by time. All of the stories will then be made to dovetail into the macro's climax, which would be the climax of the film too, thus providing meaning and closure. This way you are exploiting the actors' improvisational skills for the maximum result, creating a connected, richly layered thematic drama with a clear climax—and doing so extremely quickly.

Be careful, though, to structure the workshop so that you, not the actors, control it. Actors are trained to think in terms of one character, not many characters and many plotlines. If not controlled by a director, in their enthusiasm they may rapidly (and quite inadvertently) pull the workshop off course. It's a good idea to follow Mike Leigh's practice of assembling a proper script for the film out of the final workshopped version of each scene. It's less expensive than making the actors improvise to camera, and less risky.

Checklist for writing a tandem narrative

1   Your mottos are: 'same theme, different adventures' and 'connected stories'.
2   Before writing or even planning, clarify to yourself your film's message and themes; that is, what your film is 'about' ideas-wise. All of your stories must illustrate the same theme. Don't let characters and passionately felt ideas drag you into writing before you have planned. They may pull you in the wrong direction.
3   Consciously work against predictability. Insert twists and turns and rays of hope (which you may or may not quash) and assume a hostile audience because then you will put your arguments more carefully and convincingly. Remember that film reaches audiences first emotionally then intellectually. Set out to touch their emotions. Take them on a journey of the soul. Consider using fractured tandem, which is discussed later in the book. It's difficult but may be your best way to remove predictability.

4   Seriously consider the pros and cons of a macro for your particular film. Your idea may or may not come with a built-in macro. The macro has to be a proper plot that illustrates the theme and connects and includes all of your stories. Including a macro is probably the safest way to ensure pace and connection. Plan your macro, then peg your other stories to the macro's timeline of events, always remembering to factor in suspense and twists. Your macro will usually involve crime and death and often a ticking clock.

5   Think about whether you want to use closely plotted three-act stories throughout the film, like *Traffic*, a mixture of one-, two- and three-act stories like *City of Hope* (see pp. 203–6), or whether, like *Lantana*, your macro is strong enough to hold together, and give meaning to, less structured stories. This will probably mean you need to include death or the threat of death or violence in your macro. Three-act stories with twists and turns are probably the most reliable structures to ensure pace and suspense. If your stories are not closely plotted three-act structures, copy *City of Hope*'s trick of ending on first or second-act turning point (see pp. 205–6), or use *Lantana*'s technique of making sure that they are full of emotion and surprises, with each character having a lot to lose.

6   Consider truncating stories, but make sure they will transmit what you intend them to in a truncated form.

7   Pick characters that are typical but vividly interesting members of the group you want to depict, not stereotypes. Think real but unusual. Ask yourself why a great actor would want to play your character.

8   Devise and carefully plan each separate story as a strikingly original and powerful variation on the film's theme. Keep the stories tight. You do not have enough screen time to meander.

9   Create connections as explained above. Connections can be made at the last moment, but if you leave it this late, the connections must be extremely clever.

10   Plan how you will interweave stories before you start.

Chapter 26
City of Hope: Tandem narrative case study

JOHN SAYLES' FILM *CITY of Hope*, while suffering somewhat from the perennial problem of political tandem narrative films, predictability, is very useful in providing examples of how to run many interconnected plots in a tandem narrative. It uses many of the connecting devices listed above and employs a combination of very tightly plotted three-act stories and plots that are cleverly truncated at turning points.

Its theme is political corruption and the battle to maintain moral integrity, and it spans an entire inner-city community from the mayor through to police on the beat down to children on the street. It is told through a web of interconnected stories all set in the same small physical area. All the stories in some way touch on people exploiting either the system or their official position for personal benefit, so all are on topic, on theme.

City of Hope uses all of the standard tandem narrative devices for achieving pace, connection, meaning and closure. Its stories are on the same socio-political theme (inner-city corruption, with all of the stories exploring and ending in corruption, or in disaster caused by corruption or greed); it has a macro that illustrates the theme (corrupt officials trying to destroy a ghetto in order to build an upmarket shopping mall); it utilises geographical connections (all of the characters live and work in such close physical proximity that they can credibly walk in and out of each other's stories); characters appear in more than one story; and finally, facilitating characters provide useful backstory information about other characters.

The most interesting facilitating character is the mentally impaired man who, acting as a sort of chorus on the action, wanders through the stories, stitching them together and, at the end, is used not only to foil attempts to get help for a dying man, but to state the film's moral with his repeated symbolic howls: 'We need help.' The appearance of this apparently unimportant—indeed, in society's eyes, redundant—character as the voice of truth provides another pleasing unity, another tying up of loose ends. Closure is further reinforced by ending the film on the building site where it started.

Story structure and content

The three dominant stories are each structured in three acts and all have the corrupt mayor and/or his agents as major or subsidiary antagonists. Each provides a different example of the theme of corruption and shows a different protagonist's attempts to retain integrity and independence in the face of corruption and abuse of power. In the minor narratives, the story always involves the issue of individuals manipulating the system (or their power within the system) for personal gain. This even applies to the story of the two teenagers who lie to avoid a police charge and to the love story involving Nicky and Angela, which is brought to an abrupt end by a policeman who, abusing his power, fatally shoots Nicky.

STORY 1: NICKY AND HIS BUILDER FATHER JOE

Nicky, an overprotected and aimless young man, leaves his cushy job on his father's building site to find independence (disturbance). This leads him to an abortive robbery attempt which has officialdom after him (first-act turning point) and eventually to his fatal shooting at the hands of the ex-husband of a girl with whom he falls in love at first sight. In a final scene which incorporates both second-act turning point (his lowest point) and climax, he is reunited with his father as he dies.

STORY 2: JOE AND THE CORRUPT CITY OFFICIALS

Joe, forced to pay off corrupt city and union officials in order to continue business, tries to maintain his integrity and protect his family. He is under pressure to burn down one of his properties, a rundown apartment building, so that a new development can replace it (disturbance). He resists, but finally agrees in exchange for the police dropping the attempted robbery charges against Nicky (first-act turning point). To his horror, two die in the fire and many are left homeless (second-act turning point). Later, he finds Nicky dying. They are reconciled, but it is too late to save Nicky and he dies (climax).

STORY 3: WYNN TRYING TO AVOID CORRUPTION

Wynn, the lone African–American councillor on a conservative and corrupt city council, has to deal with the council on one hand and with militant black community members (who despise him and try to destroy his credibility at every turn) on the other. When two black youths beat up a white teacher, then lie that he propositioned them (disturbance), Wynn has to choose between exposing the lie and keeping the black community onside (first-act turning point). The pressure mounts on Wynn, and it seems he will have to lie and support the boys (second-act turning point). In the end, he persuades the teacher to drop the charges and unites the community against the corrupt mayor (climax).

One-act stories

There are three one-act stories (all ending on a first-act turning point, a thought-provoking surprise).

1. NICKY FALLS IN LOVE WITH ANGELA RIZZO

Nicky meets Angela Rizzo on the day of the robbery (disturbance) and last sees her at the story's first-act turning point, when they have sex and talk about commitment, a big issue for Nicky since Angela has a handicapped child. A three-act structure would go on to explore how irresponsible Nicky copes with an instant and demanding family. Instead, the story stops at the thought-provoking surprise. Notice how there is no sense of frustration when the story stops like this, no sense of being left in mid air. It's because we are left with the reward of a thought-provoking surprise. We can see the same thing in *The Sweet Hereafter*.

2. MIKE RIZZO MURDERS NICKY

Mike, already angry that Angela has left him, notices Nicky talking to her on the night the two meet (disturbance). He threatens Nicky, then later when drunk, shoots him (first-act turning point), thereby possibly incurring a murder charge and putting his partner, Bill, who hates corruption, into the very difficult position of either lying to protect him or being honest and seeing him arrested ('Will they get found out? Will the good cop lie?').

3. NICKY AND THE UNSUCCESSFUL ROBBERY

Two minor criminals rope Nicky in to help them rob the electrical store (disturbance). They are discovered by a security guard and arrested (first-act turning point). Again, the story stops here. There is further material about Nicky, because his father seeks to protect him, but it is the last time we see the other two robbers.

Two-act structures

There are two stories ending at their second-act turning point, hence in tragedy.

1. A GOOD TEENAGER BECOMES CORRUPTED

Desmond, a decent teenager, is hanging out with a delinquent friend. Irritated by police harassment, the delinquent suggests deliberately assaulting an innocent jogger, Wes (disturbance), which they do. To get out of the assault charge, they claim Wes propositioned them (first-act turning point). The black community is horrified. Community outrage spirals. The press comes in and a community meeting is called. On the way to the meeting, Desmond's mother suspects something is wrong and asks Desmond directly whether he lied (second-act turning point). The story stops here, just as it seems Desmond is going to confess. It is not made clear whether or not he does. The next time the matter is revisited is at the community meeting, where Wynn announces he has got the charges dropped. There is a sort of epilogue where Desmond seeks out and apologises to Wes, and it seems there is some sort of reconciliation. But Desmond has been corrupted—and that is the point of this small tragedy.

2. WES IS DESTROYED

Wes is assaulted (disturbance), hears that the boys are claiming sexual assault (first-act turning point), and is told by Wynn that his reputation will be damaged regardless of whether he drops the charges or maintains them, but that there will be less damage if they are dropped (second-act turning point). He is not seen after this. His life, tragically, is ruined. Wynn provides the information that he has dropped the case.

Skeletal three-act macro plot

Alongside all of these stories runs the macro, the story of how the corrupt mayor and his officials manage to get a major development on track. It dramatises the theme of corruption in high places. Notice that it is skeletal. This does not matter. It is there to provide connection and point to the theme. The characters concerned are the mayor, his assistant Pauley (Joe's brother), a corrupt lawyer from the district attorney's office, and an ambitious detective, O'Brien. It consists of a disturbance (the development), followed by a first-act turning point (the news that investors will back out if building does not commence immediately), a second act showing their attempts to force Joe to burn the building down and, as third act and climax, how they discover and use Nicky's criminal act to force Joe to do their bidding.

Section 2

Multiple protagonist narrative

Chapter 27

Multiple protagonist narrative: An introduction

MULTIPLE PROTAGONIST FILMS ARE about the 'adventure' of a group and the heat of the idea is the actions and personal relationships of this group. If your film idea or a film you want to use as a model concerns a group of people (for example, a troubled family, any kind of team, a group of students, inhabitants of a town), all of whom are involved in the same 'adventure' with the group's survival under threat, what you are looking at is probably not a single-hero story, but a story about multiple protagonists. Your motto here is: 'same team, same adventure'.

Multiple protagonist films are very popular all over the world because they provide a means to look at group mentality and group interaction—individuals under pressure from society—something that conventional 'one hero/one journey' does not address. Examples include *The Full Monty*, *Little Miss Sunshine*, *American Beauty*, *Revolutionary Road*, *The Magnificent Seven*, *Gosford Park*, *Crouching Tiger, Hidden Dragon*, *The Jane Austen Book Club*, *Ordinary People*, *Chicken Run*, *The Big Chill* and *Saving Private Ryan*.

When multiple protagonist scripts fail

Tragically, multiple protagonist scripts routinely fail and are abandoned. This is a very serious problem, as many cultures are extremely interested in external social pressures on individuals and small groups, equally if not more so than in individual spiritual quests.

I think there are two reasons why scripts and films like these fail. The first is that the scripts lack an action line and consist of characters in search of a plot, probably a result of the misunderstanding I pointed out earlier, whereby people believe there is a particular sort of film known as the 'character-driven' film that can operate successfully without a plot. As successful multiple protagonist stories are often described as character-driven it's easy for film-makers to feel that an interesting group of characters will *per se* make a film. However, as we've seen, character-driven means the very opposite of 'no plot'. It means 'character displayed through a characteristic story' and, while successful multiple protagonist films do have very interesting characters, far from having no plot, they are very intricately plotted and involve a mesh of interwoven action and relationship line strands in almost every scene.

The second reason that these scripts fail is because the received wisdom is that every script must be about a single protagonist on a journey into self-knowledge. A character from the group is therefore selected as the single hero and, while the group's fascinating activities and interaction (the real heat of the film) get pushed into the background, centre stage is given over to a tired spiritual fulfilment journey involving this individual with, usually, an equally clichéd romance. The reason the plot material is tired is because nobody involved with the film—writer, director or producer—is really interested in it. It's there solely because it's thought to be compulsory. For an extensive study of films that are inherently group stories but are either characters in search of a plot or are structured as single-hero stories, see pp. 421–33.

Is my film a multiple protagonist film?

The heat of a multiple protagonist film—its point—is the interaction of the group, and to service that heat you need to provide plot material that not only follows the group in its group adventure, but also depicts the individual journeys of each character, and the characters' interactions. If you don't, your film is likely to go round in circles.

You can pick whether your material is a multiple protagonist story by asking whether what excites you about it is not one individual or a relationship between two people, but one of the following:

1 a group of people
2 how an individual is limited or in some way affected by a group
3 how an individual affects a group

Several versions of the same protagonist

The most useful way to understand how to construct multiple protagonist scripts is to think of the group as being versions of the same protagonist.

Take *The Full Monty*. We follow different versions of 'the unemployed man from the North of England preparing to perform in a striptease show'. In *The Big Chill* we follow different versions of 'the radical student ten years on faced with the suicide of a charismatic leader'. In *Monsoon Wedding*, the group is 'people connected by a big wedding'. In *The Jane Austen Book Club*, all of the women are modern versions of Jane Austen heroines, and all are in a book club.

This is why there is no sense of dislocation or of 'being in a different film' when the plot switches from one group member to another (as there would be in a conventional one-hero film)—because the whole point of a multiple protagonist film is to observe members of a group. This is why in *The Full Monty* it feels perfectly natural for the action often to leave Gaz (the character who first had the idea of a male striptease show) to follow the story of other group members—such as the overweight man who is worried about showing his naked body, or the ex-manager who cannot tell his wife that he has been sacked. And not only does it feel quite natural to follow each character, it makes the film because what the film is 'about' is a group of men, not just Gaz. Some of the protagonists in the film will be more prominent than others.

The team on a group journey or adventure

Multiple protagonist structure is about several people travelling the same journey, with the story passed from one protagonist to the next, like a relay race, and each character showing a different response to the quest, siege or reunion adventure. In a normal three-act single-hero structure, changing protagonists several times would be disastrous. But there is no disjunction in multiple protagonist films when a different protagonist takes over the story because the new one is just a different version of the one we've just been following. Each is reacting in a different way to the same crisis and the same choices, which is exactly what an audience comes to a group film to see. Approaching your film as a multiple protagonist story will stop you from creating a group of characters in search of a plot. The spark of your film—its heat—is the group, so you must create plots and relationship-line material that will properly display your group.

Quests, reunions and sieges

Very conveniently, successful multiple protagonist films always seem to have the same plot material. They seem always to be about a group quest, a group reunion or a group siege (which includes emotional or psychological sieges, as in people trapped in families or social roles). This is probably because quests, reunions and sieges are ideal subject matter to explore a group since they throw the group together in close physical proximity and send it on an adventure under danger and stress with a lot to lose. All of these elements provide great scope for character exploration and interaction and, in plot-terms, suspenseful build to a climax. Often, the categories overlap; for example, *Little Miss Sunshine* and *Chicken Run* both mix a quest with a siege. A siege becomes a quest when all of the characters escape their prison. Similarly, if characters in a quest get trapped in any kind of prison, their quest will turn into a siege.

All varieties include one character who causes the quest, siege or reunion, a character we can call 'the instigator' (in *Scriptwriting Updated* I called this character 'the dominant character', but instigator is more descriptive), and which we'll look at in detail below.

The quest, siege or reunion will be the main action line—the group action line, the adventure—of the film. If your material sounds like any of the topics below, you are probably writing a multiple protagonist film. Social minorities are automatically in a siege situation with regard to the majority, and many multiple protagonist films in all categories feature social minorities (for example women, teenagers, ethnic groups). Because of this, there will be an added layer to the quest, mission or siege, because each member represents a different minority response. In cases like these, you might find you prefer to use tandem or fractured tandem narrative.

QUESTS

Quest films are about groups forced into a quest to survive and prevail. They join together to achieve a common goal. Often they start out as a team, if not, they soon become one. The instigator is usually the person who caused the quest, or leads it. Typical story topics with examples are:

ONE LAST JOB

A group of ex-colleagues reunite to perform one last enterprise, often criminal (*Ocean's Eleven* (and its sequels), *Space Cowboys*, *Crouching Tiger, Hidden Dragon*, *Sleepers*).

SOLDIERS ON A NEAR-IMPOSSIBLE QUEST

A group of soldiers or quasi-soldiers attempts a very dangerous quest. Many war stories are group stories, with each soldier being a different version of 'the soldier'. The instigator will usually be the leader (*Saving Private Ryan, Dirty Dozen, The Magnificent Seven, Stand by Me, Galaxy Quest* (which is also a reunion film), *Deliverance, Space Cowboys*).

THE CINDERELLA SPORTS TEAM

A struggling sports team enters a competition and triumphs, sometimes actually but always morally. The instigator is often a fairy godmother figure, someone new who comes into the group and leads the quest (*Mystery, Alaska, As It Is in Heaven, The Mighty Ducks, Brassed Off, A League of Their Own, Any Given Sunday*).

'LET'S PUT ON A SHOW'

This overlaps with the Cinderella team idea. A group of people, often amateurs, decides to put on a play or perform for the public. The instigator will be the person who suggests the show. The group sometimes wins literally but always wins morally (*The Full Monty, The Commitments, Cosi, Little Miss Sunshine* (which is also a version of 'soldiers on a near-impossible quest'), *Calendar Girls*).

GROUP JOURNEYS

A group on a journey of any kind—a group prison break, group holiday, group expedition etc. (*The Great Escape, The Hangover, City Slickers*).

REUNIONS

Reunions are the hardest form, because of their potential to be static. The instigator is usually the person who initiates the reunion (it may even be the corpse), or makes trouble at the reunion. Typical story topics are:

WEDDINGS, FUNERALS, FAMILY (OR *DE FACTO* FAMILY) RITUALS

This involves people assembling before or after a wedding or funeral (*The Big Chill, Death at a Funeral, Invasion of the Barbarians, Radiance, Cat on a Hot Tin Roof, After the Wedding, Monsoon Wedding, Steel Magnolias*).

THE CLUB/WORKMATES/THE CLASS

This story material is about a group of people that meets regularly, either because they work together, or because they are friends, or because they share similar interests. Examples include: *The Jane Austen Book Club*, *Love! Valor! Compassion!*, *The Dinner Guest*. However, note *The Joy Luck Club*, which is in consecutive stories form.

SEEKING OUT THE FAMILY

In this, a prodigal returns, or an upright person seeks out a disreputable family member and their friends. Examples are: *You Can Count on Me* (which is also a family siege film), *All about My Mother*. If the action stays for the vast majority of the time with one character, the film is probably a one-hero structure.

SIEGE FILMS

Sieges involve a group in some way trapped together and trying to break out—either literally, as in a prison, emotionally, as in a family, or socially, as in a social class, ethnic or gender minority, or a community. In social sieges (such as *American Beauty* and *Revolutionary Road*), the instigator will be challenging the status quo. In actual physical sieges (prisons or quasi-prisons) the instigator will be the person leading the escape attempt. Typical story content is:

TROUBLED FAMILIES (THE EMOTIONAL SIEGE)

In this, family members are emotionally (and sometimes physically) imprisoned with each other. To be a multiple protagonist story, the story must be about the whole family's interaction, following all or several members, not just one or two. Examples of family sieges are: *To Live*, *Ordinary People*, *Little Miss Sunshine* and *American Beauty*.

PRISONS

Inmates of a prison either find creative ways to cope with incarceration or try to escape. Examples are: *The Great Escape*, *Chicken Run*, *Paradise Road*, *Paradise Grove* and *Cocoon*.

SAVE OUR TOWN!

Members of a small community encounter a force for change (either from within or from the world outside) and either fear their way of life is under threat or see an opportunity for the town to benefit. Examples are: *Waking Ned Devine*, *The Swamp Dwellers*.

Subgroups use the following storylines:
- Townsfolk feel threatened by an outsider who turns out to be a

mentor antagonist, a teacher figure who shows them how to be better people (for example, *Chocolat*, *As It Is in Heaven*, *Italian for Beginners*).

- Townsfolk convert and save the person who came to destroy them (as in *Local Hero*).
- Townsfolk close ranks against one or more individuals who are trying to break the rules (for example, *American Beauty*, *Revolutionary Road*, *Mystic River*).

COMIC HEIST, KIDNAP

Bungling criminals attempting to commit a crime draw together a group of allies and opponents, who often have never met before (for example, *Burn After Reading*, *Ruthless People*).

Not all quests, sieges and reunions are multiple protagonist films

Not all stories about groups or people in siege situations (including unhappy families) are multiple protagonist stories. Many are normal three-act one-hero structures (as in *The Counterfeiters* and *Cadillac Man*), or (as in *The Shawshank Redemption* and *Clubland* aka *Introducing the Dwights*), mentor antagonist stories. Again, many disaster movies are simply a vehicle for one saviour figure. Essentially, if the film stays primarily with the point of view of one character, it's a single-hero film. The test is, if you can remove the individual stories of group members (leaving only the story of the central character) and still have a story (albeit diminished), it's a single-hero. *Four Weddings* could work with just Charlie's story because his friends' stories occur only when Charlie is present and is the primary focus. However, if you remove the team of strippers from *The Full Monty*, you don't have a film. You need to know this so you know what (and what not) to plot.

Survival macro: 'Will the group survive?'

When we were looking at tandem narrative I introduced the idea of the macro, an overarching plot that shows the film's theme in action and holds all of the stories together. Multiple protagonist films also have a macro but it is always on the same theme; namely, the survival of the group. Even in gentle versions, there is always a threat to the group, and this threat causes the group adventure, often even the formation of the group. The macro is always centred on the question 'Will the group survive?' More precisely, 'Will the group emerge from the quest, siege or reunion *intact, changed or destroyed*?.' In gentler films, the destruction or break-up of the group may not be of major concern to group members, but in serious films it can literally be a matter of life and death.

In quests, often an actual physical threat to life is involved (as in *Saving Private Ryan*, *The Magnificent Seven* etc.). In sieges, the threat is sometimes to physical survival (as in *Chicken Run*), sometimes to emotional survival (*Ordinary People*) or sometimes to both (*American Beauty*). In reunion forms, the question is whether the group will survive the reunion emotionally, or whether it will split up. The issue of survival in reunions can come about in three ways. Sometimes the reunion has been caused by the death or imminent death of a key member (as in *The Big Chill*, *Radiance*, *Cat on a Hot Tin Roof*, or, in comic form, *Death at a Funeral*) and the question is whether the group will survive the loss of this member. Sometimes an external threat has caused the group to meet or form (for example, the group of gay men in *Love! Valor! Compassion!* meet because of the external threat of AIDS, and the club in *The Jane Austen Book Club* comes together out of one character's desire to help others in emotional crisis). Finally, the threat can appear at the start of the reunion, as in *Monsoon Wedding*, where suddenly the bride-to-be is having second thoughts.

I've said that reunion films are the hardest multiple protagonist films to write. It's because they do not arrive with any suggestion of plot (there is no quest to pursue or prison to break out of). As we'll see, the difference between strong and weak reunion films is that good reunion films have a plot about a threat to the group and bad versions don't. Weak reunion films are characters in search of a plot, and the missing plot is a macro about group survival in the face of a threat to the group. We'll come back to this later.

The macro and death

I mentioned that group reunions are often triggered by death or the threat of it. Significantly, almost all multiple protagonist films, even gentle versions like *Little Miss Sunshine* and *The Jane Austen Book Club* and comic treatments like *Death at a Funeral*, *The Hangover* and the black gangster comedy *In Bruges*, involve or touch on death. Death often starts the quest, reunion or siege story, lifting the stakes and frequently being the crucial factor in the film's rising suspense and climax. Multiple protagonist films in which death arrives very late typically meander before its arrival (as do *Topsy-Turvy* and *Parallel Lives*). Sometimes the group will reinvent itself and survive in a life-affirming way after a death, as in *The Big Chill*. Sometimes the group will be destroyed (*American Beauty* and *Ordinary People*). Alternatively, the group may triumph even though its members suffer and some die, as in *The*

Magnificent Seven, Saving Private Ryan, Little Miss Sunshine and, bleakly, *Revolutionary Road.*

Roles and masks
THE INSTIGATOR
As I've outlined above, multiple protagonist films always have an instigator character like Gaz in *The Full Monty,* Lester in *American Beauty* or little Olive in *Little Miss Sunshine;* someone who creates the group's task or problem, or is in charge of it, leading its members on their adventure. Instigators cause writers a lot of confusion because it's easy to mistake them for sole protagonists who need a journey to spiritual growth. Hence, writers often produce plots that take the instigator away from the group into a separate adventure, which forces the film's heat—the group—to the margins of the story.

Some other examples of instigators are: Captain John H. Miller in *Saving Private Ryan;* Ginger in *Chicken Run;* the conductor Daniel Daréus in *As It Is in Heaven;* Jen, the young woman warrior in *Crouching Tiger, Hidden Dragon;* Alex, the suicide in *The Big Chill;* Linda Litske in *Burn After Reading;* and Ned in *Waking Ned Devine.*

Most importantly, the instigator not only creates the adventure but in most cases generates conflict within the group, often about how they are running the adventure.

In many cases the instigator is the group's salvation, as in *The Jane Austen Book Club.* In others, as in *American Beauty*, the instigator threatens the group, destroys it and is crushed by it. Sometimes the instigator is a newcomer to the group, sometimes a long-term member. Sometimes, as in *Little Miss Sunshine,* the instigator is not a leader but someone who needs the group's protection and help. Sometimes (in fact, quite often) the instigator is dead as in *The Big Chill, Waking Ned Devine* and, hilariously, *Death at a Funeral.* In *Revolutionary Road,* the husband, Frank Wheeler, starts out as the instigator rejecting the status quo, gets his wife April to join him and then returns to the group, leaving her tragically and fatally marginalised.

Just as multiple protagonist films need a macro plot about a quest, reunion or siege, so they also need an instigator to lead the quest or siege; to cause problems at a reunion and, in all three forms, to provoke conflict, dissent and divided loyalties. Without internal conflict, the group can only react to outside forces, which significantly reduces the film's interest.

Of course, the intensity and nature of feelings towards the instigator will vary enormously with the subject matter. Everyone in *American Beauty* wants to kill Lester, but everyone in *Little Miss Sunshine* wants to protect Olive, and everyone in *The Jane Austen Book Club* looks to Bernadette for support. But in all cases, the instigator provokes strong emotions. For a multiple protagonist film constructed as if the instigator is a single hero, with problematic effects, see *Bootmen* (pp. 424–5).

THE OUTSIDER

The second character type that routinely appears in multiple protagonist films is 'the outsider'. The outsider is a character who exists alongside the group but is not part of it. Outsiders are useful because they can articulate the group's rules and taboos and cause conflict either by challenging the group, trying to change it, or by seeking membership. In *The Jane Austen Book Club*, the outsider is Grigg, the sole man in the group. In *The Big Chill*, the outsider is the apparently fatuous young woman who was the dead man's lover. In *The Magnificent Seven* it is the young Mexican villager Chico, who wants to be a hired gun and is permitted to join the seven, but in the end leaves for love and a normal life in the village. *American Beauty* has Ricky Fitts as its outsider and *Revolutionary Road* has the ex-mathematician psychiatric patient, John Givings. In *Ordinary People* the outsider is the psychiatrist, and in *Little Miss Sunshine* it is the depressed academic.

The outsider is another figure who can be mistaken for a single protagonist, as in *28 Days* and *The Oyster Farmer* (see pp. 423–4, 426–7).

THE TRAITOR WITHIN

The traitor within is an even stronger force for conflict and suspense than the outsider. The traitor within is a group member who disagrees with the instigator, and tries to sabotage, discredit, overthrow or even kill them. Multiple protagonist stories about wars or gangsters will always have a traitor within trying to sabotage the leader. In *American Beauty* the traitor within is Frank Fitts. In *Ordinary People*, it is the mother. In *Little Miss Sunshine* it is the sulky son, and in *Galaxy Quest* it is Alexander Dane, the acidic, one-time Shakespearean actor. In *Revolutionary Road*, Frank Wheeler eventually becomes the traitor within.

The traitor within is also sometimes mistaken for a single hero, as in *Mo' Better Blues* (see pp. 425–6).

Characters can swap roles

Fascinatingly, characters in multiple protagonist films can take it in turns to play the role of traitor within and outsider—to great effect. For example, in the *The Full Monty*, sometimes Gaz's little son is the outsider. At other times the outsider is Gerald the ex-manager, but sometimes Gerald is the traitor within. Sometimes Dave, the chubby man who is too shy to perform is the traitor within. Right at the end of the film, Gaz himself is the traitor within—when he won't go on stage and his young son has to persuade him to go.

In multiple protagonist films with small casts, the cast will routinely swap these roles. This happens in *You Can Count on Me*, in which the multiple protagonists are a brother and sister orphaned as children trying to overcome their respective responses to the trauma; the sister being someone who always wants to please, while the brother is a weak, self-doubting wanderer. The same role-swapping happens in *In Bruges*.

Multiple antagonists

Strictly speaking, we should speak about 'multiple protagonists/antagonists form' because many group films are actually about a group of charismatic mentor antagonists who save or influence a young or helpless protagonist in what are really coming-of-age films; for example, *Tea with Mussolini*, *The Magnificent Seven* and *Saving Private Ryan*.

Another kind of multiple mentor antagonist film is the *Local Hero* model, where an outsider learns from a group which he or she joins (in which case members of the group are mentor antagonists). The reverse of this is the *As It Is in Heaven* model, seen also in *The Dead Poet's Society*, where an outsider is the mentor antagonist who transforms the group of protagonists.

Most of what I say about the structure of multiple protagonist films applies equally well to multiple antagonist films. The important thing with these stories, as with all group stories, is that the plot you use must provide sufficient opportunities to properly explore the personalities and interaction of *the group*, and many story strands dealing with group interaction need to be carefully interwoven into the fabric of the film. Multiple antagonist films always revisit the protagonist at the end of the film, even if it is only momentarily, to provide closure. The final appearance of the protagonist can provide a good final twist, as in the bookend scenes in *Saving Private Ryan*.

Chapter 28
Multiple protagonists: Preliminary plotting

CREATING A MULTIPLE PROTAGONIST film is like driving a team of dogs or horses: each team member has its own mind but you must keep them running simultaneously, at the same pace and towards the same goal.

Your writing problem is that multiple protagonist films require you take not just one protagonist on an adventure, but about six, all of whom must be explained and taken on their individual emotional journeys (as well as on the group adventure) in the screen time of a conventional one-hero film. The only way to include all of these story strands is to interweave several within individual scenes, making almost every scene transmit more than one storyline. This means you have to choose your scenes extremely carefully, with a view to how much you can pack into them, how many story strands you can take forward simultaneously. Every scene must earn its keep.

The five story strands you have to plan separately then interweave

Let's look at the five kinds of story strands you have to understand, create and interweave—adding up to a vast number.

There are two main sorts of story in multiple protagonist films. There is what happened, is happening and will happen to *the group*, and there is what happened, is happening and will happen to *each individual*. Let's look at them in *The Jane Austen Book Club*. The five kinds of storylines are:

1. THE GROUP ADVENTURE (ACTION LINE) IN THE PRESENT

This is a quest, siege or reunion involving a threat to the group which forms the group 'adventure'. This adventure (the macro) is the vital connecting element and it is a fully developed (if sometimes skeletal) three-act action line. In *The Jane Austen Book Club*, a group of people form a book club at the instigation of Bernadette.

2. THE GROUP ADVENTURE (ACTION LINE) IN THE PAST

In multiple protagonist films, this is the group's activities—its action line—in the past (for example, what a gang of thieves did together in the past). In films where the group has no shared past this can be minimal, but where it does it can be extensive and very important. It is particularly important in reunion films, which are all about unfinished business. The group in *The Jane Austen Book Club* was never a book club in the past, so there is no proper past group adventure (although there is a lot of emotional baggage from the past).

3. EACH PROTAGONIST'S ACTION LINE IN THE GROUP ADVENTURE

This is how each protagonist is physically affected by the group adventure, and what they do within it. If you have six protagonists, you will have six of these. Sometimes they will be little three-act structures, other times they will be one-act structures. In *The Jane Austen Book Club*, it is how each member reacts to the challenge of providing notes on their book, and how each behaves at group meetings.

4. THE RELATIONSHIP LINES IN THE PAST

This is how each character interacted with the others in the past. If you have six protagonists who knew each other in the past you must include plot material for each protagonist's interactions with the other five. In *The Jane Austen Book Club*, the past relationships between Bernadette, Slyvia and Jocelyn are very important to the story. The desire of Bernadette and Jocelyn to help Sylvia is central to the formation and continuation of the club.

5. THE RELATIONSHIP LINES IN THE PRESENT

These show the emotional stresses of each individual in the present. Additionally, if relevant, they will show how unfinished business from the past impacts on the present. In *The Jane Austen Book Club*, these stories in the present are very important. They are particularly highly developed for Prudie, Sylvia and Jocelyn, less so for Allegra and Grigg, and almost non-existent for Bernadette. Jocelyn's story is very much about how the past has created her and how she has to shed it. Each story also depicts how each woman is a different Jane Austen heroine.

Simple arithmetic tells you just how much backstory and exposition you have to get into these films. We will look at how exactly you can plan and handle this story material below. The point to remember here is that good character exploration will not happen just because your characters are interesting. You must create and cleverly insert situations that depict character through action and provide opportunities to visit any unfinished emotional business.

But perhaps it's tandem narrative?

How do you know your idea isn't best served by tandem narrative, which also deals with groups? Why do I say that *Lantana* is a tandem narrative film and *American Beauty* is a multiple protagonist film? Aren't all of the protagonists in *Lantana* versions of the same protagonist? Aren't both films social sieges? And does it matter?

It may. The distinction is not academic. There are significant differences in theme and message, and as a result of that, in story material, hence structure. Message-wise, tandem narrative is interested in the group for what it tells us about society, whereas multiple protagonist form is interested in the group for what it tells us about individuals in a group situation. More precisely, tandem is about a group defined by society, a group that is interesting because of the diversity of its members. In contrast, multiple protagonist form is about the interaction of a closely knit group on an adventure and under threat. These differences can be seen in the plot material of each form.

In tandem:

- The group is a social grouping (for example, people living in or visiting Nashville, people linked by a murder investigation, people linked by drugs).
- One or two group members might know each other, or get to know each other during the story, but rarely does the whole group know each other.
- There is no group quest, siege or reunion.
- Members always or mostly have their adventures away from the group with characters who are not part of the group.

In multiple protagonist form:

- Members are involved in a group quest, reunion or siege.
- Group members all know each other (either from the start, or as they band together on their group adventure).
- The individual stories are caused by the group quest, reunion or siege and normally, but not always, happen during dealings with other group members.
- One member will be causing the others trouble, in some way initiating or furthering the adventure.

- There will be a character or characters acting as the outsider and the traitor within (sometimes these roles will be played in turn by various characters, and sometimes there will be duplicates).
- Conflict between group members during the adventure is central to the film's interest.

We can see the difference by thinking about *Nashville*. As the film stands, it is a tandem narrative about the diverse inhabitants of Nashville. If all of the inhabitants of Nashville started on a group quest, or were thrown together in a siege, or had a reunion, it would be multiple protagonist form and you would need to explore their interaction.

Big casts are best served by tandem

As we've seen discussing tandem narrative, multiple protagonist films can only handle five or six characters because the form requires each character to take the limelight alone for a significant amount of time. In contrast, tandem permits several characters to be explored within each story, which means they can successfully handle huge casts.

Chapter 29
Multiple protagonists: Plotting the group action line

IN MULTIPLE PROTAGONIST FORM the group story, the macro—the quest, siege, or reunion adventure—is your lifeline because it holds everything together, giving your characters action towards a goal. Like all action lines, it is a chronological sequence of events, hence it has a timeline and can therefore form the spine of your film, giving you clues as to where to locate steps in the relationship storylines. So start your planning with it. As you go, you will be using all of the charts, diagrams, narrative sentences and basic Smiley/Thompson plans discussed earlier in the context of conventional narrative.

Work out your threat
The group story, the macro, depends on a threat to the group's survival. Once the survival threat is decided, the steps in the group's action line can be devised by thinking:

1 what situations could credibly happen, and
2 what each group member would do in response. Each individual needs a story in which they are seen to react in their individual way to the group threat.

Sketch out your three-act structure
Start by sketching out a three-act structure plan for the quest, siege or reunion, as if you were planning a conventional one-hero model but, for the moment, imagine the group as one protagonist (this is because each member will be engaged on the same action towards the same goal—they will just feel and behave differently about it). Essentially, whether it is a quest, siege or reunion, your group will be faced with a threat; they will make a plan, try to implement that plan, have problems and finally succeed or fail. Start by listing, in just a few words, the threat, plan, implementation of that plan, problems and success or failure.

Reunions, except those such as weddings and funerals that arrive with a clear progression of events, might be a bit harder, but try at least to sketch out the start, the middle and the end. However limited this is, it is your first line of defence in preventing characters in search of a plot.

Next, try to work out the group adventure's basic Smiley/Thompson structure and simple and advanced narrative sentence (of course, this is just a start, you will keep returning to this as you go). This Smiley/Thompson structure will start to lock in rising suspense and surprises, all building to climax.

The disturbance will usually be the arrival of the threat and the first-act turning point will be some event or consequence that makes responding to the threat essential. Think of this as: 'the team decides to take action'. Your climax will be an answer to the question 'Does the group survive the threat, if so, in what form, if not, what happens?' Your resolution will indicate how the world went on after the threat ended.

Skeletal action line

Because there are so many parallel stories to tell, the group's action line—the macro, the adventure—often has to be skeletal. This is not to say that it has to be trite—quite the opposite—but it cannot contain too many twists and turns because there is simply not enough time, particularly if it's an action movie. This often skeletal plot needs to be carefully planned so that what steps there are can provide maximum potential for the development of the other stories. This is akin to making sure every stop in a journey movie is impelling characters and plot forwards. I discuss the practical details of plotting the group action line later in this chapter.

Multiple protagonist form often borrows from other parallel narrative forms

For example, *Saving Private Ryan*, *Tea with Mussolini* and *American Beauty* all use bookend flashback (see pp. 175, 257–9). Bookend flashbacks don't change the way you plot a multiple protagonist film because they can be added to the plan after you've worked out the group action line.

Shouldn't you start with the characters?

One could argue that planning should start by analysing your characters in depth because multiple protagonist form is all about the conflict within a group of characters. However, starting with detailed character exploration tends to push writers into creating characters in search of a plot, so I would suggest that you start on the action line because then, when you do explore your characters, it won't be in isolation, it will be in terms of how they act and interact in the group adventure.

How to find a group adventure

Writers are often attracted by a group but don't have a group adventure to send it on. Here is how you might start to find one.

Imagine you were fascinated by the comic possibilities of a remote, anti-quated little town full of colourful characters that pride themselves on being behind the times. You want to write a comedy about it but you don't yet have a main action line. You could easily make those characters start walking around and behaving in character, interacting as they bump into each other—as many weak multiple protagonist films do. You could go slightly further and have someone returning to the town after many years—and bumping into your colourful characters as they are walking around. However, in both cases, you would really have only characters in search of a plot. Your characters are just *being*, not *doing*. You don't yet have a spine to your film, you need a group adventure.

WHAT DOES THE GROUP VALUE AND WHAT THREATENS IT?

To get a group adventure, you need to invent something that threatens the group's survival so the individuals will band together and take action. To do that, isolate what the townspeople love and value (which will need to be unique and interesting, because it defines the 'new world' we need for a good film), then work on a real but unusual *quest, reunion or siege story* that threatens it and, most crucially, threatens their survival as a group. This plot must let you explore precisely what is interesting and unique about your group, which is the heat of your idea.

WHAT DOES OUR TOWNSHIP VALUE?

Our township hates interference from the outside world, so what would bring the outside world into our township? One thing would be television. Let's choose television. The next step is to work out what the group could do in response to the threat of TV coming to their town. The group story will be a team mission, reunion or siege, so brainstorm what these might be, making the coming of TV (and the group's reaction to it) genuinely threaten the group's survival. Do they go on the attack (a quest)? Or do they go into defence (siege)? Remember that survival can be threatened not only by exter-nal threats but by internal disagreements, defections and the like.

Your group story exists to explore the characters, so find a story that gives you the best chance to do that. Brainstorm what the group of townspeople could do in the face of a newcomer with TV. Brainstorm how the group could fight back, how their fight could go wrong, and how the group might start to fracture from inside. Brainstorm the practical problems a newcomer to town with a TV would actually face and don't forget to brainstorm the newcomer him or herself. Does the newcomer have to be a newcomer? Could they be a previous resident returning? The story of a township under threat from TV is inherently a siege, but if the person with TV is a resident or a previous resident returning, it becomes an internal siege, where a member on the inside decides to challenge the status quo (as in *American Beauty* or *Revolutionary Road*). This is useful to know, because it will suggest a kind of 'civil war' dilemma and responses.

A quest might take the group to fight their battle outside of their township, as in *The Castle*, where a family whose home is under threat from a planned airport development take their case to the highest court in the land. Alternatively, a reunion might be involved, where the TV issue is linked to, say, a wedding or funeral. In the case of our township, it could be, say, a funeral where it is revealed that an upright citizen secretly had a TV.

In all of these cases, the disturbance is the start of the threat, but in some films the threat may come at the first-act turning point. Play with possibilities.

POINTS TO REMEMBER ABOUT YOUR GROUP ADVENTURE
- Except in comic or very gentle versions of the form, you need a significant threat to the group. If the threat isn't big or credible enough (a) you won't have inbuilt suspense and (b) your script will probably end up slow and/or far-fetched.
- The group action line will be the action the townspeople take, so in this case it will be a siege or quest or both.
- In structural terms, the start of the threat is the disturbance of the group story.
- Thus, in our film, the normality of the group action line is the township before the TV arrives, and the disturbance is the arrival of TV, which needs to be introduced by someone. This person is the one causing the group's problem, so is the instigator.
- The group action line will be the steps the townspeople take to get rid of TV.
- The climax will be whether the township stays the same, is changed (if so, in what way) or is destroyed (if so, in what way).
- Since this is a comedy, the comic climax will need to be very funny. Your whole film will be leading to this comic climax, so it will take work.

- The third-act battle that precedes the climax of the film will be a battle against TV, with the climax the final battle.
- The other plotlines about the individuals will all be about how the newcomer with their TV affects them and their interpersonal relationships with the group.

The opening is vital: Normality and disturbance

It is very easy for group stories to meander, which wastes audience goodwill. The audience has to know as early as possible 'whose film' it is and, since the answer is 'the group's film', the group has to be set up early, preferably in the opening moments. Additionally, the audience needs to know what the film is 'about', which in a multiple protagonist film, is the group story, the macro.

So, establish the normality of each protagonist early on and the normality of the group (if it already exists) plus the arrival of the threat (the action-line disturbance). You might actually open on the disturbance scene, implying the normality as you go.

This is harder to do than it might seem. Because film is very fast at transmitting visual information and very slow at transmitting information through dialogue, you usually need to open the film showing your many protagonists in their normalities away from each other *or* where they interact as a group. For example, if your protagonists are all members of a band, you might want to start your film with the band rehearsing, simultaneously showing each individual's idiosyncrasies and the group dynamic. You might actually want to insert the disturbance in this group meeting, before following each protagonist to their home in some interesting and original way, so the audience can learn about their domestic normality. If you do this your audience immediately knows it's in a group film and starts enjoying the individual members.

If you try to introduce your protagonists in a neutral setting, you will need to explain them via dialogue, which is very time-consuming and leads to the sense of the film going nowhere. We can see the problems that result from this in *Parallel Lives*, where the film opens at a college as people assemble for a reunion, requiring each of the characters to be explained via dialogue. This rapidly becomes boring and gets the film off to a very slow and shaky start, taking twenty minutes to establish its many characters (too many to handle in a multiple protagonist film, another unfortunate misjudgment).

By contrast, successful multiple protagonist films tend to set up their group and group threat (the disturbance) very early on. In *The Big Chill*, the disturbance of the group action line, the suicide, is cleverly set up during the opening credits by each member in their normality receiving the news of

Alex's death. Note, by the way, the clever exposition in the opening moments of the film. The little boy is singing the 1971 hit 'Jeremiah was a Bullfrog', which he must have learnt from his parents. This not only places the parents culturally and in a particular time but, along with the fact that the father not the mother is bathing the child, reveals their style of parenting.

American Beauty also uses the set-up trick of opening the film on the characters' normality, plus a shock mention of death, but in reverse, with death introduced before the characters' normality.

The comedy *Galaxy Quest* is equally brilliant in its set-up of its group of has-been actors. The film opens with part of an episode from a discontinued space-odyssey TV series in which they used to perform. It then cuts to a shopping mall where, we discover, a fan rally is being held. It then goes backstage to where the group of now has-been actors from the show is waiting to go on, discussing the past and bickering in character, each revealing their idiosyncrasies. We realise instantly that this is our group and is 'what the film is about'. By the end of the sequence, we know all about the group's past and its present. Also, although we don't realise it, the film's action line (good aliens arriving to enlist the actors' help against bad aliens) has been cleverly set up.

Significantly, a comment quite often made about the hilarious and enormously successful *Burn After Reading* is that it took a long while to start. Technically, this is probably because the group threat in the comic heist/siege plot is the discovery of the floppy disc containing the ex-CIA man's memoirs, and neither that nor the setting-up of the group itself happens until some time into the story—not a great deal of time, but sufficient for some audience members to ask: 'Where is this going?'

Chapter 30
Multiple protagonists: Plotting relationship lines

AS WE'VE SEEN, MULTIPLE protagonist films have many relationship lines to get across and very little time in which to do it. Sometimes when multiple protagonist films are discussed the various story strands are referred to as 'subplots'. This is misleading because it suggests that the film should constantly be going off at a tangent from the main group-threat adventure. The opposite is true: relationship material in these films must happen *because of* the group adventure—the group adventure forces the relationship material to happen. The motto here, as in conventional narrative, is 'what happens in the adventure causes what happens in the relationship strands'. This points you towards the story material you need and a place where you can insert it. It means, for example, that specifically *because* of a group threat, your characters will revisit old hostilities or form new alliances. And not only does the relationship matter happen because of the group threat, it happens *during* scenes involving the group adventure.

For example, you may know that during the course of your film two of your characters need to comically explore and resolve their sibling rivalry issues, but you don't know where or how or why. However, once you've sketched out your group action-line quest, siege or reunion you will be able to find reasons and opportunities for your angry siblings to fight, compete and reconcile as the group adventure is happening, and slot them in.

Imagine that your sibling-rivalry story strand occurs in a multiple protagonist prison-break story. Imagine the two rival siblings are escaping from prison down a tunnel. The stresses of escaping down the tunnel can credibly cause them to throw the past back at each other. That way, one scene is furthering the main action line (the escape) and two character lines (sibling one and sibling two). Further, since the characters' quarrel may well impact on other members of your group and cause them to react in character, suddenly your scene is carrying many character story stands as well as the macro, the group action line. Also, of course, your sibling rivalry will impact on the group adventure. For example, your siblings could be so busy having an argument that they don't hear the prison siren go off, which means the rest of the group, still waiting to enter the tunnel, get caught. Actively search for ways like this to combine storylines.

Exploring the characters
CHARACTER AND STORY STRANDS
Multiple protagonist films are always primarily character studies, often stories about unfinished business, so you need to choose and know your characters in depth so that you can create a plot that contains events capable of revealing them through action. Choose your characters very carefully, making them interesting, different, and real but unusual characters. You will have to exert great self-control not to let them run away with you and lead you into a plot that doesn't serve your ideas. Remind yourself that the heat of your story is not the group, but the group in action pursuing a specific goal. If you don't get the proper action-line plot, your interesting characters will rapidly become boring. From the start, link your character exploration by thinking what kind of quest, reunion or siege they need to best display them.

Character profiles
Most multiple protagonist stories have only about six characters because each character needs to take centre stage for so long. Create group members who have a skill or ineptitude that will be useful in your main action line and make sure characters have a basis for conflict, or else your only threat will be from the outside, which is much less interesting. The more potential for internal conflict within the group, the more scope you have for character interaction. If your characters have known each other for years, look for unfinished business that can play a part in the present.

ROLES AND MASKS
You may already have a instigator in your initial idea. If not, create an original and interesting version to initiate the task or trouble and be the focus of loyalty, animosity, rebellion or other strong emotions. Look for a similarly interesting and original outsider and traitor within, and be aware that these roles can be played temporarily by other characters. If your group is large, you may have a number of different versions of the traitor within or outsider, as happens in *Love! Valor! Compassion!*

Be careful not to create clichéd or predictable characters. Remember that if you signal a character's intentions too early on it will become predictable and stereotypical. This happens in *Space Cowboys*, where the traitor within is so obvious that all the audience can do is sit back and wait for the treachery. Very useful here are those web sites on film clichés; for example, www. moviecliches.com. Read them, wince, and delete any clichés that have crept in.

To get an interesting range of characters, consider archetypes. A good place to start is with the archetypes that Christopher Vogler mentions in *The Writers' Journey*: the mentor, the shape shifter, and so on. These are all character types that might be useful.

FAMILIES AND MOTIVE

It's helpful at this stage to start thinking of your group of multiple protagonists as a family, operating in family roles; say, the parent figure, the kid brother, the big sister, and so on. This reminds you to think of them as a group rather than interesting unconnected eccentrics and, to add to the interest and originality, consider role reversing sometimes. Try role reversals to add interest, so that, for example, your 'younger brother' character can swap roles with the group's father figure.

NOT 'AND' BUT 'BECAUSE'

A good tip is to think of your film not as 'a family of characters comes together *and* . . .', but as 'a family of characters comes together *because* . . .' This will force you to go back to the macro, which is the 'because', the crisis or threat behind the quest, reunion or siege.

CHARACTER PERSPECTIVES

The 'character perspectives' approach is another way to enrich and differentiate multiple protagonists. John Vorhaus describes the technique in his interesting book *The Comic Toolbox* (1994) in relation to TV sitcom, but it could equally apply to drama or action movies. The idea is that to create a lively, richly comic cast, you consciously choose characters with opposing world views, and set these against a mostly 'normal' character. This gives you the opportunity to create many differing but comic responses to the same problem, hence many reasons for ongoing comic disagreements. For example, one character might be obsessively tidy, another might be a slob, another might neurotically veer between the two, and the final character will provide a normal balanced approach. These characters can be in constant conflict—either in response to a group threat ('our neighbour won't take out their garbage at the appropriate time') or in addition to a group threat (say, all of the characters are trying to buy their landlord a birthday present and the issue of tidiness comes up).

WHAT THE CHARACTERS THINK OF EACH OTHER AND HOW THEY INTERACT

Your next step is to consider methodically how your characters view each other and how they interact, writing a few sentences for each character. Why? Because unless you list these interactions now you may forget to include them. You don't need to work out plots yet.

Here are the interpersonal relationships that you need to work out between your six protagonists (remember, this requires only a sentence or two of description).

- 1 and 2, 1 and 3, 1 and 4, 1 and 5, 1 and 6
- 2 and 3, 2 and 4, 2 and 5, 2 and 6
- 3 and 4, 3 and 5, 3 and 6
- 4 and 5, 4 and 6
- 5 and 6

You will need story material to cover interpersonal relationships in the present (and sometimes also the past) between all of these characters. A lot of material about interpersonal relationships will already have crept in. Brainstorm many possibilities and note them down, again not locking into any. Sometimes the relationship between two characters will be very brief— something you can handle in asides in a few lines across a few scenes—at other times it might be very dense indeed. For example, *American Beauty* has a series of little three-act plots all with 'Lester causes trouble' as a possible title. Start to pencil them in, but don't commit.

Plotting relationship lines

It's very easy to create relationship-line scenes that merely show characters bickering about the past or present, which is boring. Unless this material pays off later, it is redundant. To create a good story to illustrate the individual's response to the group threat, try the following:

1   Isolate aspects of the group threat that would impinge on the relevant character, using your knowledge of each character and their relationship with other members of the group.
2   Create a well-structured story to carry this, preferably using a three-act structure. A one-act structure will suffice as long as its turning point is strong.

As a very large part of your film's attraction will be about the alliances, disagreements and unfinished business between characters, keep looking for ways that the group-adventure line could permit this relationship material to happen and factor it in. Peg your various relationship-story strands to what is happening in the group adventure (the film's main action line), and always think in terms of scenes combining strands. The characters will behave and comment characteristically in response to events, so choose your group scenes carefully so they permit this to the full. Arguments can easily flare up in stressful situations and are good places to give the audience backstory, as are introductions and characters meeting up after time apart. Don't forget visual and sound clues.

CHARACTERISTIC COMMENTS AND REACTIONS

In the case of our TV-hating township, make the individual townspeople respond to the challenges of the group task *in character*, demonstrating their relationships with the others—thus furthering the action line and many relationship strands simultaneously. For example, say the group story involves a farce scene where the townspeople are sabotaging a TV satellite dish. Make characters 1 and 2 argue about unfinished business as they struggle to climb a roof to get to the dish. Meanwhile, make character 3, who is on guard but is prone to hay fever, have an attack. Meanwhile make character 4, who is famous for her bad temper, have a quarrel with character 5 causing character 6, who is chronically inept, to stall the getaway car.

Set-up, development and payoff

A good general rule for any kind of plotting is 'set up, develop, pay off'. So, think of your character-interaction strands as three-step narratives, even if you have only three tiny beats, that give you a set-up, development and payoff. Insert these along the spine created by your quest, reunion or siege plot. Visit the strand once (to set it up) a second time (to develop it) and a third (to pay it off).

Your 'story' could be as simple as a few sentences shared between two characters in three different scenes. Alternatively, it could be extensive; if so, the middle will be extended and you may have to use a number of separate scenes. If it is a very complex plot, such as the love affair between Carolyn and Buddy Kane in *American Beauty*, the set-up and the development will both be extended and you will have several scenes in all. But in all cases, keep thinking 'set-up, development, payoff'.

Points of view

When all of the protagonists in your film are working against a joint external antagonist, they will all be protagonists, as in buddy movies. But in relationship lines, the protagonist whose point of view you are taking will be the protagonist—for the duration of that storyline—with the other members of the group being antagonists. So, for example, if one of your storylines involves character 1 being bullied by character 2, we'll see things from the victim's point of view in certain scenes and in others we'll see them from the bully's view. This is how Lester in *American Beauty* can be the protagonist in certain storylines, but the antagonist in several other storylines.

You need to be aware of this antagonist/protagonist switch so that you remember whose point of view you need to have at any given moment; thus, what content you need to include in scenes. If you don't, you won't get the vital 'different points of view' that multiple protagonist films need, or you will get it in a blurred or muddied form or, worse still, your scenes will become just characters bickering or chatting.

INDEX CARDS
As your film start to takes shape, transfer plot beats to index cards to map out the film. Try to combine plot beats, and work always to condense. Do we really need to see the secret TV viewer sneak out of choir practice twice so as to catch the big game? Would once do? How can once be even funnier?

A writer at work
Writer/director Robin Swicord, who wrote the multiple protagonist screenplays *Little Women* (adapted from Louisa May Alcott's novel), *Shag* and *The Jane Austen Book Club* (directing the latter), has some very useful insights on constructing these films. Her approach is remarkable for its precise and extensive planning. She too sees multiple protagonist films as the equivalent of driving a team of wilful animals which need to progress simultaneously towards the same destination. Particularly, she stresses the difficulty of telling competing individual stories in such limited time, pointing out how little time the film has alone with each character away from the group—therefore how important it is to choose action that will tell the most about any given character vividly and quickly.

Her writing process involves first plotting the macro (which she calls the umbrella plot), consciously giving it a three-act structure and thinking of the group as one protagonist. Hence, in *The Jane Austen Book Club*, she very deliberately created a second-act turning point scene in which all of the members hit rock bottom emotionally (as the single protagonist does in a standard conventional narrative) followed by a third act, in which she brings all of the characters back from the brink to final triumph.

To create the emotional journey of each character in *The Jane Austen Book Club*, she plotted each progression in steps, then, using index cards, carefully chose scenes that would depict this well but economically, working out how many scenes she could allow each character away from the group. She consciously used the group gatherings as markers for herself, working out how much each club member's story needed to progress between meetings.

CREATE RISING EMOTION THROUGH THE WAY YOU JUMP STORIES

Particularly fascinating is the technique she uses to factor in rising emotion when jumping between storylines (there always being a potential problem with anticlimax when you leave a story at an emotional high point to join another). Her answer here is to link the emotional level of one scene's departure point to a similar emotional level in the next scene's arrival point, sometimes jumping to a contrasting emotion to heighten the effect. She says that this gives the illusion that each story is pushing the next scene into existence, even though the next scene comes from another plotline.

Actually, the sense of rising momentum—of each scene pushing the next—is not an illusion. The film steadily rises in emotion, with the audience becoming more invested as we build from storyline to storyline. Let's say in that in a scale of 100, scene A starts at, say, 50 and will end at 65. But scene B, in another character's story, will start close to 65 and end at 75, while scene C—jumping to another character's story—will start near 75 and end at 100. This technique is excellent not only in its efficacy but in its economy in this most time-restricted of forms. It's as if the film is pulling itself up emotionally by its own boot-straps.

On the matter of group survival, she believes that each member of the group should be propelled by a strong desire that is capable of unsettling the group to the point of threatening its survival (this is very astute: it means that emotions will always be bubbling within the group, providing ongoing conflict, hence suspense and energy). She believes, too, that these films function best when there is a hierarchy of stories, whereby the story with the highest jeopardy takes precedence, so you need to select this story, which she calls 'the jewel in the crown'.

The amount of time, effort and planning that even such an experienced writer brings to a multiple protagonist film is a salutary reminder of just how complex these structures are to create.

Chapter 31

Plotting issues in multiple-protagonist quests, reunions and sieges

Quest films

The basic steps of the group quest are identical to the hero's journey model, the basic Smiley/Thompson, the simple or advanced story sentence or any other three-act restorative structure—except it must happen to the group, not an individual.

The film will take the group of multiple protagonists (instead of just one protagonist) on an adventure/journey well away from their regular life and into realms where major and often dangerous decisions have to be made. The action will force the group of protagonists to find new strengths and over-come new hurdles, and in the course of this 'adventure'—indeed, as a direct result of it—the relationship lines happen.

STRANGERS AND FRIENDS

Quest films that bring together strangers are obviously not concerned with a group past in the way that films dealing with long-established groups have to be. With a group that has a history, the story will deal with unfinished business and/or changing loyalties. In groups of strangers, relationship lines will concern developing relationships within the quest. They may refer back to the individual's normality to show how the quest has changed that person. In *Saving Private Ryan*, this presents as an obsession on the part of the soldiers to know each other's normal social role.

BANDS OF HEROES/COMING OF AGE

Quest films often deal with heroic figures who by definition are enigmatic and charismatic and cannot be seen from the inside. Hence, the group will consist of multiple antagonists, often mentor antagonists as the protagonists will typically be minor figures whom the antagonists influence (as in *The Magnificent Seven* and *Saving Private Ryan*). Note this if you are planning a film about a group of heroic characters. You might have to create a protagonist (or protagonists) to be influenced by them. As we've seen, coming-of-age films often feature multiple mentor antagonists.

GROUP ACTION MOVIES DO NOT NEED AS MUCH PLOT

Chases, fights and escapes stop the main action-line plot in its tracks, because the action line cannot continue until we see the result of the fight, chase or escape attempt. This means that, overall, you have less time at your disposal, so your plots will need to be shorter.

THE INSTIGATOR

In quest movies, the instigator is typically engaged in forcing the others to approach the quest in a way they think is dangerous. This also serves to unite the other characters in a group survival problem. Here, the analogy is with journey movies. Unless there is conflict between the travellers, they can only react to outside forces, which means that when they are alone there is no conflict, hence no drama—nothing to quarrel about or discuss.

Reunions

In quest films there is a job to be done: a heist to be completed, a competition to win, enemy aliens to fight. In contrast, reunion films are inherently static, with much if not all of the story deriving from unfinished emotional business.

Whereas a quest clearly takes a character out of their normal environment and sends them on a physical adventure with other versions of themselves and plenty of opportunity for character-revealing incidents, a reunion takes a character out of their normal life and traps them, with other versions of themselves, in one location. The inherent immobility of reunion films makes it easy for writers to forget the need for an emotional journey with significant events. It is very easy to think of reunions just as a device to get characters together ('I'll write a film about a group of Gulf War veterans having a reunion') and stop there, forgetting that interesting character interaction depends on the group and each of its members undergoing a strong emotional journey caused by a threat to its survival—all within a physically static situation.

It's easy for writers to think that they are providing a good group action line when all they are doing is depicting 'business'; that is, scenes about eating, drinking or entertainment, without internal conflict or any ingredients that drive the story forward. This happens in *Parallel Lives*, which features a string of redundant social events such as a ball, a dormitory raid and ball games, all of which, while executed with gusto, rapidly become boring because they are not taking the film anywhere. *Peter's Friends* suffers from similar scenes.

It's easy to make the same mistake in relationship lines, making redundant chats or bickering take the place of scenes that actually progress unfinished business, resulting in unfinished business actually impacting on the present and future. Similarly, time can easily be spent establishing the characters' foibles and describing their past and personal present (their normality) without linking these things to an ongoing personal dilemma. *Parallel Lives* has many examples of this kind of redundant, unfocused conflict, which is a close cousin to the repeated normality seen in *Mr Saturday Night*. It quickly becomes boring: good characterisation and acting alone are not enough.

THERE MUST STILL BE A THREAT AND A SURVIVAL ISSUE

While the group story in reunion forms is usually a lot less dynamic and overt, it still has to deal with the problem of whether or not the group will survive the ordeal it has to experience. Your group of Gulf War veterans needs to be faced with a threat to its survival or else it is likely to end up as just a bunch of characters talking, quarrelling, entertaining themselves and going home again.

To find the group story, the threat and survival issues in reunion films, look for what caused the reunion, because the group survival issue is often raised by it and you can create a story out of that. Sometimes this will be a detective story of sorts, as in *The Big Chill*, which is about why Alex suicided and, leading from this, whether the group will survive the trauma. The film's action line puts the group and its members into a siege situation of staying together in a house (notice how multiple protagonist categories can over-lap, with a reunion becoming a siege), where events can be constructed so that individuals and the group as a whole can confront unfinished business, discuss the dead man's motives, and try to construct new ways of relating to each other. *Monsoon Wedding* creates another kind of reunion 'detective story', dealing with the bride's hesitancy about getting married.

The Big Chill gives you one model for the threat in your Gulf War veterans' reunion story (the group gathering because of a threat to its survival) and *Monsoon Wedding* gives you another (the threat to the group's survival happening at the reunion itself). Use these options as a trigger for brainstorming, and choose one that permits you to do the kind of character exploration that attracted you to the group of characters in the first place.

Having a mystery at the heart of a reunion story is very useful, inserting rising suspense to the action and linking the group as 'suspects', possibly the keepers of vital secrets, as the investigation continues, led either by an outsider or conducted from within by members. The momentum and interest can build to a final denouement as clues are uncovered. The secret can cause credible, powerful and revealing conflict—suspicions and recriminations—within the group. Be careful, though, that the secret is not obvious or the twists predictable, or you may get into cliché. Be careful too that the secret, if you use one, genuinely threatens the survival of the group now, and is not just a horrible incident from the past (although of course what threatens the group now may well be a horrible incident from the past, increasingly haunting the group with the years).

THE GROUP ON THE CUSP OF CHANGE
Good reunion stories are almost always about a group that was on the cusp of change before the traumatic event.

PLANNING
Think of the reunion as an emotional journey for both the group and for individual members. Decide where the journey starts and ends then create a normal three-act structure. Choose events not just because they are typical or odd things that could happen on a journey, but because each will advance the action line (the reinvention or death of the group) and fuel the relationship lines.

THE INSTIGATOR, TRAITOR WITHIN AND OUTSIDER
Structurally, the instigator in reunion and siege films injects a story into the film, because instigators arrive with a plan and a goal and therefore permit psychological action and movement within the 'closed walls' of the physical action. The instigator's plan and goal provide the group with internal problems that can cause conflict and shifting loyalties. Meanwhile, the outsider can do their usual job of challenging the group, articulating its idiosyncrasies and invading its privacy. Choose your outsider carefully for what they can credibly reveal about the group. The traitor within always causes good internal conflict. If the story is some kind of mystery or detective story, you may also like to consider which character, if any, holds the key to the secret.

Siege films
In terms of writing problems, siege is midway between quest and reunion. Siege films share with quest films an inbuilt survival plot with clear closure,

because in most cases the siege is an exciting event that starts and ends, and stories can be structured around that. But, for the duration of the siege, the characters are trapped in one place, as they are in reunion films, and this means the film can become static.

PHYSICAL SIEGE

The physical siege—people physically imprisoned—is a useful form for exploring character because it shows people thrown into a stressful and usually highly dangerous situation. Physical confinement creates anxiety which can insert rising jeopardy. Like groups in reunions, the group in a siege is being forced to change against its will—although it might also be on the cusp of change. Shifting loyalties, breakdown and unexpected courage or cowardice are natural subjects to explore in siege and works well to counteract the physically static nature of siege form.

Physical sieges have as their trigger (technically, their disturbance) the event that sets up the siege; for example, the decision of a gang to rob a bank. The onset of the siege will usually be the first-act turning point, because it is what the film is 'about'. For example, your idea for your bank-robbery film will be something like 'a gang sets out to rob a bank but becomes trapped inside because aliens have unexpectedly landed'. Once you know what the siege is, and when it starts, you can work backwards to create the pre-siege normality and a suitable disturbance.

The second act will normally be the duration of the siege, and it will show the conflicts within the group. Work out what emotional progression you want for individuals and the group and create a scenario within the siege to permit that, utilising your traitor within and outsider to the full, swapping these roles between your characters. The second-act turning point in the group story will be the lowest point for the group followed by the decision to fight back. The third act will normally be a battle (in this instance, to escape). Make the climax answer the first-act question of 'Will the group escape the siege and survive?' Even the most straightforward action adventure group story will show the group changed emotionally, often with some members dead.

As you structure the various plotlines, remember that they will all need to climax in and around the conclusion of the siege.

SOCIAL SIEGE

Social sieges are one of the hardest multiple protagonist forms to write. Partly this is because they are inherently static, being about people trapped in one place in rigidly restricted social roles (it's hard to create a driving story about people who want to stay boring) but partly because social sieges are often predictable. Comic social sieges predictably have the instigator winning over the group, with all ending happily. Darker social sieges are equally predictable, except that the instigator is crushed. This predictability even creeps into very fine social sieges like *Revolutionary Road* which, while poignant and thought-provoking, does not have the energy of *American Beauty*, an energy given by its whodunit ingredients and its final twists.

Because all of its members are already in a siege situation, the social siege needs a threat to its survival in the form of a trigger. This can be an internal trigger in the form of a decision by a member to reject the status quo, or an external trigger such as a catastrophic accident happening to a member or the whole group. The external trigger turns the plot into a group quest with a ready-made adventure. An internal trigger, a rebellious member, has to be dealt with differently. You need to think of the rebel as the threat to the group, just as in quest stories the enemy soldiers or the meteorite hurtling towards earth are the threat. In practice, it means that you have to give the rebel–instigator his or her own plotline (tracking their rebellion) and create plot material for the other characters that shows each fighting the instigator in a unique way, their joint goal being to stop that person and restore normality; just as, in a quest, each group member would be fighting the aliens or the meteorite.

EMOTIONAL SIEGE

Emotional sieges—usually, films about troubled families—show people trapped inside meaningless or actively destructive relationships. The trigger is often a past accident (as in *Ordinary People* or *Rachel Getting Married*), or the film may simply deal with the the group having to deal with ongoing catastrophes (as in *To Live*).

COMIC HEIST

Comic heist or kidnap sieges often bring two or more groups of protagonists into conflict. For example, a town may divide into two warring factions. But all of the protagonists will usually still be versions of the same protagonist. The group action line will be how two different factions respond to the same threat. 'Will the group survive?' will still be the key issue. Set up the two groups quickly because your story does not properly start until they are established.

INSTIGATOR, OUTSIDER AND TRAITOR WITHIN

These three character types keep the internal conflict of the siege bubbling. As in all siege situations, the instigator is a very useful character creating conflict within the group, without which there would only be the problem with the external enemy. The traitor within is an explosive, secret character, particularly powerful in siege situations because being imprisoned can credibly shorten their fuse. Outsiders, as ever, should be chosen with care so that they can reveal as much as possible about the group's rules and taboos. There may be a number of outsiders in a siege film.

Chapter 32
American Beauty: Multiple protagonist social siege

AMERICAN BEAUTY IS RECOGNISABLE as a multiple protagonist social siege film rather than a one-hero story because the action successfully and frequently leaves Lester (the instigator) to follow several other characters in their separate stories: Lester's daughter Jane, her friend Angela, his wife Carolyn, the boy next door Ricky Fitts and the boy's father Frank Fitts, a retired marine. The group story (macro) is indeed a threat to the group's survival. It is Lester's rebellion against his role as respected breadwinner, husband and father.

THE OPENING
Openings are vitally important in all multiple protagonist films. The group and group threat need to be set up early, with high energy, a difficult task when the material is about people leading boring lives: too easily, the film itself becomes boring. *American Beauty* avoids boredom by starting with the highest jeopardy and strongest hook of all: the threat of murder. The first moments show Lester's daughter plotting her father's murder. We then hear Lester in voice-over predicting his own death. The film has become a murder story, which adds continuing and building suspense to everything that happens.

FLASHBACK
The structure of *American Beauty* is actually a kind of double narrative flashback whereby the film opens and concludes in the present, and we return to the present intermittently throughout—except that in the present Lester is dead. In the present we see high-angle footage of the neighbourhood where the story is set, closing in on its characters, and hear only Lester in voice-over, speaking from beyond the grave, explaining that what his living self does not realise is that he will be dead in a matter of months.

The film ends with Lester's murder by a member of the group, which at the lowest level concludes the detective story and, in terms of the film's higher meaning, provides closure to the macro, answering the problem of whether the group will survive (it will not). Returning to the present after the long flashback is also helpful in closure, and permits a startling end to the film in which the deceased Lester talks about the moment of death.

Note how the flashback is set up and resolved in classic case history flashback style. It starts at the triggering crisis, Lester's death, which is both the climax of the story in the past and the start of the story in the present. Lester's actual death will be the film's climax, with the necessary 'Rosebud' twist (referring to the unexpected twist at the end of *Citizen Kane*, where the investigator protagonist, the journalist, never finds out the meaning of Kane's dying word, but the audience does) being that Lester, dead, actually talks about the moment of his death, and the visions he describes are shown on screen.

THE INSTIGATOR, TRAITOR AND THE OUTSIDER

The traitor within is Frank Fitts, although Lester's wife and daughter also sometimes play that role. The outsider—who, in typical outsider style, questions the functioning and beliefs of the group and introduces conflicting and new views—is Ricky, with his drug dealing, his ever-present video camera, and his compulsion to capture and hold beauty.

THE MACRO

Lester's rebellion, the film's macro, has a complete three-act action line (his career as breadwinner) and a complete three-act relationship line (Lester's crush on Angela). In the opening moments of the film, Lester's normality in marriage and at work are established. The disturbance in his action line is being threatened with retrenchment, and in his relationship line it is encountering Angela. The first-act turning points in the action and relationship lines are the triggers for his rebellion. The first-act turning point in his action line is quitting his job and in his relationship line, the moment when Angela suggests that he work out and he decides to pursue her sexually. As usual, the first-act turning point of these two storylines is what the film is 'about'.

The second act covers Lester's rebellion. The second-act turning point in his action line is when he serves his wife and her lover at the fast-food restaurant and declares that his role as husband and breadwinner is over. In his relationship line, it is when Angela tells him that she is a virgin, thereby aborting their attempt at sex. The climax of both stories is his death. There are high levels of suspense in Lester's action and relationship lines: 'Will he be murdered?' and 'Will he have sex with an underage girl?'

LESTER CAUSES TROUBLE FOR EVERYONE

Note how Lester's rebellion impacts on each individual, first irritating them, then significantly angering several people to the point where they want to murder him. In *American Beauty*, each character is involved in at least one and sometimes more well-structured three-act narratives—relationship triangles—in which Lester is the antagonist, the irritant, and which could be called 'Lester causes me trouble'. There is: Carolyn/Buddy/Lester, Jane/Angela/Lester, Ricky/Frank/Lester, Jane/Ricky/Lester and Jane/Carolyn/Lester.

The behaviour of group members towards Lester is not random, it is not just the accidental foibles of interesting characters. It is a manifestation of the group's need to destroy what is threatening it. What this gives you in terms of drama is driven individuals, people who want something, people with a goal, moreover, the same goal. This avoids characters in search of a plot, a big potential problem in all social sieges.

SAME CLIMAX, AVERTING PREDICTABILITY

Structurally, the climax of each of the relationship-line stories in *American Beauty* is, not surprisingly, Lester's death, the destruction of the threat (the exact equivalent of, say, the destruction of the meteorite in *Armageddon*, or holding back the final German attack in *Saving Private Ryan*).

The film is deliberately structured so that each character's story seems to be moving towards a climax in which one of the protagonists, we don't know which, will kill Lester. This is a masterstroke because it pulls against predictability. It is done so well that it is impossible to work out until the last moment who will be the murderer. In effect this is providing a complex whodunit, with driven potential murderers, and it provides very high levels of suspense and jeopardy. Compare the rather different jeopardy—more like dread of the inevitable—in *Revolutionary Road*, in which individuals in the group do not set out to physically harm April Wheeler, but instead voice strong disapproval, ironically the strongest disapproval being voiced by the person who was initially the instigator: Frank, her husband.

SECRET REBELLION

All of the relationship lines in *American Beauty* show people rebelling in their different ways against the status quo, often secretly. This is typical of social siege films. Frank, the supreme agent of status quo, is a repressed homosexual and a murderer. Carolyn is an adulteress, a mother who assaults her daughter, and a wife who plots to kill her husband. Jane hates her parents (even fantasising about getting Lester murdered); dresses rebelliously and takes up with Ricky, the dreamy outsider and drug dealer. Angela pretends to be a slut. Ricky sells drugs, and videotapes anything that interests him (including corpses) with no regard for normal notions of privacy or propriety. He and Jane plan to run away and live on drug money. While some of this antisocial behavior is not in the form of proper stories (the interaction between Jane and Carolyn, for example), frequently there are proper stories set up as genuine three-act structures; with a disturbance, act turning points and a climax. Carolyn's affair with Buddy is a good example.

CLIMAX OF THE MACRO, THE GROUP STORY

While some siege films permit a third-act battle and a triumph, this does not happen as such in the macro of *American Beauty*. However, just before Lester dies he seems to have found peace and happiness in himself, and particularly in the fact that Jane is in love. As he is shot, he is staring with a look of beatific peace and happiness at a family photo in which he, Carolyn and Jane present as the archetypal happy middle-American family. He seems to have transcended his lust for Angela. The look of peace and happiness is still on his face in death. Perhaps Lester's rebellion against convention and his search for beauty via sex has led him back full circle to a discovery of beauty and peace in Middle America.

CLIMAX OF THE INDIVIDUAL STORIES

In all of the 'Lester causes me trouble' stories, the climax was set up to be Lester's murder. This was what was going to reinstate the proper order of things. Only Frank's version has a climax involving murder. The other stories end with an avoidance of murder by the individual (providing a good twist ending for each) but the destruction of the group as a whole. The climaxes to these different stories answer the question raised by the first-act turning points in Lester's two stories, which was: 'How is the group going to survive this antisocial behaviour?' The answer is that the group will not survive, because the group has destroyed itself from within.

DEVICES TO PREVENT THE SIEGE BEING STATIC

To summarise, *American Beauty* inserts and maintains energy and prevents predictability by employing a high-jeopardy opening (mention of murder, flashback device revealing the protagonist is dead) and setting up a whodunit, with a range of murder suspects and a number of final twists. Additionally, each member of the group is in rebellion, open or secret, against the status quo.

The enemy of the social siege, like the enemy of political tandem narrative, is predictability.

Section 3
Double journeys narrative

Chapter 33
Double journeys

THE 'DOUBLE JOURNEY' FILM is a version of multiple protagonist form. It's always about two characters journeying either towards each other, or in parallel, or apart (emotionally or physically or both). Examples of double journey films are *Brokeback Mountain*, *Finding Nemo*, *Vicky Cristina Barcelona*, *The Lives of Others*, *The Departed*, *The Proposition*, *The Lemon Tree*, *Julie and Julia* and *The Queen*. The motto is: 'two lives in parallel'.

Because the action follows two characters in separate lives, each of the pair is a protagonist who must have an action line and a separate range of companions.

The idea of these films being multiple protagonist films will puzzle many people, who will feel that as in many of these films we know one traveller better than the other, that person is the protagonist, with the other the antagonist in a one-hero film. I'd say these films spend too much time alone with the second traveller for that structure to work: furthermore, the central concerns of these films is not one person's emotional change and one person's point of view. They are films about two individuals in a social context, and they make their point through an exploration, often critical, of how society moulds and restricts these two individuals.

The danger of thinking of these films as single protagonist stories is that you can easily forget to follow the second protagonist (which is what happens with Ada in *Cold Mountain*) with the result that one character has nothing to do.

A buddy movie?

These films are not buddy movies because buddy movies are about the tensions of two people together almost all the time on a single adventure—so all you need to plot is one adventure, not two. Also, apart from rare cases like *Thelma and Louise*, which explores society's poor treatment of women, they are not about social issues.

Whereas the friends in buddy movies meet up early (they have to or we don't have a film about their joint adventure), double journey films rarely show the two travellers becoming friends early in the film. Often they don't even meet until late in the film. Double journey protagonists who do meet early or already know each other usually relate in ways riddled with anxieties and insecurities. In these and indeed many double journey films, one of the pair will often not realise the importance of the relationship until the end of the film. At this point it is frequently and tragically too late. Normally, one character takes the lead in trying to get closer, but will initially be rejected, or feel rejected.

Opposites

As in normal multiple protagonist films, the travellers are different versions of the same protagonist; however, in addition, they usually represent different, usually opposite, responses *to a social convention or taboo*. Thus, the two men in *Brokeback Mountain* are different versions of the gay man in a homophobic community. In *Vicky Cristina Barcelona*, the two women represent different attitudes towards sexual permissiveness. *Julie and Julia* are both cooks. In *The Queen*, Queen Elizabeth and Tony Blair are two kinds of national leaders. In *The Lives of Others*, *The Proposition* and *The Departed*, the two protagonists are on opposite sides of the law. In *The Lemon Tree*, the two women neighbours are from enemy countries.

Where the characters differ gives you the theme, message and action line

The social convention, rule or taboo that the two travellers differ about provides the theme and message, and points the way towards the main action line—the macro—which is the adventure the two have together. The external events of the double journey provide the macro of the film. For example, in

Brokeback Mountain, the macro plot is how the two men first meet, then how they meet over the years for camping trips; in *The Queen*, it is the events that followed Diana's death, both within the royal family and in the public at large; in *The Lemon Tree*, it is the decision by security services to remove the lemon orchard, and the steps each side takes in response to that decision. The macro permits the relationship that you want to explore to actually happen and, of course, is closely entwined with it. Hence, we have plots like: 'the problems of two soulmates who can only meet secretly', 'the problems of a monarch and a prime minister dealing with a rival for the public's affection' or 'the problems of two women on either side of the Palestinian/Israeli divide'. Choose your macro plot so that it will permit the relationship between your protagonists to unfold in the way you want.

The macro in these films is a version of the general multiple protagonist film of 'will the group survive?'. It is 'how will the relationship emerge from this situation?', to which the answer is sometimes that it survives well (with a successful relationship and enduring love) and sometimes it does not survive (with the travellers parting).

Story content

Double journey films typically explore, challenge and often criticise the particular social conventions that are troubling the two central characters. Hence, the macro puts the characters in a position where they have to confront or play out what is troubling or dividing them. *The Lemon Tree* wants to explore the day-to-day interaction of Palestinians and Israelis, so creates a plot around a woman from each side who are, literally, neighbours. *Brokeback Mountain* wants to explore homophobia, repression and self-hatred, so has a plot that puts two gay men into a situation where a dangerous secret liaison is possible. *The Queen* wants to challenge and explore the idea of a good leader, so sets at loggerheads two different kinds of national leader with opposing views as to how to deal with the death of the Queen's rival, the 'people's princess'. *The Lives of Others* sets a cold, unartistic Stasi agent to spy on his polar opposite, a rebellious writer. In *Vicky Cristina Barcelona*, a conformist and a nonconformist travel into each other's philosophy and out again.

Several action lines and relationship lines

As well as the macro, and the relationship line that it pulls along (both of which happen when the travellers are together), the film has to give each character its own action and relationship line for those periods of the film when he or she is away from the other. Make sure these 'separate life' action lines will create the kind of relationship material that you want. For example, if you want each protagonist to have a troubled life when they are apart, construct action lines to show the precise way in which those lives are troubled.

Is my film a double journey film?

It's surprisingly easy to miss the fact that your idea is a double journey model. Some or all of the following questions may help. Ask yourself:

1 Do I have two characters journeying towards or away from each other in the way that happens in films like *Brokeback Mountain*, *The Lives of Others*, *Finding Nemo* and *The Departed*?
2 Does the story require that each of the pair spends a lot of time with other characters in another world, and little if any time with each other?
3 Is the film's main action line about one person hunting down another or trying to find another, or about two people leading similar parallel lives or being thrown together at a distance or being attracted across social conventions or in the face of taboos?
4 Is my story about two people leading parallel lives:
    - whom logic says will not grow close? And/or
    - who are either in very distant places or on opposite sides politically? And/or
    - who represent different responses to the same events or to social conventions?

The key question, usually, is whether the couple spend a lot of time apart in different worlds.

If you think your film is a double journey, instantly start thinking about and planning two plots, two journeys (involving two separate three-act mountains) that finally intersect or diverge at the last moment. Take note that your characters will usually have different and opposed views to some kind of social convention, rule or taboo. Define how and why they are in conflict. This will give you both your message and your scenario. Create a macro plot that makes them confront their difference, hence lets you explore it. All of your action lines must permit your relationship lines to happen.

Social dimension adds depth

If your idea presents simply as two characters in opposition, pinpoint the social convention that divides them. For example, *Finding Nemo* could simply have been a fun film about a baby fish who gets lost and is found again by his dad. Instead, the issue of over-protective fatherhood is added, which gives the film a much greater resonance, engaging not only adults intellectually, but even small children, thus satisfying its wide demographic.

Maintain conflict

Be careful to find sufficient conflict and difference between your two travellers, and good reasons to keep them apart. Remember they are two versions of the same protagonist. Don't make them identical twins! Give each a separate world. Pinpoint how and why they are different, and start thinking of ways that the plot can demonstrate the differences to provide conflict and increase interest. Consciously make their travelling towards each other or apart interesting.

Remember that you will have three action lines with matching relationship lines: one set for each of the characters when they are off leading their separate lives, and a third set that tracks the progression of their relationship. Because you have three sets instead of one, each will be quite short. Depending on the story, sometimes the lives your travellers lead when they are apart will be extensive (as in *Vicky Cristina Barcelona*), sometimes very little will happen when they are apart (which happens in *The Lives of Others*, where, as an important part of the film, the Stasi man has virtually no human contact in his private life at all). Find the action line for each of these three storylines and peg each relationship line to its timeline.

The storyline that will hold the entire film together will in most cases be the storyline about them when they are together. It will normally be an action line with a clear timeline of crucial events (not always, as in *Vicky Cristina Barcelona*, where the individual stories pull the action along, but frequently, as in *The Queen* and *The Lives of Others*, when what happens to the two in their public interaction drives their personal relationship). If your action line does perform this crucial central role, peg your other stories to its timeline. Make sure that each meeting of the protagonists marks a change in the relationship. Be careful not to give all of the meetings the same outcome.

A kind of love story

These films are always a story of twin souls or mirror opposites—a kind of love story or anti-love story—so, as with all love stories, the heat and suspense come from the question of whether and how the couple will come together or part, and you have to maintain that heat and suspense by keeping the travellers either apart until the last moment or, if it is a tragic version, together until the last moment. Invent social and emotional hurdles and barriers. Keeping one character a bit mysterious will help here, so the audience can puzzle about their motivation or whereabouts or actions. Dramatic irony (whereby we, the audience, know something about one traveller that's unknown to the other; for example, their whereabouts or the fact that they never received a vital letter) can also help, permitting your film to remain suspenseful.

Odyssey structure?

Quite often, double journey stories are odyssey stories. *Finding Nemo* is one such. *Finding Nemo* doesn't need to start in the middle because there is sufficient jeopardy at the start when Nemo, the sole remaining son (and an injured son, at that) is lost. However, depending on your story material, your double journey might need a central start (see pp. 370–5).

More travellers?

In the future we may see triple or quadruple journeys, as audiences become faster and faster in picking up clues and handling multiple narratives.

Section 4
Flashback narrative

Chapter 34
Flashback: An introduction

FLASHBACK, SEEN IN FILMS such as *Slumdog Millionaire, Milk, The Curious Case of Benjamin Button, Eternal Sunshine of the Spotless Mind, Memento, Cinema Paradiso, Shine, Amadeus, Michael Clayton, Annie Hall, The Home Song Stories, The Constant Gardener, The Sweet Hereafter, The Green Mile, Citizen Kane, The Usual Suspects, The Remains of the Day, The English Patient* and many others, is one of the most exciting storytelling techniques available to screenwriters. It blows open the traditional, sequential three-act narrative structure in the most radical way and offers writers a freedom and range that is dazzling. Through flashback, the audience can relive the past rather than just hearing about it. It can transmit what might have been as well as what was. It works equally well for comedy as for drama. It can give an epic grandeur to a film and it is unequalled in taking us inside a character's mind.

To see just how much flashback can enrich a film, let's look at a conventional linear version of *Slumdog Millionaire*. It would either tell *Slumdog* as an episodic three-act story starting at its chronological start in Jamal's childhood, or as a three-act story beginning with Jamal as an adult working as chai wallah. The past would be told as backstory through dialogue, typically in conflict situations like arguments (where the past can be credibly brought up) or explanations to an interrogator. This version would have run something along the following lines.

Slumdog Millionaire told as a conventional linear story

Jamal is working as a chai wallah (normality). He finds his lost brother, then Latika (disturbance), with the backstory of the three told briefly in dialogue (for example, via recriminations). His plan is to rescue Latika, but he has no money to successfully evade her gangster captor. His first-act turning point (surprise/obstacle) is getting on the show *Who Wants to Be a Millionaire?* (which might give him the chance to get the money). The second act shows him progressing successfully through the show, increasingly suspected of cheating. Between show episodes, as part of his relationship line, he seeks out Latika and Salim, as in the existing film. His second-act turning point (moment closest to death) is the police interrogation scenes, during which, in an impassioned but brief speech to his interrogator, he reveals how he knew all the answers to the questions (decision to fight back). As his third-act battle to win, he returns to the show to answer the final question. Winning (as per the existing film with, in the relationship line, Latika freed by Salim's self-sacrificing suicide), provides both action- and relationship-line climaxes.

Needless to say, this version doesn't begin to approach the richness and depth of the real movie, which actually shows us Salim's past. Of course, the committed conventional narrative supporter would respond that *Slumdog* is indeed brilliant, but flashback wrongly used is a recipe for disaster—which is absolutely right. Jumping from a story in the present to the past is always dangerous—partly because the story in the present stops for the flashback, which can cause slowing, and partly because the audience might forget where they jumped from.

So, can we set down any rules or patterns at all to identify why and how best to use flashback? Fascinatingly, and very usefully, there are definite patterns and rules underlying all successful flashback films, and these are directly related to the conventional three-act narrative. At present, flashback ranges from simple, self-contained chunks of backstory in otherwise linear one-hero films to complex structures like the eleven stories in nine different time frames we see in *The Sweet Hereafter*. Excitingly, flashback forms are developing and hybridising all the time, encouraged by audiences who are highly receptive to non-linear forms and well used to flashback from TV and online drama. There are five simple flashback forms and two complex forms, the latter we can bracket together and term 'double narrative flashback.'

Chapter 35
Simple flashback forms

REALLY, ALL FIVE SIMPLE flashback forms are just devices added to conventional, linear three-act stories to add impact. We will look at each of these in turn, and then, to show them in action, we'll look at how each could be applied to 'Cinderella'. They are:

1. FLASHBACK AS ILLUSTRATION/MEMORY
These are self-contained bits of backstory, comic or dramatic (as in the history of Butch's watch in *Pulp Fiction*).

2. REGRET FLASHBACKS
These are non-chronological fragments about an unsuccessful love relationship (*Annie Hall*, *And When Did You Last See Your Father?*).

3. BOOKEND FLASHBACK
This is a frame to add either dignity, gravitas and poignancy to a story (as in *Titanic* or *Saving Private Ryan*) or a shock at the end of a story (as in *Fight Club* or *Sunset Boulevard*).

4. PREVIEW FLASHBACK
This is a preview at the start of the film of a powerful scene or sequence within the film, often from the later part (as in *Michael Clayton* or *Goodfellas*) to hook the audience.

5. LIFE-CHANGING INCIDENT FLASHBACK
A life-changing incident is told incrementally, emerging in full and fully understandable form only close the end of the film (*Catch 22* or *The End of the Affair*).

VOICE-OVER AUTOBIOGRAPHICAL NARRATOR

All of these forms can use an autobiographical narrator, speaking in voice-over. Sometimes the voice-over is just a way of adding colour and immediacy to a character (as when a character is replying to a detective's questions, and their voice continues over the flashback), sometimes it is used to trick the audience and provide a final twist (as in *Fight Club* or *Sunset Boulevard*). Some films use a narrator who is only a minor player in the action, others use a person who is not in the film at all, a kind of ubiquitous storyteller.

Flashback as illustration/memory

Flashback as illustration/memory is just a backstory device in films set in the present. For example, a detective asks: 'Where were you last Tuesday night?' and the action depicts those events on screen, often with voice-over, before the film jumps back to the present. Really, flashback as illustration is a way following the old writer's rule of 'show, don't tell'. Except in special cases, it doesn't affect the overall structure of the film. Use flashback as illustration sparingly, and set up a pattern for the audience. For example, if you give one suspect in your murder story a flashback to illustrate their alibi, it's probably best to give all of the suspects an alibi flashback. Flashbacks that simply repeat what has just been said in words are a waste of precious screen time, as are flashbacks that simply contain information that could be transmitted via deft dialogue in the present.

Flashback as illustration appears in all kinds of film structures. It appears throughout the tandem narrative crime story *Crimes and Misdemeanors* as memories haunting a criminal. It appears in the multiple protagonist film *Crouching Tiger, Hidden Dragon* as a self-contained slab of backstory and, as I've mentioned, in *Pulp Fiction*, it appears in Butch's dream about the watch.

The rule here is to make sure that the flashback is highly pertinent to what later happens in the story, or the audience will get lost or distracted.

Whether in comedy or drama, you need to peg flashback as illustration to *a strong main story in the present*. An unconnected series of flashbacks pegged to a weak and wandering plot will get tedious frighteningly quickly.

BABETTE'S FLASHBACK

Occasionally you will find a conventional three-act film which has one complete and lengthy flashback at the start. While this is really just one big slab of backstory, it is so long that it has a structural impact. We can call this 'Babette's flashback' because *Babette's Feast* contains such a memorable example. The past lives of Babette and her sisters are told in one long flashback *before* the film's disturbance (the disturbance being Babette winning the lottery). *There's Something About Mary* does the same. The film opens with the film's disturbance—Ted falling in love with Mary—which happened thirteen years before and is introduced in voice-over by the older Ted.

HOW TO USE FLASHBACKS AS ILLUSTRATION/MEMORY IN 'CINDERELLA'

Used like this, there would be flashbacks to events in Cinderella's recent past as the story proceeds. *Babette*-style long flashbacks from the distant past would not be appropriate because the main interest of Cinderella's story is not unfinished business that needs to be fixed in the present. The interest in 'Cinderella' is what happens *after* the invitation.

Regret flashbacks

Some films use a series of illustration flashbacks, presented out of chronological order, to deliberately create a kind of incomplete jigsaw of an unhappy, unsuccessful relationship in the past that the protagonist cannot understand or get over. Two films in this category are *Annie Hall* and *And When Did You Last See Your Father?*, the first about a failed romance, the second about a man unable to connect with his difficult father during the father's terminal illness. These films end with the protagonist still bewildered and troubled by what happened. The message in both is that the relationship should have worked, and possibly would have had both parties worked harder, but, sadly, they didn't—and that's the way life is. Because regret is the dominant emotion in the protagonist and the audience, we can call this 'regret flashbacks': non-chronological flashback fragments depicting a failed relationship.

Annie Hall's flashbacks show snippets from Alvy's relationship with a range of women, and depict the entire relationship with Annie Hall, doing so very wittily, and using clever techniques like putting characters from the present into the flashback, observing themselves. Flashbacks in *And When Did You Last See Your Father?* show fragments of the pair's troubled relationship over the years, culminating in their mutual inability to reconcile.

Be aware that regret flashback films can easily meander because the flashbacks are not shown in chronological order (*And When Did You Last See Your Father?* has problems here). Make sure your flashbacks are telling, and connect them to some kind of ongoing suspenseful story in the present.

SHOULD YOU USE REGRET FLASHBACKS OR DOUBLE NARRATIVE FLASHBACK (A FULL STORY IN PAST AND PRESENT, LIKE *SLUMDOG MILLIONAIRE*)?

If you want to write a story firmly rooted in the present that concludes by showing a protagonist troubled about a failed relationship that should have worked better but, tragically, didn't, think about 'regret' flashbacks. However, if your story is about a protagonist gradually finding out crucial new information about the past that solves much or all of what's troubling them in the present it's probably better done as double narrative flashback (*The End of the Affair*) or preview flashback (*Cinema Paradiso*), both described below.

HOW TO USE REGRET FLASHBACKS IN 'CINDERELLA'

Regret flashbacks would only be useful if Cinderella and the prince had split up; although perhaps you could use it if the prince had not sought out Cinderella. You might have to invent a lot of plot because the heat of a regret flashbacks film is a person, in the present, musing over what has happened in the past. The earliest your film could start would be just after the ball.

Bookend flashback

Bookend flashbacks (as in films like *Saving Private Ryan*, *The Green Mile*, *Stand by Me*, *The Home Song Stories* and *Titanic*) are a simple framing device and involve no jumping between past and present during the film. The film consists of a complete linear story from the past inserted inside one scene or sequence set in the present. The film typically opens with a character forced to remember a crucial period in their remote past. The action then jumps back to the start of that period in their past and runs chronologically without interruption through to its conclusion (usually also in the past). At this point, the action returns to the opening scene in the present, followed quickly by a resolution and the end of the film.

Note that the ending in bookend flashback always provides a surprise—a Rosebud twist that changes the whole meaning of the film and gives a powerful last-minute surprise or climax. The Rosebud twist provides the real climax of the film, the moment when the film's final meaning is revealed. A twist is necessary because otherwise the ending would be an exact repeat of what we've already seen, hence an anticlimax. We shall see the Rosebud twist again later when we look at *Citizen Kane* and other double narrative flashback films. Usually, but not always, the Rosebud twist provides classic dramatic irony (whereby the audience knows something the protagonist doesn't). A good Rosebud twist provides very satisfying closure.

In chronological terms, the bookend scene will be very close to the film's end and often many years after the main action of the film. If you want your film to open with a scene from somewhere in its middle, then jump back to its start and progress chronologically from start to finish, repeating the scene it opened with on the way (as in *Michael Clayton*, *Goodfellas* or *Walk the Line*), this is not bookend flashback. It's probably another kind of flashback, preview flashback, which we look at later.

Bookend flashback can appear in all kinds of film structures. It often appears in multiple protagonist films (such as *Saving Private Ryan* and *Stand by Me*). Because bookend flashbacks frame a complete story, they are often inserted during editing. However, there is no reason why a writer cannot insert them in the script. Leaving any kind of major structural decisions to the editing suite is dangerous.

TWO KINDS OF BOOKENDS

There are two kinds of bookend flashbacks, ones with poignant Rosebud twists and ones with shocking Rosebud twists. When you are planning bookend flashback, you may already know your twist. If you don't, insert one of the appropriate kind because otherwise your film will fizzle at the end. Choose carefully—the message that the audience will walk away with is whatever you give them in the final twist.

1. POIGNANT BOOKEND FLASHBACKS

(*Saving Private Ryan*, *Titanic*, *The Green Mile*, *The Home Song Stories*, *Stand by Me*) The person remembering is often old. For example, the poignant twist at the end of *Saving Private Ryan* is the identity of the old man in the opening scene. In *The Green Mile*, it is the strange effect that John Coffey had on Paul, the protagonist, and the mouse Mr Jingles. In *Titanic*, it is that the old lady, Rose, a survivor of the *Titanic*, reveals to the audience what happened to the missing *Heart of the Ocean* diamond necklace.

Properly used, poignant bookend flashbacks can give a film dignity and gravitas, often pathos. However, they can also feel redundant, anticlimactic and even mawkishly sentimental (the old person hobbling away into the sunset). The secret here is a powerful story in the past and a clever twist.

Annie Hall has bookend flashbacks of a kind in addition to the regret flashbacks we discussed. It starts with a speech to camera from the narrator at the chronological end of the story and returns to the narrator at the end.

2. SHOCKING BOOKEND FLASHBACKS

Shocking bookend flashbacks, as seen in *Sunset Boulevard* and *Fight Club*, usually involve young protagonists, and the twist usually involves violence, even death. In *Sunset Boulevard*, the shocking twist is the surprise identity of the dead body in the pool as the film opens. In *Fight Club*, it is the identity and death of Tyler Durden. Interestingly, *Fight Club* and *Sunset Boulevard* both employ a voice-over from a protagonist who turns out to have tricked us: the unreliable narrator.

TURNING 'CINDERELLA' INTO BOOKEND FLASHBACK

The standard story would be inserted into the middle of a scene or short sequence from many years later in Cinderella's life. An event would have triggered Cinderella either to tell her life story to someone, or to think back about her life. Voice-over might be used. There would be a final twist, touching or shocking, which would provide the message of the film (for example, that Cinderella's new life had also been a kind of slavery—poignant—or that we don't see the narrator's face until the end when, say, it emerges, shockingly, that she is actually one of the ugly sisters, who cheated to make the shoe fit). Cinderella might be an honest or an unreliable narrator.

Preview flashback

Preview flashback occurs in films such as *Walk the Line*, *Brick*, *Michael Clayton*, *Cinema Paradiso*, *The Hangover* and *Goodfellas*. *Eternal Sunshine of the Spotless Mind* is a hybrid that uses preview flashback plus other sorts of flashback. I analyse *Eternal Sunshine* in detail later (see pp. 264–5, 323–7).

Films that use preview flashback are conventional three-act structures, but they hook the audience by inserting a powerful scene from later in the story as a tantalising preview before showing the story in a linear way, from start to finish, repeating the opening scene on the way. Visualise this by imagining 'Cinderella' starting at its second-act turning point, with Cinderella running down the steps of the palace losing her glass slipper as midnight strikes. Next, imagine the story jumping straight back to its beginning (Cinderella's normality before the arrival of the ball invitation) and proceeding uninterrupted from start to finish, repeating the slipper-losing scene in its proper context and continuing to the climax where the slipper fits.

Except in very rare cases, preview flashback at the moment does not involve jumping back and forth between time frames to an ongoing story in the present. The only flashback is at the start, so, really, the narrative is a kind of loop. The opening scene comes from either a third of the way through the film, or half way, or two-thirds of the way. Sometimes the preview section is very short, as in *Goodfellas*, other times it is quite long, as in *Michael Clayton*.

THE PREVIEW SCENE MUST BE THE RIGHT ONE

Preview flashback can go badly wrong if you open on the wrong scene. You may give the audience the wrong clue and send them in the wrong direction, with disastrous results.

The audience will naturally assume that the characters and content of the opening scene are telling them what the film is about. Hence, if the opening scene is simply an interesting scene from late in the film, the film's whole point can be lost. The preview scene should be a vital scene from the main story and it must concern the film's main point, with no possibility for audience confusion about which characters are the most important.

A film that leads the audience in the wrong direction via a preview flashback is the otherwise fine Australian film *Three Dollars*, about a good family man struggling to do the right thing by everyone. The action line is that the man becomes a whistleblower, but its core, its heart and its *raison d'être* is supposed to be his troubled but loving relationship with his wife and child. Unfortunately, the film opens with a preview flashback showing the protagonist losing his job and saying, in voice-over, that Amanda, a childhood friend, always appeared every nine and a half years to change his life. This, naturally, made many audiences feel that the story was going to be about something remarkable happening between the protagonist and Amanda. So they waited for this story to happen. But in the event, Amanda, who is visited in flashbacks to the man's childhood, has no real significance in the film and appears only at the end to save the hero in a moment of crisis.

Unluckily, such is the power of preview flashback that while the film's key scenes about the man and his family were playing, many of the film's audiences were impatiently awaiting Amanda and the start of what they assumed would be the film's real story. For these audiences, the family scenes were nicely written but repetitive and off the point. By the time it became clear that the man and his family were the core of the film, the film was over. Thus, *Three Dollars*, a potentially very fine film, ended up being disappointing for many people. Possibly *Three Dollars'* origin as a novel affected plotting decisions in the film.

Compare this film with *Walk the Line* and *Michael Clayton*, where the openings mark a genuine turning point in the protagonist's story and, when it returns, is satisfying and injects energy.

Since preview flashback is often inserted at the editing stage, when everyone connected with the film is in danger of being too close to it and therefore unable to see what a first-time audience will see, it is a particularly dangerous flashback form. If you, as writer, think your film might use it, insert it into the script. But make sure that it is leading the audience the way you want them to go.

DISTINGUISHING PREVIEW FLASHBACK FROM OTHER KINDS OF FLASHBACK

Preview flashback films differ from bookend flashback films because preview flashback films continue for some time after the preview scene has returned. By contrast, the opening scene in bookend flashbacks is close to the film's ending, sometimes only seconds away (think of *Saving Private Ryan*).

It's much harder to distinguish preview flashback from double narrative flashback films (films such as *Slumdog Millionaire*, *Shine*, *The English Patient* and *The Remains of the Day*). There are two major differences:

1 In double narrative flashback, the opening scene or sequence will trigger *two* narratives—one in the past and one in the present—with action jumping between them.
2 In preview flashback, the preview scene is merely a hook. Preview flashback films are not primarily stories about the actions in the past of an enigmatic outsider (again, think of *Michael Clayton* as opposed to *Citizen Kane*, *Slumdog Millionaire*, *Shine*, *Memento* etc.).

If you think your film has two separate stories, one in the past and one in the present, that's double narrative flashback. But if what you want is just a teaser for the audience, preview is the form you're after.

DIFFERENT SORTS OF PREVIEW FLASHBACK

There are several different sorts, and the difference is where the preview actually occurs chronologically in the story. Different positions create different effects, but preview flashback films always open on a major turning point for the protagonist because turning points combine striking action and the protagonist under emotional stress, therefore provide a powerful audience hook. Usually, the preview is the story's second-act turning point, but it can be the disturbance, first-act turning point, midpoint or climax.

1. PREVIEW FLASHBACK AS THE FILM'S DISTURBANCE

The Sweet Hereafter and *The Constant Gardener* are thwarted dream flashback films that open on a disturbance (the school bus accident and the death of Tessa). I have not been able to find a preview flashback film that starts on its disturbance, but if they don't exist at present (which they probably do somewhere) they will exist soon. Probably, using a disturbance as a preview would require a very powerful disturbance indeed.

2. PREVIEW FLASHBACK AT FIRST-ACT TURNING POINT

Brick, a murder mystery, opens at the first-act turning point surprise—the discovery of a murder victim. It then flashes back to the start of the story and shows the events that led up to the murder; hence, the whole first act is a flashback.

Brick works well, but opening a film on its first-act turning point is dangerous because the first-act turning point is the moment when the story has a big surprise that turns it in a new direction. If you give away that surprise at the start of the film, flashing back to the normality and the set-up prior to the surprise could easily seem tame. This happens in *The Well*, a film about two women who accidentally run down a man then dump his body in an old well and drop rocks on top of it. Later they hear noises, fear he wasn't killed and panic that he is coming back to get them. Clearly, the heat of the story rests in this psychological thriller aspect; that is, what happens after the man is dumped in the well. However, the film opens on the accident, then flashes back to the start of the story, showing a first act about how the women met and came to be driving along, which contributes no useful information about the past or present, so adds nothing; indeed, actively prevents the film from progressing to its heat.

The fault here is not so much the use of flashback as a weak first act. No flashback will fix inherently redundant material. Probably *The Well*'s first act should have been cut massively—so that the man being run down became the film's disturbance and the first-act turning point became the noises coming from the well, which is in fact what the film is about. Often, cutting the disturbance and making the first-act turning point the disturbance can significantly boost a film's energy levels, as we've seen earlier, pp. 139–41.

Another problem about starting at the first-act turning point is that there could be a shock effect—a jolt or hiatus—as the film comes back to where it started and jumps in its new direction. You might want that shock effect. If you do, fine. Arriaga uses that in the fractured tandem film *Three Burials of Melchiades Estrada* to deliberately spin the film in a new direction. However, if you don't want the jolt, avoid a first-act turning point start (or use a fractured tandem form that will let you flash forward to conceal the hiatus).

I suspect that *Brick* works well with its first-act turning point opening because it has a short, fast-moving first act.

3. PREVIEW FLASHBACK FROM THE MIDDLE OF THE FILM (CENTRE-SPLIT FLASHBACK)

This is when, as in *Goodfellas*, the preview flashback scene or sequence comes from the middle of the film, usually at the midpoint. Centre-split flashback adds energy to films that are inherently slow to start, such as biographies, where the start of the story is necessarily (a) the actions of a passive young protagonist, observing and being influenced by others and (b) episodic, thus potentially meandering and apparently directionless.

Centre split can be used very effectively to point to a moral, as *Goodfellas* shows. *Goodfellas* opens with the horrific and definitive event that marks the start of the protagonist's decline into complete depravity. The horrific event is concluded by a voice-over in which the protagonist says, in a shockingly cheerful way, that he always wanted to be a gangster. We then flash back to the protagonist as an impressionable adolescent starting his career in crime, follow him through to the middle and the horrific event (up until which gangsterism is largely a game), then as, increasingly brutalised, he sinks ever deeper into violence, drugs and promiscuity.

To see the strength of the centre-split flashback in *Goodfellas*, imagine the film without it. It would run chronologically, starting with the protagonist as an adolescent, then go on to show him as young man, enjoying gangsterism. The first half of the film would come across as a jaunty, episodic black comedy endorsing gangsterism. The brutalisation wouldn't start until the film's middle, by which time it would probably be too late to introduce a strong moral point. It would feel as if we had changed films, from gangster romp to cautionary tale. Starting in the middle, with a brutalised man, then flashing back to the man as an innocent young boy, provides not only a great hook but a direction for the plot (so it doesn't feel episodic) and seeds the moral ending.

As a postscript on biographies, it is very easy to forget to plot a biography as a three-act structure building to a climax. Too easily you can end up just inserting events that happened. To write a bio-pic you really need a 'take' on your central character, with events that illustrate that take.

4. PREVIEW FLASHBACK AT SECOND-ACT TURNING POINT (TWO-THIRDS PREVIEW FLASHBACK)

This is probably the most common preview flashback and it is a very powerful suspense device. Two-thirds preview flashback opens either just before or during the protagonist's second-act turning point—their closest moment to death physically, emotionally or both, followed by a decision to fight back that becomes, in act three, the battle to win.

For writers trying to seize and hold an audience, the second-act turning point of a plot is an ideal hook because the protagonist is at such a bad moment in their lives that the audience will instantly identify with them and engage with the film. Not only that, they will remember the scene, so it both grabs the audience and holds them.

Michael Clayton has a preview flashback opening at the second-act turning point. The film opens as a Mr Fixit lawyer performs his typical work—then narrowly escapes a car bomb. This instantly ups the stakes and pulls us into his story. The film then jumps back to the start of the story, the disturbance.

We can see the same sort of thing in *Walk the Line*, although here violence is only implied. The film opens with Johnny Cash about to go on stage in his famous Folsom prison concert. Frowning, he thoughtfully strokes the huge blade of a vicious-looking table saw, which is clearly bringing back bad memories. Instantly, he has our attention, the hint of violence lifting the stakes and making us intrigued to find out what happens. The film then flashes back to the start of his story.

Some films that use the second-act turning point for a preview flashback don't open on violence or the threat of it; in fact, they don't feel like a moment of crisis at all, instead they feel like the start to a story where intriguingly odd things are happening. For example, *Eternal Sunshine of the Spotless Mind* (which actually combines this kind of preview flashback with other forms) simply opens on a man, Joel, waking up, being oddly puzzled by a couple of unremarkable things, heading off to work, then impulsively not taking his normal train but catching a different one, a train to Montauk. At Monauk station he meets an attractive, eccentric woman, Clementine, who initiates a conversation, and the two seem to be moving into a relationship. It feels like a linear film, with a normality leading to a disturbance.

It's only when the sequence returns two-thirds of the way through the film that we realise, to our dismay, that Joel, far from being in normality in those opening scenes, was actually at his second-act turning point because, disturbingly, while he has just had a procedure that wiped treasured memories of his love affair with Clementine, he is not aware of it. However—and this is crucial—alongside our dismay is excitement because we realise that the reason Joel is catching the train to Montauk is because, in some deep part of his brain, he has remembered Clementine's plea 'meet me at Montauk', and although he doesn't know it, his train trip is the start of his fight against the odds, the second part of the second-act turning point.

The shock of realisation followed by a surge of excitement and suspense that comes with the return of the preview scene in *Eternal Sunshine of the Spotless Mind* demonstrates clearly why preview flashback using the second-act turning point is such a powerful tool. Its combination of the protagonist first in deep distress then deciding, with outstanding courage, to fight back creates what is sometimes termed 'a leaning-forward moment'; that is, a moment where audiences get so powerfully seized by the story that they lean forward in their seats, willing the protagonist to win. If we were to create a graph of the audience's emotions during the return of the second-act turning point, their emotions would first track down into deepest depression, then instantly soar up into optimism. This is exactly the effect we want three-quarters of the way through the film when, as we must never forget, the audience has been sitting still for more than an hour and can easily start to get restless.

Interestingly, while it's widely recognised that a preview scene inserts energy when it first appears at the start of the film (which is why preview scenes are so often used), in fact, properly used, it has most of its impact when it returns, for the reasons I've explained above. Wrongly used preview flashback doesn't have this energising effect on its return because it doesn't lead on to anything, giving us instead just a sense déjà vu, whereby we're thinking: 'Well, we're back where we started—and so what?'

CINEMA PARADISO: TWO-THIRDS PREVIEW FLASHBACK WITHOUT A RETURN OF THE PREVIEW SCENE

Cinema Paradiso (the later, director's cut version) is interesting in that it opens three-quarters of the way through the protagonist Toto's story, at the death of Alfredo, his surrogate father, *but we do not visit that scene again*. The film jumps from this opening to the start of the story, Toto as a little boy. It then proceeds chronologically through to the point at which teenage Toto leaves his hometown. It then jumps back to the present, with middle-aged Toto attending the funeral, revisiting the cinema and finding out the truth of his lost love.

Probably, *Cinema Paradiso* does not need to return to its opening scene because the second-act turning point is an emotional one, the death of Toto's father figure. Returning to his receipt of the news would add nothing. *The Constant Gardener*, in a different form, but also opening on a second-act turning point, also does not revisit its opening scene, which is also news of a death. Note that the third act in *Cinema Paradiso* is a battle to win. Toto tries to win back his lost love, but fails.

Preview flashback or double narrative flashback?

It's very easy to confuse preview flashback, particularly two-thirds preview flashback, with double narrative flashback (as in *Slumdog Millionaire*, *Shine* and *The English Patient*) and feel you need to use double narrative when two-thirds preview will do the job. As I've mentioned and will return to later, double narrative films have at least two complete stories, one in the past and one in the present, and throughout the film they jump between the two. By contrast, excellent mechanism though it is, preview flashback is really just a loop: it starts on a scene from the film, usually the middle or two-thirds through, then jumps back to the disturbance and continues uninterrupted until the end.

Don't use double narrative flashback unless you really feel you need an ongoing story in the present because once you opt to use a story in the present as well as the past you have to service that story, and that (as we'll see later) can be quite a task. A story in the present has to have a very good reason for taking up screen time and if it doesn't it will feel pointless and therefore be boring. It has to comment in some way on the story in the past, and depict a character in the present exploring or having explained to them a mystery or puzzle central to the story in the past. Stories in the present without a mystery (as in *Pay It Forward*), or that frequently feature a character passively sitting remembering (like *Nixon*), or just involve characters engaged in a normality will be boring. Think carefully before you proceed with double narrative flashback about what your story in the present would actually contribute.

TURNING 'CINDERELLA' INTO PREVIEW FLASHBACK

Our heading here is not 'how to use preview flashback in "Cinderella"' but 'turning "Cinderella" into preview flashback'. This is because preview flashback actually changes the shape of a film, whereas illustration and regret flashbacks are just backstory mechanisms inserted into a linear story. 'Cinderella' is most suited to a two-thirds preview flashback, with Cinderella running away and losing her slipper at the stroke of midnight. Preview flashback at disturbance—the invitation to the ball—would have a slowing effect; there is no need for us to see the scene twice and Cinderella's normality is not interesting enough to be worth visiting by a time jump. Preview flashback at first-act turning point or midpoint would not be very effective either, since it would simply send us back to an essentially uneventful first act, uneventful because the disturbance is not particularly surprising. Perhaps this gives us a new clue to preview flashback. Stories with a low-surprise disturbance shouldn't use preview flashback that starts on a first-act turning point.

Life-changing incident flashback

Life-changing incident flashback is one short, traumatic, life-changing scene from the past of a mysterious person at the heart of the film. It keeps recurring incrementally, showing an extra bit each time, until we finally see it in its entirety, when its final moments explain the baffling motives and behaviour of the unfathomable character and solve the central mystery of the film. Hence, your life-changing scene:

1 must only reveal its full significance in its final moments
2 is what the film is about.

If you are thinking about using a life-changing incident flashback in your film, make sure it is genuinely the mystery at the heart of the film; thus, what the film is about.

Typical life-changing incident flashback films are *The End of the Affair* and *Catch 22*. In *Catch 22*, the life-changing incident flashback is the story's disturbance. It is what causes the protagonist's story, with the protagonist Yossarian being the enigmatic outsider who is behaving oddly. The film opens on the second-act turning point (where Yossarian is stabbed for apparently no reason). As he slips into unconsciousness, we see the first moments of his disturbance, which is the incremental flashback. Yossarian is on a bomber, assisting the plane's gunner, who appears to be only slightly injured.

The incremental flashback occurs throughout the film, with a little more shown each time, until we see it in its horrific entirety. What the final moments of the final flashback reveal is that the man's abdomen has been blasted open, with fatal implications, and Yossarian discovers that the morphine in the plane's first-aid kit has been sold by profiteers. Having seen this, we realise it was what has been driving his frantic, often surreal attempts to get out of the air force.

The flashback appears in its entirety immediately before the film has come full circle back to Yossarian's second-act turning point, which is where the film opened. After this, it does not appear again (we don't need it because the mystery is solved and its job is done) and, energised by the horror of the flashback's final moments, *Catch 22* goes into its truncated third act, in which Yossarian actually pursues his lost dream, escaping from hospital and setting off in a life raft to row his way to Sweden and away from the war.

DON'T GIVE THE GAME AWAY TOO EARLY

It's crucial in all kinds of incremental flashback that you don't finish the flashback too early or have the crucial life-changing incident in the middle of the flashback. If you do, your film will fizzle. Also, you need to position the final reveal so that it happens when you are ready to take the story into its final act. The revelation—the mystery finally solved—will inject great energy, so capitalise on that.

THE END OF THE AFFAIR

The End of the Affair also opens on the story's second-act turning point (which is after the mysterious antagonist Sarah has ended the affair with the protagonist without warning or explanation) although we stay here, at the second-act turning point, much longer than in *Catch 22* before we go back to the past.

The life-changing flashback is used rather differently. This time, the life-changing incident and the flashback depicting it happen not to the protagonist, but to Sarah. The life-changing incident flashback does not start to appear until quite late in the story in the past and it is crucially important to the story that neither the protagonist nor the audience know until very late that the incident actually happened at all.

The story of the film is that some years after the abrupt end of the affair, the protagonist, vicious with resentment and jealousy, gets a private investigator to stalk Sarah and find out whether she has a new lover. Much of the pathos of the film is that, almost too late, he finds out that she ended the affair not because she didn't love him but because of a life-changing incident of which he was unaware. She has loved him all along. The 'end of the affair' in the title *was* the life-changing incident. It is—along with the philosophical message about God and religion that the incident carries—what the film is about.

This kind of story is only possible, of course, when the life-changing incident happens to the antagonist. Life-changing incident flashback form is in itself a kind of detective story, but a story involving an investigator protagonist trying to fathom the behaviour of a mysterious antagonist is actually quite common in detective stories generally, and the detective does not have to be romantically involved with the antagonist.

If you wanted to use life-changing incident flashback form in a detective story film, your film could simply involve a detective protagonist finding out the motives of an enigmatic outsider, a person who, unknown to the detective, is having incremental flashbacks to a life-changing incident or, possibly, the crime being investigated. Hence, *The End of the Affair* provides a useful template, with good dramatic irony. If you find yourself writing a story like this, with a life-changing incident flashback happening to the antagonist, you will have to think carefully about where you position the incremental flashbacks. They normally occur when the antagonist has an experience in the present that triggers a flashback.

You will also have to remember to structure your film with the investigator as protagonist, climbing the three-act mountain, and not get distracted into centring the plot around the antagonist, with the protagonist simply an observer.

INCREMENTAL DREAM

Sometimes life-changing incident flashback form is used in a conventional linear film to show the protagonist's recurring dream, often a nightmare, incrementally. This happens in *Gladiator* and *Twelve Monkeys* and, famously, *Wild Strawberries*, with the recurring nightmare in *Twelve Monkeys* providing a thought-provoking and pleasing Rosebud twist ending to the film. A chronological series of dreams being dreamt by a protagonist about their past is rather different. It is functionally the same as double narrative flashback, the form of *Citizen Kane* and *Slumdog Millionaire*. *Wild Strawberries* contains both sorts; the first, dreams of actual memories that tell us what happened in the professor's past, the second a recurring, building symbolic nightmare.

TURNING 'CINDERELLA' INTO LIFE-CHANGING INCIDENT FLASHBACK

You could not use life-changing incident flashback in 'Cinderella' because the story as it stands does not show Cinderella or anyone else acting oddly as a result of some extraordinary event happening in the past. To make it work, you would need to add a life-changing incident. Life-changing incident flashback needs to live up to its name: it needs to be the cause of shocking problems in the present.

OTHER KINDS OF FLASHBACK IN *CATCH 22* AND *THE END OF THE AFFAIR*

Catch 22 actually contains a range of different flashbacks. There is flashback as illustration, which illustrates something just stated in dialogue (when Dreedle asks whether he is indeed decorating soldiers because they have ditched their bombs in the Mediterranean, and we see on screen the event he is describing). Similarly, there is simple illustration flashback when Yossarian sees the wrecked fuselage of Orr's plane floating in the sea and remembers Orr working on a heating machine in their tent. Again, there is a dream flashback (another version of memory) where Yossarian not only dreams the life-changing flashback, but also dreams of a naked woman beckoning to him from the sea. Note the eeriness of the life-changing incident in *Catch 22*, which is shot so as to have a dream-like quality, providing a recurring, ominous moment of calm. In any film, the director calls the shots, but there is no reason why, if you as writer wanted this effect, you could not state: 'ominously calm and dreamlike' in the script.

The End of the Affair makes very clever use of a tiny snippet of flashback as illustration (so brief that it is sometimes almost subliminal) to the protagonist's memory of the first time he and Sarah made love. It also uses flashback as illustration (to show Sarah's version of events when the bomb went off), blending it with flashback as life-changing incident in the repeated and incrementally revealed use of the bomb's explosion and events immediately before and after. Note how the explosion itself recurs independently, at moments of great emotion. This is a good trick to remember: it adds mystery.

Chapter 36
Complex or double narrative flashback: An introduction

DOUBLE NARRATIVE FLASHBACK, SEEN in films such as *Slumdog Millionaire, Milk, Shine, Fried Green Tomatoes, The Usual Suspects, The English Patient, Memento, The Bridges of Madison County, The Curious Case of Benjamin Button, The Sweet Hereafter, The Life of David Gale, Citizen Kane* and many others, tells two or more stories in past and present. Double narrative flashback often fails because writers insert random flashbacks into flagging scripts in the hope of increasing energy levels. This is a recipe for disaster. The flashback does provide instant energy, but when it's over the script is still flagging and the audience has forgotten where it was. Flashbacks in successful double narrative flashback films neither contain random material nor occur at random. Remarkably, they consist of a three-act linear story (set in the past) and they appear in strict chronological order. Essentially, to create a double narrative flashback film, you construct two three-act stories, one long one in the past and one short one in the present, and jump between them at specific cliff-hangers in each story.

This pattern comes up again and again in double narrative films from all over the world and even (amazingly) appears in works that are thousands of years old, such as Homer's *Odyssey*. It is surprisingly easy to follow and recreate. We will come back to the pattern in a moment. First of all, we need to look at how you can pick that a film or an idea for a film is double narrative flashback.

Characteristics of double narrative flashback
The main distinguishing structural features of double narrative flashback are:
- **Two narratives** The action keeps jumping between one complete story in the present and at least one complete story in the past. The story in the past is usually longer and more important than the story in the present.
- **Enigmatic outsider** The film always involves a person or people in the present finding out about the past actions and motives of an enigmatic outsider in a way that explains that person's current

behaviour or situation. In autobiographical voice-over versions, the narrator might be the person examining their own actions, and may or may not also be the enigmatic outsider.

- **Wisdom born of pain, love versus duty** The enigmatic outsider usually has a wisdom born of pain and is always juggling love or personal fulfilment with duty or social obligation.
- **Epic love story** The story in the past is usually epic and often a story about relationships and great passion, particularly lost love.
- **Detective story** The film is a kind of detective story whereby, little by little, flashbacks explain (or appear to explain) more and more about an enigmatic outsider who is being asked questions by an investigator figure or sometimes a sequence of investigator figures. If the enigmatic outsider is dead (as in *Citizen Kane*), the investigator will ask the outsiders' friends and family about them, or read their letters (for example, *The Bridges of Madison County*).
- **The past is more important than present** While normally a film is written to make the audience wonder what *will* happen in response to a new event, double narrative flashback is written to make the audience wonder what happened in the past, and how the past impacts on the present and future. The film's primary concern is about what happened in the past.
- **The mystery solved** The story in the present *solves the mystery* of the story of the past or, in a twist, reveals that while the mystery seems to be solved, it isn't. This is a quick way to distinguish double narrative from other kinds of time jump stories. For example, the story in the present in *City of God* is not about solving any mysteries. It just shows how Rocket, stuck in the line of fire between a mob of gangsters and a group of police, manages to take the final incriminating photos of Lil'Z.
- **Action and relationship lines** All double narrative flashback films have both action and relationship lines in the past and in the present. For example, in *Shine*, in the present David Helfgott has an action line about his career, but also has relationship lines involving his friends and future wife. In the past, he has an action line dealing with the events of his career and also a relationship line about his dealings with his father.

A detective story of the human heart

The detective story element mentioned in the list is crucial to double narrative flashback. This form is always a 'detective story of the human heart'. That description is not whimsically poetic: it describes story content, which is 'an investigator figure, or figures, sets out to discover the dreams and motives of an enigmatic outsider'. It reminds us that the film must reveal a sequence of clues about the enigmatic outsider's past (like a detective story), and that those clues are the innermost secrets of the enigmatic outsider, the reason for their behaviour. If the film doesn't fulfil these criteria and do these things it will be boring, like *Pay It Forward* (see p. 181). The closest flashback form to this in terms of the detective story element that we've seen so far is life-changing incident flashback. However, films that use life-changing incident flashback are about the effects of just one crucial incident on the enigmatic person. Double narrative flashback is about the effect on the enigmatic person of many incidents, often the events of a lifetime.

Jumping between stories
THE TRIGGERING CRISIS
Successful double narrative flashback always jumps at major emotional moments in both of its storylines and we can pick a clear structured pattern from the film's opening moments. One family of double narrative flashback opens on the second-act turning point of the story in the past. The other family opens on the climax of the story in the past. Crucially, in both cases the events in this opening scene *are also what cause the disturbance in the present*; indeed, they sometimes *are* the disturbance. In other words, the same events and sometimes even the same scene have different functions in each of the two stories. They are the disturbance (or the trigger for the disturbance) in the story set in the present and simultaneously the second-act turning point or climax in the story set in the past. Because these events set the double narrative in action, triggering the story in the present, we can call them 'the triggering crisis'.

For example, the opening sequence of *Shine* shows an apparently crazy man banging on the door of a closed restaurant late at night. This is the disturbance of the story in the present ('an apparently crazy man persuades the staff and owner of a restaurant to let him play the piano, turns out to be a concert pianist, is a huge success, wins a loving wife and returns triumphantly to the concert-hall stage') but *the same scene is also, simultaneously, the second-act turning point of the story in the past.* It is David's decision to act—to find a piano—in a story that runs: 'David Helfgott, a child prodigy, wins fame as a pianist, has a nervous breakdown, stays in psychiatric hospitals for years, comes out, is lost, alone and desperate to play the piano, sets out to find a piano, finds one in a restaurant, persuades the staff and owner of a restaurant to let him play the piano, is a huge success, wins a loving wife, returns triumphantly to the concert-hall stage').

Another film in the same family as *Shine* is *Slumdog Millionaire*, and it opens in the same way. It opens on Jamal's second-act turning point, his arrest, which is simultaneously the disturbance of the story in the present, namely the police chief's story, the interrogation of Jamal.

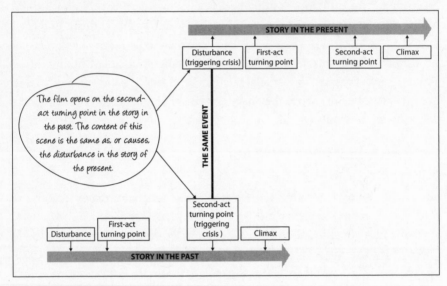

Figure 36.1 The triggering crisis in *Shine*, *Slumdog Millionaire* and *The English Patient*

Citizen Kane belongs to the other family of double narrative flashback films that open on the climax of the story in the past, in this case Kane's death, which causes the disturbance of the journalist's story in the present. *The Usual Suspects*, which is in the same family as *Citizen Kane*, opens on the moment when the enigmatic outsider, Dean Keaton, is murdered, which is what causes the disturbance of the story in the present, which is the story of Kujan, the customs officer, interviewing Verbal Kent (see Figure 36.3).

We can also understand the way the story in the past and the story in the present intersect by thinking of them as being like two of Christopher Vogler's hero's journey circles, one set inside the other and linked at one point (see Figure 36.2).

THE FIRST FLASHBACK IS TO THE DISTURBANCE IN THE PAST

After the triggering crisis, double narrative flashback films go quickly into their first flashback. Again, the content of this first flashback is crucial and is not chosen at random. *The first flashback is the event that started it all*; technically, the disturbance of the story in the past. We've seen this jump from

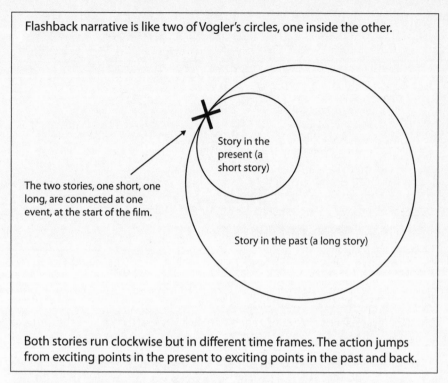

Flashback narrative is like two of Vogler's circles, one inside the other.

The two stories, one short, one long, are connected at one event, at the start of the film.

Story in the present (a short story)

Story in the past (a long story)

Both stories run clockwise but in different time frames. The action jumps from exciting points in the present to exciting points in the past and back.

Figure 36.2 Flashback narrative is like two of Vogler's circles

second-act turning point to disturbance earlier, in other flashback forms, and it is vital to keep the story on track.

In *Shine*, the first flashback is to the disturbance of David's story in the past, which is the music competition where he met his first proper piano teacher, Ben Rosen (notice it is a dynamic scene, interesting in its own right—we always have to remember our primary job is to tell a good story). The film stays in the past until the story in the past reaches its first-act turning point, which is when David's father agrees to let him start music lessons with Rosen. It then returns to the present.

In *Slumdog Millionaire*, the story is 'how a boy from the Mumbai slums wins *Who Wants to be a Millionaire?*, so the first flashback is to how Jamal was able to answer the first of the questions on the show. When it has shown us in the past the reason Jamal could answer the first question, the story jumps back to the present.

In *Citizen Kane*, the first flashback is to the disturbance of Kane's story (when he was taken away from his mother). In *The Usual Suspects*, it is to the formation of the gang, the disturbance of Keaton's story.

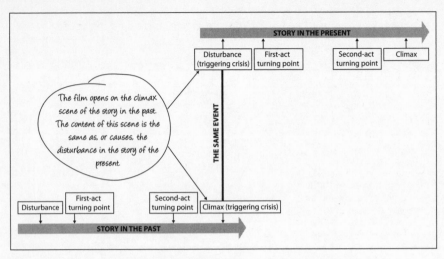

Figure 36.3 The triggering crisis in *Citizen Kane* and *The Usual Suspects*

AFTER THE FIRST FLASHBACK?

After the first flashback, double narrative flashback will continue jumping to and fro between past and present on the dramatic high points of the three-act structure in each story (making good use of the complications in the second act) until finally we see the triggering crisis scene again and the film has come full circle. Fascinatingly, once we have seen the triggering crisis again, the film heads forward chronologically to its climax with *no more flashbacks*. There may in some films be brief 'flashback as illustration' moments, but there are no long flashbacks filling in details from the past. So, once we have seen David Helfgott banging on the window a second time, the story progresses without interruption until its end. Similarly, once we have reached the point in Jamal's story where he is arrested and taken off to be interviewed by the police, his story proceeds uninterrupted to its end. Again, in *Citizen Kane* and *The Usual Suspects*, once we have come full circle to the opening scene, there are no more flashbacks.

The jumping pattern in double narrative flashback is shown in Figure 36.4.

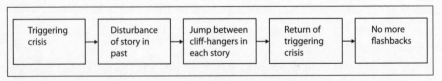

Figure 36.4 The jumping pattern in double narrative flashback

The triggering crisis injects very powerful energy into double narrative flash-backs at the same time as making sure their two stories are on track. But you must make sure that your disturbance in the present has been caused by the second-act turning point or climax of the story in the past. Does it matter whether you open on second-act turning point or climax of the story in the past? Yes, as we shall see in the next chapter.

Chapter 37
Thwarted dream and case history flashback

THERE ARE TWO MAIN families of flashback that differ in both structure and theme. The first is 'thwarted dream' flashback (for example, *Shine*, *Slumdog Millionaire*, *The Remains of the Day*, *The English Patient*), where someone is pursuing a lost or stolen dream. The second is 'case history' flashback (*Citizen Kane*, *The Usual Suspects*, *The Life of David Gale*, *The Bridges of Madison County*), which explores an enigmatic, sometimes sinister outsider, or larger-than-life character. Each presents the world and human nature in a very different way and that world view is reflected in their structure. That difference in world view explains the apparent paradox I pointed to earlier, whereby flashbacks in *Shine* showed David Helfgott as a product of his past, while flashbacks in *Citizen Kane* showed that Kane remained a mystery despite extensive flashbacks about his past. Thwarted dream, to which *Shine* belongs, uses flashbacks to transmit the view that people are a product of their environment. Case history, to which *Citizen Kane* belongs and as its name implies, uses flashbacks to transmit the view that people are not explained by what has happened to them and are ultimately mysterious, indeed often sinister.

The thematic and structural differences between thwarted dream and case history are:

- the content of the triggering crisis—what scenes are used
- the message—the view of human nature
- the return of the triggering crisis scene, and what happens after that
- the use of protagonist, antagonists and mentor antagonists

The content of the triggering crisis

Earlier, I said that double narrative flashback films opened on either the second-act turning point or the climax of the story in the past. Thwarted dream films start on the second-act turning point; case history starts on the climax—for reasons we'll look at below.

THE MESSAGE: OPPOSING VIEWS OF HUMAN NATURE

Typical thwarted dream flashback films are: *Shine*, *Slumdog Millionaire*, *The English Patient* and *The Remains of the Day*. Thwarted dream deals with an enigmatic outsider pursuing a lost or stolen dream. It's optimistic, and the flashbacks reveal the enigmatic outsider to be a good person who has suffered greatly, has a wisdom born of pain, and who now strives to overcome their past, retrieve their dream, and triumph. The motto here is 'there but for the grace of God go I'. Usually the outsider does triumph, although poignant films like *The Remains of the Day* and *The End of the Affair* depict the dream lost at the last moment.

Meanwhile, case history flashback, seen in films such as *Citizen Kane*, *The Usual Suspects* and *The Life of David Gale*, puts forward the opposite view of human nature: that human beings defy analysis and are more than the sum total of their past. They are a study (a case history) about people never being quite what they seem and, indeed, the motto for case history is: 'people are never what they seem'. The point of the story is to make the audience believe something that proves in a final twist to be untrue or unknowable. The enigmatic outsiders are products of nature rather than nurture, beings who are ultimately mysterious, unpredictable, often in positions of power and frequently menacing or even criminal. Indeed, crime or a cover-up are often part of the story, frequently as a final twist (a structural point that we'll look at later). While the investigator or investigators in thwarted dream usually succeed in penetrating the mystery of the enigmatic outsider, any investigator in case history will either not solve the mystery (as in *Citizen Kane*), be duped (as in *The Usual Suspects*) or discover that the mystery was not what they thought it to be. Even the heart-warming *Fried Green Tomatoes* carries this message.

Reason for the triggering crisis: Thwarted dream

Thwarted dream chooses the second-act turning point from the story of the past to use in its crisis because the point of the film is to show how an enigmatic outsider fights a final battle in the third act to regain a dream. Hence, a good place to start is showing that outsider at their worst possible moment. A thwarted dream film can open either on the *first* part of the second-act turning point (the closest point to death—physical, emotional or both—as in *Slumdog Millionaire*, when Jamal is being tortured) or in its *second* part (the decision to act, as in *Shine*, which opens on David trying to get into the restaurant to play the piano).

Reason for the triggering crisis: Case history

Case history chooses the climax of the story in the past as the triggering crisis for the film because its message is that even if you study the details of a person's life or even their whole life, you cannot fathom human nature *or* you cannot fathom the extraordinary individual who is the enigmatic outsider. The films aren't about the pursuit of dreams, so there is no third-act battle to win back the dream. The scenario that carries this message is always a story (tough or poignant) that follows the outsider's life, *deliberately misleading the audience* into believing something about the enigmatic outsider that is proven wrong at the very last moment, thereby proving the theme: people are inexplicable. This even happens in gentle forms like *The Bridges of Madison County* and *Fried Green Tomatoes*.

Case history films are normally about an enigmatic outsider who is dead, about to die or (like Leonard in *Memento* and Salieri in *Amadeus*) metaphorically returned from the dead. The climax of the story in the past in case history (and hence the disturbance of the story in the present) is usually someone's death, most commonly the death of the enigmatic outsider but sometimes someone else, as in *Memento*). This is sound storytelling, as death, the highest jeopardy, will always seize the audience's imagination, and so is particularly useful in a film that makes demands on its audience.

THE TRIGGERING CRISIS: SOME EXCEPTIONS

It's actually more surprising that there is such conformity in the triggering crisis than that there are exceptions, but we should note them and probably expect more in films of the future. In *Citizen Kane*, if we are to be absolutely precise, the first jump into the past is not a flashback, it is a piece of newsreel footage summarising Kane's life (thereby providing very useful backstory in a dramatic way). However, the first proper flashback is, as we've seen, the disturbance. *The Sweet Hereafter* and *The Life of David Gale* also have unusual triggering crises (see pp. 316, 319). Some films, such as *Fried Green Tomatoes*, don't have a triggering crisis at all, which gives them less initial impact, hence makes them much quieter.

After the return of the triggering crisis

Thwarted dream has a third act, a genuine battle to win, after the return of the triggering crisis. Just as in conventional narrative, the protagonist fights a third-act battle, so in thwarted dream the enigmatic outsider, often with allies, fights to win the lost dream.

The third act in the past of thwarted dream is also the entire story in the present. You can see this if you look back at the description of the third act of *Shine's* story in the past. It is identical to the description of the story in the present. Both are: 'David Helfgott persuades the staff and owner of a restaurant to let him play the piano, he turns out to be a concert pianist, is a huge success, wins a loving wife and returns triumphantly to the concert-hall stage.' So really, if we were to be absolutely accurate, Figure 36.1 would show the story in the present as being only the same length as act three of the story in the past. Everything that happens in the present after David Helfgott knocks on the restaurant door is the third act of his story, and is very much 'a battle to win', exactly as three-act conventional narrative requires. But it's also a self-contained three-act short film (lasting about twenty minutes). *Slumdog Millionaire* also has a very clear third-act battle to win (by answering the final question).

Shot of adrenalin in thwarted dream

We've seen in preview flashback how the return of the second-act turning point creates a leaning-forward moment for the audience. The same thing happens in thwarted dream. The return of the second-act turning point injects a massive shot of adrenalin into the film exactly when we want it; the audience now fully understands the enigmatic outsider's traumatic past and is deeply invested in their courageous attempt to win back the dream against very unfavourable odds. This is the massive payoff of the detective story of the human heart, so when you are writing thwarted dream flashback, you must exploit every minute of it, making your climax a real 'do or die' for the dream.

Case history finishes quickly

In case history, the triggering crisis is the climax of the story in the past. Hence, after the return of the triggering crisis, all we see is the film's resolution. For example, in *The Usual Suspects*, after the return of the triggering crisis (the fire on the ship and the shooting of Keaton) all we see is the twist ending, in which Kujan realises he has been duped.

The Rosebud twist

Because case history opens on its climax (just like bookend flashback), there is a potential for anticlimax when the climax scene returns. Case history solves this problem in exactly the same way as bookend flashback: it inserts a Rosebud twist ending after the return of the climax/triggering crisis. The twist ending is a defining and vital structural characteristic of case history flashback because it carries the film's message; namely, that people are not what they seem. The

Rosebud twist often, but not always, involves dramatic irony—whereby, as in *Citizen Kane*, *The Usual Suspects* and *The Life of David Gale*, the audience learns something that the protagonist either never knows, or else learns too late. In other films, such as *Fried Green Tomatoes* or *Amadeus*, the twist is learnt by both audience and protagonist and has its impact via shock value.

DOES THE ROSEBUD TWIST MAKE CASE HISTORY SUCCEED?

Arguably, case history flashback succeeds or fails largely on the original- ity and ingenuity of the Rosebud twist. Think of *Citizen Kane* without the Rosebud ending, *The Usual Suspects* without Verbal Kent's transformation, *Fried Green Tomatoes* without the denouement about the missing corpse or *Memento* without the final revelation of the tricks that Leonard's memory was playing on him. If you are writing a case history double narrative, work very hard to invent a clever twist. In a very real sense your film is about your Rosebud twist. However, just as in the Smiley/Thompson model, the pro- tagonist's plan in response to the disturbance should send the audience in the wrong direction so that the first-act turning point surprise comes as a much bigger surprise, make your audience expect the film to end one way, then have your Rosebud twist show it ending in another real-but-unusual way.

Diagrams of thwarted dream and case history

Above, we looked at how double narrative flashback can be usefully depicted diagrammatically by one circle inside another, touching at one point. To understand more precisely how the stories in past and present in each form intersect and see the the exact pattern of the jumping back and forth, look at Figure 37.1, which is a diagram showing the structural mechanics of *Shine*, a thwarted dream model.

THE STRUCTURAL MECHANICS OF *SHINE*

In Figure 37.1 the story in the past is a big circle, the story in the present is a small circle. Both stories run in a clockwise motion, with the action depicted as a broken line, moving between past and present. The line running off to the right at the top of the circle is the film's action after the return of the trig- gering crisis. It is a single straight line because, in double narrative flashback, there are no more flashbacks after the return of the triggering crisis.

As we know, the events that happen after the return of the triggering crisis are simultaneously the third act of David's story *and* the story in the present from after its disturbance to its end. The scene where David plays brilliantly is the first-act turning point *in the story of the present* (because the story in

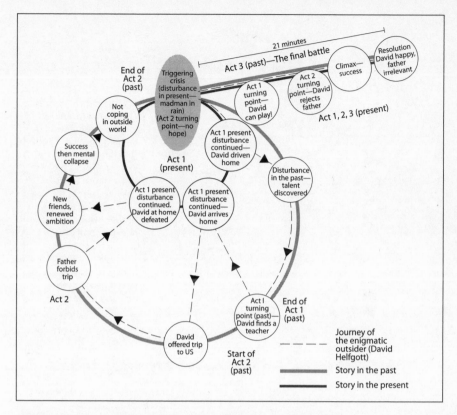

Figure 37.1 The structural mechanics of *Shine* (thwarted dream)

the present is about someone who looks like a demented derelict but turns out to be a concert pianist). The inner circle is so small because all that happens in the story of the present between the first appearance of the triggering crisis and its return is David being taken back to the halfway house, sitting in his room, then setting out in the rain to return to the restaurant.

THE STRUCTURAL MECHANICS OF *THE USUAL SUSPECTS*

Figure 37.2 is a diagram of *The Usual Suspects* (a case history model), showing the triggering crisis positioned at the climax of the story in the past and the disturbance of the story in the present, and depicting the way the film's action jumps between its stories.

This story is told in flashbacks by Verbal Kent, as Kujan (the investigator protagonist) interviews him. Kujan is convinced that Keaton is alive; moreover, that Keaton is actually Keyser Soze.

Kujan's interrogation of Verbal forms half of the story in the present. The rest concerns the interrogation of the other survivor, a Hungarian man badly

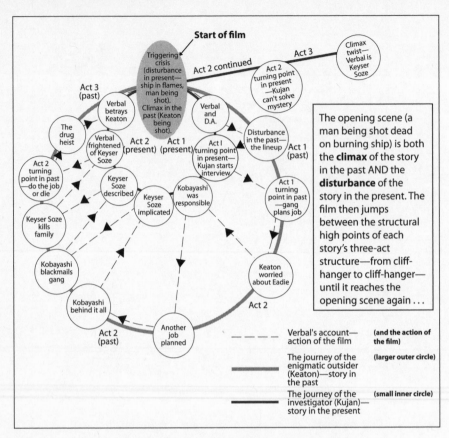

Start of film

Climax twist—Verbal is Keyser Soze

Act 3

Triggering crisis (disturbance in present—ship in flames, man being shot). Climax in the past (Keaton being shot).

Act 2 continued

Act 2 turning point in present—Kujan can't solve mystery

Act 3 (past)

Verbal betrays Keaton

Verbal and D.A.

The drug heist

Verbal frightened of Keyser Soze

Act 2 (present)

Act 1 (present)

Act I turning point in present—Kujan starts interview

Disturbance in the past—the lineup

Act 1 (past)

Act 2 turning point in past—do the job or die

Keyser Soze described

Keyser Soze implicated

Kobayashi was responsible

Act 1 turning point in past—gang plans job

Keyser Soze kills family

Kobayashi blackmails gang

Keaton worried about Eadie

Kobayashi behind it all

Act 2 (past)

Another job planned

Act 2

The opening scene (a man being shot dead on burning ship) is both the **climax** of the story in the past AND the **disturbance** of the story in the present. The film then jumps between the structural high points of each story's three-act structure—from cliff-hanger to cliff-hanger—until it reaches the opening scene again . . .

- - - - - Verbal's account—action of the film **(and the action of the film)**

━━━ The journey of the enigmatic outsider (Keaton)—story in the past **(larger outer circle)**

━━━ The journey of the investigator (Kujan)—story in the present **(small inner circle)**

Figure 37.2 The structural mechanics of *The Usual Suspects* (case history)

burned and in hospital. Verbal Kent's flashbacks depict the formation of the gang, their first successful job, the second job that goes wrong, and their manipulation by the arch-criminal Keyser Soze. Soze forces them to set up a drugs heist on a moored ship. The attempted heist brings the story full circle to the shipboard fire and Dean Keaton's death.

Like *Citizen Kane*, the investigator protagonist in the present (Dave Kujan) has learnt a lot about the enigmatic outsider, but by no means all. As in all case history flashback, there is a Rosebud twist at the end proving that human beings are unpredictable. In this instance it is a moment of dramatic irony in which, unwitnessed by Kujan, the audience sees limping, cowering Verbal transform into a striding, mysterious arch-criminal—then melt into nowhere with his offsider, Kobayashi. So the Rosebud twist in *The Usual Suspects* is that Dean Keaton was not the enigmatic outsider at all. The real enigmatic outsider was Verbal Kent.

While the story in the present is a three-act structure, it is very short.

Note how the diagram shows that much more happens between the first and second appearances of the triggering crisis in case history than in thwarted dream. This is natural, because case history opens at the end of the film, at its climax, not at the second-act turning point. This is why in Figure 37.2 there are so many word bubbles contained within the two circles.

Note too the brevity of the section of the film after the return of the triggering crisis. It runs for only about ten minutes, providing a false resolution (containing snippets of flashback as illustration) followed by a Rosebud twist that proves Kujan's theories utterly wrong.

Story content differences in thwarted dream and case history

To summarise, the differences in story content between the two forms are:

- Thwarted dream uses flashbacks to make the audience see the enigmatic outsider from the inside, as someone sympathetic who has been damaged by the past; in contrast, case history uses flashbacks to make the audience see the outsider from the outside, as an ultimately unknowable (and often sinister) specimen created by past trauma.
- In case history, the enigmatic outsider is usually dead. This is a useful tip: if you are planning a flashback film about someone who is dead, you have to use case history.
- In thwarted dream, the enigmatic outsider is capable of change. The audience very much wants them to get their lost dream and, provided this is physically possible, the outsider usually takes on the challenge.
- In case history, the outsider is incapable of change or wants to deceive. This is one of the reasons why such films have to end at the reappearance of the triggering crisis—because the outsider's incapacity for change means the film has nowhere further to go, except for an ironic twist.
- In thwarted dream, the person having the flashbacks is the enigmatic outsider. In case history, the person having the flashbacks is usually a person or persons who have known the outsider. This is obviously necessary when the outsider is dead (as in *Citizen Kane*), but it also happens when the outsider has in a sense returned from the dead, as in *The Sweet Hereafter* or *Memento*. Quite often, when the outsider has flashbacks they turn out to be misleading or deliberate lies (as in *The Usual Suspects*, *The Life of David Gale* and *Memento*).
- The flashbacks in case history give a documentary reality to the action. They make the audience a scientific observer, mystified and

often appalled by the outsider, whom the flashbacks do not explain but make more mysterious. In thwarted dream, the flashbacks explain the outsider and make them appealing. They make the audience identify with the outsider.

- Thwarted dream starts two-thirds through an unfinished story and has a final third (the third act) using new action in the present. This action is the pursuit of the lost dream. Case history starts with a story that is over except for an ironic twist.

- As a rule of thumb, if the enigmatic outsider is supposed to be a normal, likeable person damaged by life, flashback as thwarted dream is used. If the outsider is supposed to be an essentially unknowable, unpredictable person, flashback as case history is used. Flashback as case history is always used if the audience is supposed to disapprove of the outsider.

When to use flashback as case history

Over and above what is suggested above about story content, flashback as case history is commonly used in mystery or detective stories, to which its quasi-documentary feel adds a sense of reality. It is used to tell stories that are complete, except for a final ironic twist. It is seen a lot on TV. Often, a dateline is superimposed on screen in imitation of news footage. While the enigmatic outsider in flashback as thwarted dream is found to be sympathetic, and often goes on to achieve their lost dream and be changed by triumph, the outsider in flashback as case history is usually unchangeable and sometimes irredeemable, even evil. The protagonist learns a cautionary lesson from them—in fact we could describe flashback as case history as 'cautionary tale'.

When to use flashback as thwarted dream

The point of flashback as thwarted dream is to reveal the apparent coldness or mental imbalance of an enigmatic outsider as the understandable result of shocking personal experiences and thwarted dreams, and in doing so to show the outsider to be normal, sensitive and likeable. The intention and effect of flashbacks in this instance is to win the outsider enormous sympathy and goodwill from the audience, who typically feels that 'there but for the grace of God go I'.

This kind of flashback narrative often shows that what initially presented as mental imbalance is really a special wisdom, as in *Shine* and *Forrest Gump*.

Chapter 38
Flashback: Protagonists, antagonists and the enigmatic outsider

ONE OF THE HARDEST things to understand about double narrative flashback films is that there can be many protagonists and the same character can change from being an antagonist in one time frame to being a protagonist in another. The point of this is to keep the enigmatic outsider mysterious, but it is so alien to what conventional narrative teaches us about protagonists and antagonists that perhaps the easiest way to explain it is by a personal anecdote.

When I first started trying to find patterns in flashback films I was puzzled because, as I was trying to analyse *Shine*, I couldn't work out where Gillian, Helfgott's future wife, fitted in. *Shine* was clearly a film about David Helfgott, Helfgott was clearly the most interesting character, and yet Gillian felt like a protagonist. She provided a normal person's point of view of David, who was seen from the outside, presented as a lovable but essentially unpredictable and unfathomable man. We were in Gillian's shoes and it was her 'mountain' that the film was climbing. However, Gillian didn't appear until some way into the story, and before she appeared we were in the shoes of characters like Sylvia and Beryl, others who helped David, who also seemed to be playing the part of protagonist to his wild-card antagonist. So, who was the protagonist?

In the flashbacks (to David as a child and as a student) David was definitely the protagonist. We were in his shoes, something vividly illustrated by the film's first flashback to the competition where he met his first piano teacher, in which we literally see young David's point of view of the little church hall as he walks up to the platform to play. However, in the present and recent past (whenever Geoffrey Rush was playing David), except for one scene (when David is with his father in the present, and we are definitely in his shoes) we were almost always on the outside of David, seeing him through the eyes of Sylvia, Beryl or Gillian.

I found the same thing in *The English Patient*, in which Count Laszlo de

Almásy was clearly the protagonist in the past, but in the present was seen from the outside. We, the audience, were in the shoes of Hana, the nurse, seeing the mysterious de Almásy through her eyes, and even following her into her own love story, in which de Almásy did not appear at all. How could two characters like David Helfgott and Count Laszlo de Almásy, who were both so clearly protagonists in the past and so clearly the most interesting characters in the film, not be protagonists in the present?

Knowing who the protagonist is in a three-act structure is vital, because, as we've seen, that structure is based on the protagonist's journey, and the plot content needs to follow the protagonist up their three-act mountain. If we don't know who the protagonist is in our film, what plot do we include? Whose mountain do we create? How much plot do we give to other characters? And if characters who are not the film's key enigmatic outsider take over the action (as Gillian and Hana do), why doesn't the film turn into characters in search of a plot? Why don't we feel that we are 'in another film'?

To add to the problem, there were films such as *The Remains of the Day*, in which the enigmatic outsider Mr Stevens was seen from the outside for most of the story in the present (on his trip to find Miss Kenton) but after the return of the triggering crisis again took the role of protagonist which he'd had in the story in the past. In the last heartbreaking moments of the film, when he meets Miss Kenton, we are clearly in his shoes, knowing things that Miss Kenton, tragically, does not.

The enigmatic outsider is a mentor antagonist

I suddenly realised that, in the present, the enigmatic outsiders of double narrative flashback—characters like Mr Stevens, David Helfgott, Kane, Count Laszlo de Almásy—are mentor antagonists, exactly like Raymond in *Rain Man* or Merrick in *The Elephant Man*.

Like mentor antagonists, while they are the most interesting character in the film, indeed are the reason the film was written, dramatically they are best depicted in the story set in the present from the outside, as antagonists to less interesting 'normal' protagonists, to whom they teach a lesson about life. In this way, the enigmatic outsiders keep their mystery. As for characters like Gillian, Sylvia and Beryl in *Shine*, Hana in *The English Patient*, Customs Agent Kujan in *The Usual Suspects* and the journalist in *Citizen Kane* they felt like protagonists because that's exactly what they are. They are, I realised, like Charlie to Raymond in *Rain Man*: less interesting protagonists to a fascinating mentor antagonist with a wisdom born of pain or (in the case of wily case history outsiders like David Gale or Verbal Kent) of duplicity.

Hence, the way to work out and use protagonists and antagonists in double narrative flashback, both case history and thwarted dream, is to realise that *the enigmatic outsider is a mentor antagonist for most if not all of the present.*

In thwarted dream the outsider swaps between being protagonist in the past and mentor antagonist in the present

In thwarted dream, the outsider is a protagonist in the past but a mentor antagonist in the present. Hence Jamal is a mentor antagonist to the police chief and his sergeant and the show host—an enigmatic outsider with a wisdom born of pain—but a protagonist in his past. In certain thwarted dream flashback films (and *Slumdog Millionaire* is one) the outsider can become a protagonist in the present after the return of the triggering crisis. This permits them to be the protagonist as they are fighting their battle to win. If the outsider is too emotionally or physically damaged to become the protagonist and fight their own battle to win (as in *Shine* and *The English Patient*) they remain mentor antagonists for all of the content set in the present. In *The English Patient*, Hana fights the battle to win as a surrogate, because Lazlo is incapacitated.

In case history, the outsider is always a mentor antagonist

In case history at present (and it's hard to see how this could change), the outsider is always a mentor antagonist, that is, in both past and present. This is most important. It is central to the philosophy behind case history and crucial to the way you structure your case history film. *The enigmatic outsider in case history is never the protagonist.* We are never truly in that person's shoes.

We may think we are (as in *The Life of David Gale* and *The Usual Suspects*), but we are not, as we find out with a shock at the end of both films in the Rosebud twist. In films like these, in which the enigmatic outsider is deliberately or (as in *Memento*, unintentionally) lying to make the protagonists (and the audience) feel they are in their shoes, you need to create the story in the past exactly as if they were an endearing protagonist in search of a thwarted dream. You then reveal the truth in your Rosebud twist.

However, in films such as *Citizen Kane*, where the outsider is dead and therefore cannot reveal what went on in his/her mind, you need to create a protagonist to investigate them; in fact, as we'll see, often several protagonists, and indeed in some cases, several antagonists too. We'll come back to that in a moment, when we turn 'Cinderella' into case history flashback.

Why this obsession with protagonists and antagonists?

The reason we need to understand and be meticulous in our use of this pro-
tagonist/antagonist swap is so that we can stay on the outside of the enigmatic
outsider, thus create suspense, just as we had to in linear mentor antagonist
films. Without a mystery around the enigmatic outsider, the story in the
present is redundant, as in *Pay It Forward*. All of the material below about
who is and isn't a protagonist or antagonist is about the crucial storytelling
task of keeping the audience emotionally engaged. No conflict—no protagonist versus antagonist—equals no emotional engagement.

The investigator protagonist(s)

Except in rare cases, there is always, in both thwarted dream and flashback, an
investigator figure, a person who asks the enigmatic outsider questions or asks
others about the enigmatic outsider (as does the journalist in *Citizen Kane*).
This is because double narrative flashback is always a kind of detective story,
so questions always need to be asked. Naturally, the investigator figure is often
a professional investigator whose questions can trigger flashbacks—a police
officer, private eye, journalist, lawyer or the like. In other films (such as *Shine*
or *Fried Green Tomatoes*), the character asking questions of the enigmatic outsider will not be an investigator by profession, but simply a person who finds
the outside fascinating. The job of the protagonist is to find out what makes the
enigmatic outsider tick. Their questions or bewilderment trigger the flashbacks.

The rare double narrative flashback films that don't have an investigator
figure are those that have a protagonist talking in voice-over about their past
and present. There's no need for an investigator figure here because the narrator is already asking the questions and triggering their own flashbacks. The
narrator is already their own detective.

More than one protagonist

Here is where things start to get odd. Earlier, I spoke about Beryl, Sybil and
Gillian all playing the part of protagonists. This is quite common. Often there
is not just one investigator protagonist, but *several protagonists*, often one
after the other, each of whom typifies a different and normal response to the
outsider. We have already come across multiple protagonists in the parallel
narrative form of that name, where all members of the group are different
versions of the same protagonist.

In double narrative flashback the presence of many protagonists helps
make our view of the enigmatic outsider more complex and interesting. This

is evident very clearly in the opening of *Shine*, where everyone at Moby's restaurant provides a different kind of normal response to David. The waiter is amused, the waitress is concerned and the owner is disgusted and dismissive. David's future wife will represent another point of view, that of someone in love with David. *The Remains of the Day* also has serial protagonists, starting off with Mr Stevens' new employer, followed by the people Stevens meets on his cross-country drive.

Hence, while conventional narrative has one protagonist and many antagonists, in double narrative flashback, we have one mentor antagonist and many protagonists.

Many protagonists means many points of view

If your outsider travels physically, or keeps encountering new people, you need to structure the plot in the present with a number of protagonists, each having the goal of fathoming the outsider, each having a different attitude towards the outsider and each taking the story a little higher up the mountain in the present, the peak of which is the explanation of the mystery.

If you don't give the characters around the enigmatic outsider a point of view, a journey and a goal all they can do is watch your outsider while he or she steals the limelight. We see this in *Mr Saturday Night*. The comedian simply behaves as himself while others watch him. If you imagine the film with the agent and/or the comedian's brother and/or others as protagonists, each seeing the comedian from their own point of view, each having him as their antagonist, suddenly the film lifts. Suddenly these characters are actively involved in a conflict, observing an enigmatic man, rather than just watching a comedian whom we know inside out and complaining about him.

Whoever is having a flashback is the protagonist

When a person is having a flashback, by definition we are seeing the world from their point of view, so they are the protagonist for the duration of the flashback. This is easy to pick in thwarted dream because the enigmatic outsider is always the person having flashbacks, so they are always the protagonists. In *Shine*'s flashbacks, David is the protagonist. In *Slumdog*'s flashbacks, Jamal is the protagonist. In *The English Patient*'s flashbacks, Count Lazlo is the protagonist.

However, things can get very complicated in case history. In case history, as we've seen, the outsider is always an antagonist, in both past and present (that is, unless he or she is lying). He or she is always seen from outside. Indeed, there is often no choice about this because frequently the film starts after the outsider is dead! As you cannot get into the outsider's head and see their memories in flashback, to tell their story you usually have to invent characters who knew them in the past and can be found and interviewed by the investigator character. This is exactly what happens in *Citizen Kane*. The problem is, it can mean the writer has to invent an army of new characters who are sometimes antagonists, sometimes protagonists. Additionally, the writer has to take us inside then outside of those characters' heads with great frequency. The old rules of conventional narrative, whereby we stay in one person's head, with one world view for the whole film, simply do not apply.

Minor characters can switch from being antagonists to protagonists

To understand why the switch is necessary and how it happens, think of *Citizen Kane*. Kane, the enigmatic outsider, is dead, so we have to learn about him through the flashbacks of people who are being interviewed by our journalist protagonist. The flashbacks are flashback as illustration—backstory put on screen—and the interviewees are a banker, Kane's oldest friend, his second wife, his servant and so on; all interesting characters who are antagonists to our journalist protagonist. Now, imagine the film with the interviewees recounting their memories calmly and objectively, without any personal feelings about Kane or about being interviewed. The effect would be boring drama documentary, with the action drearily bouncing between past and present. It would be the difference between a real court case (witnesses impassively recounting memories) and a screen court case (lawyer and witnesses in conflict, lawyer and judge in conflict, and so on).

To maintain suspense and audience engagement we need conflict. The interviewees in *Citizen Kane* need to be in conflict with the journalist in the present and with Kane in the past. And when the film goes into flashback, it's vital that we see Kane through the point of view of whoever is having a flashback, as part of that person's past life, with that person at the centre. There can't be just a slab of Kane being interesting with no connection at all to the person having the flashback: that is documentary, not drama. It would be akin to the multiple protagonists in the present of, say, *Shine* simply watching David Helfgott without having any kind of attitude or response to him. Also, of course, the whole point of the film is to show many accounts of Kane, none of which ultimately explain either him or Rosebud, so the story has to do this.

Consequently, the interviewee having the flashback is the protagonist during the flashback. However, when the interviewee's flashback ends and the action returns to the present, things revert to where they were before.

Now we're back in the journalist's shoes. The interviewee ceases to be the protagonist and becomes, once more, an antagonist to the journalist protagonist, the two in a situation of mutual suspicion. This creates interest and suspense because we, the audience, have actually been in the interviewee's mind, whereas our protagonist has not. When his next interviewee has a flashback, they too will become the protagonist for the duration of their flashback. The result is a series of interesting, often angry, antagonists who in flashbacks, as protagonists, give us their own very personal point of view. Thus, they become characters, not mouthpieces to trigger footage of Kane.

'CINDERELLA' AS CASE HISTORY FLASHBACK

Described in the context of *Citizen Kane*, all of this may seem obvious. However, in your own case history film the point-of-view swap can easily get out of hand. The sheer number of extra characters and storylines needed to tell the case history story can be daunting. That said, you can create wonderful effects with this new army of characters. As an example, let's imagine an updated version of 'Cinderella' as case history flashback.

In the new version, Cinderella is not dead but, at her wedding, just as she was at about to marry the prince (the original 'Cinderella' story's climax), she collapsed into catatonia. To find out what has happened to Cinderella, we need to invent an investigator protagonist (like the journalist in *Kane*), so let's invent a psychiatrist, Dr Susan Smith, a leading expert on Cinderella's condition. The triggering crisis of our film will be the climax of Cinderella's story (Cinderella collapsing at the altar), which is simultaneously the start of Dr Smith's story, her disturbance. Let's have it that Dr Smith is a guest at the wedding, a friend of the prince, so is actually present when Cinderella collapses. Like all protagonists, Dr Susan Smith will need a good action line and relationship line (think of the unhappy housewife played by Kathy Bates in *Fried Green Tomatoes,* or the journalist Bitsey Bloom in *The Life of David Gale*).

Let's give Dr Susan Smith (in whom we must really immerse ourselves, so she is a genuinely interesting character) a powerful relationship line with, for example, a troubled marriage and a junkie sister. Meanwhile, in the action line, to find out about Cinderella, Dr Smith will need to interview people who knew Cinderella in the past. These interviewees will be antagonists to Dr Smith, our protagonist. However, when they are actually having flashbacks to their own past they will be protagonists, describing Cinderella who, in their past, was an antagonist (you need to recall this so that you remember to give them a plot mountain to climb during the flashback—otherwise you might just have them just standing in the background during the flashback passively observing Cinderella). Inventing interviewees sounds daunting, but actually opens up wonderful possibilities storywise. For example, let's make one of the interviewees Buttons. He was in love with Cinderella in the past, was trying to take her away from her terrible life with her sisters, and was heartbroken when she was about to marry the prince. We can do interesting things like making the ugly sisters give differing accounts from Buttons, and making Buttons give an unflattering account of the prince—all things to add to the detective story component.

ORDER OF THE FLASHBACKS

Typically, these will tell Cinderella's past in chronological order. The first flashback will show Cinderella's disturbance, the arrival of the invitation, seen from an interviewee's point of view. If you follow the *Citizen Kane* model, each interviewee's flashback takes the story forward a step.

A WRITER'S NIGHTMARE?

Adding all of these characters may seem a nightmare. However, if you look at the narrative that's emerging above, you can see that as well as telling Cinderella's story, suddenly you have a series of potentially very powerful stories in the present that can comment on the story in the past. Suddenly, you have Dr Susan Smith with her bad marriage and junkie sister. You have heartbroken Buttons, who perhaps Susan Smith feels might be lying or covering up for Cinderella in some way, or who might even have caused the catatonia. You also have the prince, the ugly sisters—and a detective story. Suddenly, you are getting a film with a genuinely interesting story in the present.

TRIGGERING CRISIS AND ROSEBUD TWIST

We need a Rosebud twist to end the story because otherwise it will simply return to the climax and fizzle out, so think hard. The twist needs to make the point that humans are not what they seem. It has to be striking but convincingly real. Whatever twist you give to the ending, the ending needs, of course, to permit resolution of the other stories. Perhaps Cinderella collapsed because the prince was wearing the medallion that revealed he was her twin, removed at birth!

'CINDERELLA' AS THWARTED DREAM FLASHBACK

Now that we have told 'Cinderella' as case history, let's retell it as thwarted dream flashback, which it suits better, as it already contains a dream lost then found.

If you were to tell 'Cinderella' as thwarted dream flashback, the best triggering crisis would be on or near her second-act turning point, which is when she runs away from the ball as the clocks strike midnight. We discussed this as a good starting point earlier, when we were looking at preview flashback. The story in the present would be a mentor antagonist story, with Cinderella as mentor antagonist, and another character as the investigator protagonist, or perhaps a series of investigator protagonists.

The story would run something like this. The opening scene shows a beautiful but distraught young woman in rags running away from a palace at midnight, chased by shouting guards. Meanwhile, in the kitchen of a big hotel, a young chef, Joe, our protagonist, is just finishing work (this is Joe's normality). Into the kitchen runs the distraught young woman (this is Joe's disturbance). She asks for a job, explaining that she has nowhere to go, but refuses to give details. Joe gives her a place to sleep for the night and, on the following day, gets her a job in the hotel kitchen alongside him, rapidly falling in love with her. Your job now is to construct a story set in the present that could be entitled 'Joe and the mysterious woman', writing it from Joe's point of view, showing how an enigmatic outsider came into his life and caused an adventure for him.

The first flashback, which happens after the story's triggering crisis, Cinderella's arrival in the kitchen (second-act turning point in Cinderella's story and simultaneously the disturbance in Joe's story), will be to the disturbance in Cinderella's story, the invitation to the ball. In flashbacks, the protagonist will be Cinderella, and the story will be seen from her point of view.

After that, the film will keep jumping between Joe's story in the present (with Joe as protagonist and Cinderella as antagonist, seen from Joe's point of view) and Cinderella's story in the past (with Cinderella as protagonist and seen from Cinderella's point of view). The jumps will occur at high points in the three-act structure of each story. Joe will be a strong character in his own right, fascinated by the stranger who has come into his life and trying to find out about her.

As in case history, the flashbacks will run chronologically. When the story in the past has come full circle and the triggering crisis scene is repeated (with the audience having their leaning-forward moment), Cinderella will pursue her dream. Perhaps Cinderella becomes the protagonist in act three (like Mr Stevens in *The Remains of the Day*). If she is too emotionally or physically traumatised by her past to act like a normal person (traumatised like David in *Shine* or the Count in *The English Patient*) she will stay the antagonist in the present.

What is exciting about thwarted dream narrative is the chance it gives you to create a genuinely interesting story in the present to run alongside your already interesting story in the past. Does Joe (broken-hearted) help Cinderella pursue her dream? Does he turn against her? Does she fall in love with him? Does he go back to his old girlfriend after all? Does she reject both him and the prince? What about all the other characters around them. Is Joe already married? Does he live at home with a demanding sick father? Is the prince someone Joe actually knows?

Joe has the potential to be as original and interesting as the frustrated woman visitor to the retirement home in *Fried Green Tomatoes* or the nurse, Hana, in *The English Patient*. Meanwhile, Cinderella in the present will be withdrawn, but she will have our sympathy because, unlike Joe, we know her story.

And of course there is always the possibility of a completely different thwarted dream model, a model like that of *Shine* or *The English Patient*, where instead of just one protagonist in the present, there are several. Perhaps Cinderella goes on the run after leaving the ball, and our serial protagonists are people assisting her in her flight.

Both Cinderella examples are light-hearted and very simple modern versions of the story, but the applications to something more serious are obvious.

Action and relationship lines in past and present

I've just been talking about relationship lines in our flashback versions of 'Cinderella', so this is a good time to think about relationship lines in double flashback narrative as a whole, and in particular how they relate to action lines.

You need to understand and make a distinction between your action lines and relationship lines so that as well as providing the action line in both stories for your key characters you make sure you include everything necessary to explain their emotional progression. The story in the past and the story in the present will both have action and relationship lines. As a general rule, the story in the present in double narrative flashback will be most concerned with action. The story in the past will be most concerned with relationships—because double narrative flashback films are essentially about motives and emotions. However, as I stressed, each story will contain an action line and a relationship line, so you must plot out each and interweave them as you would in a standard linear film.

CHANGING FROM PROTAGONIST TO ANTAGONIST IN DIFFERENT TIME FRAMES AFFECTS ACTION AND RELATIONSHIP LINES

As we've seen, characters in double narrative flashback sometimes change from protagonists to antagonists when the action moves to different time frames. This can impact on the relationship lines. For example, in the relationship line in the present of *Shine*, David Helfgott is an antagonist to Gillian and the other serial protagonists (who are protagonists in both the action and relationship lines in the present). However, in the relationship line in the past, David is protagonist with his father as antagonist. Again, this is important to make sure David stays an enigmatic outsider in the present, someone seen from the outside, a mystery. Making the serial protagonists all have their own vivid and unique response to the enigmatic outsider sharpens the drama because it gives the protagonists 'attitude'; it gives them conflict and strong emotions.

Because we are looking at successful double narrative flashback films it is hard to see the amount of damage mishandled or absent action and relationship lines can create in a script, although *Mr Saturday Night* demonstrates how boring a film can become if it simply shows one character (just being himself, while others watch) in public and domestic relationships across the years.

THE ENIGMATIC OUTSIDER APPEARS IN BOTH ACTION LINE AND RELATIONSHIP LINE OF THE STORIES IN PAST AND PRESENT

Unless your enigmatic outsider is dead, he or she will figure in the action and relationship lines in both the past and the present. When the enigmatic outsider is dead, in the past they will be the antagonist to whoever is having a flashback about them (just as Kane is the antagonist when his wife, the protagonist at that moment, relates what happened in their marriage). In the present, the enigmatic outsider will not figure in the relationship line at all (as in our Dr Smith/Cinderella example, the investigator protagonist will have a relationship antagonist, or antagonists, like Dr Susan Smith's husband and junkie sister).

Examples of action and relationship lines in past and present

SHINE (ACTION AND RELATIONSHIP LINES IN THE PAST)

Shine is a thwarted dream model. In the past, David Helfgott is protagonist in both the action line and relationship line. The action line is the story of

David's musical career from his boyhood through to his mental collapse and placement in a halfway house. In the action line his father is the main antagonist, but David's other teachers and musical mentors are also antagonists.

The relationship line in the past deals with David's traumatic relationship with his father (in which musical success starts out being necessary for love, then becomes its enemy). So David is protagonist and his father is antagonist.

SHINE (ACTION AND RELATIONSHIP LINES IN THE PRESENT)
Shine's action line in the present shows how David gets out of the halfway house and builds a new musical career. In this time frame, David is always a mentor antagonist to a series of protagonists (each representing a different but normal point of view). In the relationship line in the present, the story shows that a musical career can indeed be compatible with love (this time, via marriage). However, David is still a mentor antagonist. The protagonist, the person with a normal point of view, whose shoes we are in, is Gillian, David's wife (notice how, if we were seeing the relationship with Gillian from David's point of view there would less drama—because Gillian is not unpredictable, she is not a risky prospective partner—than can be portrayed when David is the antagonist).

The climax of the action line is the concert. The climax of the relationship line is the scene in the cemetery where David visits his father's grave with Gillian, with David now possessed of Gillian's love and thereby able to combine love with a career as a pianist, the dichotomy that caused his troubles with his father.

THE REMAINS OF THE DAY (ACTION AND RELATIONSHIP LINES IN THE PAST)
The Remains of the Day is a thwarted dream model. In The Remains of the Day, the action line in the past is the story of Lord Darlington's naive involvement with Nazi appeasement, and how this impacts on Stevens and Miss Kenton. Stevens is the protagonist, Lord Darlington is the antagonist, with Stevens staying loyal to the traitorous, racist Darlington. It vividly demonstrates Stevens' inner conflict between personal feelings and unquestioning loyalty to his employer, which he has been brought up to place above all else. The relationship line in the past concerns the unspoken love between Stevens (protagonist) and Miss Kenton (antagonist), particularly Stevens' inability to open up to love, partly because he has difficulty expressing his feelings, but largely because he feels that a love liaison between butler and housekeeper is inappropriate. Stevens' father is also a relationship-line antagonist, putting the case for duty over love.

THE REMAINS OF THE DAY (ACTION AND RELATIONSHIP LINES IN THE PRESENT)

In the present, the action line is Stevens' cross-country drive to see Miss Kenton (in which he lies about the past and allows himself to be thought of as a gentleman rather than a butler). The relationship line in the present is his voice-over correspondence and final meeting with Miss Kenton, which ends in love unfulfilled.

Stevens is a mentor antagonist with a series of protagonists (like David in *Shine*), starting with his new employer and including all the people he meets on the way. When his story in the past is told and we have come full circle, we understand Stevens. At this point, the start of the third act of the story in the past, Stevens becomes protagonist, with Miss Kenton as antagonist. There is no action line in the present now, except for the couple's meeting and parting. This swap from mentor antagonist in the present to protagonist in the present at the start of the third act, also happens to Jamal in *Slumdog Millionaire*.

CITIZEN KANE (ACTION AND RELATIONSHIP LINES IN THE PAST)

Citizen Kane is a case history model in which the enigmatic outsider is dead in the present and thus is always an antagonist, in both present and past—we can never get into his head to see his view of the past or the present. The action line in the past deals with Kane's professional career as viewed by those who knew him and is told in flashbacks. The flashbacks appear in largely self-contained chunks, each stage of Kane's life told through the perspective of one of these people in his life. Each of these people is the protagonist during their own flashback, in both action and relationship line. For example, the action line of Kane's second wife, Susan Alexander Kane, explains how she had an affair with Kane and he forced her to become an opera singer. Her relationship line is her difficult relationship with Kane.

CITIZEN KANE (ACTION AND RELATIONSHIP LINES IN THE PRESENT)

In the present, the action line is the protagonist Thompson's quest to find documents and individuals capable of revealing the identity of 'Rosebud'. Kane is the enigmatic outsider (always an antagonist) and there are a range of minor antagonists consisting of the people who knew Kane and who are interviewed by Thompson, telling him their story in flashback. As we've seen (but it's worth saying again because it's so easy to forget), to point up conflict and add drama, each of these people is antagonist until their flashback starts, when they become protagonists for the duration of the flashback. Once the flashback is over, they become antagonists again. In the present we are always in Thompson's shoes.

The relationship line in the present is very thin—in fact, we do not even see Thompson's face. The relationship line seems to consist of the responses— hostile, amused or irritated—of the people Thompson interviews.

THE USUAL SUSPECTS (ACTION AND RELATIONSHIP LINES IN THE PAST)

The Usual Suspects is a case history model with the enigmatic outsider, the corrupt ex-cop Keaton, recently killed by the mysterious Keyser Soze. The action line in the past consists of the deeds of Keaton's gang as related in flashbacks by a small-time criminal called Verbal Kent. Because Verbal is the person having the flashbacks, he is the protagonist in both action and relationship lines in the past. The relationship line is between Verbal and Keaton.

THE USUAL SUSPECTS (ACTION AND RELATIONSHIP LINES IN THE PRESENT)

The action line in the present is the investigation by police and US customs of two survivors of the burnt ship, including Verbal Kent. The protagonist is Kujan, the customs officer who interviews Verbal, who is an antagonist in both the action and the relationship lines in the present. We are in Kujan's shoes. As in *Citizen Kane*, the relationship line in the present consists of the relationship between investigator and interviewee. There is a similar relationship between Jamal and the police chief in *Slumdog Millionaire*. There is another antagonist in the present, the other survivor of the fire and shoot-out on the ship. There is a Rosebud twist, revealing that Verbal has duped Kujan both in relationship terms (by fooling Kujan that he is harmless) and in action line terms (by creating a false trail).

Chapter 39
Autobiographical voice-over flashback

I'VE ALREADY MENTIONED THAT double narrative flashback films which involve a person speaking in voice-over about their past and present don't need investigator characters because the narrator is the protagonist–detective, investigating their own past. Other significant structural differences are caused by the particular attitude the voice-over protagonist is bringing to their past—what precisely they want to reveal about it or explore. This can radically affect which characters are protagonists and antagonists in the two storylines.

For example, while we might assume that the speaking protagonist will inevitably be the protagonist in both of the stories, past and present, this might not be so. For example, in a film about the narrator's childhood, it might be that the reason the narrator is telling us about his or her childhood is to show how their child self was radically different from the adult they have now become. Hence, because the child is a stranger to the adult, when we flash back to the past, the child will be depicted as a stranger; that is, from the outside, as an antagonist. In these films, the protagonist in the past (the person whose shoes we are inside) won't be our narrator. It will be an adult mentor figure from the narrator's childhood (in Woody Allen films, the adult version sometimes steps into the flashback to comment disparagingly and comically on the younger version).

In films where the child is supposed to be a stranger, the child needs to stay a stranger and a mystery throughout—unless, say, the climax of the story in the past is whatever caused the child to change (perhaps some shocking experience) turning into the kind of person their adult self now is. In this case, we leave both child and adult as protagonists, two versions of the same person.

Everything depends, then, on the attitude that the autobiographical narrators bring to their past. There are three attitudes: either they fully understand their past and are just recounting the facts (as in *Milk*) or they think they understand it but, as in the Rosebud twist, it turns out that they don't (as in *Memento*) or their past is something which they are still trying to understand (as in *The End of the Affair*). The films can either be thwarted dream or case history, or in the case of *The End of the Affair*, thwarted dream that ends unhappily. Mostly, films like these do end unhappily.

Who is the enigmatic outsider?

All double narrative flashbacks are about enigmatic outsiders. In your voice-over double narrative flashback film, you need to know which character is the enigmatic outsider so that you can make sure that your plot keeps them enigmatic and doesn't normalise them.

Sometimes the outsider is actually the protagonist narrator, as in *Milk* and *Memento*, and, to comic effect, Woody Allen in many of his films. Alternatively, the outsider can be someone of enormous emotional importance to the narrator (often a lover) as in *The End of the Affair*. In this case the narrator stays protagonist in the story of the past, with the enigmatic outsider in their past as a mentor antagonist, the lover who teaches them something. *The End of the Affair* has the enigmatic outsider (Sarah) as antagonist in the past and present, because the protagonist recommences his relationship with Sarah after they have parted.

Case history or thwarted dream?

It will help you stay on track if you work out whether your film is following a thwarted dream model in which, in the third act, the narrator will try to regain the dream that was lost (as in *The End of the Affair*). Or it may be the flashback as case history approach, in which the point, comic or dramatic, is the narrator's scientific observation of their own past—sometimes, as we've said, with their past self as the enigmatic outsider, an antagonist, sometimes with their past self as a protagonist, affected by the enigmatic outsider who is an antagonist. Thwarted dream flashback will start at the narrator's second-act turning point then jump back to the disturbance. Case history will start at the climax and jump back to the disturbance.

Keeping voice-over under control

I suggested earlier that voice-over is probably best handled by being inserted after the film's structure has been worked out and, indeed, after the first draft is written. This applies to autobiographical voice-over double narrative films too. You will have to be aware that a voice-over needs to go in, but don't start out with it in case the joy of writing lyrical or punchy prose pulls you off course. It is always easy to go off course in a double narrative flashback film, and having to handle voice-over just adds to the problem.

'CINDERELLA' AS AUTOBIOGRAPHICAL DOUBLE NARRATIVE FLASHBACK WITH VOICE-OVER

The story would depend on Cinderella's attitude towards her past and what she wants to tell us and show us about it. Has she lost the prince but is still trying to find him (thwarted dream)? Or is this a case history story in which she's sadder and wiser (either because she married him, or because she didn't)? Is her past self a stranger? A fool?

You would have to think carefully here about the content of the story in the present. Do you need a full three-act story in the present, containing, as it will have to, a whole extra cast? Preview flashback with voice-over (starting either at Cinderella's second-act turning point or the climax) might be the more appropriate form.

Chapter 40
Planning a double narrative flashback film

FIRST OF ALL, DOUBLE-CHECK that you need double narrative. Consider other flashback forms. If you opt for double narrative flashback, work out which sort you need: thwarted dream, case history, or one of these but with an autobiographical voice-over. Double narrative flashback films are always about an enigmatic outsider and, to maintain suspense, they need a 'detective story' element, whereby a person or persons seek to find out the mystery of the past (sometimes their own). Work out the message of your film, remembering that thwarted dream and case history take different views of human nature, and autobiographical voice-over can take either stance. The list (currently accurate, but that could change) below should give you clues.

Plot content of double narrative flashback

1   Particularly in thwarted dream, the story in the past is usually an epic story about relationships and great passion, often lost love.

2   Double narrative flashback films are always about an enigmatic outsider. Except in rare cases, this person is a mentor antagonist at least in the present and sometimes also in the past.

3   In case history, the enigmatic outsider is usually dead (like Kane), mentally damaged (like Leonard in *Memento*) or lying. This is a useful tip: if you are planning a flashback film about an enigmatic outsider who is dead, mentally incapacitated or turns out at the end to be lying, you have to use case history.

4   Case history is a good form to use if you are writing the biography of a genius or larger-than-life person (as in *Milk* and *Amadeus*) because it permits the person concerned to be viewed only as an antagonist, from the outside through others, hence to keep their mystery and status and not be trivialised. *Shakespeare in Love* did the opposite, playing on the trivialising effect of making a genius an ordinary person, to great comic effect.

5   The enigmatic outsider in thwarted dream has a lost or stolen dream, which they suddenly decide to recapture. The film tells how the dream began and was lost and charts their progress to regain it. Usually, they do regain the dream.

6   As a rule of thumb, if the enigmatic outsider is supposed to be a normal, likeable person damaged by life, use flashback as thwarted dream, for which the motto is: 'there but for the grace of God go I'. If the outsider is supposed to be an essentially unknowable, unpredictable person, or even evil, use case history, where the motto is: 'human beings are mysterious, unpredictable and more than the sum total of their past'. Case history is always used if the audience is supposed to disapprove of the outsider. The protagonist learns a cautionary lesson from these films—in fact we could describe case history as 'cautionary tale', because the audience is initially duped along with the investigator.

7   In autobiographical voice-over double narrative flashback, the enigmatic outsider is usually the person the speaker is most concerned with, often a lost lover, but sometimes a former self.

8   Usually the central tension of the film concerns a conflict between the enigmatic outsider's personal life or well-being, and their professional duties; often it is love versus duty.

9   Many double narrative flashback films, particularly thwarted dream versions, insert further tension into their endings by adding 'a ticking clock'; that is, pressure of time to solve the problems of either the investigator protagonist or the outsider trying to achieve the thwarted dream.

10 In thwarted dream, the person having the flashbacks is the enigmatic outsider. In case history, usually the flashbacks are had by a person or persons *who have known the outsider*. If the outsider has the flashbacks, often they are not true. *Milk* is an exception.

11 In thwarted dream, flashbacks explain the outsider and create audience empathy. In case history, flashbacks give a documentary reality to the action, distancing the audience. They make the audience a scientific observer and, when the Rosebud twist happens, make them even more mystified by the story than when they started, sometimes appalled.

12 Case history ends with a Rosebud twist (to avoid an anticlimax).

How to structure a double narrative flashback

Plan each story separately, constructing a tight three-act chronological model in each (even though the story in the present may be truncated), complete with action line and relationship line. Both stories will be strengthened by good strong first-act turning points—genuine surprises that create the particular obstacle that drives the rest of the story—as places to boost their interest and as jumping-off points. For example, in *Shine*, in the story in the present, the first-act turning point is the moment when David, apparently just a crazy derelict, sits down at the piano in the restaurant and plays brilliantly. It is a surprise that creates the obstacle that drives the rest of the story in the present, which is 'kindly people help David Helfgott to become a concert pianist again'. If you tried to make the first-act turning point surprise be that David returned to the restaurant and fell and broke his leg before entering, that would definitely be a surprise, but it's not a surprise that would further the story of 'kindly people help David Helfgott become a concert pianist' (unless you somehow made the broken leg lead to David revealing he was a concert pianist). It would simply be an incident, and would certainly not give you enough story to fill your second and third acts.

When you have mapped out your two stories, start to think about inter-weaving, using the guidelines in this book. Think of your flashback film as two circles, one inside the other, linked at one scene—the triggering crisis—which has a different function in each story.

It helps when you are creating the plots to think of the story in the present as the film's action line and the story in the past (dealing, as it does, with the outsider's relationships) as the film's relationship line. This is because it reminds you of what sort of plot material you need to have in the present.

Points to remember about writing double narrative flashback

1   The triggering crisis in thwarted dream is the second-act turning point of the story in the past. In case history, it is the climax. In both, it is usually the disturbance of the story in the present.

2   Jump between past and present at high dramatic points in each story. In the second act of the story in the past, your dramatic high points, your jumping-off points, will be the second-act complications and twists and turns.

3   The plot in the present has to permit the story in the past to be told. This is very similar to the way, in conventional narrative, the action

line permits the relationship line to happen—as in *The African Queen*, where the journey down the river (action line) is the reason the two characters fall in love (relationship line). Your story in the present must put the outsider into a situation where their story can be told.

4   Except in autobiographical voice-over flashback, *the story in the present is not the enigmatic outsider's story; it is the story of a person who has to deal with the enigmatic outsider.*

5   In autobiographical voice-over forms, the narrator protagonist can be the enigmatic outsider, and the story can be their story.

6   Flashbacks always occur in chronological order. Choose the content of each flashback very carefully so that it takes the story in the past forward at least one beat in a dynamic way. Note how, in *Slumdog Millionaire*, the order in which the questions are asked permits the flashbacks to show Jamal's life in chronological order. None of the questions he is asked require flashbacks to jump around in his life. Flashbacks unfolding chronologically are pleasing, providing momentum towards the climax.

7   The screen time of double narrative flashback films is a potential problem because they contain at least two stories in one film. This means focused and economic plotting or the film will be much too long. The story in the past is traditionally much longer and more important than the story in the present, although this is changing. Films such as *The End of the Affair* and *The Sweet Hereafter* have very complex stories in the present, and this is probably the way of things to come. Consider truncation.

8   The story in the present is a strong (albeit often truncated) 'detective story' in the present, exploring the motives in the past of the enigmatic outsider.

9   The story in the present (and also sometimes the story in the past) usually involves a hunt, quest or journey (physical and/or metaphorical). Its structural role is to permit an investigation or revisiting of the traumatic past. Sometimes the person on the quest is the enigmatic outsider, usually in pursuit of a thwarted dream. Sometimes the person on the quest is the investigator figure (or figures), and the quest involves trying to understand the outsider. The hunt or quest is a vital and energising component of the form. In some films it takes the place of the 'great battle' that constitutes the third act. *The End of the Affair* is interesting in that while its

protagonist is not an investigator, he actually hires an investigator to pursue the enigmatic outsider (Sarah). It also, classically, involves a hunt or quest in its story set in the present.

10   Thwarted dream might require two climaxes, in the same way that we've seen in inner story/outer story films and for much the same reasons. You may need to resolve the story in the past (that is, the pursuit of the dream) in one scene, and the story in the present (the investigator protagonist's dealings with the outsider antagonist) later, in another. Sometimes both can be resolved in the same scene. This happens in *Slumdog Millionaire*, in which the past and present stories are resolved in one dramatic sequence. Jamal answers the final question on *Who Wants to be a Millionaire?* as he and Latika affirm their love. By contrast, in *Shine*, David Helfgott's dream to become a concert pianist is resolved in one scene while his relationship with his future wife is resolved in another.

11   To add to the documentary feel that many case history films seek to create—the sense that we are watching a true story—datelines are often used throughout, superimposed on screen in imitation of news footage.

12   Successful double narrative films often start with the sudden appearance of an enigmatic outsider, usually at a moment of serious crisis or danger in their lives, often (particularly in thwarted dream) figuratively or physically knocking on a door wanting to be let back into society—like David Helfgott at the restaurant in *Shine*. Alternatively, the outsider will appear and people will try to find out who he or she is. This happens in *The English Patient* (nobody knows who he is), and in *The Remains of the Day*, where the people the butler meets on his journey are intrigued by him, and persistently ask him questions. Explaining how the enigmatic outsider came to be in this situation makes up the greater part of the film—it is what is explained in the flashbacks.

13   Alternatively, to increase the audience's interest in your investigator protagonist, you could open the film on them, introducing them first. In your audience's eyes, this will make the film your protagonist's story, which will give the character extra strength to stand up to the limelight-stealing enigmatic outsider. You can see this effect in *Fried Green Tomatoes* (where the film feels like the housewife's story) and *The Life of David Gale* (which feels like the journalist's story).

Tip and reminders about protagonists and antagonists

ANYONE HAVING FLASHBACKS IS A PROTAGONIST

In all forms of flashback narrative, anyone having a flashback is a protagonist for the duration of the flashback. We see the world from their point of view.

MANY PROTAGONISTS, ONE MENTOR ANTAGONIST

Conventional linear films have one protagonist and many antagonists. Double narrative flashback has many protagonists and one mentor antagonist. There can also be minor antagonists. Also, characters can switch from being antagonists to protagonists and vice versa (see above). The point of thinking in terms of switching between protagonists and antagonists is to create strong characters, good character conflict and strong stories. You need these badly because these films have to be detective stories (to justify the story in the present), and so you have to maintain suspense and the possibility of many outcomes.

PROTAGONISTS IN THE PRESENT ASK QUESTIONS

Double narrative flashback always involves people in the present who ask questions. Even autobiographical voice-over flashbacks involve a questioner, the narrator themselves. These people are always protagonists because they represent the normal point of view, asking the questions a normal person would ask. Frequently the question-asking protagonist is an official investigator such as a journalist, police officer or lawyer. Sometimes there is a sequence of protagonists. Thwarted dream has at least one and often more investigator protagonists (for example, the people who help David Helfgott). The person they question (and often help) is always the enigmatic outsider. Sometimes, as in *Memento*, the question-asking protagonist turns out in the end to be abnormal or duplicitous.

CASE HISTORY USUALLY HAS ONLY ONE INVESTIGATOR PROTAGONIST

The story in the present in case history frequently consists simply of actual interview situations. Often large slabs of the story happen in investigation rooms. Often there is only one investigator protagonist. This usually happens if the mentor antagonist is alive (as in *The Life of David Gale*). If the protagonist is dead, many people are usually questioned about the dead enigmatic outsider. In *The Sweet Hereafter*, people are questioned about someone who has returned from the dead, the sole survivor of the accident.

In autobiographical voice-over double narrative flashback the protagonist is the person asking questions, so there is no need for an extra investigator protagonist. *Slumdog Millionaire* has extensive interview room scenes, although it is a thwarted dream version of case history.

THE MENTOR ANTAGONIST IS THE PERSON CAUSING TROUBLE

In the present, the mentor antagonist (even when dead) is the person causing trouble to the protagonist. In the relationship line they cause trouble by not answering questions, or by lying, or being enigmatic. In the action line, they are the person who has made the protagonist take their present course of action. Often, they drag the protagonist on a crazy journey, and the protagonist may protect them or even fall in love with them (as Gillian does with David in *Shine*). If you are using a static interview situation, be sure to insert conflict or a mentor antagonist throwing out some kind of challenge, otherwise it will rapidly become boring. Conflict need not be physical.

ANTAGONISTS IN ACTION AND RELATIONSHIP LINES

In thwarted dream, the antagonist in both the action and relationship lines *in the present* is usually the enigmatic outsider, although sometimes this person returns again to being protagonist in the final battle to win. The question to ask is, 'Whose shoes do I want the audience to be in at various points of the film?' In films like *Remains of the Day* and *Slumdog Millionaire* it is useful to keep the enigmatic outsider as an antagonist in the present until, along with the film's protagonists, we know their story. At that point (usually the return of the triggering crisis), turn them into protagonists, so we are in their shoes for the exciting third act. In *Slumdog Millionaire*, we want to be in Jamal's shoes for the third-act battle-to-win, not the shoes of the police chief.

MINOR ANTAGONISTS

Both case history and thwarted dream may have minor antagonists in the action line in the present. In thwarted dream the antagonist and protagonist will join forces against these minor antagonists (in *Shine*, the minor antagonists are the people who believe David is crazy). Autobiographical voice-over double narrative is different because the person asking questions is the protagonist, so they are the ones creating trouble for themselves.

The story in the present is usually the hardest to write

I have found in working with writers on double narrative flashback scripts that the most common problem is the story in the present. This is not surprising. When you are writing a film specifically to tell the past life of a fascinating enigmatic outsider, it requires great concentration to put that character aside and throw yourself into inventing and seeing the action through the eyes of a new, and inherently less dynamic, investigator protagonist to whom you give a mystery to solve and, preferably, a good strong story of their own. But you have to do this to make your film work—just as in mentor antagonist films you have to invent a less interesting protagonist to properly create the enigmatic, unpredictable wild-card character who is the reason you are writing your film.

As I've shown above in examples of 'Cinderella' retold as case history and thwarted dream flashback, the story in the present needs a lot of work. It requires new characters (often several), a new point of view and, crucially, it needs to be a detective story in which the audience, with or in advance of the investigator protagonist, pieces together clues about the mysterious past of the enigmatic outsider.

It must have mystery and threat. If it doesn't, your film will go around in circles until the action returns to the past, with characters in the present just doing 'business'.

If your character is static, there must be a threat, something at stake. For example, the story in the present in *Milk* is just Harvey Milk sitting in his kitchen dictating a memoir, but the scenes are riveting because we know he is going to be assassinated and he says that he is dictating his memoir specifically in case this happens. Similarly, while Salieri in *Amadeus* sits in a chair for most of his story, he has just tried to commit suicide and is wracked with guilt and religious doubt as he passionately tells his story.

Keep reminding yourself to pump up the film's detective-story-of-the-human-heart qualities in the story of the present. Remind yourself too that in most double narrative films, for most if not all of the time, the story in the present is not the enigmatic outsider's story, it is the story of whoever has to deal with the enigmatic outsider (as in *Fried Green Tomatoes* and *The Life of David Gale)*. This can be very hard to do.

That said, successful double narrative flashback films show just how powerful the story in the present can be, and how it can enhance—perhaps make—a successful film. If you plan your double narrative flashback film carefully you can get wonderful results with the story in the present. For example, I often ask writers I am mentoring to construct, as an exercise, a plan for a case history double narrative flashback film using their own modern-day version of 'Jack and the Beanstalk', opening on Jack in a coma after falling from the beanstalk. They inevitably return with wonderful, complex stories in the present that involve Jack's difficult relationship with the Giant's wife (whom, in the story, Jack of course betrayed), or Jack's mother, along with a variety of personal and professional dilemmas for their investigator, who is invariably some strong and interesting character in their own right.

Double narrative flashback stories can give you not just your powerful story in the past, but fine, thought-provoking stories in the present that pass comment upon the story in the past. But the story in the present will probably be the hardest thing for you to write.

Chapter 41
Case studies of flashback films: Hybrids and oddities

The Constant Gardener: Thwarted dream with extended battle to win

The Constant Gardener is an odd form of thwarted dream flashback. Like *Shine*, it opens on the second-act turning point of one story, which is simultaneously the disturbance of the other story. What's different about it is that the third-act battle to win in the story in the past (as in *Shine*, simultaneously the story in the present), is very long—twelve chapters out of twenty. The triggering crisis returns much earlier than in normal thwarted dream flashback, with the flashback to the story in the past concluded *before the middle of the film's screen time*. Of course, in normal thwarted flashback films, the flashbacks are not concluded until about three-quarters or more of the film is over.

The story in the past is the story of Justin and Tessa from their meeting through to his suicide at the end of the film. We can call this 'Justin and Tessa's love story'. The second story we could call 'Justin investigates'. This runs from Tessa's death to just after Justin's death, when the villains are brought to justice. The triggering crisis, Tessa's death, which opens the film, is thus (in classic thwarted dream flashback style) the second-act turning point in the story in the past and the disturbance of the story in the present.

It resembles the consecutive stories film *Amores Perros*, which also starts in its chronological middle.

WHY ISN'T THERE AN ANTICLIMAX?
Why isn't there an anticlimax when Tessa's story is wound up mid-film? Partly it's because the detective story about the drug company cover-up is interesting, but probably the main reason is because Justin is not an objective outsider. He isn't, for example, a journalist or police officer just doing his job. He is a heartbroken husband trying to find out not just why and how his wife died, but whether she was unfaithful to him, which, to add to the emotional impact, initially seems highly likely. Thus, what's creating the suspense of the

film is not primarily the drug cover-up story, it is the emotional jeopardy of the loving, faithful husband throughout (although of course, by the end of the film, Justin is placed in the ultimate physical jeopardy and is murdered). The film, as many people have said, is very much a love story.

The lesson here is that a powerful love story quest, technically a relationship line, can energise a detective story even to the degree of preventing a film stopping in its tracks when a preview scene returns at what is usually the least exciting of all the dramatic high points in a story, the disturbance. The film is an interesting reversal of the normal pattern whereby the action line pulls the relationship line along. In *The Constant Gardener*, the relationship line shoves the action line along, as we will Justin to find out how Tessa died. It permits the story to be much more than a detective story.

Thus, the points to take away from *The Constant Gardener* are that if you want to conclude your story in the past early, be sure there is enough emotional punch in the relationship line to pull your story forward; and that an emotionally involved investigator, particularly one with a strong vested personal interest in the mystery, adds a powerful dynamism to the plot. So, if you're wondering how to energise a double narrative detective story about an enigmatic outsider in the past, consider making the investigator protagonist personally involved with the outsider, turning the film into some kind of love story (not necessarily between husband and wife, it could be between brothers or parent and child).

Notice too the use of new flashbacks coming later in the film to poignantly expand information that we've already been given in early flashbacks. When Justin returns to the flat where he and Tessa first made love, the film cuts between heartbroken Justin in the present, a repeat of the flashback we've already seen, *followed by a new flashback* set in the same time period. Notice too that the actual disturbance scene of the story in the present, Justin being told by Sandy that Tessa is dead, does not reappear. It's not necessary, and would simply slow the film down. This suggests that we need to think carefully whether we actually need the return of the actual disturbance scene in the present. *Cinema Paradiso*, using preview flashback, doesn't have it returning either.

The Sweet Hereafter

The Sweet Hereafter is another double narrative flashback film with an interesting use of the disturbance, although 'double narrative' is not the right term since the film has eleven powerful stories in nine different time frames. Apart from the extraordinary achievement of running so many moving stories concurrently without audience confusion or loss of pace, it is particularly clever in its use of incomplete or truncated stories—one-act structures or two-act structures—to achieve effects that one would think possible only through a complete narrative. It can teach us a lot and provide a lot of new tools.

The film concerns a lawyer attempting to persuade a small town it should sue for the tragic loss of its children in a school bus accident. The easiest way to think of *The Sweet Hereafter* is to imagine it as two flashback narrative films in one. It is as if the journalist protagonist in *Citizen Kane* were to have his own flashback story and flashforward story happening during and after his investigation of Kane's life story. *The Sweet Hereafter* incorporates a number of different sorts of flashbacks. In the course of jumping between its many stories it uses:

- autobiographical voice-over flashback and flashforward (where a protagonist, the lawyer, describes in voice-over his experiences and deepening disillusionment as the father of a junkie)
- flashback as case history (the story of a young girl who is the survivor of the bus crash, an enigmatic outsider)
- flashbacks as illustration (in the evidence of the various parents of the dead children)

WHAT IS STANDARD ABOUT *THE SWEET HEREAFTER*?

The movement of each story is still generally chronological, and the story in the present moves strictly chronologically. The film also displays many of the standard features of double narrative flashback. For example:

- It involves a detective story of the human heart (several, actually).
- Its main focus is to reveal what, in the past, caused the problems of the present.
- It includes a typical investigator protagonist, the lawyer whose job it is to ask questions about the past.
- It opens at a triggering crisis (just after the bus crash) and comes full circle to end with an ironic twist (the sole survivor lying in order to sabotage the compensation suit) just after the story of the bus crash has reached its climax.

WHAT IS ODD ABOUT *THE SWEET HEREAFTER*?

The Sweet Hereafter departs significantly from the standard pattern of double narrative flashback, but works extremely well. It therefore has exciting potential as a template. Its differences are:

- It has as its triggering crisis the disturbance of the story in the past. It opens with the lawyer arriving in town immediately after the bus crash. However, the crash is not, as we might expect, a second-act turning point or a climax. Instead, the crash is *the disturbance* of the main story in the past. I deem the crash the disturbance because, using my rule of thumb whereby we describe a film's plot structure by what we can say that plot is 'about', we have to say that *The Sweet Hereafter* is not about the crash *per se*, it is about the after-effects of the crash on the community. Thus, the film starts just after the disturbance in the past, which means that the film's triggering crisis is the disturbance of the story in the past.

- The actual disturbance scene—the bus crashing through the ice— does not open the film and is actually not seen in detail at all. In other words, the triggering crisis is described through dialogue but not actually seen until much later in the film; in fact, not until the story of the past has been told full circle. Why does this work? After all, the point of a triggering crisis scene is to provide a film with a strong hook. How can a flashback film operate with such a quiet opening? One possible answer is that the idea of a bus full of children crashing through ice to their deaths in a lake is strong enough to hold our attention, so we don't need a visual to open the film. Another possible answer is that the harrowing story of the lawyer's dealings with his junkie daughter (one of the most powerful things in a very powerful film) starts in the opening scene. Also, that scene, set inside a car stuck in a car wash, opens with a view through the windshield of the car wash's brushes that look eerily like waterweed and for a moment suggests that the vehicle is at the bottom of a lake.

- A number of the stories show the town's pre-crash normality (using flashback as illustration) until the moment of the crash changed it all. Once the story has gone full circle and the bus crash has been shown on screen, the town's story reverts to the present and events leading up to the main witness giving her statement.

- It uses truncation in a very interesting way. All of the stories about the parents of the children who died in the crash are one-act stories. In these stories, the normality is life before the bus crash, the disturbance is the bus crash itself and the first-act turning point, the surprise ending of the one-act story, is an unexpected response by the parents to the bus crash, a thought-provoking surprise.

- Another example of truncation is that the lawyer Mitchell's story has no

second or third act; that is, the story of Mitchell and his junkie daughter
has no second or third act. It jumps straight from the first-act turning
point (the revelation that the daughter has AIDS) to the second-act
turning point, where we find out that the daughter is unredeemed and
Mitchell admits that his love for her is permanently destroyed by her
addiction, and ends there. We do not see the great battle to win the
dream, in this case reconciliation. The same phenomenon of a missing
third act and climax appears in tandem narrative films *City of Hope*
and *Crimes and Misdemeanors*. Truncation is an exciting phenomenon
we shall come across increasingly in the more complicated forms of
parallel narrative, particularly fractured tandem, where it appears in
films such as *21 Grams* and *The Hours*.

- The film's central story seems to be thwarted dream double narrative
  flashback, but it turns into case history at the end. It initially feels
  as if both the action line in the present—the consequences of a
  bus crash in which most of the local children are killed—and the
  relationship line concerning Mitchell and his junkie daughter will be
  examples of flashback as thwarted dream, with the thwarted dream
  being 'lost children redeemed'. However, in both cases it turns out
  to be flashback as case history. Nicole, the sole survivor of the crash,
  deliberately sabotages the court case and thus rejects the dream, in
  the process revealing a shocking family secret, and the film ends with
  a case history moral—people are unknowable. In the story about
  the lawyer and his junkie daughter, the revelation that the daughter
  was not redeemed and that Stevens cannot love her turns what we
  thought would be thwarted dream into case history: the ever-patient
  father, the father who saved his infant child's life, now hates her.

- Mitchell, the investigator protagonist, actually has several stories.
  He has two action-line stories in the present (trying to arrange
  a class action from the townsfolk generally, and from the sole
  survivor in particular), a relationship-line story in the present (his
  junkie daughter harassing him by phone), a flashback story in the
  distant past (when his daughter was a toddler) and a flashforward
  story, set two years hence, when he is visiting his dying daughter. In
  this, he plays a typical enigmatic outsider being asked questions by a
  protagonist (Allison, his daughter's school friend) with his answers,
  shown in flashbacks, explaining his bitterness and dark wisdom.
  The flashback narrative concerning the lawyer's relationship with
  Zoe, his junkie daughter, is structurally interesting because it

does not have a triggering crisis. This is probably wise because the triggering crisis scene would be Zoe actually announcing that she has AIDS. Since the film already has one opening triggering crisis that is harrowing (the bus crash), an AIDS announcement would probably be over the top.

- What *The Sweet Hereafter* shows us is that many time frames and many stories are possible, particularly using truncation. If it has enough impact, a disturbance can act as a triggering crisis, but it needs enormous impact.

The Life of David Gale: Tricks to build up the story in the present

The Life of David Gale is interesting because while in most aspects it is copy-book case history—complete with a journalist investigator (Bitsey Bloom), detective story of human motives, enigmatic outsider/mentor antagonist close to death (David Gale), and a Rosebud twist—it also uses a clever structural trick to increase the impact of the story in the present, something we always have to work hard to do. It opens in the story of the present, skewing the film so that the protagonist in the present has more dominance, making the story very much a detective story.

THE STRUCTURE OF BITSEY'S STORY

1 **Disturbance**: the invitation to interview Gale, an anti-capital punishment activist about to be executed in an open-and-shut case of rape and murder of a fellow-activist
2 **First-act turning point**: Gale's probable innocence
3 **Second act**: interviewing Gale, investigating, finding a mysterious videotape
4 **Second-act turning point**: Bitsey being too late for Gale's execution
5 **Climax** (with Rosebud twist): Bitsey finds out how precisely Gale duped her, and why

THE STRUCTURE OF GALE'S STORY

1 **Disturbance**: Gale is framed for rape, sacked and deserted by his wife and child
2 **First-act turning point**: Gale's fellow activist, Constance, who has cancer, asks him to have sex with her (and, as we later discover, hatches a plan with him to fool the legal system into executing him for her murder)

3   **Second-act turning point**: he is about to be executed for Constance's murder, which he did not commit
4   **Climax**: he is executed

OPENING ON BITSEY, NOT GALE

Although the film opens, as is standard, on the climax of Gale's story (just before he is to be executed), *it does not open on Gale*. It opens on the protagonist in the present, journalist Bitsey Bloom. It opens on Bitsey's second-act turning point, as she abandons her broken-down car and runs frantically towards town in a bid to save Gale's life because she has proof of his innocence.

The problem that this structure is solving is that Gale will easily steal the limelight, particularly as the plot demands that Bitsey spends a lot of time just sitting listening to him in the three interviews she is permitted with him (note the triplication). We need to put Bitsey in the foreground, so opening the film on her quickly establishes her very firmly as the protagonist in the present and keeps Gale enigmatic, as he must be.

Notice that the story in the present contains a time-honoured screenwriter's trick: the protagonist's companion (here, a trainee journalist) who can feed the protagonist lines and to whom she can articulate in dialogue her theories (this time about the framing of Gale). This sidekick is interestingly characterised, and conflict has been inserted between him and Bitsey about his pushiness and his smoking habit, which adds energy.

After the opening scene with Bitsey's car breakdown and her frantic running, the film cuts back on cue to the disturbance—but not the disturbance in Gale's story, as would be normal, but the disturbance in the story of the present, Bitsey's story. This is Bitsey being invited by Gale's lawyer to have three interviews with Gale as he waits on death row.

Bitsey's story is a classic double narrative detective story of the motives of the human heart, with Bitsey gradually starting to believe Gale was framed for rape and murder, and gradually getting the proof just before she misses saving him. The Rosebud twist, coming right on cue after Gale's death, is that Gale managed to fool Bitsey.

Bitsey's story is a short, tight three-act structure. The first interview flashes back, in classic style, to the disturbance of the story in the past (David's story) and concludes on the first-act turning point before jumping back to the present. Each flashback tells more of the story, with Gale finally leaving Bitsey only a day to prove his innocence, giving her a strong third-act battle to win in the story set in the present.

The slight structural differences in *The Life of David Gale* are very useful to remember for the way they push Bitsey, the protagonist who might have become simply a listener for most of the time, to centre stage.

Memento: Establishing the ground rules, differentiating the storylines

Memento is a fascinating, structurally complex flashback film about Leonard, a man who suffers from short-term memory loss, trying to find and kill the man who murdered his wife and gave him the blow to the head that lost him his memory. The film is deliberately constructed so as to reproduce Leonard's struggle to work out where he is in his hunt, and follows him as he pursues it to its end. When the film concludes, a number of threads are left tantalisingly and pleasingly untied because we are unsure how much of the film's plot was confabulated by Leonard's damaged and grief-stricken mind.

People routinely comment that while *Memento* is a very interesting film, structurally it is an oddity, with its one-step-forward, two-steps-back scene structure too idiosyncratic, too closely entwined with its subject matter to be used in other films. However, as we'll see later, the consecutive stories film *City of God* uses a similar device—starting in the middle of a sequence and returning to the start of the story that caused the sequence, to show how it all began. For example, to tell us how drug dealers important to the story came to be living in an apartment, it first shows us the drug dealers, then flashes back to the original owner before returning again to the present. As in *Memento*, it is a dynamic, energising device.

THE PLOTS

Memento jumps between four plots. The main action line (which deals with Leonard trying to hunt down his wife's murderer and finally killing Teddy) involves Leonard's voice in voice-over, is shown in colour and runs in a complex backwards motion (I'll explain precisely how in a moment). Meanwhile, the relationship line, all shown in black and white, contains three stories, two using flashbacks. The 'present' of this black and white relationship line consists of a series of scenes set in a motel, with Leonard talking on the telephone about his past to an unidentified caller. In chronological terms, this section of the relationship line actually happens and concludes *before* the start of the action line. The second story, *a disjointed flashback story*, depicts how Leonard lost his memory after being massively injured when he went to the defence of his wife, who was murdered by two intruders. The third story, another flashback story, *told chronologically*, is accompanied by a voice-over by Leonard, and concerns Sammy Jankis, a man with short-term memory loss that Leonard had to deal with when he was an insurance investigator. There are other subliminal flashbacks that are flashback as illustration, showing slightly different versions of the past.

LIFE-CHANGING INCIDENT FLASHBACK
The wife's life and death is rendered as a life-changing incident flashback that we revisit a number of times until, right at the end, after the murder of Teddy, we are given a scene which may mean that Leonard has confabulated the facts of her death, combining her story with Sammy's story.

MEMENTO AND CASE HISTORY
While the structure of the film is complicated, involving a number of stories (the main one told backwards with a mind-spinning rewind pattern), *Memento* is actually a version of autobiographical case history flashback (using voice-over), with the addition of one life-changing incident flashback, flashback as illustration and, in Sammy Jankis' story, a complete case history flashback story (hence, case history within case history) featuring the secret mysteries of Leonard's consciousness, with Leonard as an enigmatic outsider in the present and Sammy an enigmatic outsider in the past, with Leonard prior to his accident as a normal man, a standard protagonist.

Memento is definitely a detective story of the human heart. It involves an enigmatic outsider who, while not dead, is massively and irreparably changed. It employs the standard double narrative case history frame, starting at the story's climax and, when the opening scene returns at the end of the film, employs the ironic twist typical of case history flashback. The difference is that there are actually multiple twists in *Memento*, leaving the ending intriguingly ambiguous (note, incidentally, how the audience loves the ambiguity of the ending).

The Rosebud twist is that Leonard has already killed his wife's murderer—although possibly Leonard might have combined his memories of Sammy Jankis with his own, thus it might be that Leonard's wife did not die during a robbery, but Leonard himself was the person who killed her, by overdosing her with insulin. Certainly, Leonard has killed people and now is being used by the crooked policeman Teddy to kill off people Teddy wants removed. We discover that the drug dealer Leonard killed at the start of the film was one of these people.

CLEVER EXPOSITION TECHNIQUES
It would have very easy for *Memento* to be confusing instead of intriguing. To prevent this, the film cleverly establishes its internal rules within seconds of starting.

ESTABLISHING THE FILM'S GROUND RULES

The first thing *Memento* explains, dynamically, is that part of it is going to be told backwards. This is done in the opening scene (which is also the film's climax, just prior to the Rosebud twist) by the film literally running in reverse. We open at the scene of a murder, with someone holding a Polaroid photograph of a bloody corpse. The photograph fades and returns into the camera, the gun thrown down by the killer jumps back into his hands, and so on. We are instantly intrigued, but also—and crucially—we instantly know the rules.

When we cut to the first motel scene, we instantly know that we are in another story because the action is in black and white. The voice-over cleverly provides exposition at the same time as driving the story forward in the present and providing a jump-off point for the flashback. Making one storyline of the film black and white is not a new technique to differentiate plots, but it is a sound one and also usefully gives the film a documentary flavour. Note that we are not given any indication at first that the motel story has happened before the murder story but, interestingly, this does not seem to matter. We happily go along with this, content to have what is actually a crucial fact revealed later, as part of the film's final ironic twists.

ACTION-LINE PATTERN

The main action line is constructed in a 'two-steps-forward, one-step-back' fashion (see Figure 41.1) to put the audience into the shoes of Leonard, who, suffering from short-term memory loss, is constantly forgetting where he is and why he is there. The pattern is that each scene sequence starts in its middle and continues to its end. It then goes back to its beginning and proceeds forward until we reach the moment where the sequence started. The process then starts all over again. That is, we open in the middle of the next sequence, follow it to its end, go back to the start and finish in the middle, where we started. That way, we, the audience, understand what really happened, while vividly experiencing the sensation of short-term memory loss.

What's particularly worth noting about *Memento* is that the audience recognises the pattern very quickly, and goes with it. This suggests that if you establish a pattern of unusual flashbacks quickly, the audience will understand it, indeed actively enjoy it. *Memento*'s popularity is growing, indeed it is well on its way to achieving cult status, a reminder that ingenious low-budget parallel narrative can translate to big financial returns.

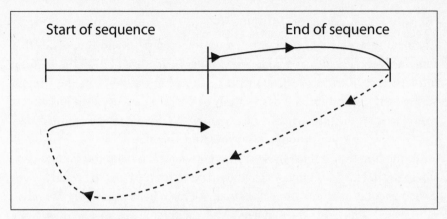

Figure 41.1 Scene sequences in *Memento*'s action line

Eternal Sunshine of the Spotless Mind: Preview flashback plus tandem

Eternal Sunshine of the Spotless Mind is a brilliant film both structurally and in terms of its depiction of love and the sacredness of memory. It combines preview flashback and flashback as illustration with tandem narrative's technique of running equally important stories on the same theme simultaneously and chronologically. The preview flashback story is the story of Joel, the man who decided to have his memory wiped of a painful love affair with a girl called Clementine, then changed his mind. The tandem narrative content is the stories of the staff at the company that is doing the memory wiping, Lacuna. The treatment of these stories is one of the ways in which *Eternal Sunshine* is so dazzling. Plot-wise, all that Joel's story requires from the Lacuna material is that the staff successfully wipe his memories of Clementine and that somehow he and Clementine find out that their memories have been wiped. However, Charlie Kaufman's genius is to use the Lacuna staff to explore the film's themes of painful love, memory, and mental manipulation in a profound and moving way.

THE LACUNA STORIES
The Lacuna staff and premises provide three extra and ingenious love stories, all about memory and unrequited love: assistant technician Patrick's unrequited love for Clementine; the nurse Mary's unrequited love for Dr Mierzwiak, and the unrequited love of Stan, the chief technician, for Mary. There is even the hint of a fourth unrequited love story, in the brief appearance of Mierzwiak's betrayed wife. It emerges in the end that Mary and Dr Mierzwiak once had an affair, but Mary has had her memory wiped and doesn't remember until she is told, at which point she is devastated.

The strength and originality of the Lacuna stories is remarkable. The Joel/ Clementine story could be almost completely removed and the stories that remained would still make up a good tandem narrative film on the existing film's themes, illustrated through the relationship problems of the Lacuna staff as they callously and disrespectfully deal with a patient called Joel who is trying to wipe the memory of a girlfriend with whom one of their members has fallen in love, and whom he is trying to manipulate.

In the film as it stands, these stories enrich and develop the themes considerably. In fact, for many people the Mary/Stan/Dr Mierzwiak triangle was as important if not more important than the Joel/Clementine story. It's interesting, technically, that the film gets a sudden burst of energy and poignancy from the insertion of the emotionally highly charged Mary/Dr Mierzwiak story just when the 'Joel and Clementine running away' scenes are starting to feel a little repetitive. Possibly, without it the Joel-losing-Clementine sequence could have made the film feel slow and directionless for a moment—always dangerous. The lesson seems to be that powerful emotion in one story can sometimes fix a slowing tendency in another. However, you have to be careful that the powerful emotion in the secondary story does not eclipse the first story. One extremely powerful scene that was deleted from *Eternal Sunshine* showed Mary discovering that in her past, before she had her memory wiped, Mierzwiak had made her get an abortion. It's interesting to speculate whether or not that scene, had it stayed, would have made Mary's story more powerful than Joel's.

On a different tack, the extreme naturalism of the scenes of Stan, Patrick and Mary having a party in Joel's flat as they perform a horrific act on his brain not only makes a symbolic point but keeps the film well and truly credible. Had the brain-wiping process been done more solemnly it would have emphasised the science-fiction element of the story.

JOEL'S STORY IN LINEAR FORM

In linear chronological form, the story of *Eternal Sunshine of the Spotless Mind* starts off with protagonist Joel Barish's discovery (disturbance) that his ex-girlfriend Clementine has had him wiped from her memory by a company called Lacuna. Joel chooses to have the same procedure (plan). The technicians, Stan and Patrick, arrive with their computers and start the procedure. As the brain-wiping process is going on, the tandem narrative multiple stories about the Lacuna staff start. We learn that Patrick is having an affair with Clementine, using her memorabilia of Joel, which he has stolen from Lacuna, to steal information that might make her love him. We also learn that Mary, the nurse, is having an affair with Stan but has a crush on their boss, Dr Howard Mierzwiak.

In the middle of the memory-wiping process, Joel starts becoming upset at the idea of losing Clementine—with whom he is interacting in his mind—and decides he wants to keep his memories of her (Joel's first-act turning point—a surprise which turns into an obstacle that drives the rest of his story). He tries to hide his thoughts from the computer, taking Clementine with him into unlikely parts of his mind, but ultimately fails, losing her from his memory just as she asks him to meet her at Montauk (the first part of his second-act turning point, his closest moment to emotional or physical death).

Meanwhile, as Joel remains unconscious, we return to the Lacuna stories and find out, at the same time as Mary, that she had an affair with the doctor, Mierzwiak, but underwent the memory-wiping procedure so does not remember this. Mary is appalled. The Lacuna team leaves.

Joel awakens, his memory wiped, and sets off for work—but impulsively and without understanding why, instead takes the train to Montauk (the second part of his second-act turning point, his decision to act, to fight back). There, he meets Clementine, who has no memory of him. They interact as strangers attracted to each other, and Joel offers to give her a lift home. She asks to sleep at his apartment, and they stop at hers so she can pick up a toothbrush. Patrick, who has been waiting for Clementine, sees Joel sitting in his car and asks him (to his bewilderment) if he is okay.

Clementine arrives back with an envelope containing her file and a cassette tape from Lacuna, sent by Mary, who has decided to send all of Lacuna's patients their files. As Clementine plays the tape, which reveals that she and Joel were lovers, they quarrel and part. Clementine later comes to his flat, and finds him playing a similar tape, sent by Mary. They quarrel some more, but ultimately decide to continue the relationship (climax).

HOW JOEL'S STORY IS PUT TOGETHER
As we've seen earlier, the story is constructed initially like standard two-thirds preview flashback, providing a powerful leaning-forward moment at the return of the second-act turning point scene that opened the film.

REGRET FLASHBACKS
As Joel's memory-wipe story progresses, we see non-chronological snippets of Joel's memories of Clementine (regret flashbacks) being wiped from Joel's memory, telling us about the relationship and graphically (and brilliantly)

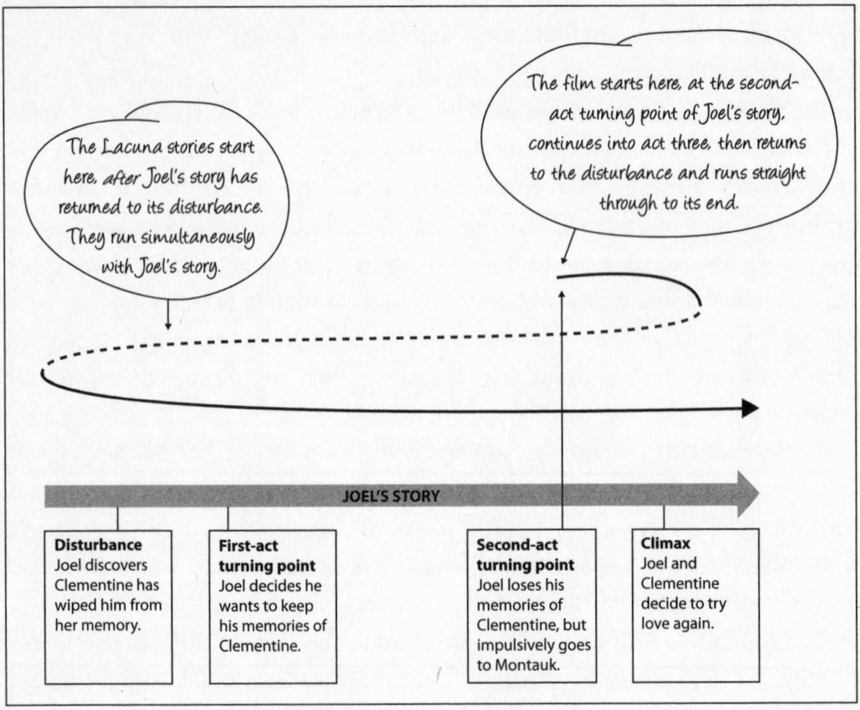

Figure 41.2 Joel's story in *Eternal Sunshine* (preview flashback)

depicting the Lacuna process in action (buildings and people disappear, and so on).

When Joel and Clementine start their surreal escape into Joel's mind, random flashbacks as illustration appear to Joel's earlier life, combined with material from the present.

COMBINING PREVIEW FLASHBACK AND TANDEM NARRATIVE

There are many fascinating things about the structure of *Eternal Sunshine*, but perhaps the most interesting is the combination of a very strong preview flashback story with an equally strong tandem narrative story. This could well be a new and very useful template, although the form is difficult, as evidenced by *Winged Creatures*, which also combines flashback (life-changing incident) with tandem but struggles to maintain pace. Since Joel's brain is really just another world or location, there is no reason why a preview flashback/tandem model could not be used for a film which, for example, depicts a tandem narrative story set in one country or town connected with a preview flashback story set in another country or town, with both stories dealing with the same themes; for example, a person living and interacting with others in a tandem narrative in town A has a preview flashback story set in town B ten years earlier.

In the light of this, it's useful to examine how Charlie Kaufman connects his tandem narrative and preview flashback stories. They link up at Joel's plan stage, just after his story has jumped from its preview sequence in Montauk back to its disturbance, which is his discovery that Clementine has had him wiped from her memory. Notice that going to Lacuna *is* Joel's plan. This suggests that the plan stage is a good point to connect the two kinds of story; in fact, is a good excuse to connect the stories. So you could make your tandem narrative story be your preview flashback's protagonist's plan. The Lacuna stories stay with Joel thereafter.

Notice how closely the Lacuna stories are physically tied to Joel's story, appearing almost always in his presence, or Clementine's, who is also part of his story. Thus, we meet the Lacuna staff and see them interacting when Joel first goes to their offices. Later, all but Dr Mierzwiak are physically at Joel's apartment for a lengthy period, with Patrick departing only to be with Clementine. This physical proximity would probably not be essential if you were using the form as a template, but it does create unities in scenario and message.

Section 5
Consecutive stories narrative

Chapter 42
Consecutive stories narrative: An introduction

Consecutive stories form describes films as different as *Rashomon*, *Pulp Fiction*, *City of God*, *The Joy Luck Club*, *Amores Perros*, *Run Lola Run*, *Paris, je t'aime*, *Night on Earth*, *Coffee and Cigarettes*, *Atonement*, *The Circle*, *Buttoners*, *Ten*, *Go!* and, less successfully, *Vantage Point*.

All of these films tell a series of separate stories (often different versions or consequences of the same event) one after the other, linking them together at the end. I used to call this sort of structure 'sequential narrative', but that caused confusion with a theory about constructing conventional narrative in sequences. I now use the term 'consecutive stories', which, if clumsy, is at least descriptive and impossible to confuse with anything else.

Sometimes these films are described as 'composite films', which is not a useful term because it is often taken to include tandem and fractured tandem films, which present very different writing problems from consecutive-stories films. Whereas tandem and fractured tandem films jump between simultaneously running stories, consecutive stories films tell semi-complete, sometimes even complete stories one after the after, creating a connection at the end. This is an utterly different plotting task.

Consecutive stories is one of the hardest parallel narrative forms to handle—precisely because it can so easily turn into an anthology of poorly connected shorts. While conventional narrative, tandem, multiple protagonist and even flashback forms all pull smoothly to a final climax and don't, as it were, end until they end, consecutive stories films have to keep concluding stories and starting new ones, sometimes actually repeating scenarios and often jumping about in time. *Pulp Fiction* actually ends on an event that happens on day one of three days. This militates against rising suspense and adds to the normal problems any parallel narrative film already has with pace, connection, meaning and closure.

Additionally—and easily forgotten—in order to maintain audience attention in this stop-start often repetitive form, each of the stories needs to be striking (often they are bizarre), and usually, as we'll see, each is structured as a suspenseful three-act structure.

The headache for writers is that in most cases the precise reason audiences come to consecutive stories films is to see how these separate, vividly interesting stories turn out to be cleverly connected. The four questions they bring are: 'Why these particular stories?', 'What point is this film making?', 'Are these stories interesting enough to merit all of this work from me?' and 'Is this complicated structure really necessary?' If those questions are properly answered, they are delighted. However, one false move and they get very critical indeed. Thankfully, there are clear structural similarities between successful consecutive stories films, and we can turn these into the beginnings of templates.

Different kinds of consecutive stories structures
We can divide consecutive stories films into three main groups, according to structure and message. Each of these is structured differently. There are also fractured versions of each of the three groups, which we'll look at later in detail.

1 **'Stories walking into the picture'** (*The Circle, Ten, Paris, je t'aime*) These are structured like 'fly on the wall' documentaries, with separate stories happening one after the other in the same location. Fractured versions include *Pulp Fiction, The Joy Luck Club* and *City of God.*

2 **Different versions/perspectives of the same event** (*Run Lola Run, Rashomon, Groundhog Day, Vantage Point*) These repeat the same scenario with modifications. Fractured versions include *The Butterfly Effect.*

3 **Different consequences triggered by the same event** (*Atonement, Go!*) Here, consecutive stories happen as the result of one action. Fractured versions include *Amores Perros.*

Typical ways of forming connections

Connections between stories are vital. The audience is coming to see how these separate, interesting stories are cleverly and thought-provokingly connected to provide one film, one coherent statement. Stories are connected in the following ways.

CONNECTIONS BY STORY CONTENT

THEME

All stories must share the same theme. This is the most basic connection. The thematic connection might not reveal itself until the last moment, in, say, a twist ending, but it must be there, or audiences will rightly ask: 'Why that story?'

PLACE AND TIME

Stories happen in the same location and/or over the same period of time, or are consequences of the same event (*Amores Perros*, *Atonement*). Often the time period is very short (as little as twenty minutes in *Run Lola Run*). Some films, however, span many years (*The Joy Luck Club*, *City of God*, *The Red Violin*). *Buttoners* uses links by place and times. The action happens over one night in Prague, 6 August 1995, fifty years to the day after the Hiroshima atom bomb, referenced in its framing plot.

OBJECT, FAMILY, COMMUNITY AND GENDER

Stories are often linked by being about the same object (*The Red Violin*), community (*City of God*), or social minority and gender (Chinese–American mothers and daughters in *The Joy Luck Club*).

SMALL GROUPS, OFTEN CRIMINAL

The stories are often about a distinct and usually small social group, often a gang, usually connected by something criminal or forbidden.

SCALE

Whereas tandem narrative films are epic in their aims and themes, deliberately portraying a wide cross-section of the community, consecutive stories narrative goes inwards into a small group, typically showing each individual's different view of the same dilemma or event.

VIOLENCE AND COMEDY OF VIOLENCE

Stories often gain suspense and jeopardy by including violence, serious accident, death or a threat of these things. When they are not present, as in *Ten*, the films are noticeably slower. Black comedy, often very violent comedy, frequently figures.

VIOLENT COMEDY VERSUS BIZARRE WIT

The amount of violence in these films worries many writers, who are concerned that consecutive stories films of the future will need to become more and more violent in order to maintain the same level of energising shock and rising jeopardy.

Possibly, *Buttoners* provides an alternative. *Buttoners* shows that bizarre wit can take the place of extreme violence and violent comedy in creating pace in consecutive stories films. In stark contrast to *Pulp Fiction, Buttoners* contains no murder and no gangsters, although it does contain two accidental deaths, and what at first seems to be a suicide. Most of the film's speed and impact comes from bizarre comedy, not violence or a reversal of male/female power as in *Pulp Fiction*.

CONNECTIONS BY STRUCTURE
FORM MIRRORS CONTENT

Most films in this form are consciously didactic and their structure deliberately mirrors their message. For example, *Run Lola Run* is about chaos theory, so uses different versions of the same scenario to illustrate how a few seconds' difference can radically change people's lives. *The Circle* aims to show how sexist laws and attitudes in Iran trap women in a vicious circle, so tells its stories of repression so that the action returns full circle to the place and story where it started; symbolically, a maternity hospital where an unwanted girl baby has been born. *Buttoners* has the theme of chance catastrophes, so uses a series of stories about the operation of chance within a framing plotline about perhaps the most powerful instance of chance: the last-minute choice (caused by bad weather) of Hiroshima over Kokura as the target for an atom bomb.

STORIES TOLD IN ONE CHUNK, OR SPECIFIC CHUNKS

Sometimes the stories are told from start to finish in one chunk (in which case they will often have their own title), sometimes the stories are told up to a turning point, to reappear at the film's end, when they are either concluded separately, or interwoven (as in tandem narrative).

Run Lola Run has an extra frame, a prologue and epilogue with voice-over and surreal footage on its chaos theory theme.

INTERCONNECTED STORIES
Often stories are interconnected, with characters appearing in several stories.

FINAL TWIST
The film will usually have a twist ending.

TRIPLICATION
If alternative versions, possibilities or consequences are involved, the number will usually be three. Triangles of three characters often appear.

DETECTIVE STORY/JIGSAW
Many consecutive stories films have a detective or jigsaw element to pump up suspense and audience engagement. Even *Rashomon*, at its base, is a whodunit.

FRAMES (SIMPLE AND FRACTURED)
Most importantly, in all forms one story normally bookends the others, creating a frame. Sometimes however, to add energy and a unifying circularity to unsuspenseful or very loosely connected stories, the framing story opens at its second-act turning point, as in preview flashback then, after all of the other stories have been told, the film returns to the second-act turning point with which it opened (again, like preview flashback) and proceeds uninterrupted to its climax. This happens in *Pulp Fiction, City of God, The Joy Luck Club* and *The Butterfly Effect. Buttoners* has a fractured frame formed of its Kokura/Hiroshima story. Sometimes, as in *Amores Perros*, the framing starts and ends in the middle of the film.

I call this sort of fractured frame a portmanteau because a portmanteau is a sturdy bag with handles, and the term describes very accurately how even very different, uneven and unconnected stories can be inserted inside one plot (just as you insert objects into a bag) with the unconnected stories being carried to pleasing closure by the portmanteau's momentum. We will look at portmanteau frames in detail later.

AN EXCEPTION: THE ANTHOLOGY FILM

One kind of consecutive stories film, the anthology film, is not intended to provide one cohesive message; indeed, it is intended to be viewed as a collection of shorts. Anthology films consist of a set of short films on the same theme or premise, each showcasing the different talents of either one director or actor, or a variety of different directors or actors. Stories may all happen in the same place, or on the same night, or involve the same objects or basic scenario. Examples are *Paris, je t'aime*, *New York Stories*, *Night on Earth* and *Coffee and Cigarettes*. Because there is no intention of the film working as one creative entity, maintaining suspense and a consistent message is not a problem, although, of course, the film must still engage its audience.

Chapter 43
Consecutive stories: Stories walking into the picture

FILMS IN THIS CATEGORY are the simplest version of consecutive stories film. They include *The Circle*, *Ten*, and the anthology *Paris, je t'aime*. I call the form 'stories walking into the picture' because, literally, that's what happens. These films set out to depict a slice of life as seen in a sequence of stories or episodes, usually told in chronological order, often happening over a short period, typically a few hours or a night. The simplest version is linear and runs chronologically from start to finish. Sometimes the message is didactic (as in *The Circle*). Sometimes the message is simply 'how interesting the people in this place are, and how talented are the directors making this film' (as in anthology films like *Paris, je t'aime*).

Usually, the films will come full circle to where they started, to symbolise a message that their characters are trapped in a vicious circle or, if more restrained, that 'this is the normality of this place'. That circle creates a pleasing frame.

Connections

The stories are always on the same theme. In typical consecutive stories style, the stories will usually involve a small group, often (except in anthologies) criminal or in breach of social taboos or rules. Other connections will be made in typical consecutive stories fashion (see p. 330) through time, place, social grouping (gender, gang, community, family etc.).

The pattern (one story appearing after another) is rhythmical. Its pleasure for the audience is in this simple rhythm. New characters with new stories keep taking over the action, one story giving way to the next, just as runners pass on the baton in a relay race. Often the films are set in public places, with new characters literally walking into shot as the camera tracks along. This technique gives a 'fly on the wall' documentary effect, an effect that the film-makers are usually actively seeking to transmit their socio-political intention.

The Circle opens in the maternity ward of a hospital on a story about a woman discovering that her daughter has given birth to a girl and not the boy the family was expecting and wanted. The camera follows this woman out into the street, where her story is interrupted by three women prison escapees trying to hide from police. The camera leaves the first woman to follow the adventures of the three escapees, until, into frame walks a woman who is trying to abandon her daughter. The camera follows her story, then goes onto yet another story concerning the plight of women in Iran—and so on. The film maintains this pattern until, finally, we return full circle to the hospital and the first story so that, as I have said, the film is framed, symbolically, by the story of the unwanted baby girl.

The film *Ten* uses walking into the picture style to tell a non-political story, the story of a young boy's access meetings with his mother. During shooting, the camera was literally attached to the dashboard of the car during their drives. It records their conversations and the people they meet as they drive along together.

Sometimes these films have a prologue and epilogue, forming a kind of frame. Fractured forms of walking into the picture (as in films like *Pulp Fiction*, *City of God*, *The Joy Luck Club*, *Buttoners* and *The Butterfly Effect*) use complex portmanteau frames either to keep their stories coherent or to overcome an inherent lack of chronologically building suspense. We will look in detail at portmanteau forms later.

Issues and danger points in linear stories walking into the picture
POTENTIAL PROBLEMS WITH PACE
Films that use stories walking into the picture in its linear form are rarely very suspenseful and often don't feature a final twist, their point being to show that life is predictable. They are intended to seize the audience primarily on an intellectual level. They eschew emotion. *The Circle* does include suspense and emotion, centred on whether the various women will solve the problems they have, but it is a limited, low-key mixture of the two, more like dread, because the film's point is that inevitably the women will suffer because of institutionalised discrimination. The film's climax is a grim anticlimax, strongly suggesting that the cycle of oppression will continue into the next generation.

A NARROWER AUDIENCE
Because of their lack of pace and surprises, linear walking into the picture films will usually attract only a limited art-house audience. Be aware if you are writing in this form that while your message may require predictability

and a gloomy anticlimax, these things can slow the film and make it feel as if it is ending in mid air. If you want a wider audience, you need to create higher levels of emotion and suspense, which means surprises, and normally the sharper, more final (hence pleasing) closure that comes from a story about a chain of events that is abnormal, not normal. Some kind of twist at the end, even a small one, might help here as might a portmanteau frame.

MAKE SURE THE STORIES ARE ALL ON-MESSAGE

Linear stories walking into the picture is the loosest of the consecutive-story forms, with a very fragile build to closure based on the pattern of thematically linked stories appearing rhythmically in sequence. Make sure you understand your message and be careful that each of your stories transmits that message, because it is very easy to get distracted into writing a story which of itself is excellent, but is not on the same theme, so does not fit. Set up the pattern and the message early.

INVENT OTHER LINKS

The more links, the more chance for audience engagement, thus the stronger the film. Consider inserting other links between the stories via:

- visuals or sound (for example, include the same images in each story, the same chiming clock)
- time (for example, make all the stories take place over a day or an evening)
- background (for example, make all of the protagonists irritated by traffic jams, cold weather)
- interconnected plots (for example, all of the connected people come to the same job-search agency, the same station—or all are friends, or relatives or enemies)
- filmic style (camera angles, cutting etc.). This is the director's territory, but you can build suggestions into the script.

Chapter 44
Consecutive stories: Different perspectives

EXAMPLES ARE: *RUN LOLA Run*, *Rashomon*, *Groundhog Day*, *Vantage Point*, *The Nines* and, in a fractured form, *The Butterfly Effect*. Films in this form repeat different versions of events either to show what might have been or may be, or to give alternative accounts of what happened, emphasising the subjectivity of human experience and the slippery nature of truth. Recently, chaos theory has come into the mix.

Rashomon and *Vantage Point* are about different perspectives on a crime. *Run Lola Run* and *The Nines* provide versions of what might have been, referencing computer games. *Run Lola Run* and *The Butterfly Effect* are about chaos theory. *Groundhog Day* is about Phil, a selfish, unpleasant man trapped in the same day until he reforms, a character not so distantly related to Ebenezer Scrooge.

Issues and danger points in different-perspectives films
REPETITION
Films written in different-perspectives form are the hardest of consecutive-stories films to write because, while they are written specifically to show repetition, repetition can quickly become boring. All films need to seize their audiences, increasing audience engagement all the way to the film's climax, creating one cohesive statement. This is very hard to do if you have to keep going back to square one and starting again, and what's more, starting again with essentially the same scenario. *Vantage Point*, which sets out to show eight different perspectives on an assassination, has problems with repetition. I discuss this and the possible reasons for it below in detail (see pp. 439–40).

PHILOSOPHICAL INTENT
Rashomon, *Groundhog Day*, *Run Lola Run*, *The Butterfly Effect* and *The Nines* employ repetition to transmit a specific philosophical message. *Vantage Point* doesn't have a message, and this is part of its problem.

HARMONY RESTORED
Usually, the film closes in the present with harmony restored.

ALL OF THE FILMS OPEN AT THEIR CHRONOLOGICAL START
Note that structurally, at present all different-perspectives films open at the chronological start of the story, as if the film is to be a normal linear film. They insert their repetitions only after a conventional linear opening. This is a great help in establishing for the audience what film they're in. Interestingly, the writer of *Groundhog Day*, Danny Rubin, says that the film originally started in its chronological middle (like *Pulp Fiction* and *Amores Perros*).

FILMS END AT THEIR CHRONOLOGICAL END
The films finish at their chronological end (if this sounds self-evident, remember that *Pulp Fiction* ends close to its chronological start).

REPETITIONS ARE LARGE CHUNKS OF ACTION
The repetitions are large chunks of action; they are not just fleeting fragments of memory—bits of flashback as illustration—although sometimes flashback as illustration appears as an extra. The size of the repetitions is a potential problem because cutting from a lengthy story to the start of a new story can stop a film in its tracks.

REPETITIONS START AT THE FIRST-ACT TURNING POINT
Fascinatingly, *Run Lola Run*, *Groundhog Day* and *Rashomon* all start their repetitions only at first-act turning point. Crucially, and very useful to know, each of their repetitions provides *a different response to the first-act turning point question*. The repetitions take the place of a normal second act; more precisely, they replace the normal barriers and reversals of the second act.

FRAME
The start of the 'different versions' section at the end of the first act means that the first act and the endings of these films form a kind of frame. The frames vary from film to film. In *Rashomon*, the story of the men talking as they shelter from the rain forms a clear frame for the whole film. The second act depicts their conversation, as each provides a different account of a recent crime involving a man, his wife and a bandit. *Groundhog Day* is similar. The frame is formed out of the first act ('Phil before his conversion') and the third act ('Phil after his conversion'), with the repetitions, the many versions of the same day, happening in the middle.

Run Lola Run is a mixture of the two. Its first act definitely sets the stage for the repetitions, as in *Groundhog Day* and *Rashomon*, and the three repetitions are definitely three possible answers to the question raised by the first-act turning point, namely, 'How can Lola get the money to save Manny in twenty minutes?' However, there is no third act in *Run Lola Run* that frames the three possible answers. Instead, the first two versions of how Lola gets the money end on catastrophe, each providing a possible second-act turning point ending to the film, in which it would be a tragedy. Meanwhile, the third answer, the happy ending, skips its second-act turning point (Lola at her worst possible moment) and third act (battle to win after catastrophe) and goes straight to a climax, where all ends well. The film does have a frame, but it is made up of a kind of prologue and epilogue consisting of material that is nothing to do with Lola and Manny's story. It features a philosophical voice-over from some kind of god-like narrator, quotations from T.S. Eliot, striking images of a clock face, comments about life as a game, and surreal footage of the cast. Note that *Run Lola Run* works very well with its truncated third version, which provides very pleasing connection, meaning and closure. This is useful to know if you're planning a 'different-perspectives' film. Probably the fact that we've already had two grim second-act turning points means we don't need a third. Some people see closure provided by a Christian message in the third version, because Lola at one point invokes God.

The Nines does not have a frame (and some people find this a problem, see pp. 340–1), although it does have a kind of explanatory epilogue in the present.

TRIPLICATION

Run Lola Run, *Rashomon* and *The Nines* involve triplication. Each film gives three strikingly different versions of the same story from the point of view of participants. *Rashomon* has a stranger providing the fourth and most likely version.

TRUNCATION

Run Lola Run, *The Nines* and *Rashomon* each show the different versions of their stories in their entirety. *Groundhog Day* needs to have many more repetitions to get its point across. It needs to show the protagonist endlessly reliving the same day. Note how it cleverly avoids boredom by starting to truncate the variations as soon as we've got the idea, then truncating more and more until the repetitions are tiny. This means we get the sense of repetition but the plot can move quickly. Truncation is an excellent device for films that need many repetitions.

FINAL TWISTS

Run Lola Run, Rashomon, The Nines and *Groundhog Day* all have a final twist.

THE REPEATED MATERIAL IS SHORT

Run Lola Run, Groundhog Day and *Rashomon* all deal with one short, self-contained event. Lola's event is a period of twenty minutes in which she has to find a large sum of money. *Groundhog Day* deals with one day, and *Rashomon* deals with an event that lasted about an hour or two. *Nines* deals with three different versions of a life, but all are short.

None of these films explores what happened *after* the key event in any depth (although each version of Lola's story also explores different possible outcomes for a range of people Lola meets as she runs). *Vantage Point* does continue its story, to problematic effect (see pp. 439–40).

OTHER DEVICES IN *RUN LOLA RUN* THAT ACHIEVE ENERGY AND CONNECTION

Run Lola Run's emotional impact is significantly increased by soundtrack effects that emphasise panic and time ticking away. The film also deliberately references video games and uses in all three stories slightly different versions of a piece of animation of Lola running. All add connection and ramp up suspense. Also employed is the classic suspense technique of the 'ticking clock', whereby the protagonist has to complete an act within a limited time or face dire consequences. In fact, her task is to cheat death, something much more confronting than anything in *Rashomon* and *Groundhog Day*. This in itself increases the suspense level.

Is different perspectives the best form for your material?

If you want a form with a lot of complex twists and turns, consider whether your material really suits different perspectives form, because it is a form that does not have the screen time for a lot of complicated plotting since the repetitions eat up the screen time. Even *The Butterfly Effect* has only a few significant scenes in the past that the protagonist keeps changing. That said, the fractured model provided by *The Butterfly Effect* (see pp. 362–4) might give you the complexity you're after.

The Nines: No frame, possibly ahead of its time

Interestingly *The Nines*, written by John August, the writer of *Go!*, is a different-perspectives film that does not have a frame, although it has an explanatory epilogue. Triplication is central: three stories appear consecutively, with the same actors playing very different characters in each, and with one actor, a man, always playing the part of protagonist, who is very different in each. In the first story he is an actor, in the second he's a writer and in the third he's a computer-game designer. Eventually, in a third story twist (as in *Run Lola Run*), we find out that this reappearing protagonist is in real life a game designer, living in the game he created, and each of the consecutive stories is a different version of the game. He is a god figure and can destroy the whole world for the people he has created.

Ultimately, he has to leave the game, but fixes things in the third game so that all the characters he likes survive and have good lives. The films bears story and philosophical resemblances to time-travel films like *The Butterfly Effect* but, typical of different-perspectives films, is about 'what if?' and possible life choices.

Interestingly, *The Nines* takes a long while to get started. It feels, disconcertingly, as if you've walked into the film halfway through. This is probably because it doesn't have a frame to set up the repetitions or warn us that the film is out of the ordinary. Perhaps this is a failing of the audience. Perhaps *The Nines* is ahead of its time. Perhaps in a few years' time we won't even notice the lack of a frame, and indeed, will find frames cumbersome.

Chapter 45
Consecutive stories:
Different consequences

FILMS IN THIS CATEGORY use stories in which one action triggers different consequences for a range of characters. Examples are *Atonement* and *Go!*

Atonement

Atonement, adapted from the novel of the same name, shows how a young girl, Briony, mistakes the identity of a rapist, which causes terrible, long-term consequences for herself, her sister Cecilia, and her sister's lover, Robbie. Structurally, it is close to the novel. It is a very clever adaptation, faithfully yet inventively transferring the novel to film. One of the things it illustrates brilliantly is how to condense a novel; how to cut. Interestingly, the makers of *Atonement* tried other structures before returning to something much closer to the structure of the novel.

It shows many elements typical of consecutive stories films, as follows.

CRIME, SMALL GROUP
The film is centrally concerned with a rape and deals with a small family group.

TRIPLICATION
The film is split into three sections, plus an epilogue, and involves three key characters. The first section deals with the wrongful accusation, the second deals with Robbie's wartime experience getting to Dunkirk, and the third deals with Briony's experiences as a nurse and her apology to Cecilia and Robbie, now reunited.

LINEAR AND MOSTLY CHRONOLOGICAL
The film tells its stories in the past consecutively then provides a final epilogue set in the present. The movement is almost chronological, but not entirely. There are some brief flashbacks in the main action and the third story (Briony grown up and a nurse) starts three weeks *before* the second story (Robbie in World War II France).

THE TRUTH AND A TWIST

Typical of consecutive stories form, the film deals with notions of truth and employs a final twist in the epilogue.

LONG TIME SPAN, BIOGRAPHICAL

Like many consecutive stories films, *Atonement* depicts life stories and spans many years.

TICKING CLOCK

There is a ticking clock in Robbie's desperate bid to get to Dunkirk, to be evacuated and return to Cecilia.

Structure

Structurally, the first section (the rape and Robbie's arrest) is in multiple protagonist form, because we do not see events from just one character's point of view, we see them from the point of view of each equally. This is worth remembering as a technique because it gives each of the three main players, Briony, Cecilia and Robbie, their own story and makes the audience invest in each immediately and at the same time. For each, the wrongful accusation is their first-act turning point—because for each, it fulfils our test for the first-act turning point of being the surprise that turns into the story's obstacle and also it is for each what their story (and the whole film) is about.

The first-act turning point is, of course, a good place to start new stories because, as we've seen, it provides a thought-provoking surprise.

During the first section of *Atonement*, there are brief 'rewinds', reminiscent of *Memento* because they first depict *the second part* of an incident between the two lovers (the bit witnessed by Briony), then immediately afterwards run the whole incident again, from start to finish, from the lovers' point of view. Note how easily audiences understand this use of rewind.

MIDDLE SECTION: PRECISE BACKSTORY TRANSMISSION

The second part of the film has jumped forward in time. It concerns Robbie, in World War II France, making his way to Dunkirk for evacuation. It leaves Robbie at what looks like the first part of a second-act turning point (closest moment to death) at Dunkirk, which turns out to be a hell on earth. Leaving a story at second-act turning point is, of course, sound storytelling. It has appeared time and again in parallel narrative and we will see it again in *Go!*

Technically, this section has to transmit a great deal of backstory explaining what happened during the time jump, and does so brilliantly. It's worth looking at for tips.

It transmits backstory through brief flashbacks as illustration as Robbie remembers his earlier past with Briony (cleverly and economically showing her crush on him) and his final meeting with Cecilia.

The latter scene, in which, just out of jail, he meets Cecilia in a café, seeing her for the first time since he was imprisoned and just before he is going to war in France, is a masterpiece of powerful but economic dramatisation. It's well worth studying. Of itself, it's clearly a highly emotional, dynamic scene, pushing the story forward. But what's so particularly clever is the way it is used to transmit, during the couple's deeply moving but restrained exchanges, both what has happened between them since Robbie's arrest and also their future plans.

We can see how clever this sequence is by considering alternative backstory transmission devices. For example, a flashback about Robbie's court case could not have carried half as much information or been anywhere near as emotionally loaded. It would probably have slowed the film down. Limits of screen time mean very careful scene choice. Transmitting backstory as part of a powerfully emotional scene is optimum.

THIRD SECTION

This jumps to Briony, now in her late teens and an aspiring writer, showing her working as a nurse in wartime London, having, as a kind of penance, given up her chance to study at Cambridge. It has elements of a third act for all three main characters, being a kind of battle to win on the part of each, with Briony meeting the other two and apologising, and all three wanting to clear Robbie's name. The meeting, bitter and heated, provides a limited reconciliation.

EPILOGUE

Many years later, Briony, now a distinguished elderly novelist about to release a novel called *Atonement*, reveals the truth of what happened in a poignant twist.

EXTRA EFFECTS

The use of typewriter sound effects powerfully suggests the fact that a story is being written. At the end, in a twist, we realise that what was being written was a whole novel.

Go!

Go! uses consecutive stories form to tell six narratives (three in detail) from different points of view (note the triplication). Typical of many consecutive stories films, all of the stories happen over one night, Christmas Eve. All deal with the dramatic and often bizarre events that happen to a (typically) small group of friends who work in a supermarket. The events are all triggered by one character's decision to take another's shift behind the cash register. The stories overlap from the start, with different stories depicting the same scenes from different points of view, and become closely interwoven at the end.

The film involves—as per usual in a consecutive stories film—crime, violence and the threat of death. While comparisons are often made with *Pulp Fiction*—and there are certainly stylistic links between the two, both having bizarre and violent black comedy, both dealing with double-crossing and revenge in the world of pimps and drug pushers, both telling apparently complete consecutive stories that come together with unexpected twists— there is no complicated time-jumping in *Go!* as there is in *Pulp Fiction*. Also, while *Pulp Fiction* ends with a surprisingly traditional moral (that even criminals can find redemption), *Go!* deliberately avoids making a moral or philosophical point (which, actually, makes it an oddity in the consecutive stories family). It ends with normality completely restored, which, unfortunately, creates what for some audiences is a disappointing anticlimax.

Go! contains high jeopardy, with each of its main characters facing death and/or prison, three for what seems initially like murder, but ultimately all of the victims survive. Note that each of its stories has a clear, albeit truncated, three-act structure. For example, the central story, that of Ronna, the girl who accepts the extra shift and becomes involved with a potentially fatal drug deal, is constructed thus:

1 **Disturbance**: Ronna accepts Simon's shift to pay for overdue rent and avoid eviction.
2 **First-act turning point**: Ronna agrees to get drugs for Zack and Adam in order to pay overdue rent.
3 **Second-act turning point**: Ronna is left for dead in a ditch after being shot by Todd and run over by Adam and Zack.
4 **Third act**: Ronna wakes up in hospital, discharges herself, goes to work, finds Mannie alive.
5 **Climax**: Ronna has the money for her rent and some left over.

TRUNCATION

Individual stories are inevitably short in consecutive stories films because there are so many of them. The place to truncate is the second-act, and third-act battle to win. The first-act turning point must stay. You could probably create stories in this form that end at their first-act turning point (a thought-provoking surprise), but you would have to make sure to unite all the stories somehow at the end.

THREE NARRATIVES TAKEN TO SECOND-ACT TURNING POINT

For structural purposes, a particularly interesting aspect of *Go!* is that it takes each of its three main narratives to their second-act turning point, stops them there, then resolves them all in a final section. This provides great jeopardy. Additionally, there is a pleasing symmetry in the fact that each story has its third act in the final part of the film.

Once again, the second-act turning point proves to be a very good place to jump between stories.

Using *Atonement* and *Go!* as templates

While *Atonement*'s structure is probably too closely linked to its content to provide an exact template, its use of a shared first act for all three stories, its final twists, its good backstory tricks, truncation, and the way it makes two of the stories overlap in time are transferable. Your subject matter would probably need to involve ongoing consequences for three characters, or people involved in three stories (three characters or stories also figure in other films about consequences such as *21 Grams*, *Three Burials*, *Amores Perros* and *The Hours* and it works well). As in the different-perspectives films *Run Lola Run*, *Rashomon* and *Groundhog Day*, the main story of the film (three stories in this case) is set up in the first act, splitting into separate stories thereafter.

Your best bet would be to work out carefully what happened to your three central characters then decide at what points in their lives you want to visit them. You will need a situation that brings them together dramatically. A Rosebud twist will add poignancy and transmit the film's message. *Go!*'s clever suspense-creating trick of stopping all three narratives at the second-act turning point of each, before resolving all in an unexpected way in the third act, is clearly transferable.

Both models call for strong, rising three-act stories planned separately before being interconnected. Robin Swicord's technique of jumping stories so that the emotional level of the scene you leave is the same as the emotional level of the scene you enter might be useful here to achieve rising suspense and emotion across storylines, although a contrasting emotion can also be effective (see p. 234).

Chapter 46
Consecutive stories: Portmanteau films

FILMS IN THIS CATEGORY include *The Joy Luck Club*, *Pulp Fiction*, *City of God*, *Amores Perros*, *Buttoners* and *The Butterfly Effect*. Homer's *Odyssey* also uses this structure. To recap, a portmanteau is a type of frame made out of splitting a plot in two to bookend a set of other stories. However, instead of opening at its chronological start, the portmanteau opens at its second-act turning point and (except in rare cares) returns there after all the other stories have been told, only then continuing to its end. Sometimes, the portmanteau story is visited between the other stories (as in *City of God*, where the portmanteau is young Rocket growing up, and *Buttoners*, where it is what is happening in Kokura and on the *Enola Gay*). Sometimes it disappears after the start, returning only at the end of the film (as in *Pulp Fiction*). I have found six kinds of portmanteau and there are probably more out there and more to come. Portmanteau frames are well worth mastering because they work wonderfully to hold together and insert suspense into loosely connected or potentially slow or repetitive stories.

As with preview and thwarted dream flashback, starting a film on the second-act turning point (first or second part) creates a detective story and a high-jeopardy hook. The portmanteau will jump from its opening second-act turning point scene back to its disturbance, thus rapidly telling audiences what film they're in. When the film finally returns to the second-act turning point the mystery is solved, creating a pleasing unity. The powerful pull to closure of one plotline carries the whole film. Paradoxically, one plot will support and sustain many plots: the lesser contains the greater.

In *The Joy Luck Club*, the portmanteau plot is the story of the young Chinese–American girl who discovers why her mother abandoned her twin half-sisters. The film opens at the moment just after the mother's death when the girl has decided to go to China to visit her long-lost half-sisters (closest moment to death or despair followed by decision to act, hence, second-act turning point).

In *City of God*, the portmanteau is the story of Rocket, the young protagonist, growing up in a ghetto in Rio de Janeiro. The second-act turning point opening of the film shows Rocket literally staring down the barrels of guns pointed at him by both gangsters and police.

In *Pulp Fiction* the portmanteau is the story of Jules, the gangster who finds God. The film opens with the planning and start of the robbery; that is, just before Jules' second-act turning point, his closest moment to death, which is when Pumpkin's gun is in his face.

The portmanteau opens up astonishing possibilities because it artificially creates pace, suspense, connection, meaning and closure in consecutive-story material that has no inherent chronological build to closure. It's particularly useful for biographical films that span many years, hence have a tendency to be episodic. In *City of God*, it holds together stories that extend over several years and include time jumps. In *Buttoners* it turns what might be simply a black comedy about the inhabitants of Prague into a thought-provoking reminder about the horror of Hiroshima, and consequently about guilt and individual responsibility. In *Pulp Fiction*, it permits the film's very effective climax to happen on the morning of day one of a three-day series of stories. In *The Joy Luck Club*, it manages to tell the stories of eight women across many time frames and many locations without the audience ever losing its place or getting bored.

The fractured frame is all the more amazing since, as we'll see, it has been in use for at least three thousand years (since Homer's time), and possibly longer.

Good structure in individual stories

Portmanteau films are just fractured consecutive stories films. Not surprisingly then, they usually contain typical consecutive stories elements. The stories:

- are on the same theme
- are striking and tightly structured in three-acts, albeit often truncated
- concern a specific and often criminal group
- contain crime or social taboos broken
- often have their own titles

Portmanteau 1: *The Joy Luck Club*

The Joy Luck Club is at base a 'stories walking into the picture' film. It uses portmanteau structure as a way to depict coherently the troubled relationships, colourful histories and final reconciliations of four sets of mothers and daughters from San Francisco's Chinese–American community. It is a particularly useful model if your film spans a lengthy period, has many loca-tions and involves a lot of similar characters. Remarkably, *The Joy Luck Club* not only manages to tell a huge amount of story set in several locations across generations without us getting lost, but also does so while involving an army of women characters, including several characters who are depicted at vari-ous ages—as toddler, little girl, adolescent, young woman and old woman. Amazingly, at no point are we puzzled about who is who or where we are. The film achieves this by a clever portmanteau and by quarantining different sets of characters in separate, self-contained stories.

All of the mothers in *The Joy Luck Club* have been friends since arriving many years ago from China and all of the daughters grew up together in the US. The portmanteau story, as I've said, is the mother–daughter relationship between one girl and her newly deceased mother. It involves the girl's diffi-cult childhood and also the mystery of why the dead mother abandoned her twin baby daughters in China.

The action jumps between a community party (being held to fare-well the bereaved girl, who is about to visit her half-sisters in China) and each mother–daughter story. The mystery of the abandoned twins provides ongoing suspense, holding all of the stories together and, in its twist denouement, providing a hopeful message about mother–daughter relationships.

The film begins with its portmanteau, opening on the bereaved girl's second-act turning point (just after her mother's death). It then goes back to the start of the girl's story, explaining her childhood. Next, the stories of the three other mother–daughter pairs are told consecutively, as complete two-part stories. In each of these, we first see the story from the point of view of one of the mother–daughter pair (introduced with voice-over). We then jump into the mind of the other member of the pair, who also uses voice-over to show us her point of view. Between each of these mother–daughter double stories we return to the party. Finally, when the three mother–daughter stories have been told, the first story (the portmanteau story of the bereaved girl) is concluded, and we learn why the dead mother abandoned her twin daughters. The film ends on the climax of the bereaved girl's story, which is when she meets her half-sisters in China.

The stories are told as in Figure 46.1. The shaded parts are the portman-teau. Notice the pleasing, rhythmic pattern the film sets up.

The film shows many typical consecutive stories characteristics. It's about a small social group, it's didactic, its stories involve crime, death, violence and even murder. It does not include triplication to the normal degree, but it

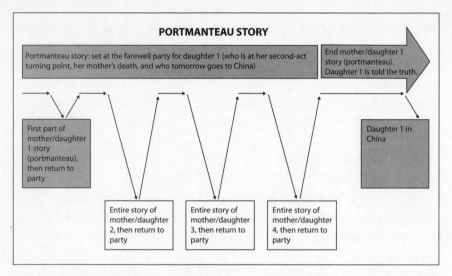

Figure 46.1 *The Joy Luck Club* portmanteau

does have three self-contained stories. It ends with a twist—the truth behind the abandonment of the twin babies. It involves a mystery story, with detective elements. There is no black comedy.

The Joy Luck Club provides several useful techniques to help the audience follow the story. They're worth learning.

1. SET THE PORTMANTEAU AT A GATHERING
Setting the portmanteau plot at a party is clever because when we return to the present from a flashback, we know instantly, visually, exactly where we are in time and place. We know who is present and we can tell everyone apart. This means the action can continue without stopping to fill in these details via dialogue. Also, the next story can start smoothly, effortlessly and credibly with the next mother–daughter pair simply coming into shot. By regularly returning to the various mother–daughter pairs *all assembled in the same room and interacting, The Joy Luck Club* constantly reminds its audience of which daughter belongs to which mother, and of how the four young women and their mothers differ. It's like getting a group photo at the end of every story.

These are basic but vital matters. It's vital that audiences know who's who, and you can't expect them to differentiate between a group of very similar-looking characters if, as well as only providing fleeting glimpses, you return to each character in a different context. Consecutive stories films present the added problem that individual characters will often have to be absent from the screen for long periods as other stories play. It's vital to provide clear, visual distinctions.

2. SLAB STRUCTURE KEEPS CHARACTERS DISTINCT
Another clever way that the film is preventing us getting lost is by quarantining each mother–daughter story. Each story, apart from the portmanteau, is told in one uninterrupted slab. This means all of the different versions of one character are confined to one story and we can tell who is who (imagine trying to keep track of which little girl becomes which woman if the action kept jumping between stories).

3. SPECTACLES, DRESS AND HAIR STYLES, MANNERISMS
The Joy Luck Club uses some of these traditional devices for helping audiences tell characters apart and pick a character at different ages. They're always handy.

THE JOY LUCK CLUB AS A TEMPLATE
Create all of the stories separately, as powerful three-act structures, taking care that the portmanteau plot happens at a gathering of all the featured characters. Be careful with time jumps and make the transitions to the next story a bit different each time, or they could become tedious. The Swicord technique of jumping stories so that the emotional level of the scene you leave is the same as the emotional level of the scene you enter can help create rising suspense, with a contrasting emotion sometimes useful.

Portmanteau 2: *Pulp Fiction*
Pulp Fiction should not work. It jumps about in time to tell a series of interconnected but autonomous stories (happening over three days) in self-contained chunks, some of which have titles. It starts and ends in the middle of the action. It kills off what appears to be its protagonist, Vincent, in a dramatic aside in the middle of someone else's story. It is extremely long. Yet, despite all these potential recipes for disaster, it is strikingly powerful, fast, suspenseful, full of well-drawn characters, and grimly comical.

Doubtless some of this is to do with the large amount of jeopardy, surprise, and quirky, often shocking, black comedy, delivered by two gangsters who much of the time interact like a comedy duo, even down to the patter. It also has a lively soundtrack. But what prevents *Pulp Fiction* from dropping into a collection of vividly original and hard-hitting short films is its portmanteau structure. This structure is immensely useful to writers. It provides us with clues, indeed a whole template for writing story material that does not have a chronological build to climax.

PULP FICTION AS A TEMPLATE

Pulp Fiction is a very useful template for consecutive stories films that:

- are really just a collection of stories about members of the same group, occurring over a few days
- are not linked by the same climax
- do not have their most dramatic point at their chronological end
- have stories that occur in different time frames
- probably do not start out having a strong message

STORIES WALKING INTO THE PICTURE/CHRONOLOGICAL SEQUENCE

Untangled, *Pulp Fiction* is in 'stories walking into the picture' form. It is not held together by its chronological sequence, which is anticlimactic, and unlike *The Circle* or *Ten*, in its chronological form it has no pleasing circular movement. Here is the action in *Pulp Fiction* set out first chronologically then in its viewing order.

DAY 1, MORNING

1   Jules and Vincent shoot the boys who tried to steal Marcellus' money.

2   A young man bursts out of the bathroom and shoots six bullets at Vincent and Jules from point-blank range—but misses. Jules speculates that this is divine intervention. They shoot the young man, and take a fourth man, Marvin, with them when they leave.

3   Marvin is accidentally shot in Jules' and Vincent's car. They go to Jimmy's to get rid of the corpse and clean up. Mr Wolf arrives at Jimmy's and removes the corpse. Vincent and Jules clean up and change clothes.

4   Jules and Vincent have breakfast at a restaurant, where Jules decides to become God's servant because he feels that the bullets missing him was divine intervention and a message from God.

5   Pumpkin and Honey Bunny plan and commence the robbery at the restaurant.

6   Jules prevents the robbery and lets Pumpkin and Honey Bunny go, intending to become an evangelist.

7   Jules and Vincent visit a bar, where Butch is getting instructions from Marcellus about fixing his fight.

DAY 1, EVENING
8   Vincent takes Mia out. She nearly overdoses. He saves her.

DAY 2, EVENING
9   Butch, asleep, dreams of the time he was given his dead father's
     watch by one of the father's war buddies. Butch wakes up.
10   Butch wins his fight.

DAY 3, MORNING
11   Butch discovers that his girlfriend has left the watch back at his
     apartment, so goes back to collect it.
12   He shoots Vincent dead.
13   Butch and Marcellus are kidnapped by rapists. Butch rescues
     Marcellus. Marcellus forgives him. Butch leaves town with his
     girlfriend.

VIEWING ORDER IN *PULP FICTION*

Here is how *Pulp Fiction* is shown on screen.

DAY 1, MORNING
1   Pumpkin and Honey Bunny plan and commence the robbery.
2   Jules and Vincent shoot two boys who tried to steal Marcellus'
     money.
3   Jules and Vincent go to the bar, where Marcellus is instructing
     Butch to lose his fight that evening.

DAY 1, EVENING
4   Vincent takes out Mia, Marcellus' wife. She nearly overdoses. He
     saves her.

DAY 2, EVENING
5   Butch, asleep, dreams of the time he was given his dead father's
     watch by one of the father's war buddies. Butch wakes up.
6   Butch wins the fight.

DAY 3, MORNING
7   Butch discovers that his girlfriend has left the watch back at his
     apartment, so goes back to collect it.
8   He shoots Vincent dead.

9   Butch and Marcellus are kidnapped by rapists. Butch rescues Marcellus. Marcellus forgives him. Butch leaves town with his girlfriend.

DAY 1, MORNING
10   A young man bursts out of the bathroom and shoots six bullets at Vincent and Jules from point-blank range—but misses. Jules speculates that this is divine intervention.
11   Marvin is accidentally shot. Jules and Vincent go to Jimmy's to get rid of the corpse and clean up. Mr Wolf arrives at Jimmy's and removes the corpse. Vincent and Jules clean up and change clothes.
12   Vincent and Jules have breakfast at a restaurant, where Jules decides to become God's servant because he feels the bullets missing him was divine intervention and a message from God.
13   Attempted robbery by Pumpkin and Honey Bunny, foiled by Jules. Jules lets Pumpkin and Honey Bunny go. He leaves to become an evangelist.

Quite clearly, there is no inherent chronologically rising suspense in *Pulp Fiction*. Instead, the film consists of a range of equally important stories, which jump in time for no apparent reason, connected only by theme and character. The film ends in its chronological middle and the only unifying plot strand is the story of Jules, the gangster who finds God.

HOW THE PORTMANTEAU SOLVES THESE PROBLEMS
The portmanteau plot is the story of Jules, the gangster who finds God. Interestingly, it is a tightly written three-act narrative on the traditional topic of perfectibility. In copybook style, the protagonist Jules is redeemed by his experiences. A narrative sentence of Jules' redemption would run like this:

> The protagonist (Jules, a ruthless gangster), faced with the disturbance (of having to execute men who double-crossed his boss) and surprised by what seems to be divine intervention (first-act turning point) is stopped from investigating the implications of this by the accidental shooting by Vincent of a hostage and the dangerous and complicated disposal of the corpse. He plans to reform, but reaches a lowest point of physical and moral danger (second-act turning point) when he is held up at gunpoint by a robber who normally he would execute. In the climax, he solves the problem by choosing the path of good, sending the robbers away unharmed.

The portmanteau works as shown in Figure 46.2

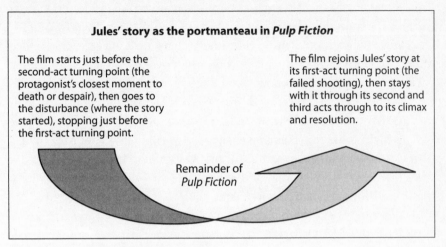

Jules' story as the portmanteau in *Pulp Fiction*

The film starts just before the second-act turning point (the protagonist's closest moment to death or despair), then goes to the disturbance (where the story started), stopping just before the first-act turning point.

The film rejoins Jules' story at its first-act turning point (the failed shooting), then stays with it through its second and third acts through to its climax and resolution.

Remainder of *Pulp Fiction*

Figure 46.2 The *Pulp Fiction* portmanteau

COULD OTHER STORIES PROVIDE A PORTMANTEAU?

If Jules' story is providing a portmanteau that holds the film together, could the other stories in *Pulp Fiction* provide the portmanteau instead? Noticeably, the two other stories are also classic (if tight, indeed, sometimes truncated) three-act narratives. Here are narrative sentences for each of the other stories.

VINCENT VEGA AND MARCELLUS WALLACE'S WIFE

A gangster, Vincent (protagonist), faced with having to take out Mia, the sexy wife of his jealous gangster boss (disturbance), is surprised by Mia snorting his stash of high-grade heroin and starting to die (first-act turning point which compounds the problem). He responds by taking her to the home of Lance, the drug dealer. He is foiled (second-act setbacks), firstly by Lance's delay in answering the phone, then his strong reluctance to help, then by bickering between Lance and his wife, then by Lance being unable to find his medical book. He reaches his lowest point of physical danger or despair (second-act turning point) when his only chance of saving Mia is to stab her in the chest with a hypodermic needle full of adrenalin. He manages it and she revives (climax).

THE GOLD WATCH

Butch, a boxer (protagonist), faced with accepting a bribe from Marcellus to rig a fight (disturbance which creates a problem), double-crosses Marcellus and is set to run away with the money. He is surprised (first-act turning point which compounds the problem) by the fact that his girlfriend, Fabienne, has left a watch of great sentimental value at his apartment. He goes back to get it and is foiled initially by Vincent, whom he shoots dead, then by Marcellus, who pursues him, causing him first to have a serious car crash, then to be shot at and wrestled with (second-act series of action setbacks, often triggered by the antagonist, but also by fate, accident etc.) until at his lowest point of physical danger or despair (second-act turning point), he ends up with Marcellus in a cellar with three sexual perverts who plan to rape him. He fights back, managing to escape. In the climax, he goes back to help Marcellus, the man he hated, robbed, and was about to fight to the death. He saves Marcellus, who lets him off the hook. He goes off happily, keeping his freedom, the money, and his girlfriend.

WHICH PORTMANTEAU?

Would the film still have worked if either of these stories had been used to open and conclude the film, using the structural breakdown shown by the Jules story? Would the film have had the same satisfactory closure?

Here is how each of the stories could have been used as the portmanteau.

With the gold watch as the portmanteau, the film could have opened with the perverted gun shop owner and his friend, Zed, getting the sexual deviant out of his cage. It could then have gone back to the disturbance—where Butch is given his instructions by Marcellus—then be put aside until all the other stories had been told, to return in its entirety starting at the first-act turning point—that is, the point at which Butch discovers the watch has been left behind. The closure would have been Butch walking free.

Alternatively, using Vincent Vega and Marcellus Wallace's wife as the portmanteau, the film could have opened with Lance, the drug dealer, and his wife bickering over the missing medical book and then getting out a syringe. It could then have returned to Vincent and Jules talking about the foot massage prior to their morning reprisal raid. Then, after all the other stories had concluded, it could return to the restaurant and the first-act turning point, which is when Mia takes the heroin at her home. It could then proceed uninterrupted until the climax, in which Vincent stabs Mia with the hypodermic needle and she revives. The pleasing closure would be when she and Vincent return to Marcellus' house and Mia tells Vincent the tomato joke from her pilot television show, *Fox Force Five*.

These two alternatives for a portmanteau seem quite possible. Each provides a structure with satisfying closure. However, it is hard to say whether either could have been made to work as well as Jules' story which, with its moral edge, passes interesting commentary on living and dying by the sword, and presents a larger moral for the film as a whole. Also, as writer–director Lisa Ohlin points out, Jules actually changes, so he is a protagonist who moves, rather than simply survives.

ADDING A FRAME WITH A TWIST: PUMPKIN AND HONEY BUNNY

I said earlier that *Pulp Fiction* starts just before Jules' second-act turning point, where Jules is faced with death in the form of Pumpkin pointing a gun at him. More precisely, the film starts a little before that, with Pumpkin and Honey Bunny discussing and starting an armed holdup. Does the film actually need that scene? Why didn't the film simply start with Jules sitting at a table and two unknown robbers trying to take Marcellus Wallace's briefcase?

It could, but starting on a discussion between two bizarre characters like Pumpkin and Honey Bunny and going to titles with the start of their robbery attempt means that the film's opening is startling and its ending is even more unpredictable because Jules is not shown in the opening so there is no warning that Jules will be involved in the robbery. Unpredictable connection is a very powerful way to end a film. So the Pumpkin and Honey Bunny opening is a technique to think about. Technically, we could say that the Pumpkin and Honey Bunny story is actually a simple frame that encloses the portmanteau.

TO USE *PULP FICTION* AS A TEMPLATE

Work out powerfully suspenseful three-act stories, using truncation if necessary. Decide on the portmanteau plot, choosing one with a final twist, but be aware that this twist will be taken to be the message of the film. Consider a simple frame (like Pumpkin and Honey Bunny) to add to the pleasure of all the stories coming together at the end. Combine the stories, employing the portmanteau second-act turning point to disturbance opening.

Portmanteau 3: *City of God*

City of God is a biographical film set in the slums of Rio de Janeiro. Really, it is a violent coming-of-age story, as Rocket, the young hero, moves from puberty to manhood in a period of gang warfare that initially threatens to engulf him but that ultimately permits him to escape the ghetto into a new life as a photojournalist.

It contains a series of consecutive complete or almost complete stories, each with their own titles. At base, it is a 'stories walking into the picture' film that uses a portmanteau formed by Rocket's life story. Just as *The Circle* dealt with the cycle of exploitation of women in Iran, so *City of God* deals with the cycle of violence that sees a boy gangster rise to prominence only to be shot dead by the next generation of boy gangsters whom, ironically, he created.

City of God is actually a double biography. In following Rocket, it also follows his boy–gangster counterpart, a mentor antagonist called Lil' Z. Lil' Z is a vicious sociopath who shapes Rocket's life. Both of them share the same disturbance and climax, because Rocket's final success in his climax is actually created by the exposure and death of Lil' Z. This makes the film a very handy template for double biographies, particularly biopics about charismatic individuals who might be trivialised or in some way reduced if seen from the inside. For example, if you were writing a biography of a great composer or painter you could tell that story in parallel with the life of an 'everyman' protagonist, thus maintaining the mentor's mystique. Another form that you could use here, as we've seen, is case history flashback, as in *Citizen Kane* and *Amadeus*.

THE PORTMANTEAU
The film opens just before Rocket's second-act turning point, which shows us Rocket accidentally trapped between Lil' Z's gang of armed ghetto kids and an armed gang of police, all guns aimed at him. We then flash back to the disturbance of both young men's stories. Next, the film proceeds through the interwoven childhood and adolescence of Rocket and Lil' Z (including stories of other ghetto inhabitants who touched their lives) before returning to the opening scene and speeding through Rocket's third-act battle to win and ultimately to the climax, which is Rocket escaping being shot, then taking the photographs which show Lil' Z bribing the police and being assassinated, photographs that will assure his career as a photojournalist.

THE WEAKER CHARACTER IS CLEARLY THE PROTAGONIST
Remarkably, *City of God* manages to keep a passive observer at the centre of the action. Lil' Z's story is clearly the more powerful of the two. By contrast, Rocket's story at base is actually an almost clichéd coming-of-age tale, complete with comic awkwardness and the obligatory seduction by an older woman. As Lil' Z sinks further and further into shocking violence, Rocket experiences unrequited love, unsuccessful attempts at crime, and ultimately seduction. It would have been very easy for this charming but bland story to have been overshadowed by Lil' Z's story. Alternatively, the film could have turned into an uneasy fit of two genres, gangster and whimsical coming-of-age. In fact, the two stories and two genres are interwoven to create a

very powerful, cohesive film in which Rocket's story, although by far the less dramatic of the two, is in the forefront and actually pulls Lil' Z's story along. Rocket is kept at the centre by a variety of structural devices.

ROCKET IS KEPT IN THE FOREFRONT VIA FLASHBACK AND VOICE-OVER

All of the flashbacks are seen from Rocket's point of view, usually with Rocket's voice-over, even if they involve events that Rocket could not have witnessed. An audience will always feel that the person having the flashback is the protagonist (particularly if there is voice-over, as there is here), hence the flashbacks establish and maintain Rocket as protagonist, even though he is passive and often absent. Astonishingly, even when Rocket himself has been out of the story for some time, when he returns there is no jolt.

ROCKET'S STORY PULLS ALONG LIL' Z'S STORY

The trick here is that almost all of the major players literally walk into Rocket's story before going on to become crucial in Lil' Z's story (this is how *City of God* is a 'stories walking into the picture' film at base). The pattern goes:

1 Characters first appear in Rocket's story.
2 Rocket talks about them.
3 Their history is shown in flashback.
4 They play major roles in Lil' Z's story.

This has the effect of putting and keeping Rocket centre-stage. Thus, the film's first flashback happens when Rocket is caught between Lil' Z's gang and the police. He then announces that to explain how he is always caught in the middle he has to, in his words, 'go back to the beginning', and we flashback to him, aged about ten playing a soccer game, as goalie, his arms akimbo exactly as they are in the opening scenes as he is stuck between gangsters and police. The soccer game is interrupted by Lil' Z (at that stage about ten and called Lil' Dice) and his inseparable friend Benny, also aged ten. The game is interrupted again, this time by three young men, with Rocket explaining in voice-over that he also needs to tell the story of these three, who are known as the Tender Trio. He tells us that they include his own older brother Goose and Benny's older brother Shaggy (this is another way of connecting Rocket with Benny and Lil' Z). We then see the Tender Trio first robbing a gas cylinder truck, then, at Lil' Z's instigation, robbing a brothel, while Lil' Z keeps watch. Unbeknown at this stage to both the audience and the Tender Trio, Lil' Z brutally murders everyone in the brothel, letting the Tender Trio take the blame.

If we stop for a moment and look closely at this section, Rocket does not participate in most of the action and when he is involved, it is marginally—as a bit player. Really, this is not his story at all. However, the way flashback and voice-over are used make it his story. If we were to ask the audience 'Whose story is this?' the answer would be, unequivocally, 'Rocket's story'. This is very clever indeed. By entering a story via a minor character's flashback (with voice-over) you can make the minor character the film's protagonist.

The pattern repeats itself throughout the film. When Rocket gets older, he joins a group of beachgoers. The group includes Angelica, with whom he is smitten, and her rich boyfriend Itiago. When Angelica asks him to buy her drugs, Rocket has to literally walk into the apartment of the drug dealer Carrot. This triggers a flashback into how the apartment fell into the hands of drug dealers—again, events that Rocket neither saw nor was involved in.

Later, when Lil' Z arrives at Carrot's apartment, Rocket tells Lil's Z's story from the murderous brothel episode onwards up to his arrival at the apartment. Still later, Knockout Ned, who will become Lil' Z's main adversary along with Carrot, is first introduced in Rocket's story.

CLEVER CONNECTIONS BETWEEN STORIES

City of God is essentially episodic. It consists of a portmanteau plot inside which complete stories run consecutively, often with titles. What prevents the film from becoming jumpy—what counteracts a stop-start effect—is two things. The first is that when a Lil' Z story finishes, the next story we jump to is the next instalment of Rocket's story, with Rocket a bit older each time. This instantly creates interest, at the same time smoothing over the time gap. The other clever connection technique is that vital information from each story is not revealed during that story, but is withheld to create mystery, being revealed only later on. Thus, we only learn long after the event (in flashbacks) that Lil' Z not only shot dead all the occupants of the brothel, but also murdered Goose. This has the effect of inserting useful suspense. Mysteries and puzzles pay off pleasingly as we go, tying together past and present, keeping our interest. Maintaining interest in these long stories is difficult, so the audience needs rewards. You can't rely on a final twist for all your film's mystery because it is too far off (this was a problem in *Winged Creatures*, aka *Fragments*).

CREATING PACE BY STEALING JEOPARDY FROM FURTHER ALONG IN THE STORY

The other trick *City of God* uses to fill in backstory dynamically is *Memento*'s technique—whereby the action jumps forward in time to a dramatic moment, then goes into flashback to fill in the missing material (see pp. 322–3). It's a kind of clawing forward movement—you hook into a later part of the story and haul the rest of the story up to join it. It's just another instance of the classic technique of successful non-linear films—stealing jeopardy from later in the story to pump up potentially slow material.

INTRODUCING NEW CHARACTERS LATE IN THE FILM

City of God makes a feature of introducing new characters even very late into the film. In a conventional linear film this usually frustrates the audience. But in *City of God* it works; in fact, it makes the film actively interesting because it gives the sense of events unfolding as in real life. Why does it work? Perhaps because we know that the film is about Rocket and Lil' Z's parallel lives and the new characters must be a part of those stories, not a new departure.

CITY OF GOD AS A TEMPLATE

As with *Pulp Fiction*, work out all of the stories. Your portmanteau will be the life story of your protagonist. Work out the internal jumps back and forth between stories to fill in clues and steal jeopardy. The pattern in *City of God*, as we have seen, is that characters first appear in Rocket's story, then Rocket talks about them, then their history is shown in flashback with voice-over, then they play major roles in Lil' Z's story.

The *Memento* trick involves first introducing characters in the middle of action, then flashing back and, with voice-over, quickly summarising their past and how they came to be where they now are, then returning to the present.

Portmanteau 4: *Buttoners* (portmanteau plus coda)

Like *City of God*, *Buttoners* uses a portmanteau and visits it during the course of the film. However, *Buttoners* has a kind of coda, extra story material, in which the ghost of the pilot who flew the plane that bombed Hiroshima comes to Prague on the night of the film's action and is interviewed by a radio talk show host. The idea of continuing a portmanteau story after the rest of the film has finished has interesting possibilities and provides a useful template.

Portmanteau 5: *The Butterfly Effect* (different perspectives)

Like *Run Lola Run*, *The Butterfly Effect* is about chaos theory and belongs to the same sub-category: different perspectives. Told chronologically, the story would be episodic and jumpy, but with a portmanteau frame it runs smoothly.

In chronological sequence, the story runs as follows.

Evan is a little boy who experiences blackouts. In particular, he blacks out during three events in his childhood and adolescence that he knows were shocking, but cannot fully remember and cannot get information about (notice the triplication). The action jumps forward several years to Evan aged twenty-one, now a punkish, A-grade college student. Evan discovers that if he reads entries in his childhood journal about the shocking events, he can physically revisit them in the past, reliving in full what happened. This is his first-act turning point (what the scenario is 'about'; also, an entry into another world, and the surprise that creates the obstacle that drives the rest of the film).

In the present, he visits two of the three childhood friends who were involved in the shocking events. Two are traumatised, while the third has only recently come out of juvenile jail. Immediately after his visit, one suicides (the film's midpoint).

As a cigarette burn that happened in his visit to the past has remained on his body in the present, he reasons that he might be able to change his friends' current unhappy present lives by changing the past. He deliberately triggers a series of returns to the past by reading the journal. But the changes that he makes create different but equally bad consequences in the present for his friends, his mother and his twenty-one-year-old self.

After his fourth horribly unsuccessful attempt to fix the past (second-act turning point, first step), he realises he is the cause of everyone's problems (decision to fight back), sets out to kill himself *in utero* (battle to win), and does so (climax) thereby giving his loved ones a happy life (resolution).

TYPICAL CONSECUTIVE STORIES FEATURES

The film involves a small group of people involved in criminal events, time jumps, a ticking clock and philosophical content (chaos theory). It also features the following:

DIFFERENT VERSIONS OF THE SAME EVENT

We keep visiting the same events, with crucial new information or changes each time. Notice that each repetition, unlike *Vantage Point*, contains a lot of new material.

TRIPLICATION

There are three shocking events in the protagonist's childhood, each of which involves a blackout, and three childhood friends. He has three other childhood blackouts, one in which he has a premonition of his future role as harmer of lives, and two others in which he has returned from the future trying to change events. However, the film contains many more versions of the main characters, because all are different in each of Evan's different lives.

THE PORTMANTEAU

The film opens on the second beat of Evan's second-act turning point, when Evan has decided to fight back, but we don't know how or why. We see him frantically trying to hide himself in an office. The first flashback, in classic parallel narrative style, is to the disturbance: Evan as a small child showing odd symptoms.

In the final moments of the film, we see the opening office scene again, then are given the typical Rosebud twist, which is that his form of fighting back is to kill himself to free his mother and friends to lead happy lives.

The film has a very long set-up and Evan's decision to change the past happens exactly halfway through, at 49 minutes, midpoint, after a suicide. Surprisingly, the section with time jumps makes up only half of the film.

THE BUTTERFLY EFFECT AS A TEMPLATE

Replicating *The Butterfly Effect*'s template exactly would give you only a copy of the film. However, *The Butterfly Effect* could be used as a template for something other than a time-travel film. For example, one could imagine a film that set up a story in the past (say, a murder, partially witnessed by the victim's young daughter) with the action then jumping forward twenty or thirty years to when the child was interviewing murder suspects and getting different versions of the same event, which we would see in flashback. This might trigger the daughter's incomplete memories, which became more coherent as the film progressed. This would give you a film a bit like *Waltz with Bashir* (although *Waltz with Bashir* does not have a section at the start where we see the past: instead; the past is assembled as the film proceeds).

If you were using *The Butterfly Effect* as a template in this instance, you should:

- be careful to make the first-act turning point the first flashback; that is, the first step back into the past (in my example this might well be the first time the adult protagonist realises that as a child she saw the murder)

- be careful to choose the content of the first flashback carefully, so that it triggers the decision that involves more investigation into the past (in my example, the adult, like Evan, would decide to investigate further)
- be aware that the first flashback (and whatever triggers it) needs to answer the question: 'What is the plot of the film about?' and will be the obstacle that drives the rest of the film

Portmanteau 6: *Amores Perros* (centre-split portmanteau)

Like several of the more successful non-linear parallel narrative films, *Amores Perros* was written by Guillermo Arriaga. With its central premise of the consequences of one event, it is actually a fractured version of the consecutive stories form used by *Go!* and *Atonement* (different consequences). Like them, it uses three stories (notice the triplication).

Unlike *City of God*, *Pulp Fiction* and the other portmanteau films we've been looking at, the portmanteau plot in *Amores Perros* does not frame the whole film. It opens and returns in the chronological middle of the three stories (so we can call it a centre-split portmanteau). It is also different in that it uses the device we've seen in thwarted dream flashback, the triggering crisis, which is when one scene has a different job in different stories.

In chronological time, the three stories in *Amores Perros* happen one after the other. However, the film starts in its chronological middle. Its triggering crisis is a car crash which massively affects three different people. The car crash is the second-act turning point in story 1 (the story about Octavio, the driver who causes the crash), the disturbance of story 2 (the story about Valeria, a badly injured victim), and the first-act turning point of story 3 (the story of a Chivo, a bystander who rescues Cofy, Octavio's dog).

After the crash, the film goes back in time and tells story 1 ('Octavio and Susana') from normality/disturbance up to the crash. It then tells the injured victim's story ('Valeria and Daniel') from its start before the accident through to its climax and resolution. Finally, it tells the bystander's story ('El Chivo and Maru') from before its disturbance through to its climax and resolution. The third act of 'Octavio and Susana' happens in 'El Chivo and Maru' and snippets of the two later stories, particularly El Chivo and Maru, appear in 'Octavio and Susana' prior to the car crash.

CHARACTERISTICS OF CONSECUTIVE STORIES FILMS

Like all consecutive stories films, *Amores Perros* concerns a small group within society, deals with criminal behaviour (also death and violence),

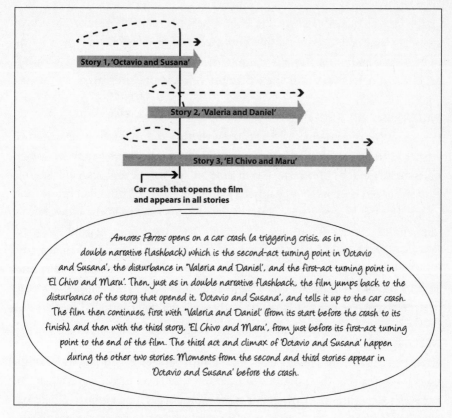

Figure 46.3 The structure of *Amores Perros*

is didactic, involves stories on the same theme (dogs influencing humans involved in troubled love affairs, often unrequited love), utilises triplication (three stories), uses twists, and has stories connected by time and place.

THE STORIES
ORIGINALITY AND PATTERNING

The three stories in *Amores Perros* are all extremely original, with surprising twists and turns, risk and emotion. None is predictable and each would be capable of forming the basis of a viable feature film in its own right. The two street stories have extremely high jeopardy, with their domestic and street violence and gory scenes of dog fighting. 'Valeria and Daniel' involves a violent injury but has lesser jeopardy and no crime.

Note that each of the three stories has a relationship line involving a human love and an action line involving a dog *which somehow brings about disaster, usually to the relationship.* As usual, the action line permits the relationship line to happen. Note that the most vividly original stories are the action-line stories. Really, love is love, so what creates a highly original love story is essentially the action line because it forces love to find new ways or to be damaged in new ways. If you are using this model, spend time creating highly original, thematically linked action lines, with clever twists and turns.

PATTERNS AND RHYTHMS
Guillermo Arriaga deliberately created a rhythm of progression between the stories. The first story, 'Octavio and Susana', is about young people and happens mostly before the crash. The middle story, 'Valeria and Daniel', is about somewhat older people and happens for the most part immediately after the crash. The final story is an old man's love for his estranged daughter, and it happens for the most part after the crash. The first story causes the second and third.

The three stories all loop back from the car crash to their normality and play through. The third act of 'Octavio and Susana' does not happen after the car crash scene returns. It is visited and concluded later in the film.

Strong three-act structures
Arriaga consciously ends scenes and jumps stories on moments of high emotion, meaning that in practice he often jumps on turning points in the three-act structure, as turning points are moments of high emotion. It's interesting to look at what strong three-act structures the three stories are.

OCTAVIO AND SUSANA
ACTION LINE

Disturbance:	Susana accidentally lets out Cofy, who kills Jarocho's dog.
First-act turning point:	Octavio decides to put Cofy in dog fights to raise money to run away with Susana.
Second-act turning point:	The car chase, impact.
Climax:	Octavio is seriously injured, his friend Jorge is killed, Cofy is taken by El Chivo.

RELATIONSHIP LINE

Disturbance:	When Susana tells Octavio she is pregnant, he asks her to run away with him.
First-act turning point:	Octavio decides to put Cofy in dog fights to raise money to run away with Susana (notice that this is the same as in action line).

Second-act turning point:	Susana does not turn up at the bus station the first time.
Climax:	Susana does not turn up at the bus station the second time.

VALERIA AND DANIEL
ACTION LINE

Disturbance:	Valeria goes in her car to buy wine to celebrate the first meal she and Richie will have in their new flat.
First-act turning point:	Valeria's leg is seriously injured in the car crash (which means she is at home and Richie her dog gets trapped under the floorboards).
Second-act turning point:	Valeria is found unconscious, after damaging her leg trying to rescue Richie.
Climax:	Valeria's leg is amputated, Richie is found alive.

RELATIONSHIP LINE

Disturbance:	Valeria and Daniel move into a flat together.
First-act turning point:	The phone rings but nobody speaks, this triggers a quarrel between them.
Second-act turning point:	Daniel telephones his wife, implying that he is having second thoughts.
Climax:	Daniel brings Valeria back to the flat. How long will they stay together?

EL CHIVO AND MARU
ACTION LINE

Disturbance:	El Chivo accepts an assassination assignment from a man who wants his brother killed.
First-act turning point:	El Chivo is stopped from the assassination by the car crash. He rescues Cofy, Octavio's dog.
Second-act turning point:	The dog Cofy kills El Chivo's dogs, sending El Chivo into despair and making him reassess his life and his role as an assassin.
Climax:	El Chivo leaves the two brothers to sort out their own problems, rejecting his role as assassin.

RELATIONSHIP LINE

Disturbance:	El Chivo reads in a newspaper that his wife is dead, decides to make contact with his daughter.
First-act turning point:	He goes to the funeral and is told by his sister-in-law to stay away.
Second-act turning point:	Cofy the dog kills El Chivo's dogs, sending El Chivo into despair, making him not only reassess his life and his role as an assassin but also realise that he can't face his daughter.
Climax:	El Chivo leaves a message on his daughter's answering machine, saying that he will come back when he has the courage to look her in the eye.

USING *AMORES PERROS* AS A TEMPLATE

Plan three high-jeopardy, highly original stories, connected thematically and also in time and place by the same catastrophic event. The pattern is a second-act turning point preview flashback story connected to two consecutive stories by the same scene, which is the disturbance in one and the first-act turning point in the other. Make the action lines cause the relationship lines to play out as they do. Notice how each story loops back after the car crash to its own normality, its start.

Danger areas of the centre-split portmanteau

A centre-split frame is dangerous to use because it ends in the film's middle, and a frame that ends in the middle of a film will always cause a change of gear and can easily create an anticlimax or a disjunction. This is fine if you want the film to have a distinct change of pace and gear—as was intended in *Amores Perros*, where the film leaves Mexico's slum streets and violent criminals and goes indoors in a wealthy area to tell a psychological drama in contrast—but not if you want to maintain the same pace. If you don't want a change of pace (and the consequent problem of trying to regain pace once you've slowed the film right down, a hard act to pull off) you will need to work hard to energise the stories that follow the return of the frame.

Bad Education is a film that shows disjunction in the middle at the point where the portmanteau frame ends. This is because *Bad Education* takes a different direction after the portmanteau ends: really, it becomes a new film. In contrast, *Amores Perros* (and as we shall see in the next chapter, Homer's *Odyssey*) sets up later stories within the portmanteau story. In *Amores Perros*,

Chivo, with his junk cart and dogs, is set up very early on in *Octavio and Susanna*.

Hence, to prevent disjunction and create momentum, try to refer to what will happen after the centre-split portmanteau has finished *before* it has finished. Another way to prevent disjunction in two part stories like *Bad Education* might be to use fractured tandem (see pp. 376–408, 440–1).

Chapter 47

Consecutive stories: Fixing journey stories with a portmanteau (Homer's *Odyssey*)

I HAVE GIVEN HOMER'S *Odyssey* a chapter of its own because, although it is not a film, it uses a specific kind of portmanteau that I think can create cohesion and build suspense in modern journey films that are in danger of fragmenting into episodes. It may also be useful for an episodic, epic feature, or for film trilogies or TV miniseries. It brilliantly conceals inherent weaknesses such as slow set-ups, episodic stories, time jumps and multiple protagonists. It might make the *Odyssey* more immediate if you think of the gods as a gang of modern gangsters who combine immense power with petulance and perverse cruelty, and of Odysseus as a flawed man caught up with gangsters.

While conventional screenwriting theory always assumes that journeys are linear and chronological, the iconic journey story of Western culture, Homer's *Odyssey* is non-linear, opens in the middle then jumps to the end, involves thwarted dream flashback and employs multiple protagonists. Nobody quite knows why the *Odyssey* has this particular non-linear structure. My hunch is that it uses non-linearity tricks to fix up its inherent plot problems because, told chronologically, it is episodic, unsuspenseful and meandering, with a lengthy, low-jeopardy set-up, tangential stories and big gaps in time.

My guess is that there are probably only so many ways to hold a live audience, and the problems that Arriaga or Scorsese face in telling episodic or exposition-heavy pieces such as *Amores Perros*, *21 Grams* or *Goodfellas* are the same as those faced by whoever created the *Odyssey* (and the many other non-linear epics from all around the world), and have been solved in the same way.

Homer's *Odyssey* uses a centre-split frame but, unlike *Amores Perros*, this framing scene does not appear in more than one story, performing a different job in each. Instead, after the opening sequence (which opens midway through the action) the *Odyssey* jumps from what is happening on Mount

Olympus to what is happening to Odysseus' wife and son, who are having problems at home as they wait for him to arrive. This adds enormous energy to the story because we, the audience, know how urgently Odysseus is needed at home. By contrast, when the *Odyssey* is told in a linear form (as in *O Brother, Where Art Thou?*), with the wife and son not introduced until the end of the story, the result is an episodic story lacking in energy and suspense. The trio of escaped convicts ricochets charmingly but aimlessly from adventure to adventure and only at the end of the film, when Ulysses, the George Clooney character, finds out that his wife is about to get married, is there any suspense, anything really at stake. Imagine the increase in pace and jeopardy if we, but not Ulysses, had known at the start that his wife was about to get married. And imagine if we also saw one of his young children wandering off looking for him, with a murderous psychopath pursuing the child, intent on murder—which is what happens in the *Odyssey*.

If you tell the *Odyssey* in its non-linear form, suddenly the journey becomes an energising force in itself, full of suspense, jeopardy and impetus. The meandering episodic quality disappears, because Odysseus' adventures from leaving Troy until he leaves the island where he was for so long kept a prisoner, are told only in parenthesis, in flashback, as in the present we impatiently wait for him to get the new ship and new crew that will permit him to get home and prevent disaster. Additionally, telling the predicament of Penelope and the story of Telemachus, Odysseus' son, before Odysseus enters means first, that the story is able to include dual protagonists, second that Telemachus' story invests Odysseus' journey with new urgency and finally that once Odysseus' story finally starts it can proceed uninterrupted to its climax, thereby preventing loss of pace and pulling the whole story forward with enormous momentum. This is exactly what happens with Jules' story in *Pulp Fiction*.

Can a story that is very slow to start be a good story? In conventional narrative, usually no, particularly if the protagonist is not established earlier. The audience will fall asleep. In non-linear, yes. Some very good stories are necessarily slow to start because either:

- the protagonist is an innocent gathering experience from mentors (as in biography—we looked at this earlier in *Goodfellas*, where a centre-split preview flashback structure prevents slowness)
- it is a mystery story, and clues have to be set up
- the protagonist is on a journey where all the jeopardy is at the end
- some stories (such as *21 Grams*) have their poignancy in a normality that can never be regained

Using the *Odyssey* as a template

Below, I break down the *Odyssey*, firstly into its chronological order (as far as that's possible, since it starts to run two stories very early on) then into its non-linear order, pointing out the problems with the chronological version and showing how brilliantly the non-linear version fixes these. Notice the detective story element that non-linearity provides.

THE *ODYSSEY*: CHRONOLOGICAL VERSION

1   Odysseus leaves Troy and has adventures, including blinding the Cyclops Polyphemus, son of Poseidon, god of the sea, which makes Poseidon his enemy. *(Poor start to the story because lengthy and episodic. No urgency to get home, therefore no suspense or momentum. Some tension via Poseidon.)*

2   Odysseus finds out from ghosts in the underworld that his wife is being pressured to marry, but then is shipwrecked on Calypso's island. *(Urgency is created but fizzles out because the journey has stopped.)*

3   Odysseus lives with Calypso for several years. *(Long, irrelevant. Stops the journey plot dead.)*

4   At the end of this time, Athene asks Zeus to let Odysseus leave Calypso and return home. *(There is a hiatus here, a jolt, as the journey story starts again. As we have a new protagonist, Athene, it feels like a new story.)*

5   Athene goes to Odysseus' home, where Penelope, Odysseus' wife, is being harried to re-marry. *(This is an interesting episode in itself, but Odysseus, who was our protagonist for a long time, has disappeared. We have new characters and story—Athene, Penelope and Telemachus.)*

6   Without Penelope's knowledge, Telemachus sets off to find his father. He has adventures. *(This is a new story with a new protagonist, Telemachus, which causes a disjunction. Where is Odysseus, our original protagonist? Whose story is this? Will Poseidon injure Telemachus as revenge for the blinding of Poseidon's son, the Cyclops?)*

7   Athene goes back to gods, again asks Zeus to let Odysseus leave Calypso and return home. *(Repetition. Has a slowing effect.)*

8   Odysseus is allowed to leave. *(It's a jolt to come back to Odysseus. We'd almost forgotten him.)*

9   Poseidon, Odysseus' enemy, whips up a storm. Odysseus is

shipwrecked on an island naked, as sole survivor. *(Interesting, exciting, informative.)*

10 Odysseus is asked to explain himself and tell his story. *(Feels slow and repetitious, because we have seen it.)*

11 Odysseus is given sailors and a ship to get home. *(Good ticking clock—but appearing much too late.)*

12 Odysseus arrives at his island kingdom just as wife is about to choose a suitor. He disguises himself to get into the palace. With Telemachus' help, he overcomes his enemies. *(Full of human interest, action and pace, but very late in story.)*

THE *ODYSSEY* IN THE ORDER IT IS WRITTEN (NON-LINEAR)

1 Athene asks Zeus to let Odysseus leave Calypso and return home. *(Who is this human hero who is interesting to dangerous beings like the gods? Instantly creates suspense, jeopardy. Putting the gods at the start places them firmly in the action, as an ongoing threat over and above all Odysseus' other problems. They are not remote, intermittent participants.)*

2 Athene goes to Odysseus' home, where Penelope, Odysseus' wife, is being harried to re-marry by suitors who have taken over the palace. His young son Telemachus is angry and humiliated. *(Ticking clock. Dramatic irony. Odysseus, this interesting mysterious hero, needs to get home—fast! We are now emotionally invested in Penelope and Telemachus very early in the story.)*

3 Without Penelope's knowledge, Telemachus sets off to find his father. He has adventures. *(Will Telemachus, whom we know and care about, get to the island where Odysseus is? Will Poseidon injure him? Dramatic irony because Odysseus does not know his son is in danger and we do.)*

4 Athene goes back to gods, again asks Zeus to let Odysseus leave Calypso and return home. *(Quick, let her release Odysseus and get him back home before Penelope marries and Telemachus gets hurt! This return visit to Zeus increases the suspense, rather than being repetitive, as in the linear version.)*

5 Odysseus is allowed to leave, sets off. *(Aha! Here is this Odysseus that everyone has been talking about, and at last he's on his way home.)*

6 Poseidon, Odysseus' enemy, whips up a storm. Odysseus is shipwrecked on an island naked, as sole survivor. *(Exciting material. Odysseus is interesting, but still a mystery.)*

7   Odysseus is asked to explain himself and tell his story. *(At last, Odysseus' story! By now we are really interested. Notice that the set-up for the flashback is identical to modern usage: an enigmatic outsider returns to society asking to be admitted, and people ask him to explain who he is. This is textbook thwarted dream flashback, with Odysseus appearing at a point close to death as he tries to pursue his thwarted dream; namely, to return home.)*

8   Odysseus leaves Troy and has adventures, including blinding the Cyclops Polyphemus, son of Poseidon, god of the sea, which makes Poseidon his enemy. *(All told in flashback. Note: because the urgent need for Odysseus to get home has already been set up, these adventures do not feel aimless, hence play slow. They are happening in parenthesis within exciting action. Withholding backstory like this increases interest and suspense.)*

9   Odysseus lives with Calypso for several years. *(As this is being transmitted in parenthesis, as a flashback, the suspense holds and the main story does not stop.)*

10   Odysseus is given a ship and crew to get home. *(The ticking clock going faster! Will Odysseus get home in time?)*

11   Odysseus arrives at his island kingdom just as his wife is about to choose a suitor. He disguises himself to get into the palace. With his son's help, he overcomes his enemies. *(Full of human interest, action, pace, excitement. Ticking clock particularly suspenseful because we have been worried about this climax for so long. Good climax, good closure.)*

Using the *Odyssey*'s devices to improve slow set-ups, central time jumps, episodic stories, dual protagonists and journey stories

- Open your film *after* the slowing events (the episodic section and the big time jump, explaining these things later in flashback).
- To increase the tension and create interest in the protagonist, open the story with an intriguing set-up between enormously powerful individuals.
- Generally, if the chronological start is slow, steal jeopardy from the ending or from events happening in another story elsewhere to inject suspense and dramatic irony that will keep the audience engaged through the slow moments.

- If your main protagonist's main quest only properly starts towards the chronological end of the action (as in the *Odyssey*, for example, where Odysseus' bid to save his wife only starts in earnest when he finally gets back to his kingdom) consider telling a secondary protagonist's story first as happens with Telemachus. This will increase the stakes for the main protagonist, punch up general suspense and permit uninterrupted momentum to climax and closure via the main protagonist's story. It's the trick used in *Pulp Fiction* where Jules' story, returning at its first-act turning point, carries the film to a good climax.

Section 6
Fractured tandem narrative

Chapter 48
Fractured tandem: An introduction

FILMS LIKE *21 GRAMS*, *The Hours*, *Crash*, *Rendition*, *Three Burials of Melchiades Estrada* and *Babel* use a narrative structure we can call 'fractured tandem' because it's like tandem narrative except chopped up. Instead of telling equally important stories simultaneously and in the same time frame, it either fractures one or all of them and tells them in a non-linear way (as in *21 Grams*), simultaneously tells stories from different time frames (as in *The Hours*) or does both *(Babel)*. *Crash* is a simpler form, with one story simply bookending the others. In essence, *Crash* is a tandem film in a frame. It's like bookend flashback except that the film proper is an ensemble film, with multiple narratives, not a one-hero model, and the frame is being used to manipulate the audience in a way typical of fractured tandem.

Guillermo Arriaga

As so many fractured tandem films have been written by the extraordinarily brilliant writer Guillermo Arriaga (*21 Grams*, *Babel*, *Three Funerals of Melchiades Estrada*) who also wrote the consecutive stories film *Amores Perros*, can we really say that fractured tandem is a distinct structural model? Is it perhaps just the *modus operandi* of one writer? I would say no. As we've seen, story fracturing goes back at least to Homer's *Odyssey* and Arriaga actually consciously employs *in medias res*. Also, fine writers apart from Arriaga are now using fractured tandem (Paul Haggis, with *Crash*, David Hare, who adapted *The Hours*—as it turns out, influenced by *Amores Perros*—and Kelly Sane who wrote *Rendition*). Given the increasing popularity of non-linear narrative on TV and the various digital platforms we can expect more writers to do the same, all adding their own modifications and taking the form further. Meanwhile, let's hope Mr Arriaga continues to forge ahead with his extraordinary experimentation.

It should be stressed again that Guillermo Arriaga says that he does not plan the non-linearity of his films on the basis of any screenwriting theories about act structure. He says he switches stories at high emotional points, something he has always done in his fiction, because interconnections of this kind are an abiding interest. I don't think the two approaches are incompatible. Turning points are just moments of high emotion in the three-act structure that have been identified and given names. Curiously, he also says that he has a innate sense of direction which means he never gets lost, even in a city that is new to him. Perhaps this mental facility for navigation translates into his ability to imagine and manipulate interconnected narratives—separate journeys—happening across time and space.

A fix for films that would not work in conventional narrative?

As well as being an excellent way to transmit multiple narrative films on the theme of consequences or unlikely and (often tragic) accidents and coincidences, amazingly the particular kind of non-linearity that we see in fractured tandem seems to permit good and powerful films to be made out of content that would not work in conventional chronological linear narrative and also (even more exciting), appears to provide a way of fixing problem films. It can:

- permit the successful telling of exposition-heavy stories and stories with a truncated second act; that is, stories that have no real 'middle'
- create connection between disparate stories that otherwise would present as two or three connected but separate 'films', sometimes even genres
- remove the hiatus in stories that have a major time jump in the middle of the action
- pump up energy levels in dark and depressing stories
- turn what would be a predictable and/or preaching film into a suspenseful detective story

Fascinatingly, fractured tandem seems to prove that certain story material that does not fit the conventional paradigm can still be effectively told, as long as the stories are split up and reconstituted in such a way that the audience gets a powerful start, an interesting development, and a climax. In other words, pace, connection, meaning and closure can be *artificially created* in stories that do not naturally have them, in some cases simply by rearranging them. Instead of linearity and a rising three-act structure giving you these things, non-linearity does it.

A detective story that plays on dread

Fractured tandem achieves its magic through creating a detective story based on dread of death or violence—often death or violence that either does not happen, or happens in an unexpected way. Although it sometimes uses a red herring to do this (as in *The Hours*), it mostly creates the dread just by rearranging its often predictable or slow story material to set up an expectation of violence and/or death—and we wait for it to happen. David Hare relates that the preview audience for *The Hours*, asked to define the film's genre, said 'it was most like a thriller because you're trying to understand what happens and pit your wits against the film as it's revealed.' That's exactly the effect most fractured tandem needs to create to overcome the potential predictability of its story content. Fracturing a story in the right way means that every time the film changes scenes the audience has to act as detective, rapidly working out which story and time frame the film is now in. Properly done, this instantly inserts interest and suspense.

The threat of death appears early on

Violent death or the threat of it always appears at the start of these films, so that from the earliest moments the audience is powerfully engaged both emotionally and intellectually by the most intense and gripping kind of mystery with the highest jeopardy: a whodunit. Suddenly the viewing experience is not only about the philosophical side of the film, which is often quite intellectual and potentially dry (for example, the meaning of life and of death, of consequences, of accident and coincidence). Instead, viewing is an emotional experience, with audiences stirred up by compassion and fear as they try to work out who died, who or what was responsible, the manner of death and all of the other brainteasers that come with murder mysteries. *21 Grams* opens just prior to an attempt at revenge killing and soon jumps to a scene in which a central character is dying horribly. *Crash* opens just before the discovery of a corpse, as does *Three Burials*. *Rendition* shows a bomb exploding in a bustling market square and in *The Hours*, Virginia Woolf suicides. *Babel*, too, has a tourist accidentally shot (although this is some way into the film).

21 Grams is full of death references

Guillermo Arriaga says he is obsessed with the impact of death on the living. Analysing *21 Grams*, I created a scene-by-scene chart of the film and, looking for reasons why the film had such energy even though all its stories were relentlessly gloomy and all had huge exposition sections (factors that should have slowed it right down), I went through the chart highlighting in red all of the scenes that related in some way to death.

The chart was covered in red. Rarely do three scenes in *21 Grams* pass without a suggestion of death. In some parts of the film there are as many as five consecutive scenes involving death or the threat of death. Similar charts for *Babel*, *Three Burials*, *Crash*, *Rendition* and *The Hours* show the action regularly returning to death or the threat of death. The effect of this is a new injection of emotion every time the script revisits death: a new injection, in effect, of dread.

Even more interesting is that when the expected death does not happen, or happens to the people we least expect, *the films still hold*, even if, in linear terms, the ending would play as an anticlimax. Does fractured tandem have to be about death? Probably not, but my hunch is that if you are writing a fractured tandem film without death or the threat of it, you would need to include strikingly original and suspenseful storylines (with good cliffhangers as jumping points between time frames) to keep up the energy level.

Chapter 49
Pace, connection, meaning and closure in fractured tandem

AS WE'VE SEEN, ALL parallel narrative films struggle with pace, connection, meaning and closure. Fractured tandem struggles with them the most.

Pace

Apart from *Crash* and possibly *Rendition*, none of the films we are discussing here would have anywhere near the same energy if their stories were told in a linear way; in fact, most would probably be predictable, repetitive and anticlimactic.

This is partly because, told in a linear way, stories about 'strangers connecting by accident or across time' are inherently predictable. Telling these stories chronologically not only means you have to set up a series of unconnected normalities (people leading their uneventful lives before the accidental encounter, something that rapidly becomes boring) but also, as the accident gets closer, things can quickly become painfully predictable ('*he's* going to the station and getting on the train, and look! so is *she*, and so is *she* . . . !').

But this isn't the only pace problem. Fascinatingly, in marked contrast to many of the parallel narrative films we've been looking at, the individual stories in fractured tandem films are often not three-act structures rising suspensefully to a climax. They are frequently wildly uneven, with long exposition sections, truncated middles and often anticlimactic endings. For example, the stories of the three major characters in *21 Grams* up to the accident take up more than half the film's running time. In *Babel*, three of the four stories end in anticlimax, as do two of the three stories in *The Hours*.

You could indeed argue that the separate stories in many fractured tandem films are just one-act films with a coda, or with a new film stuck on the end. *21 Grams* could be described as three pensive, poignant one-act films featuring three interconnected protagonists, followed by a single one-act action–revenge blood bath. *The Hours* has the same combination without the action–revenge story. *Three Burials* consists of one short fractured tandem film (written from two points of view) about an accidental killing, followed by one linear double journey film.

This is in marked contrast to the tight, suspenseful, big-climax stories in films such as *Pulp Fiction*, *Run Lola Run*, *City of God* and *The Butterfly Effect*. Remarkably, in fractured tandem films, what's causing much of the pace is the way the film as a whole is fractured. Hence, although I have been suggesting throughout this book that three-act structures are at the heart of parallel narrative, astonishingly, fractured tandem seems often to do without them.

STRUCTURAL TRICKS TO ADD PACE

Death placed at the start to create dread, combined with the extreme fracturing of the form that forces the audience to play detective in each scene, massively increases speed. Additionally, fractured tandem employs the same pace—injecting devices we've seen across parallel narrative forms; that is, the use of the climax or second-act turning point as the film's hook (often jumping back to the disturbance) and the twist ending.

21 Grams opens just before the second-act turning point in Jack's story, Paul's unsuccessful attempt to shoot Jack. *The Hours* opens with Virginia Woolf's suicide, which we take to be either the film's horrific climax or a second-act turning point (in fact it is a red herring, but we are not to know that). *Crash* opens just before the film's climax. *Rendition* opens at the climax of one story (which is simultaneously the disturbance in two other stories).

But, interestingly, not all fractured tandem films open on a second-act turning point or climax. In *Babel*, the film starts at the disturbance of the young boys' story, the sale of the rifle, which has as its first-act turning point the accidental shooting of the tourist. *The Three Burials of Melchiades Estrada* opens on the discovery of Estrada's corpse, which is the first-act turning point both of Pete, Melchiades' cowboy friend and of Mike, the border patrol officer, Melchiades' killer (because, in both cases, the death is what the story is 'about').

ARRIAGA'S FLASHFORWARD

Much of the pace in Arriaga's fractured tandem films is created by use of a unique and very clever pattern of flashforwards that not only pull the film forward but conceal joins between stories and sew what are actually two uneven halves of the film together. Another way of thinking of this flashforward pattern is as a breaking wave. We'll come back to this later.

Connection and meaning
1. THEME AND MESSAGE

All of the stories in these films have the same theme and subject matter, namely tragic accidents or coincidental connections between strangers and chain reactions. Overall, the films are fatalistic. Each looks at accidents and consequences in a different context; for example, in *Crash,* the context of race and racism, in *Three Burials,* the context of loneliness, friendship and justice, and so on.

Whereas fractured tandem's nearest relative, tandem narrative, is typically didactic, socio-political and reformist, showing how a whole community is suffering because of a faulty social system or personal failings, fractured tandem is about random accidents, about, as is demonstrated so clearly in *Crash,* individual strangers accidentally colliding.

Tandem narrative is 'we're all in the same boat' (note the 'we') and fractured tandem is 'they're in the wrong place, at the wrong time' (note the 'they'). Another thematic difference is that while tandem tends to show people acting predictably because of social mores or personal inadequacy, fractured tandem sets out to demonstrate that nobody is all good or all bad, that people are full of contradictions, that people are victims of random events, and that life is full of tragic and unpredictable ironies. *Crash,* for example, deliberately shows a deeply racist policeman risking his life to save an African–American woman he had earlier deliberately humiliated, while his non-racist partner impulsively shoots dead an African–American he misjudged along racist lines. In tandem narrative, each man would have behaved in character, because such predictable behaviour would have been exactly the point the film was making.

FRACTURED TANDEM DOESN'T NEED TO BE PROFOUND
Although current fractured tandem films all seem to involve deep philosophical content, there is no reason why all films in this form have to be profound. You might, for example, want to use fractured tandem to pump up the energy of a simple detective story that seems too predictable, as for example, I suggest on pp. 416–17 might work well for *Prelude to a Kiss.*

2. GEOGRAPHY AND TIME
Characters in fractured tandem are usually connected by being in the same place at the same time. Often, events happen within a short time period, like a day.

3. THE MACRO PLOT AND DEATH
Fractured tandem at the moment (and this might well change) is about chain reactions, consequences and unlikely connections, so the macro depicts these. The films at present are always about random or accidental death. Films such as *The Hours* and *Crash* have a theme more than a macro: 'A woman's whole

life in a single day' and 'In LA nobody touches you', but in each there is the presence of death.

4. FACILITATING CHARACTERS/CHARACTERS CONNECTED TO SEVERAL DIFFERENT STORIES

Obviously, given the theme of connection and coincidence, there is usually a lot of character connection, including connections at one remove. In *Three Burials*, the wife of the border patrol man who murders Melchiades has slept with Melchiades. In *Crash*, the Persian family and Graham the detective are linked because Graham's brother dies in the hospital where the daughter of the Persian family works as a nurse. Similarly, Graham's brother ran down a people smuggler, and while Graham and the locksmith never meet, they are connected through the nurse. *Babel* is of course centrally concerned with connections at a remove from events (although for some audiences the connection between the Japanese girl and the other stories was too tenuous).

5. OBJECT OR NATURAL EVENT

Characters can be linked by an object, like the rifle in *Babel*, or by natural events like the snowstorm in *Crash*.

Closure by means of a frame

PROLOGUE

It's worth noting that at the moment all fractured tandem films end with a thought-provoking twist, and get closure by a frame, so the film comes full circle, often to poignant effect. The film opens with a prologue and then, in its closing moments, returns to the prologue material to create an epilogue, which contains the twist, so that the message we are left with is not quite what we expected. The prologue can be a speech, text on the screen, or action. Mostly it's quite short but sometimes it's a sequence of scenes, as in *21 Grams*, where the prologue ends with Paul in hospital, saying he is in death's waiting room.

The prologue has three jobs: to present the theme in an intriguing way, to warn that the film will be serious, and to buy the audience's patience. Quite often the prologue creates a red herring, making us expect something which, in the event, does not happen.

THE TWIST ENDING

The twist ending is necessary either to insert surprise into predictable story material or because the film is returning to where it started, so needs a

384 The 21st-Century Screenplay

surprise ending, or indeed a series of surprises. *Rendition* ends with a surprising time jump. In *Crash*, a child miraculously escapes death, and the identity of the corpse is a shocking surprise. In *21 Grams*, Paul dies in a way we did not expect and, surprisingly, has fathered a child. In *Babel*, we dread that certain characters will die, but they do not. In *The Hours*, two characters are unexpectedly linked and someone suicides, but not the person we expect. *Three Burials* reveals that Melchiades Estrada was not what he claimed. In all cases, the ending is on the film's theme, but gives us an answer out of left field. Be aware that the audience will take the twist ending to contain the film's real message—so be careful that it does.

EPILOGUE/RESOLUTION

While *Three Burials* and *Babel* end quite abruptly and *Rendition* opts for a traditional 'sadder but wiser man' ending, *21 Grams*, *The Hours* and *Crash* each end movingly and lyrically in quite lengthy epilogue sections that appear after the twist ending and all feature death and moving speeches. *21 Grams* also revisits Chris, Jack and Paul in their separate lives before the accident, to poignant effect. The last words are Paul's explanation of 21 grams being the weight of life when it leaves the body. *The Hours* gives us Woolf's suicide and voice-over suicide note, and *Crash*, returning to the detective and the corpse, talks again about alienation.

THE EPILOGUE ONLY WORKS BECAUSE OF THE PROLOGUE

Probably, almost every film is written so that the writer can write the final scenes. The final scenes are often what drew them to the idea in the first place. You get the strong sense in *The Hours*, *Crash* and *21 Grams* that the epilogues articulate the reason the film was written. While all three epilogues work wonderfully well, notice that their strength derives not so much from their powerful speeches but from the fact they are paying off what the prologue set up, and paying it off in a thought-provoking, often unexpected way. In other words, to work as well as they do, these poignant epilogues need a clever prologue, and the prologue must be constructed with care to permit a clever final twist to the film.

TRIPLICATION

It's striking that so many fractured tandem films involve triplication, most obviously *The Three Burials of Melchiades Estrada*, but *21 Grams*, *The Hours* and *Rendition* all use three protagonists, while *Babel* has one story that triggers three others. Three, as ever, seems to provide a pleasing unity.

The death of the second act?

As we saw when discussing conventional narrative, in the standard one hero/ one journey film the middle, the second act, is not only the longest part of the film, but is actually the start of what the film is 'about' in terms of the plot. It contains the meat of the film. We go to *Thelma and Louise* to see what happens after two women shoot a rapist. We go to *Tootsie* to see what happens after a man dresses up as a woman to get a role in a soap opera. Notice the 'after'. Before that point, before the first-act turning point, we are still in the story's set-up. The middle, the second act, explores the characters and themes, building suspensefully on the question set up by the first-act turning point so that we will be deeply interested in the answer to that question provided by the climax.

In contrast, as we've seen, the stories in fractured tandem films often lack rising suspense, are exposition-heavy, frequently have no proper second act or middle, and, as I've said, seem quite often to consist of a collection of one-act films.

As I have mentioned, people have joked that with fractured tandem I am announcing the death of the second act. Am I saying we can have films with no proper middle? No. I'm saying that in certain cases we can create films that have a powerful beginning, middle and end by using a fractured structure.

Fractured tandem films certainly possess a middle in the sense that they have a long central section in which their entwined narratives develop and gradually rise suspensefully towards an energised final section and a powerful ending. The difference between conventional and fractured tandem structure is that the suspenseful middle of a conventional linear film *is* the suspenseful middle of the action line, whereas in fractured tandem films (apart from the simplest versions) the suspenseful middle is created artificially by three devices:

1 by making the film's hook a powerful scene from its ending
2 by clever rearrangement of their stories to make a detective story
3 in Arriaga's work, by persistent flashforwards

For example, the middle of *The African Queen*'s action line is *of itself* exciting and rising in suspense, but the middle of *21 Grams* is suspenseful because we know there is going to be a bloodbath and we want to know how these three people end up in that situation.

Chapter 50
Fractured tandem: The structure of *21 Grams*

21 GRAMS HAS ATTRACTED such interest from writers that I deal with it here in depth. *21 Grams* would not work in linear form. It would be long, slow, predictable and so depressing that audiences might well give up on it. Told chronologically, the normality of the characters, so poignant in the non-linear form, would appear as one long and apparently pointless slab as we waited for the story to start. There would be a slowing down at the point where Chris and Paul start to live together and a major disjunction at the point where Chris suddenly demands revenge and the story changes style and genre from a journey of the soul to an action thriller. Finally, its climax—a different death and different manner of death from the ones we expected—would probably feel, despite the energy given it by its violence, forced and out of focus, as if it were the climax to another story (which, one could argue, it is).

But astonishingly, in its non-linear form, *21 Grams* is a triumph, a landmark film that overcomes a central gap and blends two films from two genres. *The Three Burials of Melchiades Estrada* does much the same thing (although the gap is more evident). We need to know the techniques behind these extraordinary results.

'Forbidden' elements in *21 Grams*
21 Grams includes the following components that screenwriting theory routinely forbids.

1 It has multiple stories and multiple protagonists.
2 Not only do we jump between the three stories in a non-chronological way but each of the three stories is itself internally fractured, presented out of chronological order.
3 It has time jumps.
4 It does not fit into the normal three-act mountain structure.
5 Its stories are exposition heavy.
6 Its three stories all have tiny, truncated second acts, none properly developing from the first-act question; in the case of Paul and Chris,

the question of what happens when the man in a love relationship has the donor heart of his partner's dead husband, and in the case of Jack, what happens when a man loses his faith in God and is denied the punishment he feels he deserves.

7   Further to point 6, you could say the film is three one-act films in one genre and a fourth one-act film in another genre, switching abruptly from pensive poignant love story to revenge bloodbath midway, switching not only story but genre.

8   However you try to analyse it, the film has a serious shift of direction in the middle. It has what would normally be a fatal hiatus when Paul moves in with Chris (at the point where the first story is over and the second hasn't started).

Switching stories

Something that we tend not to notice because the film works so well is the central split, the change to a new story, whereby the film starts out as a thought-provoking gentle drama about grief and guilt and ends up as a mission of revenge, with shooting and a bloodbath. This is shown clearly in the macro, which starts out as the accident and its aftermath, then becomes 'Will two of the affected characters kill the third?'

To see how truly strange this is, let's look at what would happen in a conventional film where, at the first-act turning point, a couple fall in love after one has received the heart of the other's dead spouse. Normally, a set-up like this would lead to an exploration of that story. The plot would follow through on what later happened in the love relationship. Typical plot ideas would range over things like the possibility that Chris was only in love with Paul because he contained part of her dead husband, or that Paul felt himself turning into the man whose organ he now contained.

But *21 Grams* does not do anything like this. It does not follow through on the 'dead husband's heart' idea at all. Instead, after showing Chris returning to drugs and Paul nagging her, it turns without warning into a revenge story. Chris suddenly decides that she wants Paul to kill Jack. This is even more surprising because Chris actually rejected revenge earlier in the story. If you did this in a conventional linear chronological narrative your film would stop in its tracks.

Arriaga often does this switch of story and genre midway through the action. It also happens in *Three Burials*, where the action switches from a murder-investigation film to a double journey film, and *Amores Perros*, when he resolves the violent, non-linear dog-fighting story midway and swaps to the quiet linear story about the dog trapped under the floor.

Structural breakdown of *21 Grams*

As I mentioned earlier, my structural analysis of *21 Grams* is based on a chart that I created by viewing the film many times and breaking down its action into what I saw as its three separate stories (that become two stories, then one story), scene by scene, beat by beat. Having constructed my chart (unfortunately, too big to reproduce in full here) I then reassembled each of the film's three stories into its chronological narrative structure using the approach that I've taken throughout this book; that is, using my own tools and models and drawing on Christopher Vogler's model, on the basic Smiley/Thompson nine-point structure model and on the traditional mountain model.

I went right back to basics and asked: 'What are the plots of *21 Grams* about?' To answer this, I followed my rule of thumb; namely, that the first-act turning point is always what a story is 'about' plot-wise. I then double-checked that I had the first-act turning point by asking whether what I had pinpointed was a surprise that turns into the obstacle that drives the rest of the story. By this method, I broke down *21 Grams* into its three stories, thus providing the following descriptions of what the plot of each story is 'about':

1 **Story one: Jack's story** Jack, a Christian convert, is not charged for the hit-and-run killing of a man and his two young daughters, a crime for which he is desperate to be punished (the first-act turning point is Jack discovering that the law won't punish him)

2 **Story two: Chris's story** Chris, the widow and mother of the accident victims, unknowingly falls in love with the man who received her dead husband's heart (the first-act turning point is her discovery that she's in love with the man who has her husband's heart)

3 **Story three: Paul's story** Paul, the recipient of a donor heart, falls in love with the donor's widow (so the first-act turning point of Paul's story is the same scene as the first-act turning point in Chris's story; namely, Paul telling Chris that he is the recipient of her dead husband's heart)

Working back from the first-act turning point of each story, we can see that the disturbance in all three is the same: it is the accident. The normality of each protagonist (Chris, Paul and Jack) is their family life prior to the accident. The plan of each is their response to how they will carry on after the accident. Chris's plan is to obliterate her memories by using cocaine and alcohol. Paul's plan is to find, then help the wife of his heart donor. Jack's plan is to conceal his crime, but he can't live with this, and turns himself in to the police.

Interestingly, there's a striking resemblance here to *The Sweet Hereafter*, where most of the parents in the film had one-act stories, with the bus accident as disturbance and the response to the accident as first-act turning point.

So far so good. But if we look at what happens next in each story, we find, as I've said, that none has a second act—a proper middle—where the story develops out of a first-act question. Now there is only one question, a completely new one, and it has turned the film into a revenge movie. The new question is: 'Will the couple kill the guilt-ridden hit-and-run driver?' Certainly, the revenge movie is infused with poignancy because of what happened earlier in the film, but it feels as if we are in a different film, a different genre altogether.

So we are back to where we were earlier, with the amazing (but very dangerous) mid-film story and genre switch. What is happening here? How is *21 Grams* getting away with this? Why doesn't it fall apart?

A new film or three truncated three-act stories?

Structurally, we could describe the revenge story in two different ways. First, we could see it as a new film (almost). This new film is very short and is actually two one-act stories, one about Jack and one about Paul, merging at the end with Chris ceasing to have her own story just after her first-act turning point and becoming instead the relationship line antagonist to Paul. In this new film, Jack's disturbance is when Paul takes him into the desert to shoot him and Paul's disturbance is when he is told that his new heart is dying (there is probably just enough backstory revealed in the revenge story for those two disturbances to do their job). The thought-provoking surprise for both is where Paul shoots himself in the tussle with Jack.

However, if we regard the three stories in *21 Grams* as running from start to finish of the film, we have to say that none has a proper second act. Chris's story ends at its first-act turning point. After that, she is Paul's relationship-line antagonist. In the stories of Paul and Jack, after each man's first-act turning point (for Paul, falling in love with Chris; for Jack, being released by the police for lack of evidence), we jump almost immediately to their second-act turning point, their closest moment to death before the climax. For Jack, this is when Paul is about to shoot him in the desert. For Paul, it is when he is told that his new heart is dying.

The climax of both stories is Paul being shot (but not in the way it earlier seemed) with the resolution being Chris's discovery that she is pregnant, so a new life begins, returning the film to the theme of the mysterious nature, location and meaning of life.

Exposition-heavy stories in *21 Grams*

This is all so weird that we need to check it. Is the film as exposition-heavy as we think? The only way is to dismantle *21 Grams'* basic mechanics and count its story beats in relation to a normal film. This is tedious work, but a film as brilliant yet as structurally mystifying as *21 Grams* can teach us a very great deal.

Normally, conventional linear films use screen time in the following proportions:

- first act about 15–25 per cent (these days often less)
- second act about 50–60 per cent
- third act to end of film about 15–25 per cent

In other words, a conventional linear film has a short set-up and a big middle. However, in *21 Grams*, I count 109 story beats, of which 67 beats, quite a lot more than 50 per cent, are given to the first acts of the three stories alone. Chris's first act has 22 beats, Paul's first act has 28 and Jack's first act has 17.

Even if you analyse the film differently (as writer–director Roger Tucker does, feeling it fits a conventional film structure, albeit awkwardly) the film still ends up so seriously exposition-heavy that, told in a linear way, the audience would surely tune out (Roger Tucker's views are contained in an essay at <www.rogertucker.co.uk>, under 'articles').

Second act until the end

Things get odder. From the start of the second act in each story to the end of the film there are only 42 beats in all. Chris has 8 beats when she is on her own, plus 1 beat shared with Jack, 6 shared with Paul, and 6 shared with both men. Paul has 7 beats on his own, 6 with Chris, 2 with Jack plus 6 shared with both Chris and Jack. Jack has 13 beats alone, plus 1 with Paul, 1 with Chris and 6 with Chris and Paul.

Below, in Figure 50.1 I break down of all of the storylines by beats. Starting from the left, columns two, three and four show the beats in which Chris, Paul and Jack are either alone or are interacting with their families (but are not with each other). The next three columns show scenes that they share.

WHAT THIS CHART TELLS US
VERY LONG NORMALITY
While films usually get their normality over and done with as quickly as possible (sometimes in the first scene) so as to move on to the disturbance,

Smiley/Thompson basic nine-point structure	CHRIS Story 1	PAUL Story 2	JACK Story 3	CHRIS/PAUL Story	PAUL/JACK Story	CHRIS/JACK Story	Story beats per section
Normality	4 beats (that appear before third-act climax)	5 beats (that appear before third-act climax)	4 beats (before third-act climax)				13 normality beats in all before third-act climax
	2 beats (returning again after third-act climax)	1 beat (returning again after third-act climax)	1 beat (returning again after third-act climax)				4 normality scenes after third-act climax
Disturbance	11 beats	5 beats	7 beats				23
Plan section	4 beats	16 beats	4 beats				24
First-act turning point	1 beat	1 beat	1 beat				3
Number of story beats from start until end of act one						Total story beats =	67
Second act	2 beats	4 beats	9 beats	2 beats	1 beat		18
Second-act turning point	1 beat	1 beat	1 beat				3
Third-act turning point	3 beats	2 beats	2 beats	4 beats	1 beat		12
Climax	6 beats shared by all three protagonists, plus 1 scene repeated once					1 beat	7
Resolution	2 beats		1 beat				3
Number of story beats from start of act two to the end of film.						Total story beats =	43

Figure 50.1 The beats in *21 Grams*

21 Grams spends a total of 13 beats setting up the normality of each of its three main characters in their separate lives. This number of normality scenes in a chronologically told story would be the kiss of death.

VERY LONG DISTURBANCE
The disturbance in all three stories is the accident. It takes up a total across all three stories of 23 beats—a huge amount compared to a normal film but utterly reasonable given the film's subject material. Again, in a normal film this would cause disaster.

VERY LONG PLAN
The plan takes up 24 beats across all of the stories, again far too many for a linear chronological film.

FIRST-ACT TURNING POINT
Each story's first-act turning point is one beat. For Paul and Chris, it is the same beat. It is the scene where, after they have tenderly made love, establishing a commitment, Paul tells Chris that he has her husband's heart, and they quarrel.

For Jack, the hit-and-run driver, it is the moment where he is freed from jail, despite his admission of guilt and desperate need to be punished.

TWO STORIES BLENDING INTO ONE
After Chris and Paul make love (that is, at the first-act turning point of each of their stories), their stories blend and Chris ceases to be a protagonist in her own right. In the revenge story, Paul becomes the protagonist, with Chris an antagonist, forcing him to take revenge for her.

Is it really a new structure?
Are we sure that *21 Grams* is not just an oddly shaped conventional film? If it is, we should be able to depict it by the normal mountain diagrams, but we can't. For a start, in the first section there are three stories with three protagonists who don't even know each other, so we would need three mountains. And of course, if we start to look at the three stories, Chris's story ends at its first-act turning point after a very long normality, and the two other stories have no middle.

If you drew Chris's mountain, it would stop at its first peak, as in Figure 50.2.

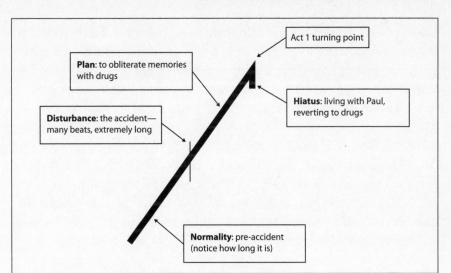

Figure 50.2 *21 Grams*: Chris's story stops at its first peak

If you drew either Paul or Jack's mountain, you would get something like this.

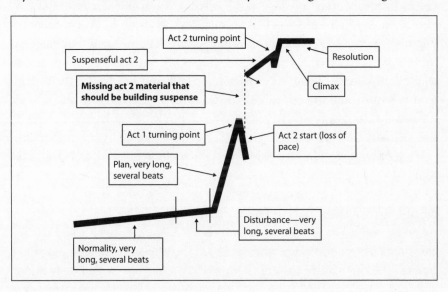

Figure 50.3 *21 Grams*: Paul and Jack's stories are not mountain structures

How *21 Grams* achieves pace, connection and unity

CHARACTERS AND STORYLINES SET UP EARLY

From the start we move methodically and consecutively between sequences from each of the four stories. The film opens at a moment late in the revenge story, jumps to Chris in her normality before the accident (at a recovering drug addicts' group therapy meeting), jumps to Jack in his normality as an aggressively evangelistic born-again Christian and finally jumps to Paul's normality in intensive care, talking in voice-over about being 'in God's waiting room'. We now have our main players in their normalities and the film can start.

INTERESTING CHARACTERS AND NEW WORLDS
All of the characters are unusual and unpredictable, each with a problem hanging over their personal life and each with the potential to act erratically which instantly inserts suspense. Notice the three unusual 'new worlds': inner-city Christian revivalist mission, drug rehabilitation for housewives and heart transplant surgery.

INTERESTING FRACTURING/DETECTIVE STORY
21 Grams needs to show a lot of the characters' domestic normality because a great deal of the film's poignancy is located in hindsight, in the contrast between their worlds pre- and post-accident. To avoid boredom, the film needs to transmit the pre-accident normalities via intriguing (but not confusing) non-linearity. Consequently, from the start the film is not only showing that we have three characters and three stories, it's forcing us to play detective as the action jumps about in ways that intrigue and involve us. First of all, Paul is healthy and in bed with a blonde woman. Then he is dying of heart disease and so deeply involved with a brunette that they are trying to conceive a child. Then he is healthy and has a gun. Then he has been shot, and the blonde woman, clearly now his lover, is shrieking for an ambulance—and so on.

KEEPING STORIES AND TIME FRAMES DISTINCT
Avoiding confusion in non-linear films is hard. Notice the vital visual story clues here—very necessary when a film jumps between stories and timeframes. The two women in Paul's life are easily told apart by their hair colour and looks. We can tell Paul is at different times of his life because his ill-health is highly visible. This basic identification matter is crucial.

DREAD AND DEATH
The mention or threat of death every third scene, as described above, means there is no opportunity for the film to slow down (if you were constructing a film like this you would need to make sure you had enough high jeopardy death scenes to keep shoving the story forward like this).

Interestingly, while the accident is not actually mentioned for some time, we quickly infer that Paul, Chris and Jack are the main players, and while we don't at first realise that a shocking accident and a donor heart are what bring Paul and Chris together, we feel dread and anxiety. Thus, the missing pieces of the story are intriguing, not irritating. The fractured storytelling creates not exasperation but dread, foreboding, and a strong desire to find out what happens. It cleverly pulls us in rather than alienates us.

NON-LINEARITY ONLY AT THE START

Surprisingly, after its strikingly non-linear opening, the film actually tells the three stories (then two, then one) of Paul, Chris and Jack more or less simultaneously and chronologically, just as if we were in tandem narrative, with only the occasional out-of-sequence scene.

If we were to take my extended chart of the film that shows the scenes in the order in which they appear on screen and colour in each scene according to where it fits in the basic Smiley/Thompson nine-point model, with normality as pale blue and each step a slightly darker blue, making the climax the darkest, there would be a general gradation from pale to dark blue, with only spots of a different shade.

What this tells us is that non-linearity at the start of the film, particularly when it involves death or the threat of death, can have enormous impact. After that, you don't need to be too worried about non-linearity and can tell your stories mostly simultaneously and in the same time frame, as in tandem.

FLASHFORWARDS

Probably the most important means that Arriaga uses in *21 Grams* to create pace, rising momentum, connection and unity is the flashforward, or more precisely, persistent and regular flashforwards in the earlier parts of the film.

Flashforwards are an Arriaga hallmark and they transmit his abiding interest in consequences. However, their technical side effect is that they tie together films that have a genre/story split in the middle. This provides a very practical application for flashforward: using it to tie together uneven films, particularly films that switch genres and/or involve big jumps midway.

The extraordinary impetus of *21 Grams* is achieved by a pattern of flashforwards that continually pull the film ahead of itself. The action keeps jumping ahead to fragments of the high-action revenge bloodbath, then returning to fill in events from before and immediately after the accident, events which, if shown chronologically, would often be bits of boring 'normality' or inherently slow because they are sad (like the funeral) but which with hindsight come imbued with deep poignancy, hence energy. Roger Tucker cleverly compares this flashforward construction of *21 Grams* to a breaking wave 'wherein fragments of future events wash up in the present before the crash of the wave'. It's a good, useful analogy—the film riding the wave, being carried along by the emotion of the future.

On the practical side, flashforwards, properly handled, permit you to leave out details and include only the crucial events from a long period, doing it, moreover, in a very unobtrusive way, with zero disjunction. This is very handy when you are running three stories.

Interestingly, as Roger Tucker points out, material in flashbacks/forwards in *21 Grams* does not depict an individual's subjective memory. The material is 'what happened' rather than events shown through an individual consciousness, a point of view. This is radically different from most flashback/forward usage, where the point is that the view is subjective.

To construct a film like *21 Grams*

Your best bet would be first to create three one-act stories about people connected by one catastrophe (each ending in a thought-provoking surprise). Then create a short section that brings all three together at the second-act turning point. Finally, create an equally brief third act and climax with a twist. Open with material from around the high-jeopardy second-act turning point area, then jump back to the three stories before the catastrophe. Jump between the three stories, progressing mostly chronologically in each, but flashing forward to create dread and add pace. Suggest death frequently. Beware of the split.

Chapter 51
Four fractured tandem films

THIS CHAPTER LOOKS AT *Three Burials of Melchiades Estrada*, *The Hours*, *Babel* and *Rendition*.

The Three Burials of Melchiades Estrada: Changing genre midway

The Three Burials of Melchiades Estrada is a poignant and deeply disturbing film about friendship, loss and the impact of the dead on the living.

Three Burials starts out as a murder mystery, opening with the discovery of a corpse, Melchiades, an illegal Mexican immigrant, who we later discover was accidentally shot by Mike, a border guard. As the dead man's friend, Pete, tries to discover who killed Melchiades, the film flashes back to the lives of Pete, Melchiades and Mike in the period leading up to the shooting. Once everything that happened up to and including the killing is fully explained through flashbacks, the film, in the present, has reached the midpoint, and switches genre. It turns from a fast-paced, flashback detective story into a linear double journey movie, a thoughtful but very different film, a journey of the soul as Pete forces Mike to accompany him across the desert to bury the decomposing corpse of Melchiades in Mexico. In the journey section there is just one brief flashback.

For some audiences there was too much of a jolt when the film switched to a different genre. The jolt in *Three Burials* is deliberate, probably in order to be confronting (the film was meant to be confronting in many ways). Whether you want jolts or hate them, it's important to know why they happen and how to create or remove them.

WHY IS THE SWITCH NOTICEABLE?
1. TWO STORIES BECOMING ONE
As well as involving a switch of genre, two stories merge into one. We start with the two separate stories before the shooting (Pete and Melchiades, Mike and his wife), then switch to one, the journey across the desert. Notice that both stories share the same first-act turning point (Melchiades' death), the

same midpoint (Pete captures Mike) and same climax (from slightly different angles) when Melchiades is finally buried. Before Melchiades' death, Mike and Pete inhabit different worlds.

2. NO FLASHFORWARDS

21 Grams also involves separate stories merging into one, but it uses flashforwards to conceal the changeover; that is, we see bits from the end of the story very early on, which prepare us for the change—in fact, we're interested to see it. *Three Burials* has no flashforwards, therefore the central split is much clearer, thus much more confronting to the audience. Journey stories always have a tendency to be slow and episodic. The *Odyssey*, as we've seen, makes liberal use of the flashbacks and jumps between storylines, both to cover gaps and to increase jeopardy.

3. FAST TO SLOW

Three Burials goes from an action story to thoughtful, lyrical story, whereas *21 Grams* does the reverse. Fast to slow is probably always going to be hard.

4. FLASHBACKS START AT THE FIRST-ACT TURNING POINT

The film does not open on its second-act turning point or climax and then go into flashbacks. Instead, it opens on its first-act turning point (the death of Melchiades) and its flashbacks depict the first act of the story. As we know, the first-act turning point is a natural hiatus point because it is where the film changes direction, so starting flashbacks on it is always dangerous. The genre switch actually happens at midpoint, when Pete is told that Mike is the murderer.

PLANNING A FILM LIKE *THREE BURIALS*

At present, audiences resist gaps and loose connections and are uncomfortable with changes of narrative style and mood. This might change, but be aware that at the moment, if you don't use flashforwards to cover the gap (that is, if you don't insert tantalising material from later stories into the earlier ones), there will be a jolt in the narrative. If that's the effect you want, fine. However, if you don't, the flashforward and the 'breaking wave' structure of *21 Grams* (which we'll also see later in *Babel*) is probably the safest way to close a gap. A flashforward gives the audience a bridge to the final meaning and point of the film.

TO STRUCTURE A FILM LIKE *THREE BURIALS*

Your best bet would be to imagine the film as two films, split in the middle, the first film involving two stories that merge in the second. If you wanted a direct replica of the pattern, your film would need to include an investigation of a murder crime, but the pattern doesn't have to involve a crime and doesn't need to involve a murder. It could be the discovery of a terrible lie, for example. Death, of course, provides the highest jeopardy.

Start by plotting your equivalents to Pete and Mike's stories separately, in a linear way. One will be the investigator, one the perpetrator of the crime or misdeed. Make sure that each of your two stories has the same first-act turning point (discovery of the crime), midpoint (investigator confronts criminal) and climax. Make your film open on the discovery of the crime. Use your investigation story in the present as the spine of the film, attaching to it firstly scenes from the present depicting the perpetrator's guilt and remorse and secondly, flashbacks to the lives of all the main players before the crime or misdeed, explaining how the crime or misdeed happened. These flashbacks will be told in chronological order. There are no more flashbacks once the crime is fully explained. Now the revenge/journey begins. Henceforth tell the story in a linear way.

If you want to conceal the split, insert flashforwards to the journey during the first part of the film, before your Pete character captures your Mike character. Remember to insert a final twist, in fact, a couple.

The Hours: Manipulating the audience's expectations

In my view, *The Hours*, written by David Hare based on Michael Cunningham's novel, consists of three intercut one-act films, each about a different woman, and a coda, all bookended by a prologue and epilogue showing Virginia Woolf's suicide by drowning (a real event) with her suicide note in voice-over. Each of the stories ends at its first-act turning point in a thought-provoking surprise, and each provides a variation on themes in Virginia Woolf's novel *Mrs Dalloway*.

HOW THE PROLOGUE MANIPULATES THE AUDIENCE

Remarkably, the film gets its suspense and momentum by a prologue that sets up dread by making us expect that all of the stories will feature suicide. It exploits our sense of pattern, our search for a uniting theme, to send us in the wrong direction. Seeing the film open with Woolf's suicide, then cutting between the desperation of each of the three women, we naturally assume that one or more are going to suicide. The stories play on that misapprehension, creating misplaced dread for the whole film. Only right at the end of each do we discover that Virginia does not suicide on the day in question, and neither do either of the other two women. The suicide that does happen is all the more of a shock precisely because we are not expecting it. The film is most certainly a detective story playing with dread; remarkably, dread created in a few moments at the start of the film and maintained by holding back the three first-act turning point surprises until the very last moment.

THE THREE STORIES

The Hours jumps about within three different time frames and uses a fourth for Woolf's drowning. Like *21 Grams* it uses three protagonists. Extraordinarily, while all three stories end in an anticlimax, with the women not suiciding, this is not a let-down; in fact the endings are energised and positive because our fears are not realised.

In 1951 in Los Angeles, Laura is desperately trying to be a perfect wife for her husband, son and unborn daughter, but cannot. She goes to a hotel to commit suicide but (and this is the anticlimactic first-act turning point surprise) she cannot. In Richmond, United Kingdom, in the 1920s, Virginia, who we think will kill herself, has just decided to write a novel, with a heroine, Mrs Dalloway, who suicides. The first-act turning point surprise (again anticlimactic) is that Virginia herself does not suicide on the day in question, but instead decides to make the poet in her novel die, not Mrs Dalloway. In Clarissa's story, set in present-day New York, Clarissa, a modern version of Clarissa Dalloway in Woolf's novel, struggles with thoughts about the inadequacy of her life as she arranges a party for her one-time lover Richard, now dying of AIDS. The first-act turning point surprise here is that the person we least expect suicides.

As in *21 Grams*, there is no proper second-act development of these three surprise/obstacles. The stories simply jump to the end, after each unexpected suicide. The final coda section involves two of the three stories coming together, physically and thematically, through an unexpected connection between Laura and Clarissa.

THEMES AND OTHER CONNECTIONS

Connections between the stories are legion, and keep referencing *Mrs Dalloway*. The three women are all living out a day in their suffocating lives. All are preparing for a party or to entertain guests, all the stories involve suicide and woman–child relationships. As it is often pointed out, Virginia is writing the novel, Laura is reading it and Clarissa is living it. The film cuts repeatedly between stories—from an image, line of dialogue or action in one story to the same or a very similar image, comment or action in another.

STRUCTURE

David Hare calls the structure 'triangular' and comments in an interview with Sheila Johnston: 'What's wonderful about a triangular structure is that you never know where you're going next'; that is, it's a detective story. The three stories do all come together to one point, in the coda which, with its remarkable coincidence, sounds, out of context, like soap opera, but in context works excellently. Partly this is because of the sheer quality of the writing and the clever intercutting, but I'd suggest that it's also probably because of the effect of the bookend, the prologue/epilogue of Woolf's suicide and the detective story based on dread. Remarkably, this dread increases the suspense so much that we don't seem to notice plot implausibility and anticlimax; in fact, we experience the anticlimax as relief. This trick of deliberately sending the audience in the wrong direction, making them expect the worst, also appears in *Babel*.

'THIS WAS NOT A FILM THAT WAS CREATED IN THE EDIT ROOM'

Thus said Stephen Daldry, the director of *The Hours*, adding, 'We knew how the stories were going to connect thematically, intellectually and emotionally before we shot them. Sometimes we'd even know how we'd cut from one story to another.'

There could not be a better way to create a fractured tandem film because the order of scenes and the way one scene cuts to the next is not only vital but is in delicate balance.

TO CREATE A STRUCTURE LIKE *THE HOURS*

Your best bet would probably be to create three one-act stories (each ending in a thought-provoking surprise); next, a brief section that blends them in an unexpected way. Finish the three one-act stories as late as possible, to maintain suspense. Bookend all of this with a prologue that sets up intense dread and an expectation of disaster and an epilogue with a final, powerful twist. Predictability as you move between stories may be a problem, hence flag this, and avoid exact repetitions.

Babel: Dread, the ripple effect and our expectation of pattern

Babel plays the same trick with our expectations as *The Hours*, creating a lasting and extraordinarily high level of dread about what will happen, then, right at the end, providing a twist. Because we see from very early on that the film is about the ripple effect of one specific event, we automatically presume that the death of one of the boys in the first story will be mirrored by deaths in all the others, particularly deaths of children. But this does not happen. We think the injured tourist will die or at least have her arm amputated, but she doesn't. We think the two little children will die in the desert, but they don't. We think the Japanese girl will suicide or be raped or murdered, but none of these things happen. Fascinatingly, as in *The Hours*, none of these incomplete, anticlimactic endings plays as anticlimaxes. To the contrary, they fill us with relief because the dread and sense of foreboding has been so intense.

This is done through the techniques we've already seen in *The Hours*. The film creates and maintains dread via misleading opening scenes and by holding back the stories' denouements until the last moment. Only in the last moments of the nanny's story do we know that the children were rescued unharmed. Before that, we are convinced they will die. Only in the closing moments of the Japanese girl's story do we learn the tourist survived unscathed (as an aside, really—we see it on a TV monitor in a café where the detective reads the girl's note), and only in the final moments of the film are we sure the Japanese girl survives.

Note that in neither the shot tourist story nor the nanny story do we see a third-act battle to win. We don't see the tourist in hospital recovering or being told she will survive, and we don't see the discovery and rescue of the children.

HOW THE DREAD IS SET UP

As in *The Hours*, the opening sequence is crucial. The first four sequences are as follows:

1 The boys' story, running uninterrupted until its first-act turning point; that is, when they see the bus draw to a halt, hit by the bullet, CUT TO

2 The nanny receiving the call from the distraught husband at the hospital many hours after the shooting (which is the normality + disturbance of the nanny's story and simultaneously the second-act turning point of the tourists' story), CUT TO

3 The tourists in Morocco first discussing marital problems; next, on the bus when the bullet comes through the window and hits the wife (this is the normality + disturbance of the tourists' story), CUT TO

4 The Japanese girl at basketball, then angry with the boys at the café (this is the normality + disturbance of the Japanese girl's story).

Notice that the film stays with the Moroccan boys until the shooting and *only then* jumps to other stories. So the film's triggering event is established immediately. The sequence that follows is not, as we might expect, the tourist getting shot, but a scene from much later in the action, the Mexican nanny's story's first scene; namely, the nanny, in her normality, receiving a phone call from the distraught tourist husband, telling her to change her plans. This creates the nanny's disturbance and tells us that the shooting prank in Morocco has had effects on the ground there but will also impact on the nanny. The next sequence shows the tourist actually receiving the bullet (disturbance). Next, in striking contrast to the blood and panic on the bus, the sequence that follows is the Japanese girl's normality, in which she interacts with her father and friends, then (disturbance) gets angry with the boys in the café. The Japanese girl's sequence is sensibly placed after the bullet coming through the window because, put earlier, it would undermine the horror. It's also too long to be put earlier. The film would take too long to show the shooting and there would a loss of energy.

This set-up has a number of effects:

- It establishes all stories and significant characters.
- It tells us that the film is non-linear and sets up the theme (the consequences of one act on specific individuals around the world).
- Via its non-linearity it creates a detective story.
- Playing on our logic and experience of films, it sets up an expectation that, as one story shows a catastrophic accident, so will the rest.

THE BREAKING WAVE
Note the shared turning points, reminiscent of *Three Burials*, making the film jump at moments of very high emotion in each story (this is also Robin Swicord's technique, see p. 234). Hence, the shooting is the first-act turning point of the boys' story but also the disturbance of the tourists' story. Similarly, the disturbance of the Mexican nanny's story (getting the phone call telling her to stay with the children on her son's wedding day) is also the second-act turning point of the tourists' story (just after the husband has been told his wife might not survive). The Japanese girl's story disturbance is not related to the other stories.

STORIES FROM DIFFERENT TIME FRAMES JUXTAPOSED
Apart from the husband's phone call, there are no repeated scenes, and each story is told in a linear way, chronologically. However, stories in different time frames appear next to each other. Hence, scenes from the Mexican nanny's story and the Japanese girl's story appear alongside scenes from the other stories, although chronologically they happened later. This is another

example of Arriaga's flashforward technique with its breaking wave effect, whereby the film is drawn forward by bits from later in the action being inserted earlier on.

PROGRESSION

Adding to the breaking wave caused by the positioning of the stories is the forward progression of the action in all the stories: the domino or ripple effect. Just as the three stories in *Amores Perros* are a progression, with one happening mostly before the accident, one happening immediately after, and the third mostly some time afterwards, so in *Babel* the triggering story, the shooting, sets off one story, which sets off another, and so on.

CAN WRITERS BE INVOLVED IN THIS DETAIL OF EDITING?

Isn't this cutting something that happens in the editing room in the absence of the writer? Perhaps, as in the creation of *The Hours*, the writer can and should be involved in such detailed work. The story jumps in fractured tandem are so crucial that in my view writers should seek discussions with the director. At the very least, writers should briefly and unobtrusively indicate in the script the reason behind the existing order of scenes, so that the breaking wave effect is known about, and can be included, even with a different scene selection. Creating a fractured tandem film in the editing room would be very risky indeed.

THREE-ACT STRUCTURE

21 Grams and *The Hours* use one-act structures with truncated second acts. *Babel* uses three three-act structures. The boys' story has a strong three-act structure (disturbance: purchase of rifle; first-act turning point: shot tourist; second-act turning point: police shoot-out; climax: boy shot dead). The shot tourist story has a three-act structure, but slows after the first-act turning point (getting stranded at the village) and ends in what in a linear presentation would be anticlimax. The nanny's story is a three-act structure with a powerful disturbance (she must stay with the children and miss her son's wedding), first-act turning point (her nephew drives through the border checkpoint), second-act turning point (she and the children will die) and anticlimax (all are rescued). The fourth story, belonging to the Japanese girl, has only a disturbance (the girl angered by taunting boys). The story doesn't progress after that, although it keeps feeling as if violent turning points will happen. It ends in anticlimax: the girl stays alive and unharmed.

POINTS TO NOTE ABOUT *BABEL*

- Non-linearity and theme are set up very early.
- While the detective story element is so important in all fractured tandem, it seems that knowing the precise time differences between the stories or exactly what was happening when doesn't really interest or worry audiences. Where criticism was made of the film, it was made about the Japanese girl's story, which people felt was insufficiently connected. It seems that major thematic connections are more important to people than the fine details of chronology. This might be very different in films like, say, murder thrillers where chronological details such as who is where exactly when could be of crucial interest.
- There is a slowing in the shot-tourist story when the husband and wife are in the village that worried some, but not all, audiences who found it had a slowing effect.
- There is no prologue and epilogue in *Babel* (hence no frame), yet remarkably the film holds.

STRUCTURING A FILM LIKE *BABEL*

Plan a triggering story and three chain-reaction stories separately, as three-act structures, but with a twist at the end. Establish the film's non-linearity and theme very early on. You will be achieving pace and suspense by the high dread level, so set that up—that is, set up an expectation of a series of disasters, and delay revealing the final twists in each story as long as possible. Connect the different stories at turning points in each. Make sure all the stories are consequences of the triggering story. You are after a breaking-wave effect featuring rising emotion.

Rendition (2007)

Rendition (not to be confused with *Extraordinary Rendition*) is a political thriller that uses fractured tandem to create a surprise twist ending, which is that while we assume all three stories (note: again three) are happening at the same time, in fact one story happens about a week before the other two. So all three stories are running simultaneously, but one is happening six days or so before the other two. At the last moment we discover that the climax of one—a love story where the young man turns out to be a suicide bomber who blows himself and his girlfriend up in a busy market square—is the disturbance of the other two stories; it is what triggers them. The first story deals with a man who is mistakenly picked up as a terrorist connected with the suicide bombing, and his wife's attempts to get him freed. The second story is about a CIA man who, as a result of the suicide bombing, is forced from his desk job out into the field to interrogate the mistakenly arrested man as he is tortured. The film spans about a week.

The two time frames are linked, very much like *Babel*. The opening scene is repeated, as in *Crash*, the second time revealing its true position in the action.

Interestingly, while the film certainly makes a strong comment on the inhumanity of the CIA and the horrors of rendition, the film is not using fracturing and time jumps to provide any thought-provoking insights, but simply to surprise us. It needs that element of surprise because, like many didactic political films that set out to shock audiences by showing the inevitable happening, if you untangle all of the stories in *Rendition*, they are actually linear and predictable: the boy contemplating becoming a suicide bomber does so, the CIA man is horrified by the CIA's practices and throws away his career by setting free the wrongly arrested man and the wrongly arrested man is freed, and returns to his wife and child.

A WAY TO INJECT ENERGY INTO PREDICTABLE FILMS

Rendition shows that what in chronological terms would be a predictable tandem narrative film can be rendered exciting by clever fracturing. Whereas audiences watching tandem narrative know that the worst will happen, audiences watching fractured tandem *fear* the worst will happen. They are caught up in the detective story based on dread, their interest held until the very last moment, often boosted by a twist ending.

While the clearest application for fractured tandem is to add interest to predictable tandem narratives, there is no reason why it should not be used to add new life to all kinds of films, particularly films in well-worn genres, such as the heist movie, gangster movie, war movie—even the love story.

STRUCTURING A FILM LIKE *RENDITION*

Your best bet would be to create each of the three stories in its linear form, then interweave them. Since the film is about events happening in split seconds you would need to make sure your three stories interwove so they suggested the split-second timing the film requires. Be sure the final twist is worth the effort the audience has to put in to fractured tandem films to follow them.

Guidelines for writing a fractured tandem narrative

GENERAL

1. Your mottos are: 'a detective story that plays on dread of death', 'wrong place, wrong time' and 'in fractured tandem, we *fear* the worst will happen but in tandem we *know* it will'. The energy of this form is in dread and suspense.

2. These films need careful planning. Be certain of the theme ('consequences' and 'unexpected accidents' work well), create vividly real but unusual stories in 'new worlds' on the theme and make sure that you have a macro that links all the stories together.

3. Plot out each story separately and plan how they interweave before you start. Your stories may be exposition-heavy, and have a very truncated middle. They may end at a first-act turning point. Make sure your first-act turning point in each is a thought-provoking surprise.

4. Set up the non-linearity and theme very early.

5. You have limited screen time. Even though your stories may need a lot of exposition, use as little as you can; make sure all content is telling. Fractured tandem films are about connections. Audiences can be alienated by stories they feel to be unconnected.

6. Using flashbacks/flashforwards always means that you can leave out details and include only the crucial events from a long period— very handy when you're running three stories. Jump stories at dramatic high points. Jumping from climax or second-act turning point to disturbance works well.

7. If you have a major hiatus anywhere in your film—a big time jump, or a change of story and/or genre—consider a flashforward and/or starting just after the hiatus, because these can help close the gap. Most audiences find a mid-film hiatus confronting (fine if that's the effect you want).

8. Think about the breaking wave, or domino, effect. Get strong starts to your stories by connecting the stories at their turning points as in *Babel*.

9. In falling-domino stories, setting up the trigger incident first works well.

GOOD OPENINGS AND GOOD ENDINGS

1   Fractured tandem films need a strong hook to keep the audience interested despite all of the jumping and the puzzling they'll do. Seriously consider introducing all of your stories in the set-up, considering carefully what scenes you choose and how you arrange them. Insert death or the threat of it and/or false expectation of disaster early, and keep returning to it—keep maintaining the dread. Construct the prologue in full knowledge of your twist ending, deliberately and cleverly directing the audience away from the twist.

2   The jigsaw or 'detective story' is essential. Set it up early. Don't make the story too hard or too easy to understand.

3   Avoid confusion. Your audience may have only seconds to identify characters before the action jumps between stories, particularly at the start, so specify that characters look physically different (hair colour, spectacles etc.) and make the backgrounds very different. Having one story in black and white not colour might help.

PROVIDE A GOOD TWIST ENDING

1   Good twist endings rely on clever set-ups that send the audience in the opposite direction. Having several twists is good. The audience will assume the film's message is in the twist. Check that yours is.

2   Conclude stories as late as possible (to maintain dread).

3   Sad scenes and normality scenes are slow, so put them in *after* you've flashed forward to more dramatic events. That way the slow material is invested with hindsight, and is therefore poignant, not boring.

4   If your message is particularly didactic and means that your material is extremely predictable, don't just rely on structure to fix this. Consider introducing some unpredictable elements into the mix, probably via events in the action line, the macro, since this is where you will have flexibility.

5   Successful fractured tandem films typically involve a close collaboration between writer and director on the matter of how the film is cut. Pursue this.

Part 5
Lost in the Telling: Films with Structural Flaws

Chapter 52
Conventional narrative films with structural flaws

LOOKING AT FILMS WHICH in many ways are fine but have structural weaknesses is a very helpful way to understand how structure works. Readers may of course disagree with my choice of films here. These things are always subjective.

Falling in Love
PROBLEMS
- no first-act turning point
- weak antagonists
- low jeopardy

Falling in Love is about two married people who meet on a commuter train, fall in love, and eventually decide to leave their respective partners and stay together. Both lead actors give fine performances, the direction is sensitive, and the film is well shot. Unfortunately, for most audiences, it does not engage.

Generally, the problem presents as low jeopardy. It is hard to see why the decision to leave their respective partners is so difficult. Neither of these partners is sympathetic and there is little left in either marriage (although some time but little weight is given to the problem of Robert de Niro's character leaving his two children). Neither of the lovers has a moral or religious problem with divorce. Right at the end of the film there is an issue over whether the de Niro character will move away or not, but it comes at the point when the film has slowed too much for it to have a great deal of impact. The response of audiences, justifiably, is: 'What is their problem?'

This hits the nail on the head. There is no problem. Specifically, there is no first-act turning point—no surprise/obstacle which complicates the protagonists' problem, turns the action in a new direction, and thereby lifts the jeopardy. A good first-act turning point—like the piano getting bogged in *The Piano* or, in *The Player*, the wrong person getting murdered—provides a whole range of complications that fuel the rest of the film. In fact, as we've seen, the first-act turning point is what the film is 'about'.

Falling in Love would have been greatly energised had it been about 'two people who fall in love and something major (moral or physical) comes in their path, forcing them to battle and agonise over their love', rather than simply 'two people who fall in love'. Without a proper first-act turning point to put the lovers' relationship under genuine strain, *Falling in Love* does not have enough at stake to make an audience properly worry or empathise. The film would also have been helped by stronger antagonists in the form of the two jilted partners. Had they been more engaging or in some way more needy, the film would have had greater jeopardy.

The Insider
PROBLEMS
- wrong protagonist?
- mentor antagonist?

The Insider features excellent performances and production values but nevertheless puzzled many audiences because they thought they had come to see a film about a whistleblower, Jeffrey Wigand, who exposed the tobacco industry. Instead, they found that the film was centered on the TV journalist to whom the whistleblower took his story, a man called Lowell Bergman, and Bergman was the protagonist. Audiences felt left in mid air when the film's climax showed Bergman resigning (because the TV network had compromised his journalistic integrity), while Wigand's much stronger story was left at what feels like a second-act turning point, with Wigand betrayed, abandoned, bereft of wife and children and mortally endangered.

My feeling is that the film is structured around the wrong protagonist. It has been turned into a film about a journalist resigning over a matter of principle, when in fact the more natural protagonist, the more interesting character, the heat of the film, is the whistleblower—because he is in the greater danger and has everything, including his life, to lose. In any film the character with the highest jeopardy will steal the limelight (unless special devices are utilised to prevent it, as in *City of God*), quite simply because they are more interesting.

Unless you are using a mentor antagonist figure (which could have been done in *The Insider*, but only by keeping the whistleblower and journalist together on screen for the greater part of the film) the most interesting character—the one in most danger, with the most to lose—has to be the protagonist. Even if you don't make this character the protagonist, he or she will steal the show by default.

The Insider was based on a true story, written up by a journalist. While *The Insider* source material is clearly centred on Wigand—it is his story— adaptations of both fiction and fact often have problems with protagonists because the source material is written from the point of view of the narrator, so those adapting it often automatically make the narrator the protagonist, even though frequently the most interesting person is the person the narrator is writing about. In cases like these, the narrator, technically, is very much like the passive protagonist in a mentor antagonist film. We the audience are in their shoes, being shown their point of view of an enigmatic outsider.

When you adapt a narrator's account of an interesting character for the screen, consider whether you need the narrator at all. If you do, consider whether your material would be best served by being created as a mentor antagonist movie.

Jaws 3
PROBLEMS
- not identifying the protagonist early enough
- not making the protagonist's problem clear enough (unfocused action line)
- passive protagonist who is not central to the action (unfocused action line, poor understanding of genre)
- weak hunt element (unfocused action line, poor understanding of genre)
- lack of strong antagonists
- poor research

In *Jaws 3*, a mother shark goes on a death rampage after her baby has become accidentally trapped in a lagoon that also accommodates a spectacular underwater aquarium and dolphin pool. Because the owner of the resort denies there is a problem, many people are killed, the shark threatens the dolphins and, in a big climax, the underwater aquarium is smashed apart by the giant shark which is eventually blown up by the protagonist.

Jaws 3 takes twelve minutes to properly identify its protagonist, Mikey, during which a large number of characters are given screen prominence of a kind that suggests they might be the protagonist. It would have been quite possible to cut the first twelve minutes and sneak exposition in later.

The problems *Jaws 3* has in establishing its protagonist, and therefore in getting started, reflect an unfocused action line and a weak protagonist generally. Far from driving the action, Mikey has little to do until the climax, when the shark is actually terrorising people in the aquarium. Only here is he at the centre of the action, being the hunter/defender protagonist essential to successful monster films.

While protagonists in monster films often follow the typical hero's journey model—being initially reluctant to 'play hero'—their reluctance is short lived and normally they accept the quest very quickly. There is a good reason for this. Monster stories only really start when the hunt starts. The whole point of monster movies is to create an exciting two-way hunt between the protagonist and vicious monster (or monsters), each bent on destroying the other. The hunt is the core of the monster movie, just as the core of a romance movie is the meeting, problems and final partnering of the lovers. Unfortunately, *Jaws 3* does not contain a proper hunt at all, and the protagonist is an essentially passive onlooker. Instead of a hunt there are many shark attacks, mostly on characters who have never appeared before and who therefore have little emotional pull on the audience.

There are three lessons here. The first is that in any story, monster or otherwise, the identity of the protagonist must be established early, because until it is, the story cannot start and the audience gets bored. The second is that the protagonist must be centrally involved in the action, otherwise the story is unfocused and cannot properly build. The third is that monster stories need to get the hunt started at an early stage.

Another weakness in *Jaws 3* is the lack of a strong human antagonist with powerful allies who load the dice against the protagonist. In all films, monster or otherwise, the protagonist and the jeopardy is only as strong as the antagonist and their allies. The original *Jaws* gained enormous suspense from the fact that the mayor and business community of the town, acting as the shark's allies, would not listen to the protagonist and stop the monster's killing spree. There is the basis for this in *Jaws 3*—the owners are foolishly materialistic and will do anything to save the aquarium—but because the protagonist in *Jaws 3* is not a proper hunter engaged from the start with a proper mission, the antagonists cannot properly do their job of putting barriers in his way.

The problem of a weak action line with no proper role for the protagonist can be picked at an early stage by creating and applying a narrative sentence to describe the action of the story in terms of what the protagonist is doing. Development strategies on protagonist and antagonist (numbers 12 and 13, pp. 83 and 90) will help to establish a strong antagonist and also the antagonist's allies. The genre equation (Development Strategy 3, p. 22), which pinpoints the genre to check audience expectations, will help identify the necessary plot components.

Another problem with the plot of *Jaws 3* is its inaccuracy. While the plot is based on the idea of a mother shark protecting her offspring, great white sharks do not mother their young. They desert them immediately after birth. It is not worth losing audiences for the sake of an hour's research. One chortling member of the audience can wreck your film.

Guarding Tess
PROBLEMS
- delayed first-act turning point
- repeating the normality
- inappropriate action line
- unconvincing climax
- better told with preview flashback?

Guarding Tess is about a US government agent (Nicolas Cage) who has to guard Tess, a wilful but likeable ex-First Lady (Shirley MacLaine). Ultimately, Tess gets kidnapped and the agent has to find her. The agent is the protagonist, and Tess is the charismatic antagonist.

Guarding Tess has a very late first-act turning point (the kidnap). Prior to that, the film simply displays a range of different examples of the same normality, which is: 'Tess infuriates the agent by her wilfulness'. While each example of this is interesting and humorous in itself, the repetition becomes boring.

The repeated normality problem in *Guarding Tess* is probably caused by the poor choice of action line. The point of interest in *Guarding Tess* is a mother–son relationship. Unfortunately, the chosen action line (the woman kidnapped) is inappropriate. A relationship film requires the two main players to be kept together so they can interact. A plot where one of them is kidnapped necessarily separates them and so prevents this. In *Guarding Tess*, the temptation is to spend as much time as possible on the normality because once the plot starts, the couple will be separated. This is exactly what happens.

The relationship line would have been much better served by the classic action line of films that are primarily about relationships, which is that events force the main players together in some joint enterprise, during which their relationship develops, moving from distance—even hostility—to closeness, often deep love. Almost every 'relationship film', comic or serious, displays this formula. Just a few examples are: *Driving Miss Daisy, Crocodile Dundee,*

Strictly Ballroom, The African Queen, Witness, Planes, Trains and Automobiles and *Romancing the Stone*.

It is very easy in scripts that are primarily concerned with relationships to forget the importance of the action line and the fact that a relationship cannot change until events force it to change. Without an action line, the relationship is jammed in one spot. Structurally, the moments in a script that force a relationship to move out of its normality are the turning points and shifts in the action-line plot (the disturbance, first-act turning point, second-act complications, second-act turning point, and climax).

The kidnap movie can be a vehicle for a developing relationship, but the relationship will be between kidnapper and victim (*Ruthless People*) or kidnapper and ransom target (*Ransom*). It cannot be between the victim and the person who is trying to find them.

A clear sign of this poor choice of action line is that the agent's profound emotion upon finally finding Tess is just not believable because it hasn't been set up. An intense response like this has to be earned over the course of the film by a complex, developing relationship. This is what happens in *Driving Miss Daisy*, which plot-wise has almost the identical ingredients and intentions as *Guarding Tess*. The difference between the two films is that the central relationship in *Guarding Tess* is trapped at the normality stage. The inappropriate action line of the film has not permitted Tess to demonstrate any likeable, admirable or lovable qualities that would justify the strong affection her bodyguard ultimately displays.

PREVIEW FLASHBACK OR FRACTURED TANDEM?

Guarding Tess might possibly have been helped by the careful use of preview flashback, with a high-jeopardy scene from the end (cut in a way that did not reveal the proper ending) placed at the start. It would, though, still be seriously hampered by its inappropriate siege plot and its overly long set-up. Fractured tandem might be a better solution, but that would mean much more time and story given to the US government agent's search, which would turn the agent into the film's central character.

Prelude to a Kiss

PROBLEMS

- delayed first-act turning point
- possibly better told through fractured tandem?

Prelude to a Kiss stars Meg Ryan and Alec Baldwin in a love story about a man (protagonist) who falls in love with a beautiful and unconventional woman. They decide to get married. At the ceremony, a strange old man appears. The bride gives him a good luck kiss—and faints (surprise/obstacle or first-act turning point). After this, she starts behaving like a suburban housewife. Her husband is initially bewildered, becoming gradually hostile as he grows convinced that an impostor is somehow located inside his wife's body. Eventually, the old man turns up at the husband's favourite bar. He reveals that his body now contains the soul and personality of the wife, and vice versa. The old man's body is dying, and unless the body swap can be reversed, the wife's soul and personality will die with him. This seems inevitable (second-act turning point). Finally, the reversal is achieved (climax).

The story of *Prelude to a Kiss* is a fascinating one and the film contains fine performances. Unfortunately, it soon becomes boring because the first-act turning point does not occur until a very long way into the film. Too much time is spent after the initial meeting and falling in love (the disturbance) on showing the lovers actually in love which, structurally, is really just a new 'normality'. There is a reason for this. The filmmakers have to set up details that will later prove the woman to be an impostor. Unfortunately, the process takes much too long. The effect is of the plot 'treading water', and the audience response is to ask, justifiably, 'What is the point of all this?' The film has lost so much momentum by the time the first-act turning point does occur that the moment does not have the impact it deserves. It is actually a good and striking first-act turning point—one that lifts jeopardy and turns the film in an unexpected and interesting new direction. The rest of the film is also interesting. Unfortunately, many viewers simply do not persist long enough to see either.

PRELUDE TO A KISS AS PREVIEW FLASHBACK OR FRACTURED TANDEM

Because its storyline demands that it is exposition-heavy (and also because it involves dread of death) *Prelude to a Kiss* might have worked better in preview flashback or fractured tandem form.

AS PREVIEW FLASHBACK

If its current first act were preceded with a powerful death-connected scene from the end of the film (preview flashback style), dread and a detective story would instantly be set up. Possibly that high-jeopardy hook alone would provide sufficient momentum for the film to proceed in its current linear way to climax, although it would need a Rosebud twist at the end to insert surprise. The twist could be set up by clever cutting of preview flashback opening scene, sending the audience in the wrong direction.

AS FRACTURED TANDEM

As fractured tandem, the film could open in the chronological middle of the story, at an exciting moment after the body swap has happened, utilising flashbacks to show the woman as she really was. Flashforwards could add cohesion and unity here. Another option would be to fracture the story even more, as in *21 Grams*. The aim would be to find a way to energise the long, slow section showing the woman's off-beat personality.

Chapter 53
Parallel narrative films with structural flaws

Winged Creatures (aka *Fragments*): Tandem narrative

PROBLEMS

- slowness in second act caused by
- insufficient story development, characters stuck on same beat, repeating different versions of the same beat

Winged Creatures is a tandem narrative utilising life-changing incident flashback to show the emotional after-effects of a mass-shooting on five survivors, each survivor a protagonist in their own story on the same theme, as all the stories unfold simultaneously. It is very much a case of 'same theme, different adventures'.

The shooting is the film's disturbance and also the life-changing incident flashback. Shown in part at the start of the film, it appears incrementally, while we see the survivors engaging in a variety of abnormal and in some cases highly dangerous behaviours. In the final moments of the film, the shooting is seen in full, explaining the odd conduct of three of the survivors. The film starts well and builds dread effectively until it slows down in the middle. Technically, the cause is that each survivor's story is stuck on the same beat: the odd behaviour they commenced after the shooting. Hence, the person who became a born-again Christian just keeps being a born-again Christian, the man who turned to gambling just keeps gambling, and so on. Each finally moves on to the next beat, and the film speeds up at its climax (although some questions about the gambler remain unanswered), but not soon enough to stop the central slowness. This moral here is that the most harrowing incremental flashback will not boost a story where, in the ongoing story, a protagonist is repeating different versions of the same action. *Winged Creatures* doesn't have enough story; more precisely, none of its stories have enough complications—they don't take the characters into sufficient building complications before coming to a close.

Eternal Sunshine of the Spotless Mind combines flashback (preview flashback) and tandem more successfully. For more information on handling beats, see pp. 133–7.

Syriana (tandem narrative)
PROBLEMS
- didacticism militating against suspense
- redundant characters
- plot information unreasonably concealed
- better told as fractured tandem?

Stephen Gaghan, the writer/director of *Syriana*, set out to inform audiences about the endemic corruption and unscrupulousness of US oil companies and their executives, basing his script on the autobiographical books of an ex-CIA officer. The film certainly succeeds in transmitting its intended message. However, as a feature film, it divided audiences. Many loved its complexity, but many found it overly complicated and rejected it, which is unfortunate because the film's topic is of major importance and there is a great deal in the film that is fine.

Given that discussion of the film always centres around its complexity, it's interesting that actually the plotlines are not complex at all. They are predictable—because of an over-zealous commitment to the film's message that all of the social-political catastrophes that happen were bound to happen. To show this the film has no surprises and the characters, well drawn as they are, are actually stereotypes (good prince/bad prince, disillusioned CIA operative, exploited young men becoming terrorists etc.). It is clear from the start that the American oil executives are crooked. It is clear that the two exploited young Muslim oil workers will become terrorists; in fact, their story is so linear it is like a documentary. It is predictable that the upright lawyer Bennett Holiday will become compromised and that the rumpled CIA man, Bob (George Clooney) will have to act alone because his superiors are cynical and manipulative liars. It is no surprise at the end when the CIA frames Bob and, despite Bob's frantic attempts to prevent it, assassinates the good prince, Nasi, leaving his vicious brother to rule.

Lacking plots with surprises and twists, *Syriana* searches for suspense and audience engagement by making it very hard to work out what is happening and what is and isn't important. For example, Danny Dalton, a key player, introduces himself by name in a TV news bulletin that is playing very much in the background during a tense scene between Bennett Holiday, the lawyer, and his alcoholic father. Dalton's name will keep coming up, so we really need to know who he is. But there really is no way that a first-time audience can tell from this scene that Dalton is of any significance; in truth, we are liable to have forgotten the TV bulletin completely because we were so focused on Holiday and his father. The only way to pick up the crucial information about Dalton is to re-watch the film. Meanwhile, the film persistently spends a lot of time on irrelevancies. For example, there is a scene where the good prince is seen talking to a man about getting the man's son a house. Man, son and house turn out to be completely irrelevant, but the audience has naturally focused on them, assuming their prominence means they must be important in the story.

The audience is persistently being led astray like this, but not in the normal way of thrillers; that is, by a complex plot that will unfold satisfactorily at the end. Instead, we are taken into emotional blind alleys. The most striking of these is at the start, with the harrowing death of a child. This is powerfully done, but it takes up a lot of time and really has no bearing on the plot proper, except to explain why his bereaved father throws himself obsessively into work. Again, after Bob is horribly tortured, we cut to Bennett being called to a bar to pick up a man slumped on a table. We naturally assume that this is Bob, and that Bob and Bennett will form an alliance, but it is not Bob at all. It is Bennett's father.

Possibly, these frustrating plot issues were created during editing, possibly not. It doesn't really matter. What matters is that many audiences simply gave up, which is a great shame because the film has important things to say.

SYRIANA AS FRACTURED TANDEM?

The plot of the fractured tandem film *Rendition* bears marked similarities to *Syriana*, in terms both of content and (because both films are didactic and want to show the inevitable) of the predictability of its plotlines. Both have a nice young man becoming a suicide bomber and a disenchanted CIA man disobeying his cynical, inhumane superiors to save a good man. Both have a man narrowly escaping death in foreign parts and returning, shattered, to wife and child in the US.

While the choice was made in *Syriana* to create a detective-story effect by concealing clues, fractured tandem would have been another option, whereby clever rearrangement of a plot could have turned predictable, anti-climactic storylines into our classic fractured tandem detective story playing on dread. Fractured tandem would have permitted red herrings and other surprises within the existing material. Opening the film on a scene about violent death from the end of the film (perhaps the moments before the convoy is blown up, or before the suicide bombers hit the ship) would have inserted dread and pumped up the energy instantly.

Were *Syriana* to be rearranged into a fractured tandem film, it would need a Rosebud twist, but this could be done quite easily by cutting an opening scene in a way that misled the audience.

Syriana's themes, in a fractured tandem version, would need to be rethought only a little because the film already looks at tragic accidental connections (one of the recurring subjects of fractured tandem) in the context of terrorism and corruption.

Another option for creating suspense would be *Gomorrah*'s use of hope and double-crossing (see p. 196).

Multiple protagonist films

All of the multiple protagonist films I discuss in this chapter suffer from the lack of a proper 'team adventure'; that is, a main action line for the group caused by:

- story material that is inherently suited to a multiple protagonist film being constructed as if one of its protagonists is the single protagonist in a conventional one hero/one journey film
- lack of a group action line, a macro
- lack of character development

Quite possibly, all of these problems could have been picked up at a very early stage had it been accepted that the multiple protagonist film is a common and valid form, and that sometimes the star will get the best part not by playing a single hero on the usual journey towards self-knowledge, but as one of a conflict-ridden group on a quest, in a siege or at a reunion.

Unfortunately, most scripts that show these problems are so distorted by them that while they are often full of good writing, they never make it to the screen.

MULTIPLE PROTAGONIST FILMS CONTORTED INTO THE SINGLE-HERO MODEL

The belief that every film needs a single protagonist on a journey to self-knowledge is so deeply ingrained that filmmakers, faced with story material that is inherently a group mission, reunion or siege, will often mistake either the instigator, the traitor within, or the outsider for this traditional single hero and construct a story around that character. Often, that character will be played by the biggest star, so there is added pressure to keep him or her firmly in the limelight.

In films like these, the story will pursue this single hero in isolation, away from what really is the heat of the idea (the group), on a plotline usually involving uninteresting and often clichéd material about spiritual growth and a troubled love life. The result is that there is simply not time or plot left to properly explore the group. Hence, when the group appears, it is not as part of a proper story but in random, colourful scenes focusing on what are really snapshots of its members. Consequently, the film springs to life when the group and the instigator are together on the screen, but slows to a halt when the instigator is off pursuing his or her extraneous story. Technically, these films have no proper action line because the action line their idea calls for—a storyline specifically about the group—is not in place. There is no shared cause, no group adventure.

You can very often pick these films by the curiously weak and clichéd nature of the hero's love life—something the writers probably did not see as clichéd because they were feeling the strength of the group material which, ironically, they never properly explore. You get the real sense in these films that the writers were simply going through the motions in constructing what is deemed an obligatory love interest, subplot material they know was boring but was assumed to be compulsory.

Doesn't the star require a big part? Of course, but often the attempt to give the star the giant's share of the action actually results in a weaker role. The star will have a much better chance of a great part if they are in conflict with their team (like Gaz in *The Full Monty*) rather than mooching off and worrying about uninteresting lovers, as happens in *28 Days*, *Bootmen*, *Mo' Better Blues* and *The Oyster Farmer*, each of which I think is treating one of its multiple protagonists as a single hero, and damaging the film in the process.

28 Days
PROBLEMS
- multiple protagonist story constructed as single-protagonist film
- the outsider (also the star) as single protagonist

In *28 Days*, Sandra Bullock plays Gwen Cummings, an alcoholic who is sent into rehab for twenty-eight days. Once there, she joins a funny and endearing group of reforming addicts who are attempting to put on a show as part of their therapy. When Gwen and the group are on screen, the film sparkles. But when the group is off screen, all Gwen has left to do is complain to her psychologist (talking heads) or deal with her unrepentant alcoholic boyfriend (who, actually, is well drawn). However, nothing is really happening on screen during these episodes, so they get boring, and Gwen, who has nothing to do except grumble, appears irritatingly self-indulgent as a consequence.

The heat of the idea is 'petulant woman alcoholic gets incarcerated for 28 days with other abusers and turns her life around by interacting with them as they all put on a play'. It is a group story featuring many versions of the same protagonist, a drug addict trying to reform. Since this is missing, the film has no group action line, no adventure to which the relationship material, including Gwen's growth, can be pegged. Had the film been constructed around what it is clearly pulling towards—a multiple protagonist group quest of the 'let's put on a show' variety—there would been a clear, dynamic, funny team adventure with built-in rising tension that would have permitted a dynamic exploration not only of Gwen's reformation but, through all the other versions of alcoholics, the topic of alcoholism itself, surely one of the film's points.

Arguably, the film is pulling towards being a 'coming-of-age' film, with Gwen being the person who learns from multiple mentor antagonists.

Bootmen
PROBLEMS
- multiple protagonist story constructed as single-protagonist film
- the instigator (also the star) as single protagonist

Bootmen is another example of a lost 'let's put on a show' group story. Lacking a team adventure, it has no strong central action line. Directed and co-written by Dein Perry (from the dance troupe *Tap Dogs*) and intended to showcase the macho tap-dancing style that he and his group pioneered and made world famous, the film comes alive when the macho dancers are interacting. It has some great dancing and the group does put on a show right at the very end, but ultimately it fails to properly pursue the heat of the material (a group of great tap dancers, as they rise to fame) because it spends so much time on a clichéd plot about a single protagonist, Sean, a young working-class tapper-cum-steelworker who blows his chance of tap dancing in Sydney and returns to his native steel city only to find that, as well as getting into crime, his brother Mitch has stolen his girl.

Mitch's problems proliferate and Sean eventually leads his troupe to success, but so much time has been spent on the tired steel town story and the redundant love story that by the time the big show happens the film's energy has been compromised.

Strictly Ballroom dealt with one aspiring dancer and appropriately used a single protagonist structure about a man fascinated by dancing and determined to succeed. *Bootmen* should be about the same thing—except

that in this case it's a group of aspiring dancers fascinated with dancing and determined to succeed. The dancers are much more interesting
and original than the bland 'love interest' girlfriend or the hoods Mitch
gets involved with, or anything in the brotherhood story. Like *28 Days*,
Bootmen gets distracted from what is original and interesting in its story
material—the group—by its assumption that every film has to be about a
single hero. It ends up with a plot that for the most part has nothing to do
with its most saleable commodity; a commodity, ironically, that is clearly
mentioned in the title. The title is not *Bootman*, it's *Bootmen*, and the heat
is the idea of great dancing from a great dance troupe. The plot that would
best serve the material (indeed the plot the script is clearly already pulling
towards) is a *Full Monty*, multiple protagonist quest story, vividly original
and centrally concerned with the adventures and internal conflicts of a
group of great and unlikely dancers as they are led to fame by Sean, in the
role of a Gaz-like instigator and undermined by Mitch as 'traitor within'.
All the ingredients are there.

Mo' Better Blues
PROBLEMS
- multiple protagonist story constructed as single-protagonist film
- the traitor within (also the star) as single protagonist

Spike Lee's film *Mo' Better Blues* has an almost identical problem to *Bootmen*.
It is another 'let's put on a show' group story (this time about multiple versions of an African American musician) contorted into a one-hero film, with
a traitor within turned into a sole protagonist. The traitor within rendered as
protagonist is Bleek (Denzel Washington), a brilliant trumpeter, who plays in a
jazz band consisting of old friends and managed by Giant (Spike Lee), another
old friend, who is not only a hopeless manager but also a hopeless gambler.
Bleek's dilemma is whether to stay in the band with his friends or leave the
band to fulfil his obvious star potential. Whenever the band and Giant make
an appearance with Bleek the film comes alive. But when Giant and the band
are not around, all Bleek is given in the way of a plot is the choice between two
equally uninteresting girlfriends, presumably because, as in *Bootmen*, it was felt
that the hero had to have the obligatory love interest as his relationship line.

Actually, like Sean the dancer, what Bleek the musician needs as his relationship line is the group; in Bleek's case, a study of his divided loyalties in a
group adventure. This sort of story would cover the interaction of the group
as the band prepares for or puts on some kind of special show, or goes on a

special tour, with Giant as the instigator and various band members playing outsider, (including perhaps, the white girlfriend of a band member currently in the existing script in an interesting but underdeveloped race-related story strand). But nothing like this happens. The film has no real action line because there is no team adventure. Despite some fine performances, *Mo' Better Blues* becomes essentially talking heads.

It finally ends with a curiously clichéd plot that has nothing to do with Bleek's dilemma about the band or the girlfriend. Bleek's lip is injured in a fight when he comes to the rescue of Giant, so much so that he is no longer able to play the trumpet. The plot has become, literally, 'I'll never play again', with Bleek's final moments given over to another cliché, where we leave him bullying his little son into practising the trumpet.

The Oyster Farmer

PROBLEMS
- multiple protagonist story constructed as single-protagonist film
- the outsider as single protagonist

All of the three films above were clearly halfway to being 'let's put on a show' group quests because they already involved teams of dancers, musicians or actors engaged in performing. In *The Oyster Farmer*, the director–writer Anna Reeves deliberately set out to make a film about the colourful community of characters who live and work on the picturesque Hawkesbury River near Sydney. While *The Oyster Farmer* is beautifully shot with some great performances, unfortunately the riverside community comes across merely as a group of wonderful characters in search of a plot. The problem is that the chosen plot does not properly illustrate the community through action. There is no group quest, reunion or siege involving the whole community. There is no team assembled for an adventure. Instead, the central plot involves Jack, a young outsider who, having attempted to commit the perfect armed robbery in order to pay his sick sister's hospital bills, puts the stolen money into an envelope and posts it to himself on the Hawkesbury, where he gets a job and waits for the envelope to arrive. As the young man goes about his life on the river, the colourful riverside people, including Vietnam veterans, make occasional appearances, behaving eccentrically in fragments of a plot about the problems of oyster farming.

When the river people are on screen, the film is full of energy and vitality. Unfortunately, so much time is devoted to the bland young man and his problems—none of which is particularly original or interesting and none of which is unique to a river community as both love story and 'perfect crime' plot could have happened anywhere—that there is no time to properly explore the genuinely original and interesting river people. The film stops when Jack and the crime story are in the spotlight. Meanwhile, the river community is in the background, just, really, being itself.

It's hard not to feel that Jack's crime story was inserted because of the perception that all films must have at their centre a single hero with their own plot, regardless of how weak that plot is. If the river community *as a whole* had been involved in the perfect crime (with Jack as instigator or outsider) and/or the community had been faced with a threat or a benefit that could have galvanised them into action, the film would have had a group adventure permitting full exploitation of its heat, the river people, and Jack could have had a rich relationship line involving them (including the river girl he falls in love with).

As often happens, a clue to the disjunction between idea and storyline here is in the title. Just as *Bootmen* is about only one dancer, so *The Oyster Farmer* is not about one oyster farmer. There are actually several oyster farmers (in fact, the most interesting part of the film is the battle between two oyster farmers, husband and wife), and Jack only becomes an oyster farmer right at the end of the film. While the director wanted to write about oyster farmers, the central *story* is not about being an oyster farmer. It's about hiding out after a robbery and getting a job as a labourer on an oyster lease.

Possibly, Jack started out being a 'literary device' (see p. 145–6).

Lack of a proper macro

Earlier, describing multiple protagonist films, I mentioned that they all have the same macro plot (an action line that dramatises the question: 'Will the group survive?'), and that death or the threat of it often figures, even in comic or optimistic versions. I want to look at the lack of survival macro in *Peter's Friends*, *The Ice Storm* and *The Thin Red Line*.

Peter's Friends and *The Ice Storm*
PROBLEMS
- multiple protagonist story lacking macro
- death threat too late

Both *Peter's Friends* and *The Ice Storm*, very fine as they are in many ways, lack energy and the action in each seems to be circling in search of a plot. Neither puts its group under threat of survival except by implication in the closing moments, when death makes an appearance. Although each is clearly a social siege and both seem to contain characters who feel like the instigator, outsider and traitor within, neither has a proper group action line, a proper survival macro, so there is no quest, siege or reunion that forces the characters to reassess and explore their relationships. Excellent as many of the performances are, and poignant as the stories turn out to be, both films are a matter of characters in search of a plot—beautifully written but ultimately disappointing (because pointless) social vignettes.

It's interesting to speculate whether putting the death material that currently appears at the end of each film (AIDS in *Peter's Friends* and the electrocution in *The Ice Storm*) at the start, as the cause of a specific quest, siege or reunion, would have provided a better way to explore the tensions and unfinished business of the group. As we've seen, death invariably appears in multiple protagonist films, and often in the opening moments of social siege films, to which *Peter's Friends* and *The Ice Storm* clearly, I think, belong (think of *American Beauty*, *The Big Chill*, *The Jane Austen Book Club* etc.).

The films *Topsy-Turvy* and *Parallel Lives* seem to suggest that death inserted early would have fixed the meandering. Both films circle randomly between characters being themselves until death appears, in *Topsy-Turvy* as a near-fatal illness, and in *Parallel Lives* a murder (which happens over an hour into the film).

Inserting the news of death at the start would of course, have created very different films out of *Peter's Friends* and *The Ice Storm*, with very different styles and content. Perhaps both films intended to be slow, lyrical and open-ended, and certainly many people enjoyed them very much indeed. However, it's possible that their genuinely interesting characters would have been richer and more complex if the film had given them major issues to explore and illustrate during the course of the action, rather than just, as at present, the ennui and quiet desperation of their lives. They would not have been stuck just being themselves, acting characteristically to no end or point. In other words, they would have had a story. *The Ice Storm* would have ventured into the territory of *Ordinary People*, with the adult and child members of the group exploring their feelings about the dead boy. *Peter's Friends* would have started with a shock as the threat of death was announced. Its reunion might have played a little like *The Big Chill* as the group sought to comfort Peter and regroup to fight the threat. Perhaps it might have explored impending death by AIDS in a way akin to *Love! Valor! Compassion!* Notice that *The Ice Storm* is constructed as preview flashback, as if it is feeling it needs to set up death.

The Thin Red Line

PROBLEMS

- multiple protagonist film lacking clear macro
- choice not to have strong plotlines?
- instigator, outsider, traitor within?
- too many characters?
- ongoing normality?
- characterisation?

I have put question marks next to the list of problems above because for some audiences they were not problems at all. For many people, *The Thin Red Line* is the ultimate anti-war film, moreover a film that broke new narrative ground to powerfully and lyrically transmit a sense of futility and repetitiousness of war using an excitingly large cast. However, other audiences had a mixed response, feeling that while the film clearly had many strong points, it was flawed. Common criticisms were that there were too many characters who were under-developed and hard to differentiate (particularly when they were in helmets); that the film was slow and repetitive; that there was insufficient plot and that the voice-overs were intrusive and sounded like the same soldier.

These criticisms are interesting because they all relate to structural matters we've looked at in the chapters dealing with the creation of multiple protagonist films. *The Thin Red Line* has deliberately made certain very risky narrative choices in order to transmit its message. Some audiences loved the effect, others hated it. Just as it was important to us as writers to understand how *Short Cuts* created its open-ended effects, so it is important to understand the narrative choices made in *The Thin Red Line* and the risks those choices might bring.

TOO MANY CHARACTERS?

Realistically, you only have time in a multiple protagonist film to follow about six or seven characters in the depth that audiences expect. If you try to include more, as *The Thin Red Line* does, you end up spending a lot of time setting up characters you then cannot explore, risking leaving the audience doubly frustrated.

INSUFFICIENT PLOT AND CHARACTERISATION?

While the film is definitely about whether a group of soldiers will survive the war, so might seem to contain the survival macro that multiple protagonist films need, in fact it contains no clear group action line—no specific new mission, siege or reunion. This is deliberate. It has been done to illustrate the film's philosophy about the pointlessness of war and the frustration of individuals trapped within its endless repetitive cycles, and it certainly does that. Unfortunately, this is a double-edged sword. It also works to reduce energy levels because without a threat that puts the group at risk there can be little suspense. Audiences are used to having suspenseful storylines, so to eschew that is to throw down a major challenge. And *The Thin Red Line* throws down a major challenge indeed. There is such minimal change in the course of the film that it would be possible recut it so that scenes from the end went into the beginning. Similarly, if you fast-forward the film for most of the time you can guess what characters are saying to each other. This is not what audiences expect and it will alienate many.

Another problem created by the lack of a group action line is how to characterise. Characterisation in film is normally done by showing characters forced to act in response to a change in their lives. Without a proper quest, siege or reunion group story to throw characters into conflict and self-revelation, the relationships between characters are inevitably jammed in one spot. Additionally, as far as individuals themselves are concerned, each character stays in the same emotional normality because there is no external force to make them change. Each has the same problems and world view they had when the film started. They simply demonstrate different versions of the same behaviour. Hence, we will see a cynical sergeant reacting to a situation in his cynical way, we will see an ambition-crazed colonel reacting to a situation in terms of his ambition, we will see a man obsessed with his wife daydreaming about her every time he goes into battle, and so on. It is very well-written but ultimately unproductive character study. The characters are simply repeating their own normality, as in *Mr Saturday Night*. This is what is causing the 'vignettes' effect, which some audiences loved but others found frustrating.

One place where the film does seem to have paid a high price for its decision not to use proper storylines is in the treatment of the soldier sustained by love for his wife. The man finally receives a letter from her telling him she is in love with someone else. This is a heart-breaking moment and we expect to follow him, seeing its consequences, tragic or hopeful. But this does not happen. We never see him dealing with it in any way at all. Possibly this odd avoidance of the expected storyline has its origins in the book the film was based on. Prose often depicts character by thought, not action. Possibly the soldier's story was satisfactorily resolved in a paragraph of moving prose. In the film, we feel left in mid air.

INSTIGATOR, TRAITOR WITHIN AND OUTSIDER

There is no proper instigator (because there is no group adventure caused by such a person) and without an instigator and a quest there can be no traitor within. It seems initially that one character will be the instigator, but he soon disappears from prominence, to re-emerge at the end as the group's saviour, a status he does not earn through the action and which consequently feels a little contrived. The lack of an instigator (and a threat) makes *The Thin Red Line* like *The Ice Storm*, but *The Ice Storm* has more emotional movement because of plot elements like the sexual experimentation between both adults and children and the final death of the likeable child. There is no clear outsider because part of the film's aim is to depict all of the soldiers as outsiders.

This brings us to a matter pointed out by many, namely that the characters don't feel like different versions of the same protagonist—'the soldier stuck in war'. Instead, they feel like the same protagonist—the *same* soldier stuck in war. The voice-overs definitely create this effect. As many people have said, they all sound like the same thoughtful, wistful and poetic man in slightly different moods, so much so that it is often hard to work out which character is actually talking in voice-over. Often the different voices are only distinguishable by their accents, not their world view, and without the camera pointing at the speaker we could not tell them apart. Was the voice-over based on the narrative voice of the novelist? In a novel, a strong, intelligent and unique prose narrative voice can hold together all manner of structural weaknesses. In a film, which shows rather than tells, uses plot rather than soliloquy, it can't.

HELMETS

We should not leave storytelling issues in *The Thin Red Line* without noting a small but vital matter. As many people have mentioned, it is often hard to work out which soldier was which in scenes where all are wearing helmets. We looked at identification problems caused by uniforms, and possible solutions, on p. 146. It's very easy to forget such basic storytelling matters in the complexity of writing the script.

Parallel Lives

PROBLEMS

- no survival macro
- no instigator, outsider, traitor within
- poor relationship lines
- too many characters

- ongoing normality
- delayed disturbance/first-act turning point
- redundant conflict
- poor climax

Many writers are drawn to write film scripts about reunions of friends, family or colleagues for births, marriages, deaths or holidays. The advantages are clear: reunions provide the opportunity for a range of interesting, equally weighted characters, a particularly attractive option in days when ensembles of actors make good box-office sense. Also, because of the unfinished business built into any reunion, the story has ready-made conflict. But many reunion films fail, and many others are abandoned at early stages, because they are unfocused, slow and, in the worst cases, actively boring, all the result of having no macro—no action line involving a threat to group survival. This is a major problem in *Parallel Lives*.

Parallel Lives is about a college reunion and was promoted on the basis that it was the *Big Chill* of the nineties. It features twenty characters (ex-students of the college) who play a significant part in the action, and two others who appear at the end. After all of the characters have been set up (which takes a long time—characters are still being introduced twenty minutes into the film), we see reunion activities such as a dance, a raid on the women's dorm, and a sports carnival. Close to the end, the much-disliked seducer, Peter, is found dead in his car in the river. Many people have a motive for his murder, and one woman, a senate candidate, was actually in the car. Her father, an elected senator, covers up. Everyone goes home, with many of the relationship subplots unresolved. Unfortunately, despite a stellar cast, fine acting and interesting characters, the film is boring.

Parallel Lives assumes that a reunion is of itself a good structure, and therefore does not bother about a survival macro until well after an hour into the action, when it seizes on the cliché of a murder. In a proper structure, the murder would be the disturbance or the first-act turning point. It would be what the film is 'about', in the way that *Gosford Park* is 'about' a murder which permits explorations of the nature of the group and the motivations of individuals. In *Parallel Lives*, the murder story should provide the means through which the characters reveal themselves. As it is, it serves no useful purpose at all.

Instead of character being revealed through the pressure of events in the macro, the group action line, character exploration in *Parallel Lives* is conducted through a vast number of scenes in which two characters discuss the past. Often the unfinished business between the characters is unconnected to their relationship at college, which means that their relationship dilemma is pulling away from the action line of the reunion. For example, one of the major relationship lines seems to be a love–hate relationship between two tough journalists, Wynn and Nick. They once slept together and Nick published a scathing article about the event, but since none of this happened at college it is not informing the premise of the film; rather, it is pulling the film elsewhere.

Similarly, the events that do happen to the group—the ball, the raid on the dorm and the sports carnival—are not used to take the characters anywhere either. They are used merely to show the characters behaving in character; in other words, repeating the same normality, as happened in *Mr Saturday Night*. Like *Mr Saturday Night*, *Parallel Lives* assumes that good characters with good conflict and interesting unfinished business will automatically make a good story—moreover, the more good characters, the better. In fact the vast number of characters makes the film very difficult to follow, and the concentration on talking-heads relationship scenes in place of an ongoing action line that involves all the characters, makes the film slow and tedious. The film is very much a matter of characters in search of a plot.

That a film can be tedious despite good characters, good conflict, complex unfinished business and good acting demonstrates that multiple protagonist films do not happen without planning and a good survival macro that will force the group and individuals on an emotional journey. *The Big Chill*, which *Parallel Lives* set out to emulate, is at all times vitally concerned with the group's past and its endangered future—indeed, its ideals and worth as a whole—and there are issues brought into prominence by the suicide of its most charismatic member. The individuals are dealt with in terms of their role in the group in the past, the present, and the future.

Parallel Lives would also be helped by useful multiple protagonist character types like 'the traitor within', 'the outsider' and the 'dominant character'.

Double journey narrative: *Cold Mountain*
PROBLEMS
- passivity of one of the two travellers
- redundant opening (battle scene)

Talking earlier about journey films, I mentioned that sequences in *Cold Mountain* can be moved around the film without problem, which in any film is a clear and worrying indication that the characters do not change. Another serious problem in *Cold Mountain* is that Ada, the woman waiting for Inman, has nothing to do except wait. While the book may have been different, the film of *Cold Mountain* is inherently a double journey film. We can see this in successful double journey films such as *Brokeback Mountain*, *The Queen*, *The Lives of Others*, *The Departed*, *The Lemon Tree* and *Finding Nemo*. Double journey films demand that the action follows two characters separately, which means that each of the two needs their own narrative and their own adventure. You cannot have one of your two travellers just waiting, as Ada does. Ada is so passive that the action on the home front eventually has to be taken over by a new character, the dynamic, proactive housemaid, because all that has been happening for some time is that Ada has been gradually and passively starving to death.

Notice too that the film has a very expensive opening battle sequence that is entirely redundant plot-wise because it triggers nothing and the only point it makes is that war is hell. Not only is this a huge waste of money (crucial in many film industries), but it squanders the precious first moments of the film. The next scene, the flashback to the first meeting of Inman and Ada, is similarly wasteful of time, as very little is transmitted about the two protagonists.

Perhaps a version of the non-linear *Odyssey* model (the woman being forced to marry, while the male lover has to reach her before the marriage) would have worked better for *Cold Mountain* (see pp. 370–5, Consecutive stories). In the existing version, the villainous bully Teague is already lusting after her, but this storyline is not pursued.

An even better story option might have been for Ada to have her own mission (like Telemachus, or Nemo in *Finding Nemo)*, either in addition to or instead of the forced marriage or rape involving Teague.

Perhaps because *Cold Mountain* was adapted from a novel, changing the story content in such a radical way was not an option. However, all film adaptations must work as films and in a film you cannot have an actor just standing there. Again, the widespread belief that a film needs and can have only one protagonist probably contributes to passive 'travellers' like Ada because Inman was probably perceived as the film's one hero.

Flashback: *Mr Saturday Night*
PROBLEMS
- poor use of double flashback narrative
- repeating the normality
- weak action line

- redundant conflict
- life story in place of proper structure
- character study in place of plot
- wrong protagonist?

Mr Saturday Night is the life story of a stand-up comedian (Billy Crystal) whose ego continually forces him to commit acts against his own professional and personal interests. We meet the comedian in old age, unable to get work because he has offended so many people. His life from adolescence onwards is depicted via flashbacks, while the story in the present follows his attempts to get work with the assistance of a young theatrical agent (Helen Hunt). Finally, he is given the chance of a comeback: a role in a film being made by an important director. Typically, he rejects the role as not good enough. There is a subplot about his difficult relationship with his daughter and his bullying treatment of his brother. At the end he is reconciled with both.

Billy Crystal wrote, directed and starred in the film. Unfortunately, despite an acting *tour de force* from Crystal, fine performances from his supporting cast, and finely characterised individual sequences and scenes, the film does not engage. The reason is structural. The film does not provide a story in which the protagonist is faced with a dilemma and moves through its ramifications to a climax. Instead it provides a range of different versions of the same normality, which is: 'good comedian bullies his brother and acts self-destructively'. This is ultimately boring because each version of 'good comedian bullies his brother and acts self-destructively' is providing essentially the same information. What is being shown is a character study, not a character driven to action by outside events.

Instead of being 'good comedian bullies his brother and acts self-destructively' (which is a character in search of a plot, a character jammed in its normality), the film should have been 'good comedian who acts self-destructively is presented with a dilemma which will test him—and he is tested and resolves the problem successfully or unsuccessfully'. The difference can be pinpointed by asking what the film is 'about', as this question will usually provide the first-act turning point. It will describe a surprising event (a surprise that turns into an obstacle). If a description of what the film is 'about' results in a character description rather than a surprising event, there is a major problem. It means that at best the plot lacks a first-act turning point. In the case of *Mr Saturday Night*, the film does not have a useful action line at all.

Certainly people in real life do get stuck within the same normality. They do fail to change and they do repeat the same mistakes and the same jokes. But in a film, a little repetition goes a long way. If *Mr Saturday Night* was intended to show a character who could not change, a better way might have been to give one or two examples of his repetitiveness within a plot in which special circumstances seem to give him no option but to change although, at the last moment, it turns out he can't. For example, a genuine dilemma would be if his marriage depended on him taking a role that he felt was beneath him and which, despite everything, he couldn't force himself to take. Putting a character in a dilemma engages the audience. They can empathise. A character not in a dilemma is ultimately boring.

Actor–writers, whose training is so heavily biased towards character analysis, are particularly prone to mistake character study for plot, to mistake scenes that depict character foibles for a scenario. The point to remember is that a plot places the protagonist in a dilemma that he or she has to resolve by action. If there is no dilemma, there is no story. Using a narrative sentence would have helped pinpoint the lack of an action line driven by the main character.

The need in a film for a heightened, selective reality and a specific dilemma, is why a character's life story is not of itself suitable for a film. It is easy to assume that a character's life is a ready-made structure but it is not, just as a journey is not automatically a ready-made structure. To successfully depict a life (as in, for example, *Shine*), life-changing events have to be selected that will properly propel whatever interpretation of the life the writer wishes to depict. In *Shine*, each scene moved the story forward, and each flashback started and ended at a structural high point. The same thing happened in *The Remains of the Day*.

Unfortunately, *Mr Saturday Night* assumes that major events from a life— as opposed to *life-changing* events from that life—provide a good structure, which results in plot sequences that are interesting of themselves but that, having no forward movement, slow the film and leave the audience without a story to follow. Again, identifying the film's narrative sentence would have pinpointed these weaknesses.

The film's relationship line in the past, which features the difficult relationship between the comedian and his brother, wife and daughter, also suffers from repetition of the normality. They are all jammed in the same interaction. A proper, dynamic action line would have permitted the relationship line to move.

Mr Saturday Night is also a useful example of redundant conflict. While the film is full of conflicts and quarrels, the conflict is redundant because the quarrels are all essentially the same quarrel, and nothing is changed by them.

With its failed protagonist in search of success, *Mr Saturday Night* seems ideal for double narrative flashback (thwarted dream). The film already uses flashbacks, but they are not successful, partly because of the film's lack of a strong action line in the past, meaning there are no strong turning points where flashbacks can start and end, partly because the story in the present is not 'a detective story of the heart' and also because, in the present, the protagonist has not experienced a second-act 'death' from which he is reborn with a new agenda and the energy to restart the quest. These are all problems that cause low jeopardy.

The first question to answer in a situation like this where double narrative flashback appears to be an option is whether flashback of any kind is the right structure to use. The answer depends on what story is to be told. If the story is primarily about the present, then double narrative flashback is probably not the answer. But if the intention is to tell of an attempt to achieve a lost ambition, then thwarted dream would be suitable. Similarly, if the story is about someone who persistently damages himself, then possibly case history would be appropriate. In both cases, the plot would have to be radically restructured in order to create proper turning points and in particular a good triggering incident.

Another issue raised by an unsuccessful 'character-based' film like *Mr Saturday Night* is whether the right protagonist has been chosen. While the obvious assumption is that the comedian is the protagonist, the film structure might well work more successfully if the comedian—who is *par excellence* an unchanging, infuriating but charismatic character—were the mentor antagonist to a 'normal' protagonist, such as his daughter or the literary agent. The pattern then would be similar to *Scent of a Woman*.

The comedian as mentor antagonist is compatible with either of the double flashback narrative structures. Using thwarted dream flashback, the comedian would be the protagonist in the past and an unknowable mentor antagonist in the present, with his daughter or the young agent being the detective protagonist. In case history flashback, the comedian is charismatic mentor antagonist in both past and present.

The lessons to be learnt from *Mr Saturday Night* are that flashbacks without a narrative structure become boring, that a life is not necessarily a ready-made structure, that an ongoing normality gets boring, that even the most fascinating character becomes boring unless placed in a dilemma that creates a series of choices and builds to a climax, that conflict needs to be productive and that the most interesting character is often better handled as a charismatic mentor antagonist rather than a protagonist.

Gods and Monsters

PROBLEMS

- central character's motives and past not properly explored
- possibly better told through double narrative case history flashback?

Gods and Monsters is a deeply moving film about the last days of James Whale, the enigmatic director of films like *Showboat*, *Frankenstein* and *Bride of Frankenstein*, who, born into poverty with a brutal father, invented a past for himself in which he was the son of a genteel cleric. As *Gods and Monsters* won many prizes, including the Academy Award for Best Screenplay Adaptation, what is it doing in a section entitled 'Lost in the Telling'? The reason for this is that while much of the heat of Whale's story lies in why such a successful man felt the need to lie, and what really happened in his past, particularly in his traumatic childhood, the film barely touches this, instead it spends a lot of time firstly showing that Whale was homosexual and a sexual predator and secondly, depicting the relationship between Whale and a young man who acts as an artist's model for him; all things which, while they tell us something about the man, don't really take us very far and could have been dealt with in a few scenes. This disappointed many audiences.

Gods and Monsters does contain some fleeting but ultimately uninformative flashbacks to Whale's childhood. There is also the suggestion throughout that the character of Frankenstein's monster was in some deep way significant, even symbolic, in his life. However, what the monster actually symbolised precisely is unclear. His father? His sexuality? War and death? His need to confabulate?

Given that the film is setting out to tell the story of a famous and very talented enigmatic outsider who dies with his lies unexplained, it's tempting to speculate that case history double narrative flashback, or perhaps preview flashback, would have been a more useful way to get across more facts while maintaining the man's essential mystery. In a double narrative case history, the film would be a little like *Citizen Kane* or *Amadeus*. The film would open on the death of Whale and, rather than being a protagonist, Whale would always remain an unfathomable mentor antagonist. We would find out about his past through the accounts of people who knew him across various areas of his life, told in flashbacks to an investigator figure. The great triumph of this form is not only that it would have permitted everything that is currently in the film but also much that isn't (for example, much more about Whale as a director, surely the main reason we are interested in him) but also, and, satisfyingly, in the end Whale, like Kane and Mozart, would remain ultimately inexplicable. This way, the man's mystery and contradictions would become a feature of the film, rather than a gap in the story. Case history flashback is an excellent form for biographies of famous and/or enigmatic people whom, like Whale, you might wish to leave, at the end of the story, still unfathomable.

Consecutive stories: *Vantage Point*
PROBLEMS
- repetitious
- action movie not suited to consecutive stories form?

Vantage Point uses repetitions to show different witness views of an assassination. You would think this would be a very suitable topic for a different-perspectives structure, but the film actually angered many audiences who felt its repetitions were tedious and added nothing but instead became an end in themselves.

Probably not enough new information is revealed in each of *Vantage Point*'s repetitions to warrant so many retellings. The repetitions simply add to the facts of what happened, whereas the repetitions in *Rashomon, Run Lola Run, The Nines* and *Groundhog Day* show very different versions of the facts and raise a whole series of new questions. More ruthless truncation (as in *Groundhog Day*) would probably have helped, as would, probably, fewer characters having their perspectives depicted. Additionally, there is no real twist at the end of *Vantage Point*, although one person we think will die is saved.

CONSPIRACY ACTION THRILLER PERHAPS NOT SUITED TO THIS STRUCTURE?
Arguably, the film just has too much story. It seeks to be not just a film about different versions of what might happen, like *Run Lola Run, Rashomon* and *The Nines*, but also a conspiracy thriller that shows the criminals caught at the end after a dramatic car chase and crash. There is not enough screen time for this. The repetitions required by the different-perspectives approach do not leave enough screen time for the complex twists and turns of plot required by a conspiracy thriller. After all the repetitions are completed, there is only time for a chase and a capture. Moreover, because the audience knows both that a car chase is coming and what is going to happen at the end of the car chase, the only suspense in the car chase lies in its physical danger, with many critics comparing it to a computer game.

But aren't James Bond films conspiracy thrillers crossed with action movies ending in a third-act chase? Yes, but James Bond's problem is set up in act one, and the second and third act provide a complex adventure that solves it. In contrast, *Vantage Point* structurally is all set-up and climax—and no middle. It never even gets to a proper first-act turning point—though the shock identity of the assassinated man feels like a first-act turning point it is not pursued. Unlike *Run Lola Run*, *Rashomon* and *Groundhog Day*, the repetitions in *Vantage Point* start at the disturbance, not the first-act turning point, and stay there, circling, as we try to work out how the assassination was done. We then jump straight from this extended disturbance and plan to climax.

When all is said and done, the mystery is actually solved quite easily, by the protagonist linking two events. By the time he has done that (after all the repetitions) there is no time for a developing suspenseful middle and exciting third act. Consequently, the film splits into two: long set-up plus final chase. Fractured tandem films can work with plots that have truncated second acts and a change of story in the middle, but their story content and structure is very different, and their specific kind of non-linearity artificially creates 'a middle' (in terms of rising suspense) in the middle of the screen time.

Perhaps the moral for consecutive stories films about different perspectives is: 'Don't think of the repeated events as the start of the movie, think of them *as* the movie'. That is, your film is about the question of different perspectives, not what happens as a consequence of them.

Fractured tandem: *Bad Education*
PROBLEM
- central disjunction, possibly avoided via fractured tandem?

While *Bad Education* has a devoted following, some people have a problem with its story switches, in particular with the jolt that occurs with the return of Manolo and the consequent change in the film's direction. Pedro Almodóvar spent a long while planning the episodic structure of the film, so clearly wanted this jolt. The problem with story switches—and why writers are warned off them—is that they make the audience care about one set of issues and characters, only to rob them of these issues and characters before resolution, and force them to transfer their interest to other stories, issues and characters that are completely new. For many people, the story switch in *Bad Education* is unsatisfactory for exactly those reasons.

Bad Education features an opening in the present, a long exposition-heavy flashback to the past, a return to present, some time spent in the present, then a switch of story when Father Manolo, the paedophile priest from the past, suddenly reappears, reformed and contrite. Interestingly, it's hard to describe *Bad Education*—with its flashback and central story switch—without feeling that it is pulling towards the kind of story-switch structure we've seen in *21 Grams*. In fact, it's intriguing to look at the idea of restructuring the film as fractured tandem, with flashforwards around midpoint to Manolo's later appearance to sew its stories together, concealing the gap.

Restructuring the film into fractured tandem would not be hard at all. The content wouldn't need to be changed, simply the way it's arranged. As well as having flashforwards, it would probably work well if it opened like *21 Grams*, with a strong, ominous scene near the second-act turning point (after the story switch—to jump the gap) preferably a scene involving death, so death and the threat of it could permeate the film. The ending would need the usual surprises and twists, something that *Bad Education* already has, because it is already a kind of detective story, as fractured tandem requires. The film also already includes the requisite unexpected death. With this and with its unavoidably top-heavy set-up (you have to know about the child sexual abuse to understand the motivation of the adults) the film is a very clear candidate for fractured tandem, as much as, if not more so than, *Syriana* and *Prelude to a Kiss*.

Part 6
Getting It on the Page

Chapter 54
Scene writing: Exposition, backstory and subtext

THIS PART OF THE book deals with the details of the individual scene: how to write dialogue with good exposition, backstory and subtext, and how to write camera and acting directions. Exposition means transmitting information. Backstory is what happened before the film started. Subtext is what is going on in a character's mind behind their expressions, behaviour or words, often in direct contrast to these.

Just generally with scene writing, don't drop into automatic pilot. You will always be able to write a scene. The issue is whether it's useful (see also Part 3, Practical Plotting).

Opening scenes

You have the audience's maximum attention and goodwill in the opening scenes, so exploit it. We've discussed the clever openings of *The Big Chill*, *Galaxy Quest* and *American Beauty*. Make your film, like these, quickly establish the identity and normality of the protagonist(s), hence what and whose story we're in, by transmitting a lot of facts unobtrusively via scenario, dialogue, backstory, sound and visuals. You need to establish the protagonist's social and personal background (their job, class, marital status, country and era they are in etc.) and what sort of person the protagonist is, with some hints of both their good points and their failings.

Starting and ending a scene

Ideally, the opening of the scene, like the opening of the film as a whole, should 'hook' in the audience with an interesting idea or event. The traditional motto is: 'a scene should open at the last possible moment beyond which it becomes unintelligible and leave at the earliest'. I would amend that to 'come in with a twist (a striking moment, or just before a striking moment) and go out with a question or implied question.' This adds pace, because each scene has added surprise caused by the sudden entry, and suspense caused by the sudden, thought-provoking exit, an exit that makes the audience want to see want happens next.

The 'watershed' line

In important scenes, there is often a line of dialogue that causes the world to change for the characters. Exit the scene after the delivery of that line. When you get to second draft you will often find that the start of a scene is redundant and you can cut it. Guillermo Arriaga says he never writes a scene longer than a page or a page and three-quarters if it contains dialogue. He adds: 'One page makes you very careful of what you are telling. One page pushes every writer to know what the scene is.'

Transition scenes

Transition scenes are often redundant, clichéd and waste screen time and money. For example, almost every scene in which the protagonist is on a plane doing nothing except receiving a drink is redundant.

Exposition and backstory

Transmit these with subtlety and don't forget visuals and sound. Never make characters volunteer information beyond credible limits. If you find yourself writing speeches that could be entitled 'The story so far', or 'What is going to happen', you have exposition problems.

HIDDEN EXPOSITION

In the published script of *Being John Malkovich* (Charlie Kaufman, *Being John Malkovich* (2000, London, pp. 16–17)) there is a short scene in which Craig and Lotte are preparing dinner in their cramped apartment while a parrot yells 'Shut up!' and 'Sorry, honey!', a dog barks, a neighbour bangs on the wall and Elijah the pet chimp jumps around in his nappy. The scene is remarkable for the amount of relationship information it transmits. The two are not arguing, but it's clear that Craig is impatient with the animals, and that Lotte knows this and is ineptly trying to endear herself and the animals to him, particularly by discussing Elijah's forthcoming trip to his psychiatrist. At the end of the scene, Lotte asks whether Craig has thought further about the two of them having a baby. Craig hedges, saying that this is not a good time to think about such things because of their financial situation. What the audience knows, but Lotte doesn't, is that immediately before this Craig was attracted to another woman, so the scene ends on a very clear question: can the relationship survive?

Let's look at how Charlie Kaufman does all this. Firstly, he has chosen to make us encounter the characters in their normality, which instantly tells us a great deal visually. Additionally, sound here also tells us a huge amount. The fact that the neighbour can hear the animals and that we can hear the neighbour immediately tells us that Craig and Lotte are living in cheap and crowded premises. Also, for the parrot to have learnt words it must have heard them many times, hence we know that Craig has said 'Shut up!' a lot and that Lotte has frequently replied 'Sorry, honey'.

Elijah's appointment with the psychiatrist shows first that Lotte is the sort of person who takes a monkey to see a psychiatrist, second that the therapy has been going on for a while and third, how out of touch Lotte is with Craig, who clearly couldn't care less about Elijah. But there is a fourth function at work here: the information actually sets up a later pay-off, when Elijah's traumatic memories impel him to help Lotte escape. Hence, a character point is simultaneously seeding a plot point. The same technique is used at the start of *Crouching Tiger, Hidden Dragon*, where a lot of plot information and backstory is transmitted while the audience is focused on the subtext of the conversation, which is the unexpressed passion between the two warriors.

Sixth draft syndrome

In the current script, this scene is followed by a brilliantly written awkward dinner-party scene with Lotte's friends. This scene doesn't appear in the film, rightly, because it does not further character or plot. So why was it there? I suspect the reason is that it had its origins in an earlier draft of the script in which there was no discussion of pregnancy. Presumably, the original point of the dinner party was to show that Craig was testy and the relationship between Craig and Lotte was poor. However, once we know that Lotte wants a baby and Craig doesn't, and furthermore that Craig is actively interested in other women, the dinner party is redundant; indeed, would have a slowing effect. This theory is borne out by a draft of the script I happened across on the internet, before publication of scripts was—rightly—restricted, in which pregnancy was never mentioned. It's very easy to leave in scenes that have been rendered pointless by later amendments. It is an example of sixth draft syndrome (see p. 148). However good the scene, if it has no function in the story it is likely to drag.

Arguments, productive and redundant conflict

People throw the past back at each other in arguments, so arguments are excellent places to transmit information dynamically, rapidly and while demonstrating character. In *Donnie Brasco*, the time frame and nature of Donnie's undercover work are first revealed in detail throughout an argument with his wife.

However, conflict in individual scenes must move the story forward, either plot-wise or in terms of how the characters understand their situation: productive conflict makes something change. Redundant conflict occurs when the characters are simply batting the same arguments back and forth: 'You're a bad father!', 'I'm a good father!', 'No, you're a bad father'. Nothing has changed at the end of that exchange. Productive conflict is: 'You're a bad father!', 'I'm a good father!', 'No, you're a bad father because . . . I overheard you/mother told me about/I found a letter . . .' Better still, instead of having your character repeating 'You're a bad father', have them go straight to their reasons: 'I overheard you . . .' etc.

Redundant conflict works to stop the plot in its tracks because the plot cannot move until the 'Yes, you did'/'No, you didn't' static material is concluded. The quarrels between Allnutt and Rose in *The African Queen* are productive because they move the characters in a new direction. The quarrels in *Mr Saturday Night* are redundant because they are all essentially the same row, and because nothing is changed by them. Linda Seger has excellent material on conflict in *Making a Good Script Great* (3rd edition), Chapter Eleven, 'Finding the Conflict'.

Avoid talking heads

Avoid talking-head scenes in which characters sit lengthily swapping information. The 'walk as they talk' sequence (used frequently in *The West Wing*) is an old writer's trick of adding movement to lengthy exposition. Another trick (when you can't have movement), is to have characters finishing each other's sentences (but don't overdo it). If budget demands impose a static scene on you, consciously seek ways to add psychological movement. Try putting the information into the first active scene as part of some action. For example, if the story demands that two police have to catch a criminal, it is normally more interesting to open with them in the car on the way to catching the criminal, with you filling in exposition and backstory as they go, rather than having them sitting in the cafeteria telling the audience the story so far.

Don't rush exposition

It's commonly said that newer writers put in too much exposition and experienced writers put in too little. Sometimes delaying explaining a character's behaviour provides for interest and suspense. For example, in *Thelma and Louise*, we don't find out Louise's motives for running from the police until very late in the action.

Budget and naturalism

Write scenes with a view to budget limitations and act each scene as you write, reading aloud for pace and authenticity.

Chapter 55
Dialogue

DIALOGUE IS THE PRIMARY way to transmit complex exposition and backstory and is a vital part of characterisation. Visuals and sound can only do so much.

Good dialogue ultimately depends upon a good scenario. It is very hard to make a clichéd or boring scene jump off the page. Generally, keep speeches short. One or two sentences is the norm. Use long speeches only rarely.

One of the most frequent problems new writers have with dialogue is writing it in 'real time', as if they were recording what would happen in real life. Dialogue is not conversation, it is an elaborate artifice resembling conversation that carries plot, theme and character. Even natural dialogue writers need training to learn the requisite economy. To understand this, look at these lines from a first draft scene: 'Stop doing that. It drives me crazy. Can't you see how that sends me nuts?' The good writer will delete the first two, because the third implies the first two (which are functionally almost identical) but takes the relationship dynamically to a new and intriguing stage. Moreover, the pause permits the camera to come in close for a pause on the actor's expression. Look out for sets of three lines like this in your work, by the way. They often appear, and are just you workshopping the same thought as you write. The third line will usually be the best.

Short speeches and pauses can work magic. Look at this weak, rambling bit of dialogue.

                         MARY
              I feel trapped. You won't let
              me do anything on my own. I'm
              frightened of you.

                         FRED
              I work my guts out for you. I'm
              not taking any more of this, I'm
              going to Bill's.

Look what happens when you split it up.

                    MARY
          I feel trapped.

                    FRED
          I work my guts out for you.

                    MARY
          You won't let me do anything on
          my own.

                    FRED
          I'm not taking any more of this.
          I'm going to Bill's ...

                    MARY
          I'm frightened of you.

Weirdly—because all I've done here is split it up—suddenly Mary is impulsively making a shocking statement, creating a watershed moment in the relationship, hence suspense and interest. The actor playing Fred would stop in his tracks, and the scene would take a new direction. Short speeches and pauses let the actors act.

Subtext

Character is defined by what it does not say as much as by what it does—subtext. Dialogue is as much about the thought progressions between the lines as the lines themselves and is written to attain the screenwriter's Holy Grail—that silent close-up of the actor showing, simultaneously, myriad emotions. But how exactly do you create subtext? Imagine that you are creating two characters who don't say what they feel (as in the scene from *Being John Malkovich*, discussed on pp. 446–7). The trick is to work out the sequence of thoughts going on in Character A's mind in response to what Character B is saying (and implying) and to the situation generally. Next, instead of having Character A speak their sequence of thoughts aloud, make them speak only every third or fourth thought. The audience will fill in the gaps and the scene will instantly become fast and suspenseful. For example, in the *Being John Malkovich* scene we've been talking about, to shut up the noisy parrot Lotte takes it out of the room. We hear it shouting off screen, 'Help! She's locking me in a cage!' after which Lotte re-enters saying, 'Isn't that cute? I just taught him that.' Craig replies, 'Adorable. What time are they supposed to be here?'

In the short space of time between Lotte's line and Craig's 'Adorable', Craig has rapidly thought something like, 'I could strangle that parrot', 'Why can't she see I hate these animals?', 'I won't lose my temper but I want to put her down not only because she's so idiotic but also because she can't see that I hate them', 'I want her to realise that I'm putting her down, but she probably won't realise it.' Between 'Adorable' and 'What time are they supposed to be here', he has rapidly thought, 'And on top of all this I have to put up with her irritating friends. How they annoy me!' If Craig spoke all of his thoughts aloud the scene would be boring but leaving out steps in his thought progression (and in Lotte's, when it's her turn to speak), makes the scene crackle with energy and pushes the whole script suspensefully forward.

Notice, by the way, how much more energised the scene is by the fact that Craig suppressed rather than expressed his thoughts. Paradoxically, scenes in which a character is repressing anger or other strong emotions usually have higher suspense levels than scenes in which characters actually let their emotions go. Revealingly, the speeches anyone remembers from fairytales are always moments immediately *before* the violence, for example, 'Who's been eating my porridge...?', 'Oh Grandmamma, what big hands you have...', 'Mirror, mirror, on the wall...' and 'Fee, fie, foe, fum...' For a brilliant analysis of how subtext drives good scene writing see Robert McKee, *Story* (1999), 'Scene Analysis'.

Examples of flawed dialogue writing

Good dialogue technique is easier to understand by looking at bad dialogue. What follow are variations on two different scenes—'Going on holiday' and 'The break-up'—that each display a wide range of typical dialogue problems, exaggerated for ease of identification. For easier reading, the dialogue column in the following examples of scripts is wider than it would normally be in a real script.

'GOING ON HOLIDAY' (VERSION 1)

Unnecessary

```
INT. LUCY'S BEDROOM - MORNING - PAN LUCY'S
ROOM - MS LUCY IS STANDING BY HER BED.
```

Repetition

Unnecessary / detail

```
LUCY is standing by her bed wearing a short
pink and white floral dress with a lace collar
and belt matched with white, lace-up shoes and
tan-coloured pantihose. She sighs, tips her
```

head to one side, then, smiling warmly, picks
up a grey stuffed elephant, hugs it, kisses it
on its trunk, and puts it down again.

                    LUCY   *Redundant—has*
                  (Happily)   *slowing effect*
Clumsy
exposition   I am so happy! It is the first
               day of holidays and Auntie Jenny
               is arriving in five minutes to
               take us to her holiday cottage!

Lucy looks out of the window.   *Time consuming—*
                                      expensive and redundant

LUCY'S POV — THE STREET BELOW WITH ITS TREES.
A BLUE CAR PASSES.
                                  Repetition—and unnecessary
                                  because dialogue should
BACK TO LUCY — SMILING.   *indicate mood*

ACROSS TO BELLA — SITTING ON HER BED WITH A
HAPPY LOOK.   *This is prose fiction*
                                        writing.

BELLA is sitting on her bed with a happy look.
She gets up, walks to one corner and swings
to face Lucy, a look of immense excitement
spreading across her freckled face.

                    BELLA   *Redundant*
         (Excitedly, standing with her hands on
                    her hips)
               The journey takes three hours
               but the cottage is so beautiful!
Clumsy   I am so excited! But I do hope
exposition   Uncle Bill has fixed the motor on
               the boat in case it breaks down
               and the tide carries us out to
               the island!
                                      Redundant—'real
                    LUCY   *time' writing*
              (Bending to tie her shoelace)
               I must do up my shoes!

BELLA
(Bending to tie her shoelace)
Me too.

Redundant—'real time' writing

Redundant

LUCY
(Sighing with happiness, sinking onto
the bed)
I really love holidays. I love
to wake up in the morning and
think there is no school and
hear the waves in the distance
and know that I can be happy all
day.

Repetition—needs tightening

Prose fiction

Lucy sighs to herself, remembering last year
when she was at the cottage and picked flowers
every morning. She hopes the grumpy neighbour
will have moved.

Redundant

BELLA
(Sighing, pulling a suitcase out from
under the bed, putting her books in it)
I think I will pack my books
in this suitcase. This lock is
always so stiff. There we are!
Open! Now, where shall I put
this one? Oh yes. Right here!
(finishing her packing) There! I
have finished my packing! Shall
we take the cases downstairs?

The action will show this.

'Real time' writing. People talk like this but it is bad dialogue.

Redundant

There has been no time to pack the case.

Scene should end here. Nothing else happens from now on.

LUCY
(Grinning at her)
Yes, let's take the cases
downstairs.

BELLA
All right.

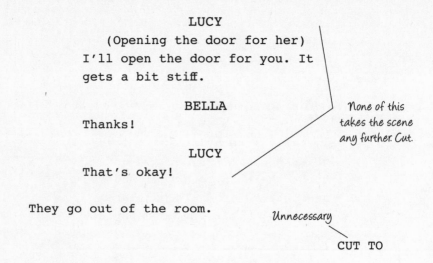

LUCY
(Opening the door for her)
I'll open the door for you. It
gets a bit stiff.

BELLA
Thanks!

LUCY
That's okay!

They go out of the room.

None of this takes the scene any further. Cut.

Unnecessary

CUT TO

Figure 55.1 'Going on holiday', version 1

COMMENTS ON 'GOING ON HOLIDAY' (VERSION 1)

This scene contains too much 'directing on paper' in terms both of acting and camera directions. These slow down the reader in the vital task of reading the script for its playing speed, credibility and emotional impact. Actors and director must be given the freedom to do their job. Note how repetitive the piece is and how like prose fiction narrative the directions often become. This is redundant. Stage directions are not prose narrative, they are notes on a plan. The problems with this piece of screenwriting are:

- The instructions as to what is seen out of the window must be relevant to the plot or cut.
- The instruction CUT TO at the end is redundant because a cut is implied by the fact that this is the end of a scene.
- The dialogue frequently states what is self-evident: 'I am excited.'
- The dialogue does not use common spoken contractions like 'can't' and 'I'll'.
- The exposition is very clumsy. When putting in exposition, try to get it across in fragments and avoid letting characters repeat the same piece of information unless it is a real springboard for delivering more information.
- The passages about doing up shoes and opening the door are repetitive and do not take the scene further. If either action is a set-up that will pay off later, they should be included but in a much more subtle way.

- Lucy thinking about picking flowers and the whereabouts of the grumpy neighbour are not transmittable to the audience. If it is important, it should be put into the dialogue.
- Nothing is happening while Bella packs her suitcase; moreover, there is no indication that the writer is imagining the action or thinking what is happening on screen while it is going on. The writer seems to have forgotten that packing a suitcase will take valuable screen time. If an action is specified in the script, enough time should be allowed for it to occur, and other action should occur as it is going on. If the action seems to be slowing the scene down, either get rid of it or imbue it with a point that will move along character. Seriously question its use in the film as a whole.
- Both characters have exactly the same speech mannerisms, and the speech mannerisms sound robotic rather than realistic. The dialogue is not credible as that of young people.
- The scene is giving us very little in terms of information about either plot or character.
- Often the dialogue and action are dropping into 'real time' dialogue—that is, what people would say or do in the same situation in real life. This simply slows the scene down.
- The scene is repetitive and boring because there is no real characterisation and no real plot movement after the first few speeches. It is not telling us anything about these girls after these speeches. It could be cut back massively.

The task here is to seed the plot while subtly transmitting as much character material as possible.

PLOT POINTS THAT COULD BE REVEALED HERE ARE:
- more about last year and what the girls expect
- relevant detail about the uncle, aunt and cottage
- more about the geography of the area they are going to have their adventure in
- details about their ability to cope with the adventure

CHARACTERISATION POINTS THAT THIS SCENE COULD EXPLORE ARE:
- whether the girls are related or just friends
- whether they generally get on well
- what social class they belong to

- where they live
- how old they are
- their possessions (which reveal character)
- how tidy/untidy they are
- whether they are timid, brave, poetical etc.

'GOING ON HOLIDAY' (VERSION 2)

This is the start of a better example of the scene.

```
INT. LUCY'S ROOM

                                          CUT TO

   Map of coastline, finger tracing the coast.
   Rock music blasts out.

                     LUCY
                    (V.O.)
   See, we could take the boat out
   of the inlet here ...

   Pull back to show LUCY scanning a map spread
   out on the bed and Bella, surrounded by heaps
   of unpacked clothes, wrestling with a suitcase
   clasp. It's the room of a wealthy middle-class
   teenage girl.

                     BELLA
   Lucy, will you hurry up!

                     LUCY
   ... and this time I am checking
   the boat!

                     BELLA
   They're coming in five minutes!
```

Combine plot with characterisation plus interesting visual

Use sound to add information.

Establish both characters.

Use visual to establish characters through possessions.

Low-level conflict adds interest and makes characterisation easier because characters can describe other characters to audience under the guise of irritation.

Get info across via a character point. Seeds info about Bill's incompetence which we can play up on later.

Info transmitted through character point and conflict.

> LUCY
> Remember picking all those
> flowers last year!

Info through character point— her happiness about going to the cottage is implied in the remark.

> BELLA
> (Scathingly)
> Remember that weirdo from next
> door last year!

Use teenage sarcasm to add plot point and character point.

Figure 55.2 'Going on holiday', version 2

COMMENTS ON 'GOING ON HOLIDAY' (VERSION 2)

Information is being transmitted via dialogue, visuals and sound, often simultaneously, and the lack of redundant dialogue means the pace is much faster. Notice how low-level conflict is used to transmit backstory, character and relationships. Note how Bill's incompetence is seeded so that it can be developed later on.

'THE BREAK-UP' (VERSION 1)

The task here is to write a scene about Marie confronting her husband, Peter, in his office about his infidelity with a colleague, Stephanie. Peter confesses, but is torn between Marie and Stephanie. Marie leaves, saying that she and the children will be staying at a friend's. Left alone, Peter wonders how he will tell his beloved children.

```
INT. PETER'S OFFICE - NIGHT


PETER is on his own. MARIE enters.

              PETER
    Marie! What are you doing here!
    I wasn't expecting to see you!
    I'm really surprised!

              MARIE
    I have just had a telephone
    call from Stella. She rang from
    the tennis club to tell me that
    you had been seen kissing that
    tall dark girl from the fifth
```

Repetition. Each of these three statements is really the same.

Clumsy. Use 'I've'.

Clumsy exposition

floor, Stephanie. I feel deeply
betrayed. I feel shattered and
alone. How could you do this to
me?

Repetition. The last two sentences are the same statement in essence.

                    PETER
I meant to tell you but I was
feeling a mixture of guilt and
regret that our marriage was
over. Now I feel good that at
least it has come out into the
open.

Clumsy. Emotions too overtly expressed.

                    MARIE
How can you be so cold!

Redundant conflict. "Tennis game" argument battled back and forth.

                    PETER
I'm not cold!

                    MARIE
You are cold!

Tighten— too overt

                    PETER
I am not cold! I am feeling so
confused. Part of me still wants
our marriage to work. Another
part of me feels that I want to
spend the rest of my life with
Stephanie.

                    MARIE
When are you going to tell the
children?

Stiff

                    PETER
I don't know. Why are you asking
me all these questions? I didn't
choose for this happen. I am so
upset and confused.

Clumsy

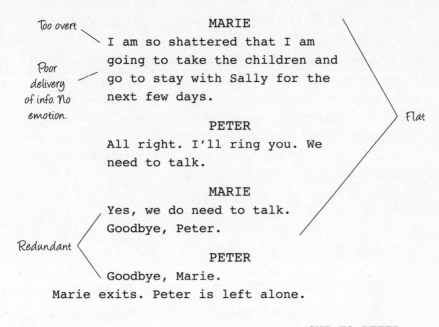

Figure 55.3 'The break-up', version 1

COMMENTS ON 'THE BREAK-UP' (VERSION 1)

Generally, this version is very poor because the characters are expressing too many of their feelings in words; moreover, they are saying things that are obvious (for example, 'I am so upset and confused'). The 'thoughts between the sentences' are not being considered at all. Specific problems are:

- The writer has missed the opportunity to characterise Peter when he is on his own.
- The writer has been so concerned to get across information that characterisation has been forgotten.
- The tennis game of 'You're cold', 'No, I'm not', 'Yes, you are' is redundant, and thus reduces the scene's impact.
- The actor is not being given enough room to act. Sentiments like the following could almost be done through body language alone: 'I am not cold! I am feeling so confused. Part of me still wants our

marriage to work. Another part of me feels that I want to spend the rest of my life with Stephanie.'

- By setting the scene at night, the writer has missed the chance to have other people in the office who could raise the stress level by overhearing or interrupting. Even if the budget for this scene does not allow for other characters to appear, never miss the chance to imply they are there, if it helps the drama.
- The use of voice-over at the end is poor. Peter should either express himself through direct words or gestures.

'THE BREAK-UP' (VERSION 2)

INT. PETER'S OFFICE - DAY

PETER is on his phone.

>   PETER
>   Yes ... mmm ... mmm ... yes ...

MARIE throws opens the door.

>   PETER
>   Marie! (To phone) I'll call you
>   back ...

Melodramatic

>   MARIE
>   Oh, don't hang up on my account!
>   I suppose that was her, was it?
>   Little Miss Stephanie from the
>   fifth floor?

Cliché ——

>   PETER
>   I ... I ... don't know what you
>   mean.

Melodramatic —

>   MARIE
>   Stella, Peter. She told me. She
>   rang me up and told me that you
>   were having an affair!

Weak direction—leave actions to director and actor.

Peter gets up, walks about distractedly.

Melodramatic

MARIE

Well? Are you going to tell me
it's not true?

PETER

Marie ... I love you and the
children ...

Cliché.
Melodramatic.

MARIE

Ha!

PETER

I do! I just ... confused. Part   *Too overt*
of me wants the marriage to
work. Another part wants to be
with Stephanie for the rest of
my life.

MARIE

You creep.

PETER

Don't call me that!

MARIE

Aren't you a creep?

Redundant
conflict. Batting
argument back
and forth.

PETER

No, I am not a creep. I'm a
human being with needs and
feelings! Something you seem to   *Melodrama*
forget, Marie!

Cliché

Marie slaps him around the face.

Melodramatic,
implausible   PETER
response   I didn't deserve that, Marie.

MARIE

When are you going to tell the
children? Or should that be 'Are
you going to tell the children'?

                              PETER
                 I'll tell them. I just need a ——— *Cliché*
                 little time.

                              MARIE
                 I'm taking them with me to
                 Sally's. We'll stay there.
                 You'll hear from my lawyers in
                 the morning.

        Peter steps forward to touch her.

                              PETER
Cliché ——— Marie, I ...

                              MARIE
                 Don't touch me!

                              PETER
                 But Marie, you can't ...

                              MARIE
                      (interrupting)   *The drink's a*
                 Can't what, Peter?   *cliché.*   *Cliché*

        She stares at him for a moment, then exits. He
        sinks, shattered, into his chair. Music as he
        catches sight of the photo on his desk of his
        kids and Marie. He pours himself a drink. He
        throws the glass to the ground, smashing it.

                                                              ——— *Cliché*

Figure 55.4 'The break-up', version 2

COMMENTS ON 'THE BREAK-UP' (VERSION 2)

This version incorporates all of the action clichés of melodrama: face slap-
ping, pouring a drink, glass-breaking and photo-surveying (staring into a
mirror is another cliché). The characters are very verbal and very sure of
themselves, and tend to say what everybody wishes they could think of to say
in such conversations. They talk in clichés and platitudes ('I...I...don't
know what you mean', 'I didn't deserve that, Marie', 'You'll hear from my
lawyers in the morning') and there is little subtext or unscripted thought

progression between the lines. While certain kinds of serial dramas operate on the overt and honest expression of emotions, this version of scene 2 is not acceptable even within such conventions. As well as wall-to-wall clichés, the scene shows a lot of redundant material. The opening phone conversation is redundant because it tells us nothing about the character or his state of mind. The tennis game of redundant conflict over the 'creep' accusation is also poor.

'THE BREAK-UP' (VERSION 3)

```
INT. PETER'S OFFICE - DAY

PETER is on the phone. He's looking through
papers as he speaks. He's calm, in control.

                    PETER
          No, I need delivery by the fifth
          or not at all ... I ... (He sees
          Marie approaching) I'm sorry,
          what? Look, can I get back to
          you? Thanks, bye.

He hangs up, gears himself to look normal.
MARIE enters.

                    PETER
          Hi!

She just stares at him. Peter gets up and
closes the door. Marie realises why, and gives
a contemptuous snort. Peter comes back behind
his desk. Tense pause.

                    MARIE
          Stella rang this morning.

Pause.

                    PETER
          I was going to tell you.
```

Marie sighs - 'the hell you were'. Pause.

>   MARIE
>   I'm taking the children to
>   Sally's ...

>   PETER
>   (Interrupting, stressed)
>   Oh, don't do that!

The phone has started to ring.

>   MARIE
> *Cut?*   (Cutting in)
>   When are you going to tell them?
>   Are you going to tell them?

Beat.

>   PETER
>   It's not as simple as that.

>   MARIE
>   I think it's bloody simple!

>   PETER
>   Oh, shit. (Snatching up the
>   phone) Masters? (He's watching
>   her every movement, but it's his
>   boss.) Oh, Mr Carter ... Yes ...
>   (Marie waits a moment then gets
>   up to go.) Look, I'm extremely
>   sorry, sir, can I call you
>   back? (The boss is clearly not
>   pleased.) Thank you, sir.

He hangs up and grabs at Marie as she gets to
the door.

>   PETER
>   Marie ...

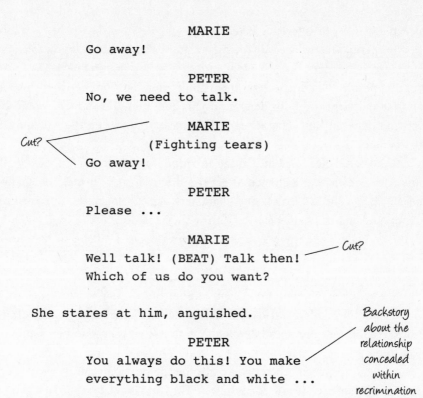

MARIE

Go away!

PETER

No, we need to talk.

Cut?

MARIE

(Fighting tears)

Go away!

PETER

Please ...

MARIE

Well talk! (BEAT) Talk then! *Cut?*

Which of us do you want?

She stares at him, anguished.

Backstory about the relationship concealed within recrimination

PETER

You always do this! You make

everything black and white ...

He can't keep it up. He looks away. Her face
flashes anguish then pride — and she's gone.
Left alone, Peter knows he's just lost the
marriage and his kids.

Figure 55.5 'The break-up', version 3

COMMENTS ON 'THE BREAK-UP' (VERSION 3)

The scene is better because there is more characterisation, subtext and
unspoken thought progression for the actors to utilise. Generally, the scene
seems more rooted in reality. Peter seems to be existing in a real office with
its interruptions and gossip-minded colleagues. The phone call at the beginning has dialogue that tells us something about Peter's job and the way
he does it. Moreover, it permits him to be seen reacting to Marie's arrival.
There is also the opportunity, implied but not specified in the opening, that
Marie's progression through the office towards Peter's room could be seen
on screen.

The scene's drama and suspense levels (jeopardy) are lifted because Marie is actually seen to interrupt Peter's work and Peter is shown being aware that they could be overheard. The mental jumps and matters left unsaid add suspense to the scene because we are not sure what is coming next. The interrupting phone call adds tension through putting Peter on the spot—his job and his marriage are both demanding his attention. The camera would be moving between both characters at this stage, monitoring their unspoken interaction.

At the end, Peter's inability to say anything is more dramatic than a weak line and gives Marie a chance to act her grief and hurt pride. His change of tack at the end is credible and characterising. It also sneaks in backstory about how he thinks she behaved during their relationship. Marie's outburst at the end is a bit soapy but acceptable because she has been so restrained earlier.

The scene could be further cut back if required. Other possible versions might include an interruption from another office member, or other such tension-builders. Many writers would reduce the number of acting directions, feeling that they inhibit actors. Of course a real scene in a real film would present the writer with opportunities to seed later events or pay off material set up earlier. There would also be the possibility to develop character in a more precise and focused way. The bad language would have to be removed if this scene were to be screening as a family film.

Chapter 56
Treatment/outline writing and the script as an instruction manual

AS WELL AS A piece of drama, a script in all its forms (including treatment, outline, beat sheet and scene breakdown) is a technical instruction manual for everyone involved in the process of creating the film. This means it has to be written and laid out according to industry conventions. The scripts in the previous chapters have been laid out differently for ease of reading in a book format.

Acting and camera directions

Unconventional acting and camera directions should not matter, but they do. Script layout guides with full glossaries of camera terms are available from organisations such as the Writers' Guild in your country. Limits of space prevent their inclusion here.

Writing well for the camera means transmitting information about what is appearing on screen in an economical, vivid but unobtrusive way. Putting in a lot of acting and camera directions is called 'directing on paper' and actors and directors hate it, partly because it pre-empts their input, partly because it interrupts the flow of the script, making it impossible to read for flow and running time. The script should take the same time to read as it takes to play on the screen and should play in the mind's eye in the same order as it would on screen. Don't make readers rewind. Never put any information in directions that is obvious from the action or dialogue.

Below is an excellent example of good writing for the camera. It is written by Cliff Green (*Picnic at Hanging Rock*, *Boy Soldiers*) and is an extract from an episode of the ABC television drama serial *Something in the Air*. Notice the economy, wit and minimal formal camera directions used to transmit a large amount of visual information, including detailed actions and characters' emotions. From this tiny scene we learn a great deal, not only about each character, but about the relationship.

```
INT. MERINDA/BEDROOM - DAY 1
DOUG, JULIA


We see, in BIG CU, a pair of tweezers pulling
an individual hair from a large nose.
WIDEN to see DOUG sitting on a chair and
JULIA plucking nasal hairs with as much loving
compassion as the circumstances allow.
Suddenly one really hurts.

                        DOUG
        Ow!


He pulls back.

                        JULIA
        They'll be doing close-ups. They
        always do close-ups.

                        DOUG
        They can come as close as they
        like.


His face cupped in her hands. Julia on guard
for signs of any other facial debris.
```

Figure 56.1 Extract from 'Getting to Know You', episode 5, *Something in the Air* © 1999 Beyond Simpson Le Mesurier Productions and ABC TV.

Make sure directions don't lead people off track

While you must not over-describe, don't under-describe either. Be sure your tight acting directions properly transmit plot. Many writers, particularly writer-directors, will write something like 'a muscle in her cheek twitches' and assume that the reader will recognise this as the crucial moment in which the woman decides to leave her boyfriend and go to Peru. It might, when shot. On the page, it can pass completely unnoticed, particularly if you are using subtext, so that people are not saying what they really mean. To transmit what you mean, state the emotion or decision, not how it should be acted. So, say 'Joe's stunned'. This also permits the actor freedom, because while some actors would act a stunned character via body movements and changing facial expressions, others might show it through, for example, stillness or a slight tremor.

Treatments and outlines

The precise meaning of treatments and outlines varies a little between film cultures. Basically, they are prose summaries of a proposed film or other piece of screen drama. They are often selling documents, in which case their purpose is to provide potential investors of all kinds with a text that will let their mind's eye see the proposed film or telemovie as if they were sitting in a cinema watching it happen on screen. A treatment for a full-length feature film or telemovie is normally about 35 pages long, although when used in Hollywood as a pitch it may be considerably shorter. Outlines are shorter and more succinct. Of course, shorter films require shorter treatments. Treatments and outlines are always written in the present tense and their closest affinity, stylistically and in function, is with stage directions.

Treatments and outlines are notoriously difficult to write because at the same time as being meticulously precise and economical, unless they are created just for the writer's own use or for in-house distribution only, they must be 'a good read'—a piece of prose that jumps off the page. Treatments and outlines must depict simply, vividly and without any ambiguity, not only what the camera is seeing but also the order in which it sees it, so that no mental 'replays' have to be done. In addition, the writer must be completely invisible because nothing, including an awareness of the narrator's sensibility, however unique or acute, must distract readers from the film or telemovie screening in their heads. As we've seen, distractions mean the reader cannot maintain a proper sense of the planned film's pace or duration. With every distraction, the film running in the reader's head risks losing its impact, suspense and emotional build.

A good spine for a treatment or outline is the advanced narrative sentence (see Development Strategy 6, p. 66) because this forces you to create and describe a building story—rather than rambling on, and, as often happens, describing the opening ten minutes in enthusiastic detail then summarising the remaining ninety in a couple of vague paragraphs. Of course, like all other pieces of scriptwriting, treatments and outlines are a personal thing. Some writers will include snippets of dialogue. Others will open the treatment with a striking and detailed description of the script's first scenes, so as to excite and capture the reader. Others will be chatty, or in rare instances where the writer feels there may be mileage in it, openly idiosyncratic in description (although idiosyncrasy of this sort is perhaps best avoided by new writers). Despite these differences, all treatments obey the same general rules as scripts about making sure readers can view the film in their heads undistracted.

Linda Seger has very useful material on writing treatments and out-lines in *Making a Good Script Great* (3rd edition), Chapter 1, 'Gathering Ideas'.

What distracts readers from the film in their heads?

The most common distractions are: repetition, redundant detail, out-of-sequence description and intrusive narrative voice. Distractions can be minimised by working out in advance what information the reader has to be given to be able to visualise and understand the full import of each sequence. You need to work out the following.

- What is the sequence about?
- What happens in this sequence?
- What information is it vital that the reader receives?

The reader needs to know precisely and economically what is happening on the screen *in the order it happens*.

Emotional state of the characters

It may or may not be necessary to describe the characters' emotional state. This is something that must be treated with caution. If the sequence is showing something not emotionally charged, then there is usually no need to describe emotions. Again, if it is obvious what the characters are feeling from their actions or from what has just happened, there is usually no need.

New details that will be important later

If a detail that will be important later in the drama occurs in this scene, make sure it is neither submerged nor too heavily emphasised. Be aware that read-ers will assume details are significant. If the treatment or script mentions that the camera lingers on something, particularly at the start of the film, the reader will assume they are being given a clue. If, as often writer–directors do, you insert a clever shot like CU—THE LIGHT CATCHING THE SOLE OF HIS SHOE AS HE FALLS, realise that the reader may well assume the shoe is a vital clue and be waiting for a payoff.

Position: Where in the film does the sequence occur?

If the sequence is close to the end of the film, we will know the characters well and therefore not be in need of material descriptive of character. Conversely, if the sequence happens early in the film, character details (gender, age, response) might well need to be spelt out.

Mood

Capturing the mood of what is to be seen on the screen is vital. The treatment must do justice to the material. The reader must be engaged on an emotional level. If the sequence is an exciting chase, the description should be exciting to read. If the sequence shows a family after a death, the writing should capture the mood of grief. Similarly, comic scenes need to be described so as to show the reader how they will be funny.

Exercise in treatment technique

Here is a sequence that needs to be turned into part of a treatment. Here is what the sequence is about.

ACTION

Protagonist, Joe, snatching up Old Harry's shotgun and running from his hotel through pouring rain to make sure that his girlfriend, Jenny, has not been attacked by a serial killer.

EMOTIONAL STATE OF THE CHARACTER

Joe is distraught and feeling guilty that he didn't heed Jenny's warnings.

NEW DETAILS IN THE SEQUENCE THAT WILL BE IMPORTANT LATER

None.

POSITION

This is a sequence late in the action, when we know Joe well. It is also just before the big climax, in which Joe and Jenny join forces against the serial killer.

MOOD

Excitement, suspense.

Poor treatment writing

Here is the sequence poorly written, with comments.

Never mention the camera by name and try to make any vital shots part of the text. This direction is redundant, telling us nothing more than the obvious. If you want to specify exactly what we are seeing, you can say 'stay with JOE.' or, for close-ups, constructions like JOE, panting and desperate, his face splattered with mud . . .' etc. Be sparing with this sort of writing. Do not 'direct on paper'.

Weak word, inadequate.

We know it's raining. Use only the most descriptive word, and use it once.

Repetition. We know he has just run out.

Out-of-sequence description. We already have a mental picture of him running out of the hotel—without a shotgun.

Redundant detail. We don't need to know about the leaves unless they are important to the plot.

The camera shows JOE hurrying out of the hotel and being annoyed to find it raining. The rain is slashing down. It's pouring. Joe runs out of the hotel grounds, carrying Harry's shotgun, which he picked up in the hotel lobby. He dashes out along the street, which is carpeted with rain-sodden leaves in every colour from yellow through red to dark brown, all fallen from the grove of plane trees planted by Old Harry sixty years ago to overhang the road. The gutters are running. Trees, dark sentinels of the night, are dripping. Cursing the rain, Joe jogs on down the black, glimmering road. Cars fly past, splashing him. His foot goes into a puddle and he turns his ankle. A car almost runs him over. He arrives at Jenny's house and runs through the rain up the drive and to the front door.

Intrusive narrative voice. This is distracting, adding nothing to what we are visualising. Its only purpose is to draw attention to the way the writer sees the world.

While some of this detail might be powerful, too much could be distracting, becoming a red herring because the emphasis placed on it leads us to feel it must be important.

It is too late in the script for exposition. If the planting date of the trees is important it should have been set up earlier. If the trees and Harry are not of relevance here, cut, or risk distracting the reader and losing pace.

Figure 56.2 Poor treatment writing

Better treatment writing—alternative versions

Here are some alternative versions that use much better treatment writing technique.

VERY TIGHT

> JOE snatches up OLD HARRY's shotgun. He runs
> frantically out into the slashing rain and up
> the road to JENNY's.

While extremely tight, this might be all that is needed if this is merely a link to the big climax and speed is of the essence. This version contains all the required elements. It maintains the mood of excitement and fear. It is colloquial rather than formal and literary. It is appropriate for its position in the script. It shows action in proper sequence. It shows the character's emotional state. It contains no distractions. Note that its shortness suggests a short sequence. Avoid depicting a short sequence at great length, because lengthy description will make the reader imagine a lengthy sequence.

SOME DETAIL

> JOE snatches up OLD HARRY's shotgun. He runs
> frantically out into the slashing rain and
> up the road towards JENNY's house. He's to
> blame for this, and he knows it. Cars fly past,
> hooting and splashing him. One narrowly misses
> him, and he slips, plunging down into a rut in
> the road. His ankle is twisted badly. He's in
> agony, but he struggles to his feet and forces
> himself on. He reaches JENNY's house.

This version addresses all the necessary points, but adds more detail on the specifics of the action and Joe's emotional state. Close-ups of Joe's face have been implied through saying that we see him in agony and that he feels guilty. This version gives both the director and actor more to work with without telling them how to do their job or cluttering up the page with distracting camera or acting directions. Notice that the actor and director are told Joe's emotional state without being given specific—and distracting—instructions as to how these emotions are to be shown; for example, 'Joe's mouth quivers, his knees buckle, he sobs, raising his eyes heavenwards . . .'

Note also that this version suggests to the reader that the sequence takes longer than the first version, and that Joe's frantic run will be used in the film to raise suspense. But the sequence still feels like a link to the next main action point, namely, encountering the serial killer.

VERY DETAILED, MAKING THE SEQUENCE VERY SIGNIFICANT IN JOE'S EMOTIONAL MOVEMENT

```
JOE snatches up OLD HARRY's shotgun. He runs
frantically out into the slashing rain and
up the road towards JENNY's house. He's to
blame for this, and he knows it. Cars fly past,
hooting and splashing him. One narrowly misses
him, and he slips, plunging down into a rut in
the road. His ankle is twisted badly. He's in
agony, but he struggles to his feet and forces
himself on. The road seems endless. He's eaten
up with despair. He's realising how much JENNY
means to him and how likely it is that he will
be too late. He staggers on. JENNY's house
comes into sight. He wills himself toward it.
Near collapse, he staggers up the drive.
```

Here, the added detail about action and emotional state suggest a longer sequence and one which is crucial to Joe's emotional development. As it is now written, the run to Jenny's house shows Joe realising, with pain, that he loves Jenny and that he might have lost her. The writing makes us imagine more close-ups because the film needs to display Joe's increasing distress. We can even imagine music.

Points to remember

The longer and more detailed the description of a sequence, the longer readers will expect it to play, and the more significance they will attribute to it. It can be tricky to describe fast, action-packed scenes briefly.

Do not accord all sequences the same amount of space. Go for variety based on the running time of the sequence. Try always to get the 'feel' of the film—funny, poignant, grim etc. It is easy for treatments to become too dry. Remember, the treatment is a selling tool. It must be 'a good read'. Think always of the film running in the reader's head. Avoid distractions in terms of redundant detail, intrusive narrative voice, repetition and out-of-sequence description of action requiring a mental 'replay'.

Scene breakdowns, beat sheets, outlines and stage directions

Treatments and scene breakdowns must, like stage directions make the action screen vividly and without interruption in the reader's mind. So everything above about distractions in treatments is equally applicable.

Like treatments, scene breakdowns and stage directions are also pieces of technical writing which must give all film personnel the information they need to do their job. Your best training here is to read as many scripts as possible to see standard industry practice.

Index